Religion and the New Ecology

Religion
and the
NEW ECOLOGY

*Environmental Responsibility
in a World in Flux*

EDITED BY
David M. Lodge & Christopher Hamlin

Foreword by Peter H. Raven

University of Notre Dame Press
Notre Dame, Indiana

Manufactured in the United States of America

Library of Congress Cataloging-in-Publication Data

Religion and the new ecology : environmental responsibility in a world in flux /
edited by David M. Lodge and Christopher Hamlin.
    p.   cm.
Includes bibliographical references and index.
ISBN-13: 978-0-268-03404-7 (pbk. : alk. paper)
ISBN-10: 0-268-03404-4 (pbk. : alk. paper)
1. Human ecology—Religious aspects. 2. Religion and science.
3. Environmentalism—Religious aspects. I. Lodge, David M. II. Hamlin,
Christopher, 1951–
GF80.R454 2006
201'.77—dc22
               2006018597

∞ *The paper in this book meets the guidelines for permanence and durability of*
the Committee on Production Guidelines for Book Longevity of the Council on
Library Resources.

CONTENTS

FOREWORD

The theme of caring for creation is one that runs through all of the world's major religious and philosophical systems of thought, and has been recognized widely as the central contribution that we can make on Earth. To varying degrees, achieving sustainability by preserving the Earth in a robust and resilient condition at least equivalent to that in which we find it when we are born is seen both as an obligation in and of itself, as well as a precondition of another: accepting social justice as a norm for our collective behavior. It has been suggested that caring for the environment, and for the human race that functions as a part of that environment, ought to be accepted as a new central tenet around which much of our religious and philosophical outlook could be focused. The task of exploring these relationships, however, is an ongoing one, often impeded by a lack of understanding between disciplines—a problem that this timely and excellent collection of papers addresses very cogently.

Concepts of a balance of nature in which human beings play a minor role have given way as the world human population has exploded to its present level of some 6.4 billion people. The several million people who inhabited the whole planet 10,500 years ago, at the time when crop agriculture was developed and domestic animals were being formed into herds of increasing size, certainly affected the planet more than most other species, but they could not have conceived a world like that which exists today. Eventually, as our numbers grew twenty-fold over two thousand years, from several hundred million at the time of Christ to our present six billion, we began to study with increasing precision the environment within which our activities take place. The concept of a balance of nature was postulated, implying a set of rules that governed undisturbed ecosystems, and human beings were seen as upsetting that balance. The dichotomy between "natural" and "human" that was envisioned in medieval and Renaissance times became the subject of much philosophical discourse, and by the late nineteenth century "nature" became the subject of a powerful conservation movement, spurred by a newfound sense of loss.

Historical examples of ecological upset by humans abound. For example, the great migrations of Polynesian peoples and others over the islands of the Pacific destroyed a major proportion of their biota rapidly, including the extinction of an estimated two thousand species of birds (of a world total now estimated as less than ten thousand species). A few hundred years later, European colonization of the world began in earnest, and the kinds of agriculture that had proved successful in Europe were exported to the Americas and Australia, with consequent major damage to the ecosystems there. Gradually people in Europe and North America began to visualize a paradise being lost—a vision of an earlier paradise being converted before their eyes into something much less nurturing and gentle. The settlement of the United States, involving the clearing of forests and the breaking of prairie sod over thousands of square miles raised concerns from Colonial days onward, but has especially done so over the past 125 years or so.

People have begun to realize that the Earth never was a stable paradise—such as that symbolized by the Garden of Eden—but rather a dynamic system in flux, and that human beings were a part of that system, clearly playing the major role in its evolution in modern times. As Professor Daniel Janzen of the University of Pennsylvania has suggested, the world can perhaps best be viewed as a garden, and we are all its gardeners. We are responsible for its form and its future as we are for our own home gardens, but with much greater implications for our children and all those who will follow us. Bill McKibben's book *The End of Nature* symbolizes the end of the nature-human dichotomy and recognizes our collective responsibility in a way that has attracted the attention of many profound thinkers in recent years. And Mathis Wackernagel and his colleagues have calculated that we are using the productivity of our home planet at 120 percent of its capability, a situation that, along with many perverse indicators over the last half-century, emphasizes the fact that we are not even remotely managing the richness of our world in a way that is sustainable. Whether we do so or not is, as Williams College Professor Kai Lee put it, "perhaps the central test of whether we shall turn out to be a species with the determination to cultivate a world in which we can live together."[1]

This notable collection of essays brings together our current state of understanding of the science of ecology with the human values that underlie our actions, and should inform our actions, which will determine the condition of the future world. The salvation of our world threatened by human consumption lies in an understanding of the world, and that fundamental knowledge may increasingly be seen as constituting the roots of our individual destinies and contributions. Understanding the way the world functions as seen through the eyes of religious tradition is essential to the constructive management of that world, just as is understanding its function by means of scientific investigation. Both views must be objective as they strive to bring into their view other ways of evaluating a common set of phenomena.

In a practical sense, what complicates our ability to manage the Earth sustainably is its changing nature. As our planet fills with people, our consumption patterns and choices of technologies profoundly affect the way the world functions. The morally abhorrent social inequities that mark the world, where one in eight people is literally starving while the richest two percent of the world's people controls more resources than the remaining ninety-eight percent, also have profound impacts on the capacity of the planet to sustain itself. The hurricanes that severely damaged several areas of Florida in 2004 would have not even been noted had they occurred 150 years earlier, when Florida was nearly empty of human infrastructure. Similarly, the results brought about by global warming of the kind we are both causing and experiencing in the early twenty-first century would have been of little consequence four hundred generations ago, ten thousand years back, in the early years of agriculture, when small human populations could adapt to changed conditions by moving from place to place, seeking improved sources of food, and adapting their living patterns to warmer (or cooler) temperatures. Now the sea level rise of some eighty meters that will occur when the polar ice caps have melted, if we prove to be foolish enough to neglect climate change that long, will have extraordinary consequences for a large majority of the world's people, with many other serious ones along the way.

Of particular concern from a religious or moral viewpoint is the rapidly increasing rate of extinction of the species of organisms that share this planet with us. Comparing the fossil record with the written record of the past few centuries and with contemporary calculations, we can determine that habitat destruction, invasion by alien species of plants and animals, and climate change have accelerated the rate of extinction of our fellow passengers on this planet from perhaps a dozen species a year to thousands. By the middle of the century we have just entered, only about five percent of the tropical moist forest is expected to survive. Overall, our actions, if continued as they are now, are projected to result in the extinction of perhaps two-thirds of all terrestrial organisms by the end of this century, an event last matched some 65 million years ago when the dinosaurs became extinct and the whole character of life on Earth changed profoundly. Clearly, the actions we are taking do not constitute caring for creation, and in fact in some religious traditions are considered grave sins. They are perhaps no worse than our collective indifference to the plight of many people living in the world's poorer countries, but they are irreversible and condemn future generations to live in a world that is less beautiful, less diverse, less sustainable, and far less filled with potential for human development than the one we inherited. Do we have a right to deal with the world in this way, for our short-term gratification?

Filled with vital attempts to deal with the relationship between religious and moral values on the one hand and environmental ones on the other, this book makes an important contribution to a crucial discussion. We can neither understand our place in nature nor how we should deal with and understand the world around us if we lack values; those values in turn are informed by our experience as a part of nature—the context within which those values, and our attitudes and very consciousness, were formed. The world and our future in it badly need further refinement of those attitudes, an effort that needs to be informed by the best available scientific information and religious thought. Only by the kind of marriage between these traditions can we achieve a life that is worthy of us. To that end, this outstanding volume makes a valuable contribution, and one that will amply repay careful reflection and further development in what we can hope will be an ever-widening circle of participants.

Peter H. Raven
Missouri Botanical Garden
Washington University in St. Louis
March 2005

NOTE

1. Kai N. Lee, *Compass and gyroscope: Integrating science and politics for the environment* (Washington DC: Island Press, 1993), 201.

This book results from our conviction that only deep and sustained conversations among specialists from different disciplines can overcome the intellectual balkanization that characterizes many contemporary colleges and universities. By "deep" we mean conversations that eschew oversimplification of any discipline, out of respect for the knowledge and values embedded in each discipline. With "sustained" we recognize that appropriate nuance and respect emerge only from repeated efforts to learn the goals, language, and methods of another discipline. When the past, present, and future of environmentalism are in such ferment as they are now, it is particularly important that we examine dispassionately what the roots, contemporary currents, and possible future bases for environmental ethics might be.

Without such conversations, we often find that the knowledge we value highly in our own discipline is caricatured in other disciplines, sometimes to the point that it is unrecognizable. This tendency exists in some of the burgeoning literature on problems of the environment, including publications aimed at audiences from the popular to the specialized. This would be unfortunate in any intellectual context, but in the present environmental situation—where urgent local, regional, and global decisions about natural resource management are intellectually downstream—the situation is downright dangerous.

In response to conversations with many of our colleagues at the University of Notre Dame and elsewhere, we wanted to foster a rigorous conversation among scientists, historians, philosophers, theologians, and others interested in environmental matters, especially as they pertain to environmental ethics and natural resource management. It is, of course, common for ecologists to talk among themselves about such matters and for ethicists to communicate with each other about environmental issues. Our conversations over the years convinced us, though, that the portrayal of the scientific understanding of nature among environmental ethicists, for example, bears little relation to the conception that practicing scientists hold. Similarly, the way in which scientists often talk about ethics and how they might relate to environmental management and policy often seems horribly superficial to those in the humanities. What is especially valuable, then, about this volume is that it opens a more serious conversation among disciplines about nature and the role of humanity in nature.

We believe that only by rooting a multidisciplinary conversation in the core wisdom of each discipline can there be any hope of a sustainable ethic for a sustainable environment. Taking this approach requires patience and more than idle curiosity, but we believe that the reader will see that central questions of environmental ethics require an exploration of some longstanding core intellectual issues in multiple disciplines that cannot simply be ignored or glossed. We invite you into this vital conversation. Join us and the other authors of this volume in recognizing the mutual importance of science, history, philosophy, theology, and the practice of religious faith in providing a foundation for decisions about managing our small planetary home.

This book reflects many important financial contributions and intellectual influences, which we gratefully acknowledge. Without encouragement from historian Jim Turner and fellow members of the Local Advisory Board of the Erasmus Institute at Notre Dame, David Lodge would not have nurtured the core ideas of this enterprise. If historian Phil Sloan had not shoved under David's nose the 1999 request for proposals for national research conferences from the Lilly Fellows Program, the conference that led to this book would not have occurred. For major financial support for the February 2002 conference (http://www.nd.edu/~ecoltheo/) on "Ecology, Theology, and Judeo-Christian Environmental Ethics," held at Notre Dame, we thank Arlin Meyer and the Lilly Fellows Program, based at Valparaiso University (http://www.lillyfellows.org). For many other financial contributions to the conference and the subsequent development of this book, we thank the following leaders and organizations at the University of Notre Dame: Jim Turner and the Erasmus Institute; Nathan Hatch and the Provost's office; Vaughn McKim and the Reilly Center for Science, Technology and Values; Chris Fox and the Institute for Scholarship in the Liberal Arts; Frank Castellino and the College of Science; Mark Roche and the College of Arts and Letters; Jim Merz and the Graduate School; and Chuck Kulpa and the Center for Environmental Science and Technology. During the final stages of revision and preparation of this book, David Lodge was supported by a Sabbatical Fellowship at the National Center for Ecological Analysis and Synthesis. For support of research reflected in the introduction and conclusion,

David Lodge thanks the National Science Foundation, NOAA Sea Grant, the Great Lakes Fisheries Commission, EPA STAR program, and USDA Ottawa National Forest.

The following participants in our fall semester 2001 graduate student seminar on ecology and religion helped us sharpen our thoughts and broadened our intellectual horizons: Terry Ehrman, John Drake, Michele Evans-White, Laurie Kellogg, Cindy Kolar, and Sadie Rosenthal. Theologian Matt Ashley, philosopher Don Howard, psychologist George Howard, philosopher Kristen Shrader-Frechette, historian Phil Sloan, and historian Jim Turner all offered excellent advice and service on the steering committee for the conference.

Many of the two hundred participants in the 2002 conference also made important contributions to our thinking. We are particularly indebted to those who offered formal comments at the conference: ecologists Calvin DeWitt, James Elser, Robert McIntosh, Lawrence Slobodkin, and Kenneth Tenore; theologians Steven Scharper and Gerald McKenny; political scientist Irene Diamond; and philosophers and ethicists Carl Mitcham and Kristin Shrader-Frechette. In acknowledging the stimulation we derived from these and other participants, we do not imply that any of these scholars necessarily agree with the views we espouse in the introduction and conclusion or the opinions expressed by other authors in their chapters.

Finally, we thank the other authors of this volume for their willingness to engage in a cross-discipline conversation during the development and revision of their chapters, in conversation with us and other authors, and in response to external reviews and suggestions. This development of ideas is, we believe, worth the effort and time, and we thank the authors for their patience with the process.

In addition to this book, the conversation continues in other ways that have and will continue to bear fruit. A 2003 double special issue of *Worldviews: Environment, Culture, and Religion* (7:1–2) contained ten contributed papers from the 2002 conference. And in November 2004, a conference on *Faith, Ethics, and Environment*, organized by theologian Matt Ashley, continued the conversation at Notre Dame, with many outside participants also. We welcome you, the reader, to this conversation, which we hope will inform wise management of our environment.

David M. Lodge, Christopher Hamlin
April 2005

Beyond Lynn White: Religion, the Contexts of Ecology, and the Flux of Nature

Christopher Hamlin and David M. Lodge

What happens to environmental ethics when the empirical context of moral responses is changed by the facts of science? In this book, we explore how to reframe moral responses to a new paradigm in ecology, one stressing the flux and unpredictability of nature rather than its stability. We are particularly concerned with the shape of that response from the religious communities most prominent in the United States: Christians and Jews. The authors of this volume do not look for a framework in terms of the distinctive doctrines of any particular faith tradition; we do not, for example, seek to discover how Baptist doctrine differs from Lutheran on environmental issues. Rather, we explore the issues in a widely shared but rarely articulated common context: we respond to public issues of environment and ecology within a heritage significantly shaped by public religion.

In particular, we explore the implications of the Jewish and Christian heritage to environmental attitudes. While we build on the common context of the Jewish and Christian traditions, we are cognizant that it is misleading to speak of a "Judeo-Christian tradition." The predominant Jewish perspective draws on law and is intensely concerned with the details of situations. To this extent, the Jewish perspective resembles an Islamic perspective more than it does most Christian perspectives, which are linked to redemption and rooted in the general.

Whatever we call it, and however we understand its origins, a common Jewish and Christian context continues to inform public discourse on the environment and on American higher education in the liberal arts. It is this context, for example, that is expressed by colleges when they assert concern with the education of the whole person. But the reality in colleges and in society at large is that the parameters of most discussions of environmental matters are narrowly technical or narrowly esthetic. We still know too little of how connections should occur where ecology, theology, history, and philosophy converge. While the institutional forces in academe and in society discourage scientists from talking about the moral status of nature and theologians from accrediting knowledge of nature as a valid basis on which to build arguments, the many authors in this volume have all climbed out of the disciplinary ghetto to address that common context. They do so not by leaving aside their expertise, but by applying it to important public conversations. We recognize that each discipline, though, brings not just its special expertise—not just a piece of the puzzle—but a whole version of the puzzle, often with important unstated assumptions. The challenge, then, is not to fit the pieces together in one plane. Rather, the challenge is to add dimensions to the puzzle, ultimately completing a richer, multidimensional version of human experience with respect to the environment and our responsibilities to it.

SETTING: THE HERITAGE OF LYNN WHITE, JR.

In his 1967 plenary address to the AAAS, Professor Lynn White, Jr., pioneering historian of medieval technology, indicted Christianity as the culprit for "our ecologic crisis" (White 1967). In White's view, Christianity valued the next world more than this one; indeed, the attitude of some early Christians had been labeled *contemptus mundi*. From the late Middle Ages onward, White claimed, Christians had been preoccupied with translating God's instruction to subdue the earth and take dominion over it into technologies of shortsighted environmental change. Moreover Christianity and Judaism (Islam was overlooked by White) were singled out as monotheistic faiths, in which a supreme male god was separated from a material earth, which he had created. That earth was thus an object to be altered according to our will. (Although White did not offer a gendered reading, others would note that this earth object was often gendered female, while the will that acted on it was male.) The polytheism, pantheism, animism, or mysticism of the East, by contrast, had a better record, White argued, by stressing harmony rather than domination. For practical purposes, White seemed to equate the religions of the book with the West, seen as monolithic, except for good St. Francis, who would become the exemplar of biocentrism.

White's thesis was simple and pithy. In many quarters it became gospel (Whitney 1993). It furthered the political reconfiguration of American environmental politics. The dominant value system of Western civilization thus joined the chemical industry (seen as the purveyor of pervasive toxins after Rachel Carson's 1962 *Silent Spring*) as threats to the public good. "Environment" became a key battleground in the war between establishment and counterculture. Along with "chemical," "capitalism," and "technology," "Christianity" and "Judeo-Christian" quickly became dirty words in certain quarters. Christianity and capitalism had already been insightfully linked by the sociologist Max Weber (Weber 1930) and the historian R. H. Tawney (Tawney 1926). Hence, to find Christianity (and by association Judeo-Christianity) as a key player in the assault on nature was not wholly surprising.

Before 1960, the political location of conservation and preservation movements was complicated (Fox 1981). After 1970, "environment" would increasingly imply "radical": to identify oneself as an environmentalist was to invite suspicion that one was atheist (or at the very least adhered to an "alternative" religion), socialist, and antimodern (Albanese 1990). Indeed, the historian Thomas Dunlap has recently argued that environmentalism itself became an alternative religion (Dunlap 2004).

By and large, historians, who might have been expected to complicate the White thesis, did not. A few criticized it, but the historical relations of religion and nature did not become a major focus of research (Barbour 1973; Spring and Spring 1974). The White thesis was vast and vague; it involved assumptions about causation with which historians were uneasy. With a few exceptions (Glacken 1967; Black 1970), environmental history barely existed; any thorough test of the White thesis would have required a mix of skills—in the history of religion, intellectual history, and the history of technology—that few historians possessed.

Mainline churches responded with a good deal of defensiveness, which manifested itself in three ways. The first was an admission that, regarding historical Christianity, White was somehow right: an environmental crisis did exist and the church was implicated. God's creation, made for the good of all, was being despoiled by societies that professed to be godly (and also by other societies not considered by White). That condition signified spiritual failures—pride; greed; cruelty; materialism; injustice to others, human and nonhuman; and a failure to appreciate the sacredness of life. Second, many theologians associated with those traditions found it important to reexamine the scriptural passages that might seem to promote or condone environmental despoilment. Perhaps these passages had been poorly rendered, taken out of context, or could be read to illuminate current issues in unanticipated ways. "Stewardship" became a familiar if not wholly satisfactory term. It endorsed an anthropocentric standpoint but made clear that humans had obligations to God in their uses of the earth. Third, other theologians, recognizing the ongoing adaptive character of their discipline, focused on the possibilities of an ecotheology of the future. How, they asked, could we use the traditional bases of theological knowledge to build a robust theology that would meet the need for identity and direction at a time when cooperative action among all cultures was needed to meet a global problem (Bakken, Engel, and Engel 1995)?

THE ASCENDANCY OF ECOLOGY

In one sense, the solution to this crisis was simple: all we had to do was to respect nature, which embodied beauty, sublimity, productivity, and diversity. All that was required was to stop our pollution and allow the "integrity" or "health" of fragile but resilient "ecosystems" to return on its own. Nature's hallmark was stability—an equilibrium or balance—a tendency to recover those qualities after a temporary human or natural disturbance. Such images were implicit in the central dogmas of the science of ecology, for example, in equilibrium population models, in the theory of niches and community assembly, in equilibrium island biogeography, and in the model of succession where disturbed nature returned to beauty and stability (Chesson and Case 1986; Hagen 1992; Kingsland 1995).

In this milieu, the move from ecology to environmental quality was short. The natural ecosystem according to Aldo Leopold was complex and beautiful, and always to be preferred to the simplified ecosystems that humans created (Leopold 1970). The appeal to nature as guarantor was hardly new, but it was very persuasive and reassuring. The concepts were easily popularized because they fit so well what people wanted to hear. "Ecology," "ecologist," and the adjectives and adverbs derived from them became widely applied beyond the science of ecology, applicable to whatever could be construed as nature-friendly. "Environmental" and "ecological" became interchangeable in many contexts. Lynn White's title, referring to an "ecologic" rather than an "environmental" crisis, indicates the degree to which that conflation had already occurred.

And yet there was, and is, a crisis of sorts within the science of ecology. Ecologists found themselves in a complicated and contested setting. Many felt a duty to apply their expertise to environmental management while at the same time wishing to distinguish themselves from non-ecologist environmental activists, who were, with considerable success, co-opting the name of their discipline. While some took a prescriptive, even activist stance on various issues, many others saw a need to demarcate ever more clearly the distinction between the natural science (the business of which was determining what nature is and how it works) and social activism (which was concerned with changing things). This left problematic the question of how their knowledge was to be applied. The more readily they crossed from the scientific question of "is" to the normative question of "ought," the less secure was the "is." Even attempting this crossing illustrated a willingness to commit the logician's naturalistic fallacy, to argue that "is" implies "ought" (cf. Callicott 1982).

At the same time, many ecologists worried deeply about modes of environmental use that seriously threatened the well-being of humans and other forms of life, and might, therefore, properly be designated as environmental problems. As professionals, they, uniquely, were in a position to recognize whether proposed solutions were more or less likely to succeed. They could only hope that a well-informed public would make wise choices. These tensions were longstanding. In the 1950s it became clear that the Ecological Society of America could not serve both missions. It would emphasize scholarly research on ecology while the Nature Conservancy would emphasize environmental concerns. The gap between science and activism widened further during the 1960s and 1970s.

Exacerbating the situation in the United States was that ecology was under fire through its close association with evolutionary biology. Evolutionary biologists were finding it increasingly difficult even to teach the "is" of their science. In state after state, well-organized groups were arguing with considerable success that evolutionary biology was itself a value system being imposed on America's children. For biologists, both jobs and intellectual integrity were (and are) at stake. One way to guard the position of ecology (and biology more broadly) as a social authority was to dissociate it from environmentalism and eschew practical problems for ivory tower research. The voice of the science of ecology was thus squeezed out of the public square.

By no means was ecology unique in facing the problem of how to go from "is" to "ought," but other twentieth-century sciences negotiated the divide less self-consciously and painfully, in part because they had long been doing so. Post-war atomic physicists settled more or less comfortably into the role of makers of foreign policy: to let politicians negotiate over or generals deploy weapons whose properties they did not fully understand was unthinkable. The biomedical sciences had long been shaped by the good of improving human health; physiology and pathology fit together seamlessly (Conant 1951, 344). And in every science where new knowledge could be patented, the border was constantly crossed: to request a patent was to make a claim of utility, of good. If ecology bore the brunt of complaints about the departure from value-free science, it is probably because it was being enlisted on behalf of interests hitherto underrepresented in policy making (Proctor 1991).

THE CHALLENGE OF FLUX

The most recent element of the crisis emerged in the guise of flux. Even at the time White wrote, some ecologists were finding that the concepts of stability and equilibrium were not wholly adequate, and many more came to that conclusion during the subsequent two decades. An axiom of science is that all knowledge is provisional, and the integrating principles of balance, too, had to be subject to criticism and revision. Taken too far, the seductive image of a stable nature that would guarantee a harmony for right-living people was incompatible with the recognition that nature changed. Increasingly, this seemed more than just a matter of timescales, with evolutionary biologists differing from ecologists by talking in terms of thousands or millions of years rather than tens or hundreds. The master model of nature was changing. The picture of a resilient system, full of subtle buffers and negative feedbacks that would dampen oscillations and restore equilibrium was giving way to an image of nature in flux, even when humans did not interfere with it (McIntosh 1987; Wu and Loucks 1995). In this new view, nature consists, at least in part, of temporary and unstable states, which are often subject to fluctuations; steady long-term changes; and sudden shifts into quite different (only partially predictable) states, sometimes prompted by minor disturbances (Scheffer et al. 2001).

And yet with regard to the public face of ecology, this revision was and is problematic. In the earlier period—when the metaphor of the balance of nature reigned—it had been easy to commit the naturalistic fallacy, for those willing to do so. Nature's way was right. On the other hand, the images of flux and chance too have a heritage in Western culture, but a more complex and ambiguous one. The traditions associated with Heraclitus (all is flux) and Epicurus (all is the chance joining and separation of atoms) rather than that of the Stoics (all is harmony ruled by a universal soul) variously inspired skepticism, fatalism, materialism, quietism, fideism, nihilism, hedonism, mysticism, and romanticism (Glacken 1967; Foster 2000). Particularly in America, where notions of providence, destiny, cosmic order, rationality, and progress loom large, the master image of flux is difficult to assimilate into public discourse (Stoll 1997). As the philosopher Stephen Toulmin has argued, these traditions continue to supply master narratives for human relations to nature, yet they require adaptation. For example, Heraclitus and Epicurus were thinking about how to respond to what nature threw at humans, not what humans throw at nature (Toulmin 1982).

Thus we are now in the situation of asking, again, what is to guide us in the use of nature. The abolition of the balance of nature as an exemplar to be imitated–even if it was always an ideal–leaves a host of open questions with no obvious routes to answers. It is not a matter then of doing things nature's way, but rather of deciding which of nature's ways or forms we want to establish, maintain, restore, or change. Certainly a recognition of nature as flux should not be taken to imply that all states of nature are equally good, or that human actions are inconsequential because it is all a muddle anyway. On the contrary, as we shall explore later, the recognition of flux magnifies the inescapability and enormity of moral decisions about how humans should live, because we must give up a concept of a nature that would guide us, reward our virtues, and fix our blunders.

One of the two foundational issues most requiring moral consideration is human population. More than most species, humans cause environmental change, and the more there are of us, the more change results. It is difficult enough to know which questions regarding human population should be asked: "How many people can the earth hold?" or "What must human population be to achieve some other good, for humans or for non-humans?" or "Why that level of good rather than some other level?" No matter which question is asked, answers do not follow straightforwardly, especially because the first issue (human population) cannot be addressed independently from the second issue, that of quality of life: how much and what kinds of environmental impact should each person have (Cohen 1995)? This question spawns a host of more detailed questions about the multitude of what we usually call environmental issues.

Combining the two issues leads to questions like: "Should we have 24 billion humans on the planet eating corn gruel or should we have 7 billion with the current US standard of fossil fuel and food consumption?" Of course, the situation as it currently exists is that a few hundreds of millions of people are consuming a large proportion of fossil fuels and food, while the other five-plus billion people are eating corn gruel or its equivalent. How humans relate to the rest of nature is intimately connected to issues of justice and equity among humans. If the "is" and "ought" were ever comfortably joined, the new paradigm rips them apart as choices and trade-offs abound.

Choices about human population size and per capita environmental impact are made more difficult by the fact that trade-offs must be decided in the face of uncertainties—uncertainties that loom especially large in the ecology of flux. Even apart from human impact, environmental changes are occurring on all temporal and spatial scales. For example, geophysical and atmospheric scientists have an increasing understanding of several-year El Niño cycles, decades-long sunspot cycles, and centuries-long earth orbital cycles. But the magnitude of each is affected by interactions with the other cycles, making the conditions at any one time difficult to forecast. Irreducibly random year-to-year variation, and the sometimes large and always unpredictable impacts of volcanic eruptions, must also be added to the equation. Finally, anthropogenic climate changes—certainly real but still inadequately understood—cause additional interactions with natural cycles and natural variation of climate. Thus, even before the enormously more complex biotic interactions are considered, the basic geophysical climatic template that shapes all life must be recognized as highly uncertain (Sarewitz, Pielke, and Byerly 2000). On top of that, the biotic interactions—involving millions of species and billions of individuals—confound the sort of predictions that would make environmental management easy. This is particularly so when even deterministic interactions can result in unpredictable outcomes—so-called chaos (Lewin 1992)—and when small changes can lead to large shifts in ecosystem state (Scheffer et al. 2001).

In this milieu of radical uncertainty in the trajectory of nature, one may argue that the new paradigm fosters a more honest ecology by ceasing to disguise those moral problems as somehow resolved in the natural order of things. But in their relations with the public, ecologists find themselves in the worrisome situation of Dostoevsky's grand inquisitor (Dostoevsky 1970, bk. 5, chap. 5). To much of the public, their discipline is the one uncorrupt science, the source of the authority and skill needed for humans to live rightly with nature, a locus of faith and hope for an earth in which we can live with joy and without guilt. But that status continues at the cost of being hobbled by generalizations now regarded as outdated and inaccurate. The notion of the balance of nature appealed to a public that had learned the ecology it had been taught as truth and was thus confident that it knew the scientific basics as well as the ecologists did, even if it was the ecologists' critical, skeptical, falsificationist methods of science that symbolically authorized that confidence. If we follow Dostoevsky, the right thing for ecologists to do might be to keep the unsettling new truths secret, to recognize that stable equilibria are the bread and circuses of our time, and that faith and hope are essential to human sanity, however ill founded.

We prefer to embrace the new ecology of flux as a description with a closer correspondence to reality. This new ecology is terrifying because it exposes the inadequacy of our normative systems. However, it is somewhat comforting to recognize that the situation is not unique. It arose a century earlier in evolutionary ethics. Against those who would extract from nature an ethic of social Darwinism, Thomas Henry Huxley declared that you could not get morals from nature (Paradis and Williams 1989). Humans decided what moral codes they were willing to enforce; they always had and always would. The situation arose, too, about the same time in psychology, as moralists sought to square Freud's naturalistic picture of the mind with the continuance of morality. The idea of flux also can seem an invitation to continue to commit the naturalistic fallacy, but in a different way: since nature is *amoral* it is acceptable for us to be *immoral.* It makes no difference what we do, because nothing is guaranteed anyway. No god or anything else—that is, nature—is in a position to enforce any prescription or proscription. In large part, however, humans have resisted that temptation in theory, if not in practice.

It might help also to recognize that we do have well-developed approaches to addressing those normative questions in the fields of applied ethics. In our consideration of options, we are now much better able to explore the implications of particular choices: What values, risks, and assumptions are we privileging if we take a certain choice? If we hold particular values, what actions are either implied or unacceptable? But the ethicists cannot ultimately tell us which values to have, even if they may be able say what is good about certain sets of values.

The answers to these questions are more personal. For a great many people in the United States and elsewhere, religious faith is the locus of such values (Guth et al. 1995). Religion, even if it is often an institution that perpetuates social stability, is also sometimes transformative, occasionally more powerfully so than education, politics, or technology. The character of an ecotheology that accounts for flux is then an important question. Certainly some elements of earlier balance-of-nature ecotheology will be harder to apply. What would we mean, for example, by a biblical obligation to stewardship of the creation, if that creation itself is constantly changing, only partly from our own actions, in ways we can only partly predict?

THE LILLY FELLOWS CONFERENCE AT THE UNIVERSITY OF NOTRE DAME, FEBRUARY 2002

An ecotheology of flux was the central problem of the conference whose conversations this book extends. The chapters herein develop conversations from presentations, commentaries, questions, and workshops at a conference on "Ecology, Theology, and Judeo-Christian Environmental Ethics," held at the University of Notre Dame in February 2002. The chief sponsor of the conference was the Lilly Fellows Network, a group of American church-related (Christian) colleges and universities. The 170 conference participants represented 46 member institutions and 43 non-Lilly institutions. They included faculty, administrators, and graduate and undergraduate students from research universities and small liberal arts colleges affiliated with most Christian denominations. All participants shared a recognition that the problems of environment and the human future were serious, pervasive, and central problems for religious people. They also shared a desire to see that the bodies of knowledge and ways of approaching problems within their various disciplines be integrated and made meaningful to the students they taught.

The main constituency of the conference—educators in institutions committed to the integration of learning and religious faith—is certainly an important one, and yet, partly for reasons already suggested, it is also a complex and problematic context in which to address environmental issues. First, as we have already noted, in the 1960s, "environment" became a part of the politics often looked upon as elitist and leftist. Among American institutions of higher education, the church-affiliated institutions of the Lilly Fellows Network are certainly on the more conservative end in the students they attract and the outlooks and values they embody. Rachel Carson's influential *Silent Spring* had appeared (in shorter form) in the *New Yorker,* a magazine addressed to an affluent, liberal, and highly educated audience (Carson 1962; Graham 1970). From then on, environmentalism would largely be the possession of certain parts of American society; to other parts it would seem at best an effete luxury, at worst an attack on strongly held values and ways of making a living (Tucker 1982; but see Gottlieb 1993).

Second, Lynn White had convinced many that Christian faith was the problem. In the context of this book, that faith is being pressed for a solution in the absence of a standard from nature. As we have noted, eco-theologians have pointed out that ancient texts and Christian and Jewish traditions have more to offer than had been previously recognized, but few Christians have been sensitive to either the linguistic nuances that occupied the scripture scholar or the metaphor and metaphysics of process theology. The historical Christianity that White blamed was the Christianity the average believer lived.

Finally, some Christian traditions delivered an ambivalent legacy about environmental activism. In one sense, the message was complacency: God was in charge; faith was faith in providence; the great problems of environment and the human future were perhaps only apparent; and the greater the problem, the greater the demand for trust in God's goodness. And, after all, the end of the world was promised as something to look forward to.

It is true that since the 1970s, the political polarization of environmental matters has diminished, but at a cost in immediacy and importance, in the precision with which problems are described, and in the detail in which solutions were considered. Earth Day, initially an occasion for display of the unity and power of an environmental counterculture, became an occasion for a generic gesture of concern for a public ideal that could be celebrated so long as it did not mandate particular changes in our ways of living. Commercial culture co-opted nature. Just as "masculine" for a long time meant smoking Marlboros while riding through the desert in a cowboy outfit, so enjoying the environment now means driving an SUV across it.

It may help to characterize the full magnitude of the problems that face us by thinking in terms of a series of transparent overlays (Hamlin and Shepard 1993). First is the physical state of the world's dynamic systems. There our knowledge is only partial, but it is less partial than we sometimes pretend. Wherever we look, human impact is overwhelming.

Second is the overlay of geopolitics. In a world sharply demarcated by inequality, "environment," "endangered species," "population control," and "economic growth" are heard differently by haves and have-nots. Even among the haves, these terms will be heard quite differently depending on how threatening they are to one's immediate livelihood.

Third are the institutional and physical structures. It is hard to maintain values that one has no opportunity to express and must violate regularly. It is hard to worry about carbon dioxide when we live twenty miles from work or school and there are no means of public transport. And it is hard to scrutinize the tendency of capitalism to commodify everything when the access our children will have to higher education, not to mention our own retirement, depends on the growth of capital.

Fourth are the images of nature that ecologists and others offer us. Somehow, we must find means to translate the nature revealed by science—that of flux—even if stated in terms of natural capital and ecosystem services (Daily 1997), into a sense of human identity, purpose, and values.

Fifth is the complex landscape of cultural politics, particularly in America. Within this are multiple layers: the legacy of polarization following Lynn White, the place of wild nature in the formation of our identity as a nation, the contradictory legacy of millenarian Protestantism eloquently outlined in this volume by the historian Mark Stoll, the multiple traditions of relations with nature in the many groups that make up a pluralistic society, the way in which "secular" and "faith" are defined as a permanent and pervasive opposition, and even the bizarre conventions that have arisen with regard to the acceptability of religion in public life (the most conspicuous invocation of God occurring after touchdowns on the football field).

Sixth is the challenge we face as intellectuals and citizens to use the many "ways of knowing" to produce knowledge that is descriptive *and* normative. The ideal is to build on what is of value in each epistemic tradition, retaining the critical demands for precision, clarity, analysis, evidence, and logical argument while avoiding the wholesale reduction of all disciplines into one. The reality is that interdisciplinarity too often is a cacophonous display of unintegrated approaches that will only convince students or citizens that their professors or quoted experts, respectively, however knowledgeable they may be, simply cancel out each other.

Seventh is the relation of what intellectuals teach to what students and citizens do. An assumption of the American tradition of liberal arts education, one particularly important for church-affiliated colleges and universities, is that students integrate knowledge from different disciplines. The Lilly Fellows Program describes its support of this goal as the fostering of a sense of vocation. The terms differ in different contexts: we may speak of "formation" or "adult commitment" or "education for citizenship" or "education for life," but what we mean is that students leave college able to assess issues thoroughly, to respond to them by well-warranted and deeply held commitments, and to act effectively. Most students will not be academics, and most citizens are not experts. From the point of view of nature, what they do is more important than what intellectuals know.

Presentations, questions, conversations, and workshops at the Lilly Fellows conference moved among these several levels. This book focuses mainly on the fourth through the seventh—how images of nature may be related to adult commitment in the context of contemporary American higher education. In the chapters that follow, we present some of the conference plenary presentations in the contexts of the conversations they were part of—not just the comments and questions directed to particular papers, but with regard to issues that arose in earlier or later sessions as well. These conversations, in our view, are what warrant the order of the following chapters, which represent distinct approaches among several disciplines. We focus in this volume on how we should do interdisciplinary work and how we expect students and citizens to learn and integrate what we write.

Themes of the Volume

Three themes are especially conspicuous in this volume. First is the importance of historical perspective. Second is the centrality of language as a medium of scientific practice and as mediating between humans and nature, between humans and God, and between scientists and a broader public. Third is a transcendence of disciplinary imperialism without an abandonment of disciplinary authority, which appears in the book as a hermeneutical circle, a recognition of the way each of the disciplinary approaches informs, and is informed by, another. We develop these themes in introducing the chapters below.

Chapters 1–3 are from historians. Elspeth Whitney begins by taking issue with the White thesis. Integrating the work of a number of historians, she finds that White is wrong for three of the most basic of reasons: the chronology doesn't work, Christianity did not uniformly espouse the doctrines White assigns to it (mechanistic, instrumentalist, exploitative views), and there are culprits other than Christianity in the economic and social changes that comprised Western civilization. Enchantment with the domination of nature by technical means preceded the rise of Christianity and existed outside it; animistic ideas and pagan practice continued within it. Whitney's critique is conceptual as well as empirical. She recognizes that medieval Christianity was not a monolith, dictating beliefs and actions. Rather, it was an interactive institution. It both challenged and accommodated its world, and served as an institution of reassurance in which people made sense of their lives. This suggests that we miss the function of religion as a mode of cultural practice, a system for the creation of meaning and the mediation of existential issues if we focus only on doctrine. White's thesis should no longer set the parameters for the discussion of religion and the environment in the West.

Mark Stoll examines similar themes in an American context in chapter 2. He illustrates two apparently contradictory themes that emerged from the millenarian Protestantism brought to North America primarily by English and Scots-Irish settlers: a belief in the limitless capacity of nature to be molded by capital to human will, expressed as market demand; and a belief that wild nature represents the Eden available to us if only we can overcome the sin of greed. Both themes were nurtured by the evangelical movements that so profoundly shaped American culture. Stoll locates that militant Protestantism in the backgrounds both of environmentalists like David Brower and of ecologists like the Odums. He suggests that we cannot see environmentalism as an external and secular threat to religion; rather, the issues of purpose, destiny, and providence that are conspicuous in environmentalism are genuinely religious matters. It follows that these matters are dealt with implicitly even by faiths that are silent on the subject (a concern we see in the later chapter by Van Houtan and Pimm).

Historian Gene Cittadino, in chapter 3, treats the broad topic of the rise and transformations of ecological science in America and its relations to social thought. Along with most contemporary historians of science, Cittadino finds that it is impossible to treat sciences as abstractions, decontextualized and universal products of a disembodied scientific method that chugs along dropping out bales of knowledge. Instead, Cittadino observes, American ecology emerged initially in Nebraska and Chicago, and later in a number of distinct and relatively independent incarnations—at Yale, Wisconsin, and Minnesota, in particular. At the beginning, it was much concerned both with finding a stasis or at least a pattern underlying flux and with making diversity a source of productivity. These themes mirrored the great social problems of America at the time, particularly acute in places like Chicago, struggling with the Americanization of immigrants. Metaphors of community were passed back and forth among at least three disciplines simultaneously pioneered at the University of Chicago: ecology, human geography, and sociology. Those conversations shaped both Clementsian community ecology and Gleasonian individualism as its antithesis. They alert us, too, to the heuristic importance in science of models and generalizations that may be borrowed from social and other sources; these heuristics then guide research and serve as templates for assessing evidence. Cittadino, however, rejects the implication that some find in such contextualism—that it implies a pernicious epistemic relativism or, worse, delegitimates ecological knowledge as some socially constructed pretender to scientific authority. The problem is hardly specific to ecology. That all knowledge is situated and embodied doesn't make it any less knowledge. It does call upon us to appreciate the implications of context, and to consider the conceptual work involved in moving from generalizations to specific investigations and back to generalizations.

Chapters 4–6 are from ecologists. In chapter 4, Kyle Van Houtan and Stuart Pimm challenge American Christian churches to respond explicitly to the crisis of species extinctions. To an unusual degree among ecologists, Van Houtan and Pimm move easily from "is" to "ought." In their view, we cannot study species distribution and extinction without recognizing that we as a species are perpetrating an irreversible, unnecessary, dangerous, unconsidered, unwarranted, and cruel change on the earth. It would seem obvious, they argue, that faith in the power and goodness of God should imply respect and protection for God's creation. But such a view does not prevail in many Christian quarters. Classifying the responses of the churches and religious groups on the basis of their programmatic statements, Van Houtan and Pimm find a range of responses: some subscribe to an Earthkeeping view; many others ignore biodiversity issues altogether; others mount a hostile skepticism toward contemporary environmental science, denying the bad news that ecologists bring; still others acknowledge the problem but deny its crisis status by giving other issues higher priority. Van Houtan and Pimm argue that those groups that marginalize environmental problems are, in essence, not religious enough. They are single-issue pressure groups, or—as in the case of the Cornwall Declaration—they have set themselves up as institutions of countervailing expertise. But Van Houtan and Pimm suggest that an institution that understands itself as embodying a moral response does not have the luxury of picking what it wants to be moral about. Even if each of us has limited time to act, we don't become more virtuous by acting justly in some matters and contemptuously dismissing others. To ignore is effectively to condone, and to condone is to support. And there is abundant irony in a religious group arguing that we need not take difficult actions until we have greater certainty. Besides diverting attention to the uncertainty, this position ignores the fact that taking action in the face of uncertainty is the normal condition of human decision making.

In chapter 5, ecologist Gary Belovsky illustrates how Old Testament events and teachings were affected by contemporaneous environmental changes that biblical authors clearly did not recognize. Drawing on recent scholarship that unites history, biology, anthropology, and climatology, Belovsky examines the relative lack of concern among biblical authors with anthropogenic environmental change. Rather than understanding that humans both cause some changes in the landscape and also respond to other long-term global environmental changes entirely beyond their control, the biblical authors focus much more on God's use of nature as an instrument of punishment. This contributes, Belovsky suggests, to a perception of nature as hostile to the human enterprise. He argues that recognition of geographical and climatic conditions in the Near East at the time these authors wrote—a period of significant climatic variability—helps us understand how an image of an angry, powerful, and sometimes arbitrary Jehovah could develop. Had the Israelites been able to recognize causes of climatic events, had they had a science of probability and appreciated lag times between cause and effect, they might have been able to see these events, and their own uses of nature, as an expression of natural laws—the sort of recognition the Babylonians achieved in astronomy. Some may worry that such an approach explains away scripture, in the same way perhaps that Cittadino's attribution of central approaches in ecology to interactions among the human and life sciences at the University of Chicago may seem to undermine the authority of that science. In contrast, we believe that Belovsky's creative approach—unusual applications of mathematics and the physical sciences—is not inherently different from many traditional theological investigations. Climate is as much a part of the conditions in which the Bible was composed as are the ancient languages used by biblical authors. We can think of such work in terms of calibrating one's instruments: how we interpret a signal is our own business, but we cannot interpret it at all unless we have confidence that the instruments are properly calibrated. By placing biblical history in climatic and ecological context, Belovsky illustrates why so little biblical teaching directly concerns environmental matters. That dearth of teaching, in turn, contributes to the indifference and downright hostility toward environmental concerns expressed by some contemporary churches—the phenomenon lamented by Van Houtan and Pimm.

Peter White, in chapter 6, demonstrating the profound presence of flux in purportedly stable ecosystems and the potential of relatively minor disturbances to cause major change, exemplifies the shift from the balance of nature to the flux of nature. White is one of the seminal figures in exploring the implications of this new ecology of flux. One of his critics is the eminent environmental historian Donald Worster. Worster questions the necessity and motives of this change in master narrative from the balance of nature (which Worster locates in the concept of ecosystem) to flux (which Worster characterizes as chaos) (Worster 1997). Surely, he suggests, ecologists have always known that nature changes. Since there is both stability and change in nature, why promulgate the gloomy prospect of chaos and flux? Worster expresses concern for the implications of ecological flux narratives for environmental protection. But the practical effect of his criticism would be to impose on science a set of concepts that its practitioners find are unwarranted and no longer helpful in the development of what the philosopher of science Imre Lakatos calls "a progressive research program" (Lakatos 1970). As both White and Worster recognize, language is not neutral. But that recognition itself does not undermine either the history or the science. Rather, it should help to focus the subsequent critical discourse on issues that are central to both ecology and environmentalism, as White's chapter illustrates.

Writing as a philosopher of science, Patricia Fleming points out in chapter 7 that the issues that arise in connection with flux are usefully considered in terms of several classic philosophical problems. Among these are the naturalistic fallacy itself: that even if we must find ways of going from "is" to "ought," "is" does not imply "ought." Another is the quandary of realism: when we say "flux," or equally when we say "ecosystem," what kind of real existence do those entities have? Are they in fact entities or models? A third is the problem of underdetermination: we must learn, notes Fleming, that decision making in a climate of uncertainty is a normal, and not a pathological, condition of science. Tension between these poles is inherent to science: we do not resolve these problems, but an awareness of them is essential to the enterprise of critical thinking.

In chapters 8 and 9, two ecotheologians explore the implications of a master metaphor of flux. John Haught finds the concept helpful in moving beyond two valuable but limited approaches in previous ecotheology: the focus on apologetics (discovering biblical evidence of environmental concern) and on sacramentalism (seeing creation as incarnation and as a means of communion with the divine). As a complement to these approaches, Haught offers the central eschatological element in Christianity—the idea that the human enterprise is unfolding toward some end. Recognition of flux in nature brings ecological science into compatibility with a religious perspective: both are the working out of an "unfinished universe." Haught's perspective offers an alternative to those many forms of green utopianism that have sought a radical withdrawal to a former stasis in nature—some form of social organization that embodies Christian precepts, nourishes human virtues, and maintains the integrity of God's creation. Haught's argument, in contrast, relies on traditional theological themes in eschatology that embrace change, though not just any change. For Haught, the theology of promise, linked with the more traditional ecotheological approaches—the reflection on scripture and an abiding sense of incarnation—will help guide that change.

In chapter 9, Larry Rasmussen uses Christian social ethics to raise well-founded concerns that flux is an open invitation to "anything goes." To Rasmussen, though, the withdrawal of guarantees from nature suggests that we must act *more* carefully, not less so, and that we must find ways to recognize environmental protection as good and right in itself, regardless of clear expectations about the response of nature. Rasmussen finds particularly worrisome an emerging perspective that he calls "ecomodernity," in which the nonhuman is decidedly secondary, its diversity significant only for the genes we can extract from it. This perspective, according to Rasmussen, along with other elements of modernity and postmodernity, privileges exploitation, alienation, imperialism, and consumerism. Ultimately, it sustains an enormous contempt for life—human as well as nonhuman. This perspective is contradictory, Rasmussen argues, with the Christian notion of human identity developed by Augustine and reiterated by great modern theologians in the tradition of Barth and Bonhoeffer. This historical Christian notion challenges self-pride rather than celebrating it. Rasmussen focuses on elements of Christian traditions that will need to be accentuated in a world characterized by flux. These overlap with Haught's suggestions, and include asceticism, sacramentalism, mysticism, and prophetic and liberating community practices. These elements of the religions of the book are often seen as outré or archaic, but perhaps only because they are so incompatible with ecomodernity.

Rasmussen's direct query—how must we live?—returns us to the Van Houtan and Pimm question of what is going on in mainline American churches, and to Whitney's invitation to think harder about the history in which we find ourselves. Christianity as an institution did not inspire environmental degradation, Whitney argues. That does not change the fact that environmental changes of the magnitude and scope that now concern us are largely the product of the globalization that emerged in a Western civilization, most of whose members understood themselves as inheritors of traditions originating in the Bible. Whitney recognizes that the fascination with world-reshaping technology was not uniquely linked to religion and was not a product of any doctrine. At the same time, as Stoll reminds us, those who championed such technologies saw their advocacy, and indeed, their identity, within a religious narrative. Religion will (and should) continue to be the framework in which we think about the use and design of technology. The challenge is to find, within religion, a framework for making the choices with which Van Houtan and Pimm and Rasmussen confront us.

ECOLOGY, FAITH, AND CITIZENSHIP

We began with the assertion that any significant environmental change in America will take place in a religious framework. And yet religion is generally regarded as conservative, while change—increase in concern for the environment in particular—is often associated with the secular and radical critique of American conservatism. An ecology emphasizing flux may seem even more threatening to religious people than one focused on stasis, because it may seem to imply no standards and no roots, just as relativistic physics seemed to imply moral and epistemic relativism. Yet the representation of religion as conservative is at least partly misleading. Historically, religion has been an enormously powerful transformative agent. One need only think of the many social movements we call the Reformation or the successive evangelical "awakenings" or the movements to abolish slavery and establish civil rights. Those transformations affected not only learned people in universities, but people in all walks of life, and in profound ways.

With regard to what specific changes in attitude and practice are appropriate—the right response to flux—the issue is more complex. Does anything go? Thomas Huxley, we noted earlier, urged us not to look to nature for morality. Huxley ended up seeing the human enterprise as the replacement of nature's valuelessness with the human values of compassion and expansive responsibility. In two respects Huxley's solution seems no longer satisfactory. First, in comparison with Huxley, modern scientists recognize more ways in which actions by the increasing number of humans affect and are affected by biogeophysical systems. It seems clear that the premise Huxley used—that the human relation with the nonhuman is a zero-sum game in which humans only win when nature loses, and vice versa—is an unwarranted and risky one, albeit one that still holds sway in many quarters. Increasingly, it is obvious that human welfare is inextricably tied to the welfare of nature (Toulmin 1982; Daily 1997). Second, many religious and nonreligious people now reject Huxley's forthright agnostic cultural imperialism as exemplifying hubris. Instead they see beauty and unfolding prophecy in wilderness, in natural diversity, or in evolutionary change. If they differ on how and when nature should be restrained, they are also often convinced that unrestrained human ambition is not good for humans. The concept of flux, frustratingly, suggests no easy way out of that muddle: it does not lend itself to the establishment of clear rules or doctrines to be taught and enforced.

Flux requires profound intellectual, cultural, and religious changes. Religion will be an important vehicle of those changes not only because it remains so important for so many Americans, but because the necessary transformations are properly understood as religious—they involve changes of human identity. Those changes are both familiar and foreign. For many, they will involve radical reckonings with conservative Christian tradition, which are prefigured in the analyses and prescriptions of Haught and Rasmussen. In brief, they will require increased attention to tenets that most religious leaders have urged upon their followers throughout the ages: a sense of one's own earthly impermanence; membership in and responsibility to a community; constant susceptibility to sin; a sense of sacramental communion with the rest of creation; a sense of participating in a great unfolding drama; and the translation of all these senses into actions that embody respect, connection, care, and hope. All these imply a greater accountability—a degree of accountability that sits uncomfortably with contemporary American culture but that is familiar to religious people. If translated into cultural changes and political structures, however, the changes could be profound.

One of the most unsettling aspects about environmental responsibility in a framework of flux is the displacement of expertise (Ludwig, Mangel, and Haddad 2001). If we believe that there is a static, ideal nature around which we must model our societies, we necessarily privilege the rule of the experts who best understand that ecological paradise. If, on the other hand, we believe that nature is in flux and that we cannot guarantee outcomes (though we can make prudential judgments), we are privileging something else. That something else is not expertise as it is usually understood, nor is it democracy, nor anarchy, nor rugged individualism. It is, in a broad sense, communitarian—it requires that prudential judgments will be made by individuals, working singly or in groups, who are skilled in a variety of different, but not mutually exclusive, modes of analysis, including scientific, religious, economic, cultural, and ethical analysis (Ludwig, Mangel, and Haddad 2001).

Some of these intellectual approaches are represented in this book. Because this is a first attempt to establish a framework for appropriate interdisciplinary analysis of nature in flux, the book does not rise to the crescendo of a simple conclusion. Rather, chapters are recursive, highlighting an existential dilemma: In the recent past, our disciplines were independent fortresses of authority defended by the canons of specialized knowledge. The university classroom and the public square were compartmentalized, giving authority to one sort of expertise on a given topic. Religion was a barely tolerated holdover from a time of superstition, and personal faith was illusion. The rejection of such authorities by modernists and postmodernists was driven by the need to recognize other cultures and other forms of knowledge. Partly the critique was epistemic. It recognized the multiplicity of ways people construe reality. It focused on the power of language and on cultural context, just as many of the chapters in this book do. This is an appropriate and constructive perspective if it is not taken to the extreme of forsaking confidence that we can approach reality more closely through intellectual exercise, experiment, and experience. Without dismissing the technical prowess of disciplines and the knowledge of experts, we must respect and seek to integrate the perspectives of all relevant disciplines.

Nature in flux poses substantial challenges to the science of ecology, but the challenges posed to the management of biodiversity and ecosystems are even greater (Lodge and Shrader-Frechette 2003). For a response that satisfies human needs and adequately addresses human responsibilities to nature, society must muster its religious and scientific resources in a collaborative effort. In the conclusion to this volume, we respond to the imperative to account for the flux of nature with several recommendations for our individual and collective behaviors as inhabitants of earth. Drawing on traditional religious resources that are not contingent on the balance of nature, we first advocate looking inward to avoid the disastrous personal, societal, and environmental consequences that follow from the ecomodernity described by Rasmussen. Then we illustrate how these religiously rooted personal resources can inform practical issues of environmental management in ways that carefully incorporate both the "is" and "ought." It is our hope that this volume opens the door to more such collaboration that is both intellectually rigorous and of great practical importance in guiding human treatment of creation.

Works Cited

Albanese, Catherine. 1990. *Nature religion in America from the Algonkian Indians to the new age.* Chicago: University of Chicago Press.

Bakken, Peter W., Joan Gibb Engel, and J. Ronald Engel. 1995. *Ecology, justice, and Christian faith: A critical guide to the literature.* Westport, CT: Greenwood.

Barbour, Ian, ed. 1973. *Western man and environmental ethics.* Reading, MA: Addison-Wesley.

Black, John. 1970. *The dominion of man: The search for ecological responsibility.* Edinburgh: Edinburgh Univeristy Press.

Callicott, J. B. 1982. Hume's is/ought dichotomy and the relation of ecology to Leopold's land ethic. *Environmental Ethics* 4:163–74.

Carson, Rachel. 1962. *Silent spring.* Boston: Houghton Mifflin.

Chesson, P. L., and T. J. Case. 1986. Overview: Nonequilibrium community theories; Chance, variability, history, and coexistence. In *Community Ecology,* ed. J. Diamond and T. J. Case, 229–39. New York: Harper and Row.

Cohen, J. E. 1995. *How many people can the earth support?* New York: W. W. Norton.

Conant, James B. 1951. *Science and common sense.* New Haven, CT: Yale University Press.

Daily, G. C. 1997. *Nature's services: Societal dependence on natural ecosystems.* Washington DC: Island Press.

Dostoevsky, Fyodor. 1970. *The Brothers Karamozov.* New York: Bantam.

Dunlap, Thomas R. 2004. *Faith in nature: Environmentalism as religious quest.* Seattle: University of Washington Press.

Foster, John Bellamy. 2000. *Marx's ecology: Materialism and nature.* New York: Monthly Review Press.

Fox, Stephen. 1981. *The American conservation movement: John Muir and his legacy.* Madison: University of Wisconsin Press.

Glacken, Clarence. 1967. *Traces on the Rhodian shore: Nature and culture in western thought from ancient times to the end of the eighteenth century.* Berkeley: University of California Press.

Gottlieb, Robert. 1993. *Forcing the spring: The transformation of the American environmental movement.* Washington DC: Island Press.

Graham, Frank, Jr. 1970. *Since "Silent spring."* Greenwich, CT: Fawcett Crest.

Guth, J. L., J. C. Green, L. A. Kellstedt, and C. E. Smidt. 1995. Faith and the environment: Religious beliefs and attitudes on environmental policy. *American Journal of Political Science* 39:364–82.

Hagen, Joel. 1992. *An entangled bank: The origins of ecosystem ecology.* New Brunswick, NJ: Rutgers University Press.

Hamlin, Christopher, and Philip Shepard. 1993. *Deep disagreement in U.S. agriculture: Making sense of policy conflict.* Boulder, CO: Westview.

Kingsland, Sharon E. 1995. *Modeling nature.* Chicago: University of Chicago Press.

Lakatos, Imre. 1970. Falsification and the methodology of scientific research programmes. In *Criticism and the growth of knowledge,* ed. Imre Lakatos and Alan Musgrave, 91–196. Cambridge: Cambridge University Press.

Leopold, A. 1970. A *Sand County almanac with essays on conservation from Round River.* San Francisco: Sierra Club/Ballantine.

Lewin, R. 1992. *Complexity: Life at the edge of chaos.* New York: Macmillan Publishing Co.

Lodge, D. M., and K. Shrader-Frechette. 2003. Nonindigenous species: Ecological explanation, environmental ethics, and public policy. *Conservation Biology* 17:31–37.

Ludwig, D., M. Mangel, and B. Haddad. 2001. Ecology, conservation, and public policy. *Annual Review of Ecology and Systematics* 32:481–517.

McIntosh, Robert P. 1987. Pluralism in ecology. *Annual Review of Ecology and Systematics* 18:321–41.

Paradis, James, and George C. Williams. 1989. *Evolution and ethics: T. H. Huxley's "Evolution and ethics" with new essays on its Victorian and socio-biological context.* Princeton, NJ: Princeton University Press.

Proctor, Robert N. 1991. *Value-free science? Purity and power in modern knowledge.* Cambridge, MA: Harvard University Press.

Sarewitz, D., R. A. Pielke, Jr., and R. Byerly, Jr. 2000. *Prediction: Science, decision making, and the future of nature.* Washington DC: Island Press.

Scheffer, M., S. R. Carpenter, J. A. Foley, C. Folke, and B. Walker. 2001. Catastrophic shifts in ecosystems. *Nature* 413:591–96.

Spring, D., and E. Spring. 1974. *Ecology and religion in history.* New York: Harpers.

Stoll, Mark. 1997. *Protestantism, capitalism, and nature in America.* Albuquerque: University of New Mexico Press.

Tawney, R. H. 1926. *Religion and the Rise of Capitalism.* New York: Harcourt, Brace, and Company. Repr., Harmondsworth: Pelican, 1972.

Toulmin, Stephen. 1982. *The return to cosmology: Postmodern science and the theology of nature.* Berkeley: University of California Press.

Tucker, William. 1982. *Progress and privilege: America in the age of environmentalism.* Garden City, NJ: Doubleday.

Weber, Max. 1930. *The Protestant ethic and the spirit of capitalism.* Trans. Talcott Parsons. New York: Scribner's.

White, L. 1967. The historical roots of our ecologic crisis. *Science* 155:1203–7.

Whitney, E. 1993. Lynn White, ecotheology, and history. *Environmental Ethics* 15:151–69.

Worster, Donald. 1997. The ecology of order and chaos. In *Out of the woods: Essays in environmental history,* ed. Char Miller and Hal Rothman, 3–17. Pittsburgh: University of Pittsburgh Press.

Wu, J., and O. L. Loucks. 1995. From balance of nature to hierarchical patch dynamics: A paradigm shift in ecology. *The Quarterly Review of Biology* 70:439–66.

CHAPTER I

Christianity and Changing Concepts of Nature: An Historical Perspective

Elspeth Whitney

From our vantage point at the turn of the second millennium it appears clear that modern Western science and technology, for both good and ill, have transformed the world in myriad and extraordinary ways over the past thousand years. The implications of these changes, for both the earth on which we dwell and for human life, are still not completely understood; given the constantly accelerating rate of technological change, they may never be fully comprehended at any point in the present. The past, however, at least appears to be a more stationary target. Historians and philosophers of history attempt to explain changes in the course of human society on both the local and specific and on the grand scales. Their explanations of the distinctiveness of the Western model of technological progress and its apparently ever-increasing control of nature hold out the hope not only of understanding past events and conditions but of offering useful commentary on contemporary environmental issues. In dialogue with conclusions drawn by scientists and scholars of religion, environmental ethics, and philosophy, the historical perspective can help anchor discussion in present as well as past experience.

In this chapter I will examine some aspects of the commonly held thesis that the values of medieval Christianity explain the utilitarian and aggressive attitude toward the natural world that has characterized the modern West. This interpretation, articulated in its most well-known form by the American historian of technology Lynn White, Jr., and generally known as the "Lynn White thesis," has dominated discussions of the historical roots of modern Western conceptions of nature, technology, and the environment over the past forty years. In suggesting some alternatives to White's thesis, I do not intend to eliminate religious ideas and values as a moving force in history; religion, without question, has played an enormous role in history, including setting the perimeters of both prescribed and discouraged behavior toward the nonhuman world. Rather, I wish to suggest that religious beliefs and practices are themselves to some degree shaped by the societies that espouse them and must be considered in conjunction with their social, economic, and political contexts. In other words, theological doctrines, even though largely determined by internal logic, do not stand alone and in isolation from other aspects of cultural and social experience but are anchored in concrete, time-bound historical contexts. Nor can we ignore the mechanisms by which beliefs are put into practice; religious values must be embodied in cultural and institutional practices to have a lasting and far-reaching effect beyond the individual. Overall, it seems more faithful to human experience to conceptualize values, religious and otherwise, as in a state of continual interaction with economic, political, and social conditions rather than as free-standing, completely autonomous agents of historical change.

Ideas about proper human relations with nature, other humans, and God, moreover, are conditioned by powerful but often unstated epistemological assumptions: the terms "human nature," "nature," and "culture," are, in one sense, semantic constructs that carry significant value-laden baggage from the past into the present (Herron and Kirk 1999). White's use of these constructs, on which his thesis explicitly and implicitly relies, must also be critically examined if we are to properly evaluate the relevance of the White thesis to contemporary environmental ethics.

Modern Western society has pursued technological advance with such systematic and pervasive determination that we can today with some justification speak of the "end of nature" (McKibben 1990). Yet environmental and other historians, following the lead of White, have argued that a pattern of Western aggressiveness in controlling nature was set first not in modern times but in the Middle Ages. Although technology and industry "took off" also in the sixteenth and seventeenth centuries and again in the nineteenth, historians of technology are generally agreed that later European development was to a large extent dependent upon, and contingent to, the precedents set roughly between the years 1000 and

1500. If the changes during the Industrial Revolution of the nineteenth century, for example, were more obviously dramatic, complex, and widespread, they nevertheless rested on prior attitudes, conditions, and innovations dating back to the medieval period (Landes 1969, 12–22; Campbell 1995). During the early Middle Ages new agricultural techniques resulted in the improved food supply and population growth that formed the basis for later European urbanism. The twelfth and thirteenth centuries saw new developments in the use of wind and water power, advances in engineering, and the expansion of mining and land clearance, as well as more mundane but important inventions such as the rotary crank, the wheelbarrow, the spinning wheel, the chimney, and eyeglasses. By the end of the Middle Ages, four fundamental inventions that would help change the course of world history had appeared: the compass, the mechanical clock, cannon and the first firearms, and the printing press. Perhaps even more importantly, Europeans by 1500 had demonstrated a systematic effort to adapt older techniques to new conditions and to actively seek out new and improved technologies. A well-known case in point: gunpowder was first invented in China, where it was used as an explosive, but it was in late medieval Europe, over the course of a half-century, that craftsmen put out the determined effort that resulted in the first effective handguns (Hall 1997; on medieval technology see also White 1962; Crombie 1959, 1:175–238; Gimpel 1980; DeVries 1992; Dohrn-van Rossum 1996; Magnusson 2001; Gies and Gies 1994; Mark 1990). Similarly, it was in the Middle Ages that the social, political, and economic structures that economic historians have linked to the genesis of modernization and industrialization began to take shape: fluid and flexible patterns of landholding and property ownership, a range of possible economic choices, multiple and overlapping centers of power, and localized and often competitive economic networks. The European West was so successful at technological and economic development that by the fourteenth century Europe had already suffered a series of environmental problems including polluted cities, decreased grain harvests, and severe pockets of deforestation (Gimpel 1990, 75–92; Coates 1998, 40–48).

The discovery of medieval technological accomplishments helped shake prior assumptions about medieval "backwardness," assumptions that are now generally banished from academic discourse but still surface in the popular press. The discovery of the dynamism and innovativeness of medieval technology also spurred a reassessment of ideas and attitudes about nature in the Middle Ages. Paradoxically, the overwhelming influence of religion—the very quality that once had been held up as the reason why the Middle Ages were dark, oppressively otherworldly and devoid of progress—now emerged as the primary reason behind medieval advances in science and technology. Lynn White and other scholars from a range of disciplines found in medieval Christianity the source of a new rationalistic attitude toward nature and a concern with reforming the conditions of human life—these together encouraged and sanctioned an aggressive approach to the natural world. White, in particular, persuasively articulated the thesis that modern technological inventiveness and exploitative attitudes toward nature grew out of the mental habits inculcated by medieval Christianity. Christianity, he claimed in his famous 1967 article "The Historical Roots of Our Ecologic Crisis" (hereafter "Roots"), therefore bore "a huge burden of guilt" for the current environmental crisis (White 1967, 1206). European monks, White argued, believed work to be an essential form of worship and embodied this assertion not only in the *Rules* governing their lives but in their practice of their faith. Monastic communities spearheaded new and improved technological techniques, developed tightly organized economic practices, and ploughed their wealth back into their economic and pastoral enterprises. Furthermore, White argued, medieval religion promoted moral approval of technology. Christianity, White argued, "in absolute contrast to ancient paganism and Asia's religions . . . not only established a dualism of man and nature but also insisted that it is God's will that man exploit nature for his proper ends" (White 1967, 1206). Latin cathedrals, in marked contrast to Byzantine churches, he pointed out, were typically decorated with mechanical clocks and organs, two of the most complex machines known prior to the early modern period. Additional evidence that medieval Christianity sanctioned technological advance can be found in manuscript illuminations, such as a ninth-century illustration of David's army using a rotary crank driven knife to sharpen their swords while the heathen enemy uses an old-fashioned whetstone. White also pointed to the late medieval emphasis on temperance, often associated with the clock as a symbol of moderation, as the chief virtue. His evidence included a 1450 illustration of a personification of Temperance depicted standing on a windmill, a bridle in one hand, spurs on her feet, wearing spectacles and with a clock on her head. The verse that accompanies the illumination begins, "He who is mindful of the clock is punctual in all his acts," and ends, "The mill which sustains our bodies never is immoderate" (White 1978b, 199). This kind of evidence, taken together with the record of medieval technological invention, White argued, demonstrated that "psychic foundations" embedded within Latin Christianity made the pursuit of technology appear morally virtuous, leading ultimately not only to Western technological dominance but to the continuing impact on the environment of an aggressive and exploitative stance toward nature.

In attributing the dynamism of medieval technology and society to "cultural climates" and deep-seated modes of thought connected to religion White and others were drawing on a well-worn explanatory paradigm. In many ways, they were simply updating a master narrative that had its roots in eighteenth-century ideas of progress celebrating human achievements in technology, politics, and science. At least since the work of Max Weber in the early twentieth century, many Western scholars have seen Western economic and political success as a direct result of a mental habit of "rationalization," the application of certain kinds of rational principles to human activities allowing precise calculation rather than traditional or personal practices to govern decisions. Weber, the chief architect of this view, argued that in order for the full force of the "economic impulse" to be expressed, economic and material relationships had to be guided by an ethic that sanctioned the pursuit of gain, disregarding traditional religious ties while preserving social norms. He found the source of such an ethic in the Calvinist idea of the "calling," which allowed for the assimilation of work and economic gain into an ideal of worldly asceticism, thus eliminating the traditional Christian tension between piety and economic success. Weber argued that Protestantism's rereading of Scripture encouraged the "spirit of capitalism" not only by endowing ordinary daily activities with a religious purpose and encouraging thrift and hard work as religious virtues, but also by sanctioning personal economic success as contributing to the general good and as a sign of God's favor.

The rationalization of economic behavior assumed that human activities legitimately took place in a secular world for worldly, as well as otherworldly, ends. Nature, likewise, was increasingly detached from the sacred and seen as an object capable of manipulation or control rather than as a living or divine being. The "disenchantment of the world," in Weber's famous phrase, therefore paradoxically had its roots in the Protestant interpretation of the biblical tradition, a tradition that contained within itself the seeds of a secularized vision of Christian providence.

Lynn White, on the other hand, found the origins of these same attitudes in medieval religious sanction of technology and the disciplined life. Despite his negative assessment in "Roots," in the larger corpus of his work he frequently asserted that technology was a fundamentally humane and liberating force. Indeed, he implicitly suggests an image of an inherently dynamic, progressive, and Christian West in which "values" rather than politics or economics determine history. By emphasizing the reformist aspects of earlier Christian practice and theology, White neatly transposed Weber's ideas back into pre-Reformation Catholicism, making the medieval monk, rather than the Puritan businessman, the pivotal figure promoting the rational and efficient use of nature.

The impact of White's updating of Weber's thesis was extraordinary. Because he addressed first the scientific and general community, rather than a specialized group of historians, White reached a wide and diverse audience. White was personally a strong believer in the potential of the humanities to play an important role in public discourse; moreover, he himself was professionally committed to advancing the liberal arts in the public arena (Hall 1989, 196–97). It was appropriate, therefore, that White published his thesis first in *Science* several years before writing more detailed and nuanced versions in academic journals. It is also significant that, unlike almost every other published writing by White, the argument of "Roots" is couched as a criticism, rather than an endorsement, of the effects of Christianity and technological advance (Whitney 1993).

By breaching disciplinary boundaries, White made his thesis a focal point for debate among environmental historians, scholars of religion and environmental ethics, and the general public. Less than seven pages long, "Roots" nevertheless galvanized an entire segment of the American public that had recently awakened to the possibility of environmental disaster. Reprints of the article appeared in numerous anthologies, textbooks, and the popular press, including such diverse venues as *The Boy Scout Handbook,* the *Sierra Club Bulletin,* the *Whole Earth Catalogue,* the hippie newsletter the *Oracle,* and *Horizon Magazine.* In 1970 both *Time Magazine* and the *New York Times* featured summaries of White's essay, and in 1972 Senator Alan Cranston quoted Lynn White approvingly to Congress (Whitney 1993, 157–59).[1] It was translated into German, Spanish, and Italian; inspired a sociological study on the relationship of church membership to attitudes toward the environment; and was the target of an academic parody. The great historian Arnold Toynbee paid White the compliment of appropriating its argument twice without acknowledgement (Hand and Van Liere 1984; Fudpucker 1984; Toynbee 1973).[2]

More importantly, "Roots" has been credited with being instrumental in creating the field of ecotheology, which developed into a major arena of scholarly debate on the relationship of religion and attitudes toward nature, and of being one of the founding texts of the Deep Ecology movement (Sessions 1995, 101, 171–72). White's criticism of Christianity as ultimately responsible for the environmental crisis sparked a widespread and concerted defense of Christian values as mandating stewardship and moral responsibility for the earth and all its creatures, in contrast to White's emphasis on exploitation. Today "Roots" remains a focal point for discussion. In the burgeoning industry of textbooks on environmental ethics, for example, White's ideas remain a staple talking point, and "Roots" is routinely included in collections of writings on environmental issues. A profile of White was included in a 2001 guide, *Fifty Key Thinkers on the Environment*, along with Aristotle, Black Elk, and Rachel Carson (Nelson 2001, 200–205). The claims made for the impact of White's thought are sometimes startling. A 2003 anthology for classroom use, for example, includes one essay calling White "perhaps the most influential" writer in the country on the negative impact of the Judeo-Christian tradition on the environment and another crediting White with sparking the "articulation of an explicitly Islamic environmental ethic" (Schwarzschild 2003, 300; Foltz 2003, 359).

Today, over thirty years after White published his major work, the debate between those who argue that the Judeo-Christian tradition has had a predominately negative effect on environmental values and those who argue that it is an important reservoir of stewardship ethics continues to elicit strong interest (Kinsley 1995). This debate has been useful in clarifying contemporary attitudes toward the environment; it has been far less helpful in sorting out the historical origins of modern attitudes toward nature. By and large the conversation about "Roots" has been conducted in terms of the abstract content of Christian values, rather than by looking at shifting understandings of these values in different times and places in the context of medieval environmental and technological practices. Yet if we are to ascribe historical causation to values, we need to clarify not only what those values are but to look carefully at how, when, where, why, and by whom these values were put into practice. Above all, the question to what extent theology helped create a rationalized and utilitarian approach to nature in the Middle Ages or, conversely, largely reflected the habits of a society that had found practical success in exploiting natural resources has yet to be systematically addressed. In part, the failure to come to grips with White's thesis is due to the failure of scholars to draw upon cross-disciplinary approaches that integrate research from the history of technology and economic and social history with the history of ideas, biblical scholarship, and cultural studies. There is also a deplorable (from the point of view of a medievalist) lack of serious attention to the complexity and range of medieval thought and life. It is significant that the great majority of both the champions and the critics of "Roots" have not been historians and, particularly, have not been medieval historians. In the present chapter I hope to point to some areas that warrant continued investigation.

The question of cause and effect goes to the heart of the difficult issue of the relationship between cultural values and social practices in shaping the individual and collective actions of people in a particular society at a given time in history. At bottom, discussion of whether theological sanction of technology was the *source* or merely an *effect* of technological development is one of prioritizing causes for complex events, the most difficult yet most essential task of the historian. An historian's identification of causes is likely to reflect not only his or her selection of the relevant factual evidence but also deep-seated personal and philosophical attitudes and habits of thought; these in turn are often shaped by the historian's own historical circumstances. Powerful historical interpretations, such as those of Weber and White, need to be examined not only in the light of empirical evidence for and against the argument but also in the light of the assumptions guiding the historian's choice of primary and secondary causes. Only then can we fully appreciate how our explanations of change in the past hold important implications for our understanding of our own situation in the present.

My intention here is not to substitute economic or other kinds of determinism for a reliance on religion as the primary spring of historical change. Religious ideas and values have clearly had, and continue to have, profound effects on human history. Rather, I would like to suggest ways in which our account of the sources of medieval technological dynamism can become more nuanced by considering how the interplay of a variety of factors may have worked together to encourage technological development in the Middle Ages. In the remainder of this essay, I will focus on two particular issues important to the Lynn White thesis and suggest how recent work by medieval and other historians problematizes White's identification of Latin Christianity as the single and only cause of medieval technological dynamism. The first issue is the significance to technological development of the shift from an animistic view of nature, identified by White and other historians with paganism, to the notion of nature as an object, which they associated with the Judeo-Christian tradition. This example illustrates how close attention to the specifics of timing and place can afford a corrective to plausible but overly general interpretations of historical change. The second issue I take up is a consideration of the relationship of ideas and "values" to economic motivations as they can be examined in medieval monasticism and elsewhere in medieval rural life. A survey of scholarship on this issue suggests that religious and economic interests can mutually reinforce each other, to the point that it is difficult to pin down one as the "cause" of the other. Finally, I will look at the rhetoric of White's writing in order to highlight some of the as yet unexamined implications of White's argument for the development of a persuasive environmental ethic in the present.

The emergence of the mechanical model for natural processes during the course of the Scientific Revolution was a crucial development in Western conceptions of nature. By the eighteenth century a view of nature as a machine, a vast clockwork operating according to morally neutral natural laws, had largely replaced the earlier concept of nature as a living organic entity, possessing its own "ends" or desires. The metaphor of nature as a living body current in the premodern world took many forms and can be found in a variety of religious practices, both folk and learned, and philosophical and scientific systems, including Stoicism, Aristotelianism, Neoplatonism, gnosticism, and alchemy. The idea that the earth was animated by an immaterial soul or vital principle, which we can loosely subsume under the rubric of "animism," meant that all things, including those that modern science regards as inanimate, were seen as possessing spirit and thus were regarded as potentially possessing degrees of autonomy, the power of self-direction, and intelligence. Overall, it is the animistic view of nature that historically has been the prevailing one; the relatively late emergence in the modern West of an alternate view of nature as a machine is the exception.

We can see the broadest difference between these two concepts of the natural world if we juxtapose an ancient Mesopotamian prayer, "O Salt," (roughly 2500 BCE)[3] with Descartes' description of the "man-machine" written in 1664. In the prayer to Salt the petitioner asks Salt to release him from an enchantment that he suffers under: "O salt, take from me the bewitchment . . . and I shall extol thee" (Frankfort et al. 1977, 24). Here the (to us) inert material salt is given the powers of an intelligent living being, including susceptibility to praise and flattery. Far from being "dead," salt is seen as intensely alive. In contrast, Descartes writes of the human body and its functions as if it were a purely mechanical, lifeless object. "All the functions which I have attributed to this machine," he writes, "such as the digestion of food; the beating of the heart and arteries; . . . the reception by the external sense organs of light, sounds, smells, tastes, heat and all other such qualities; the imprinting of the ideas of these qualities in the organ of common sense and imagination; the retention or imprint of these ideas in the memory; the internal movements of the appetites and passions . . . they follow naturally in this machine entirely from the disposition of the organs—no more nor less than do the movements of a clock or other automation, form the arrangement of its counterweights and wheels" (Descartes 1972, 113). In this passage, even the human faculties of sensation, imagination, and desire are presented as mere by-products of the motions of a robot-like mechanical device; the physical body, sense impressions, and even emotions are reduced to the workings of a machine.

Descartes, a complex thinker, elsewhere in his work qualifies this picture of human physiology and psychology as wholly mechanical; indeed, as I show below, the distinction between an animistic and a mechanical view of nature is less clear-cut than it first appears. Nevertheless, by the time of Newton in the late seventeenth century, European thinkers increasingly represented the universe as a whole as a vast clockwork rather than as an organic body. Composed of solid, massy particles of matter moving through space according to immutable mathematical laws, nature in the mechanistic worldview possessed no inherent qualities of any kind. Immediate human observation and experience were of little use in comprehending this natural world; rather, its workings could be understood only through methodical inquiry, experiment, and mathematical analysis.

It is worthwhile to draw out some of the contrasting implications of these two very different views of nature. In the animistic view represented by the prayer to salt, the natural world is made up of an infinitely varied multiplicity of living things, each one of which can and should be dealt with on a personal and individual level. The universe and natural phenomena are living entities, possessed of inner sources of movement and vitality and hence possessed also of spirits and even personalities. Humans lived in the world cognizant of its many potential threats to human life but nevertheless at home. Nature, the gods, and men were not all that different; indeed, from the modern Western perspective it appears that ancient thought created nature in the image of man. Or to be more precise, in the image of woman, for ancient writers identified the earth, and matter in general, with the feminine; the earth, often constructed in ancient writing as a bountiful mother, was modest but deceitful, protective of her hidden mysteries, and should be respected lest her reproductive capacities be diminished by human greed. As developed by thinkers in late antiquity, all beings were seen as linked in a hierarchy or "great chain of being," from the lowest, such as rocks, made up largely of matter, to the highest, composed entirely or almost entirely of pure spirit or mind. "Why then should we not judge the world to be animate and endowed with wisdom, when it produces animate and wise offspring?" asks the Stoic Cicero, quoting Zeno (Cicero 1967, 145). Most classical thinkers understood nature in terms of analogies drawn from purposive activity. Like humans and other biological organisms, all material things, up to and including the stars and planets themselves, were propelled by their own inner directiveness and desire to fulfill their potentiality for their own perfection and excellence.

In contrast, as the mechanized worldview became increasingly dominant in the early modern era, scientists set nature apart as a thoroughly impersonal and "other" realm to be approached not by building rapport through sympathetic insight but by manipulation through experiment. As a metaphor for the cosmos the body was replaced by the clock. In the language of some scientists, most notably Francis Bacon, nature, usually constructed as female, must be forced and dominated to suit the purposes of the human experimenter, almost always constructed as male. At the same time, the mastery of nature through technology, which was becoming increasingly visible in the West, was also being used more and more as evidence of the superiority of the Western male over animals, women, and non-Western peoples, even as images of Mother Nature increasingly depicted her as coyly submissive (Adas 1992; Merchant 1980, 189–91; Ruether 1994, 192–99). In Carolyn Merchant's formulation, the "Baconian-Cartesian-Newtonian project" presupposed a notion of fallen Nature, encoded as female, which was to be controlled by male science and technology and organized by a male-dominated state (Merchant 1995, 31, 32).

White and others have often asserted both that Christianity destroyed animism and that the end of an animistic viewpoint was an important and essential part of the "rationalization" of Western culture. Christian theology took from Judaism the concept of a transcendent creator God, outside and beyond a created, material, and therefore secondary natural world. Animistic beliefs and practices were identified by early Christian authorities with paganism and drew harsh penalties as constituting idol-worship. The natural world, described in the book of Genesis as distinct both from its divine creator and from the human beings given dominion over it, manifested God's goodness but no longer possessed its own autonomous source of life and being. Similarly, it is often claimed that the substitution of a concept of nature as an inanimate object would automatically encourage technology. Devoid of spirits and increasingly objectified, nature could more easily be seen merely as a means to an end, to be mastered and controlled but not necessarily honored. Lynn White argued this point unequivocally: "To a Christian a tree can be no more than a physical fact. . . . [F]or nearly two millennia Christian missionaries have been chopping down sacred groves which are idolatrous because they assume spirit in nature" (White 1967, 1206). Carolyn Merchant, speaking of the mechanistic worldview that prevailed in the sixteenth and seventeenth centuries, remarks in *The Death of Nature,* "Because nature was now viewed as a system of dead, inert particles moved by external, rather than inherent forces, the mechanical framework itself could legitimate the manipulation of nature" (Merchant 1980, 193). Similarly, David Landes, noted historian of the Industrial Revolution, writes "as long as every tree had its dryad and every fountain or stream its naiad, man was intimidated and inhibited in his confrontation with nature" (Landes 1969, 24). As long as nature herself could be identified with the divine, the argument ran, it smacked of hubris or overweening pride to interfere with her internal processes; once nature had become a mere dead object, there was little or no intellectual restraint on human efforts to shape natural objects for their own purposes.

While this argument is intuitively plausible, it is difficult to maintain that there has been any simple historical relationship between the erosion of animistic or organicist worldviews and an interest in technology. A short overview of philosophical and religious concepts of nature and attitudes toward technology from antiquity to the early modern period shows that, at least prior to the eighteenth century, there has been no clear-cut correlation between animism and a rejection of technology or, conversely, between a mechanistic view of nature and technological advance.

In the first place, pagan ancient civilizations to varying degrees combined an animistic viewpoint with a practical interest in controlling and harnessing nature. Although antiquity may have not been especially technologically innovative, there is abundant evidence of a broad interest in military technology, agriculture, the use of water power, and building, reflected both in treatises on these subjects and in the practical use of mechanical devices (Long 2001, 24–45). For example, archaeological research done in the 1980s (and largely unknown to White) shows that the Romans used the water mill far more than White had believed and that the crankshaft, which White had thought was invented in the ninth century was also known to the Romans (Holt 1996, 106; Squatriti 1997, 125–32). The ancient world was aggressive enough in its use of natural resources to suffer an array of environmental issues (Hughes 1994).

Classical animism, moreover, far from being a crude belief in "spirits," reached subtle and intellectually powerful philosophical understandings of nature that were not incompatible with the idea that nature should serve humankind. The Greeks themselves made fun of cruder versions of animism; Herodotus, for example, heaped scorn on Xerxes, the would-be Persian conqueror who ordered the Hellespont whipped after a storm destroyed the bridge he had built across it. Greek thinkers centuries before the advent of Christianity articulated the notion that man should cultivate the mind and master the body and the physical environment, even if matter was regarded as ultimately alive and "ensouled." The elevation of the transcendent realm of the rational mind over the disorganized sphere of the material in Greek philosophy privileged the pursuit of purely abstract knowledge yet also at times valorized the control of the physical world as an expression of human reason. The Aristotelian conception of art, for example, conceptualized both nature and human skill as shaping matter. Overall, the approach to natural resources by the ancient Greeks and Romans may have been more manipulative than reverential (Coates 1998, 39).[4] The Stoics, for example, both argued that the universe was permeated and informed by reason and vitality and consistently expressed praise for human art and its ability to reshape the environment, creating as it were a "second nature." "This earthly part of the universe," runs one Hermetical text, "is kept in order by means of man's knowledge and application of the arts and sciences. For god willed that the universe should not be complete until man had done his part" (quoted in Glacken 1967, 146). As a reflection of the mind of God, the natural world was beautiful, orderly, and purposeful, created as a unified whole to perpetuate itself but also to serve the needs and desires of men and the gods. In contrast, the ancient Hebrews, who rigorously enforced monotheism and a ban on "nature worship," and articulated a radical distinction between man and the rest of God's creation, demonstrated no special interest in technology.

Secondly, it is not clear how effectively or quickly the Christian tradition eliminated an animistic worldview. Throughout the Latin Middle Ages Christian attitudes toward nature were less a monolithic structure of cut-and-dried theological doctrines than a fluid repository of contested beliefs and attitudes (Coates 1998, 40–66; Salisbury 1993). Medieval peasants demonstrated an interest in innovative agricultural techniques even during the early Middle Ages when their religious values were arguably still heavily influenced by pagan beliefs and practices. Early medieval shrines, churches and holy places often incorporated parts of earlier sacred objects, including trees and stones. Indeed, Karen Jolly has persuasively argued that the seventh through the twelfth centuries were characterized by a view of nature influenced by Germanic animism that merged the natural and the supernatural: "this is a world in which earth can be anthropomorphized and addressed as a principle created by God, and with no sense of contradiction with the Christian cosmology" (Jolly 1993, 235). Magical practices depending on belief in the presence of spiritual forces in plants and ordinary objects remained common among the peasantry throughout the Middle Ages, and even among the more educated the line between prayers and magical remedies was often elusive. Among theologians and philosophers reverence for nature, often interpreted through the Neoplatonic notion of divine immanence, competed with the notion of nature as completely separate from God. While the dominant theological tradition may have enforced a rigid demarcation between humans and the rest of nature, including animals, other strands within Christian thought, most notably that of St. Francis and some later Franciscans, suggested a loving kinship between men, women, and nature, expressed in such hymns as "Brother Sun, Sister Moon."

Western science and philosophy, moreover, continued to be informed by classical thought into the eighteenth century, long after the medieval

West had demonstrated its interest in technological development. Aristotelian physics and biology, loaded with animistic assumptions, was fully accepted until the Scientific Revolution. Investigation into the "occult sciences," notably alchemy, astrology, and learned magic, often depended on a sophisticated understanding of matter as permeated by spiritualized essences and hidden forces; these sciences, which shared with technology the stated aim of controlling nature, may have contributed more immediately to an ethos of the domination of nature than the modern sciences of physics and celestial mechanics (Newman 2000; see also Long 2001, 143–74; H. Cohen 1994, 169–83; Osler 2000; Henry 1990; Copenhaver 1990). Indeed, the rediscovery of the full corpus of classical writing during the Renaissance helped prompt a new interest in vitalistic scientific theories, at precisely the point at which the pace of European technological development was increasing. In the writings of Paracelsus, Della Porta, Agrippa, and others, for example, the cosmos was viewed as "a vast organism, everywhere quick and vital, its body, soul, and spirit . . . held tightly together" (Merchant 1980, 104). Based on chronology alone we would have to say that an acceleration of technological progress preceded, rather than followed, the development of mechanistic philosophy. Moreover, echoes of the earlier animistic view of nature continued throughout the Scientific Revolution, surfacing, for example, in Henry More's notion of the "spirit of nature" and the writings of Anne Conway and Ralph Cudworth. Even Newton, one of the prime architects of the new mechanistic conception of the universe, found it difficult to avoid giving matter quasi-vital properties.

Given the historical record I have outlined, attributing the triumph of aggressive attitudes toward nature directly to the destruction of animism by Christianity seems untenable. Other aspects of Latin Christian thought that have been cited as playing a general role in promoting technology might also be carefully examined in the light of specific case studies. White and others, for example, have pointed to the biblical mandate in Genesis 1:28 giving mankind "dominion over the earth," Christian compassion for the individual, and the activist strain within Western Christian ethics as encouraging a distinctively exploitative approach toward nature. Yet historians who have attempted to examine how these values were manifested in particular aspects of medieval culture and society have generally found a far more complex picture than that painted by White. A number of scholars, including Susan Power Bratton, Clarence

Glacken, and Paul Santmire, for example, have found a continuing appreciation in the Middle Ages of nature in and of itself as a site of contemplation and appreciation of God's creation (Bratton 1988; Glacken 1967, 173–75, 176–87; Santmire 1985, 117–19). The activist and rationalist bent of orthodox, male-dominated Latin Christianity must be placed alongside the minority strands of female mysticism in which the binary oppositions of male/female, soul/body, and spirit/matter were often elided (Bynum 1987; Petroff 1994, 61, 106, 217–19). An exhaustive study of medieval commentaries on Genesis 1:28 demonstrated that premodern Jews and Christians rarely, if ever, saw the verse as applying to technological domination of nature at all; rather, the exegesis of the verse typically dealt with issues related to God's covenant and human sexuality (J. Cohen 1990; Harrison 1999).

A second fundamental area of controversy is the relationship between ideas or "values" and practice. White, as a devoted Christian as well as a follower of Weber, was convinced that religious values were the moving forces of history. Moreover, he seems to have assumed that these values existed "below the level of conscious thought" and would exert their influence through an unconscious process of osmosis. He was less interested therefore in exploring either how values were translated into actions or how a desire to transform nature might be translated into an effective ability to do so. As pointed out in a recent updating of White's argument, "the main defect of [White's] article is its inability to clarify the relationship between ideas and social practice" (Marangudakis 2001, 259). A start in this direction is made in the same piece in which the author, Manussos Marangudakis, argues that materialism, arising from a theologically based rationalistic and utilitarian worldview, was spread in the medieval West by clergy and monks in their double roles as bearers of the faith and economic and political actors. According to Marangudakis, Western theology was born and developed in a social environment that included a "psychological predisposition toward changing and manipulating matter and the natural environment" from the sixth century onwards. Marangudakis emphasizes the importance of the Latin Church in supplying an ideology that legitimized and organized "the rational and intrusive investigation of the world" represented by science and technology (Marangudakis 2001, 247, 254). Yet the bulk of the article, while providing an analysis of the rationalist and secularist tendencies in Western thought and theology, with special attention to Thomas Aquinas, does little to flesh out how theological premises were actualized in social practice. Moreover, an additional problem arises in that White had characterized medieval philosophy, in contrast to medieval religion, as almost uniformly hostile toward technology (White 1978c, 328).

One place to take up an examination of how values might have been put into practice is an aspect of White's argument often neglected by nonhistorians: his argument that the shift toward a more exploitative attitude toward nature took place in a highly specific social milieu, the medieval monastery. White was certainly correct in associating monasticism with an interest in technology, although I will suggest later that the reasons behind monastic success in technology may be more varied and complex than White allows. St. Benedict of Nursia, the founder of Western monasticism in the sixth century, incorporated manual labor into the daily life of the monastery and regarded physical and spiritual labor as interdependent aspects of the life of the monastic community (Ovitt 1987, 104–5). European monasticism was actively involved in the expansion of technology and in the vast projects of land clearance, swamp drainage, and cultivation of new lands that characterized Europe from the twelfth century (Coates 1998, 44–46). The Cistercian order, founded in 1098, for example, not only cleared huge tracts of land for sheep-raising, wine production, and other forms of agriculture but became one of the leading producers of iron in Europe. Moreover, the Cistercians pioneered the use of water power throughout Europe not only to run iron mills but for a variety of industrial projects. Other monastic orders also made use of new technologies in support of their communities, although not on the grand scale of the Cistercians. One minor order, for example, founded by St. Benezet, was devoted to bridge building. They not only developed new techniques but constructed bridges with a combination chapel and toll station at one end, the better to combine pastoral care with a steady input of cash. The economic success of medieval monasticism and the consequent challenges to the ideal of monastic poverty have been well documented: St. Francis, who began an order of beggars was, ultimately, made the patron saint of merchants (Little 1978).

Research by medieval historians, however, has tended to qualify the simple equation between monastic spirituality and interest in technics and productivity made by White. For example, George Ovitt, Jr., has argued that, as technological and commercial activity increased over the course of the twelfth century, the Cistercians and other monastic communities increasingly removed manual labor and technological endeavors from the realm of the spiritual. While continuing to depend economically on the aggressive use of natural resources, they ceased to see manual labor and technological development as an essential part of the monastic spiritual mission; instead, this work was turned over to hired laborers or to lay brothers, while the church itself located its privileged position as one outside and above the pursuit of wealth (Ovitt 1987, 143, 159, 163). The French medievalist Jacques le Goff has explored the contradictions between the antimaterialist ethics articulated by the early Church, which condemned most forms of labor *except* agriculture as leading to vice, and the new, more commercial economy taking shape in the twelfth century. In his view, the emergence of a more positive theology of labor (directed toward nonclergy) in this period reflected, rather than caused, economic and technological expansion (Le Goff 1980, 58–70, 114–21). Similarly, Lester K. Little finds the emergence of the new profit economy to have been profoundly disturbing to church leaders, requiring an intense, at times even violent, reorientation of traditional ethics (Little 1978, 164–69). Nor should we forget that, as White himself has shown in other contexts, aggressive use of new technologies took place also in peasant villages, urban centers, and on the lands of secular lords, outside, as well as within, monastic communities (White 1962; Gimpel 1980, 38–44, 81–86).

Recent microstudies of how specific technologies were used in specific places have shown that medieval peasants and landlords did not necessarily enthusiastically pursue new technologies, undercutting White's argument that a psychological climate promoting mechanization and technological change permeated medieval life. Rather, a variety of complex social and economic factors came into play among different social groups that helped determine if and how technological innovations were adopted. According to Michael Toch, an historian of medieval agriculture, for example, agricultural productivity increased in the Middle Ages not because of technological change, as White had argued, but because of the more intensive use of human labor (Toch 1997). Toch demonstrates, moreover, that even in the later Middle Ages "adaptations in crops, breeds, and cultivation techniques were . . . more important than new tools" (Toch 1997, 168). Other regional studies of technology use in the Middle Ages suggest that the use of the horse, rather than oxen, as a draft animal was less important in medieval agriculture than White had suggested and that the diffusion of water mills in early medieval Italy was conditioned less by religious values than by complex local labor conditions as well as cultural expectations that the use of mills and white flour would bring prestige (Toch 1997, 161; Squatriti 1997). Similarly, two studies by Richard Holt document that mills of all types were less common, less productive, and less universally appreciated in the Middle Ages than White had argued (Holt 1996, 1997). In a detailed examination of the use and economic impact of mills in medieval England, Holt concludes that "there is no sign of the growing enthusiasm for the various forms of the mill which Lynn White and others have imagined"; instead, limited markets, the small-scale production of household craft workshops, and the competing economic interests of landlords and peasant farmers served to severely limit the use of water- and wind-powered mills by medieval people (Holt 1997, 157). Nor was monastic practice or motivation with regard to the exploitation of resources always consistent. Clarence Glacken, for example, finds that the attitudes of monasteries toward the clearing of land varied according to their individual economic interests. According to Glacken, monks often negotiated their rights to land and its resources with an eye to efficient management and local power politics, not necessarily developing the land to its fullest (Glacken 1967, 314, 330–33). Monasteries in practice were rarely totally isolated from local communities but interacted with them on a continual basis; abbots and monks therefore had multiple roles and had to consider their actions from a variety of perspectives including, but not limited to, their position as exemplars of the religious life.

In sum, it appears difficult if not impossible to isolate religion as a motivating force for the pursuit of technology from other aspects of human life in the Middle Ages. No medievalist has denied that there was an association between religion and technology in the Middle Ages, in part because religion acted as a filter for virtually all reflective thought in the medieval period. Yet association does not prove a causal relation or explain how desires shaped by values were translated into an effective ability to transform the world through technology. Another approach would be to consider how economic and social conditions, as well as religious values, may have encouraged the church and other groups toward an aggressive approach toward nature and to look closely at the economic and political aspects of religious institutions. Economic and social historians have just begun to look closely at how medieval institutions and labor relations may have helped or hindered industrial and technological development. Peter Laslett, for example, has recently argued for the importance of the unique pattern of late marriage in medieval Europe and the consequent necessity for every potential head of household to acquire sufficient training and savings prior to marriage (Laslett 1988). Other historians have shown how the structural complexity of basic economic units—the family, kinship ties, and the community—in late medieval and early modern Europe facilitated flexible economic choices and the consequent range of economic possibilities. Richard Holt, one of the few historians of medieval technology to look closely at the economic context of the diffusion of water and windmills in the Middle Ages, goes so far as to assert that "if the people of the Middle Ages did indeed have any genius for innovation, it was in the organization of the human resources rather than the material resources of their society" (Holt 1996, 120). Historians have pointed to the existence of multiple and overlapping centers of political power that allowed both for local independent action and competing markets as important prerequisites for economic, and hence technological, expansion (Mann 1988; Musgrave 1999). Economic historian E. Ashtor has pointed to such mundane factors as the migration of foreign workers and the consequent introduction of new techniques as crucial to technological development in the later Middle Ages (Ashtor 1989). One might also contrast the frontier-like conditions of early medieval Europe with the far more rigid and hierarchical social structure of the Byzantine Empire as part of an explanation for why the medieval West was more open to and appreciative of technological innovation. On the other hand, some of the regional studies by Holt and others cited above have shown that labor conditions and the competing economic interests of different social groups have often inhibited the adoption of new technologies or made new technologies economically irrelevant.

The most striking thing about White's argument and much of the response to it is the degree to which history, that is, the location of events and ideas in the specifics of time and place, became irrelevant. Much of the initial appeal of White's argument was in its seeming historical specificity: Western dominance of nature could be located in the European Middle Ages, particularly in medieval monasteries. Yet upon closer examination this historical anchor dissolves under the pressure of White's belief in the overriding influence of timeless religious values. Much as White's groundbreaking 1962 book, *Medieval Technology and Social Change*, has been criticized as technologically determinist (Sawyer and

Hilton 1963; Roland 2003), White's logic in "Roots" and elsewhere expresses a religious and cultural determinism that works at cross-purposes with his historical argument.

Few histories of Europe today would define Western society only in terms of religion. In White's account, however, the Western world emerges as both Christian and technologically based from its inception and by its very nature. Bert Hall has shown how White, influenced by his mentors, became caught up in the effort of medievalists to fight against the prevailing image of the Middle Ages as culturally antithetical to modernity; as a result, White insisted that medieval religion was not only uncompromisingly rational but also fully consistent with modern values and even identical to them (Hall 1996; Whitney 1993, 153–54, 157). In White's rhetoric, moreover, the values of Latin Christianity promoting technology existed "below the level of verbal expression" and were "so taken for granted, so axiomatic, that they largely elude expression in writing." In fact, there is considerable attention, both positive and negative, to values relating to technology in medieval philosophical and theological texts (Whitney 1990). So strong is White's belief that "culture" is made up of inherited unconscious values, rather than deliberately articulated ideas, however, that he refers to "cultural genetics," Christianity's spontaneous "genetic mutations," and the "recessive genes" of minority Christian views (White 1978c, 201, 239, 318, 134, 253; White 1978a, 105). Western culture in "Roots" and other of White's writing, therefore, takes on a life of its own, as if culture existed independently of social, economic, and political factors and remained essentially unchanged through time; in other words, White himself fails to historicize the terms of his argument. In treating Christian values as wholly autonomous, moreover, White effectively, if perhaps unwittingly, erases human agency. Such an approach, while illuminating in many ways, tends to obscure and gloss over important issues related to the playing out of economic interests, political power, and social difference in human relations, including the implementation or rejection of new technologies.

The vision of Western culture as permeated with a rationalist and utilitarian approach to the natural world rooted in Christian values, however, has great appeal, in part because the self-identification of the West as normally "rational" and progressive flatters Western sensibilities. Whatever caveats individual historians might introduce, the movement toward modernization, industrialization, and the domination of nature often seems to take on an aura of inevitability and universality. As Langdon Winner has perceptively remarked in explanation of the attraction of White's ideas, "There is something oddly appealing in the idea that the troubles of our technological age stem from a perverse streak in the very identity of Western man" (Winner 1977, 115). Furthermore, historical interpretations of this type often unconsciously tend to conflate the specific experiences of the West with human experience in general. In its cruder versions, the West, explicitly or implicitly, is treated as the bearer and flagship of human destiny, and modern Western practices and attitudes as the appropriate endpoint of history. Such an approach is unlikely to provide useful critiques of current environmental problems.

In contrast, recent historical perspectives have tended to suggest that the undeniable economic, political, and technological successes of Western society are not inevitable outgrowths of Western values but are in part contingent and fortuitous, one possibility among other possible outcomes. European technological dominance may have emerged largely because of luck and the fortunate convergence of a number of factors, many of which either were not under people's control or were unplanned. If this is accurate and if we wish to use the past as a guide to the present, we need to look closely at the particular intersections of politics, economics, and local and global interests, as well as cultural values, to address current environmental problems.

I would further suggest that taking economic and political factors, such as governmental policies relating to globalization, as well as cultural factors into account in fact broadens the role of religiously based ethics and morality. Environmental problems have disastrous effects on human populations as well as on animals, plants, and the earth itself. Every major religion advocates the moral responsibility on the part of its followers to care for those weaker and less-well-off than themselves. As Larry Rasmussen (chapter 9, this volume) suggests, Christian ethics must incorporate the notion of a community of life encompassing the human and the earth. Broadening the concept of stewardship to include "people and other living things in their environments" and to include examination of political events as well as underlying "attitudes" would enable us to tackle more effectively difficult questions in which economic justice and well-being appear at odds with environmental concerns. A more complex picture of the past, and an appreciation of how the interaction of many different types of choices have resulted in our present state of crisis, can perhaps aid us in

48   Elspeth Whitney

finding a path out of our current difficulties. White, who once remarked
that "it is better for a historian to be wrong than to be timid," would only
have applauded our efforts (White 1978c, xx).

NOTES

1. Gowan and Schumaker (1980) list 185 publications relevant to White's
"Roots," including 36 under the rubric, "The Judeo-Christian Tradition Defended." I have counted over 240 articles citing "Roots" since its publication in
1967.
2. I am grateful to Professor Bert Hall for alerting me to the satiric nature of
the piece attributed to Fudpucker.
3. Although we are concerned here with animism as it continued to influence
Western ideas about nature into the early modern era, the Mesopotamian example offers an exceptionally vivid picture of how animistic thought endowed even
the most ordinary natural objects with spirit and agency.
4. A similar point has been made about native or indigenous societies that
practice traditional religions predicated on animism and have also been widely
credited with an ethic of living in harmony with nature. This assessment has been
recently questioned by sociobiologists, who argue that human beings are biologi-
cally disposed to aggressively appropriate natural resources, and anthropologists,
who have suggested that hunting patterns of hunting and gathering societies reflect attempts to maximize yields rather than any innate respect for nature (Flores
1999).

WORKS CITED

Adas, Michael. 1992. *Machines as the measure of men: Science, technology,
and ideologies of western dominance.* Ithaca, NY: Cornell University Press.
Ashtor, Eliyahu. 1989. The factors of technological and industrial progress in the
later Middle Ages. *The Journal of European Economic History* 18:7–36.
Bratton, Susan Power. 1988. The original desert solitaire: Early Christian monasticism and wilderness. *Environmental Ethics* 10:31–35.
Bynum, Caroline Walker. 1987. *Holy fast and holy feast: The religious significance of food to medieval women.* Berkeley: University of California Press.
Campbell, Bruce M. S. 1995. Ecology versus economics in late thirteenth- and
early fourteenth-century English agriculture. In *Agriculture in the Middle*

Ages: Technology, practice, and representation, ed. Del Sweeney, 76–108. Philadelphia: University of Pennsylvania Press.

Cicero. 1967. *De natura deorum.* Trans. H. Rackham. Cambridge, MA: Harvard University Press.

Coates, Peter. 1998. *Nature: Western attitudes since ancient times.* Berkeley: University of California Press.

Cohen, H. Floris. 1994. *The Scientific Revolution: A historiographical inquiry.* Chicago: University of Chicago Press.

Cohen, Jeremy. 1990. *"Be fertile and increase, fill the earth and master it": The ancient and medieval career of a biblical text.* Ithaca, NY: Cornell University Press.

Copenhaver, Brian P. 1990. Natural magic, hermeticism, and occultism in early modern science. In *Reappraisals of the Scientific Revolution,* ed. David C. Lindberg and Robert S. Westman, 261–302. Cambridge: Cambridge University Press.

Crombie, A. C. 1959. *Medieval and early modern science.* 2 vols. Garden City, NY: Doubleday, Anchor Books.

Descartes, René. 1972. *Treatise of man, French text with translation and commentary by Thomas Steele Hall.* Cambridge, MA: Harvard University Press.

DeVries, Kelly. 1992. *Medieval military technology.* Peterborough, Ontario: Broadview Press.

Dohrn-van Rossum, Gerhard. 1996. *The history of the hour: Clocks and modern temporal orders.* Trans. Thomas Dunlap. Chicago: University of Chicago Press.

Flores, Dan. 1999. Nature's children: Environmental history as human natural history. In *Human/nature: Biology, culture, and environmental history,* ed. John P. Herron and Andrew G. Kirk, 11–30. Albuquerque: University of New Mexico Press.

Foltz, Richard C. 2003. Islamic environmentalism in theory and practice. In *Worldviews, religion, and the environment: A global anthology,* ed. Richard C. Foltz, 358–65. Belmont, CA: Wadsworth/Thompson Learning.

Frankfort, Henri, H. A. Frankfort, John A. Wilson, Thorkild Jacobsen, and William A. Irwin. 1977. *The intellectual adventure of ancient man: An essay on speculative thought in the ancient Near East.* Chicago: University of Chicago Press.

Fudpucker, Wilhelm E. 1984. Through Christian technology to technological Christianity. In *Theology and technology: Essays in Christian analysis and exegesis,* ed. Carl Mitcham and Jim Grote, 53–69. Lanhan, MD: University Press of America.

Gies, Francis, and Joseph Gies. 1994. *Cathedral, forge, and waterwheel: Technology and invention in the Middle Ages.* New York: HarperPerennial.

Gimpel, Jean. 1980. *The medieval machine: The industrial revolution of the Middle Ages.* New York: Penguin Books.

Glacken, Clarence J. 1967. *Traces on the Rhodian shore: Nature and culture in western thought from ancient times to the end of the eighteenth century.* Berkeley: University of California Press.

Gowan, Donald, and Millard Schumaker. 1980. *Subduing the earth: An exchange of views.* Kingston, Ontario: The United Church of Canada.

Hall, Bert S. 1989. Lynn Townsend White, Jr. (1907–1987). *Technology and Culture* 30:194–213.

———. 1996. Lynn White's *Medieval technology and social change* after thirty years. In *Technological change: Methods and themes in the history of technology,* ed. Robert Fox, 85–101. Australia: Harwood Academic Press.

———. 1997. Weapons of war and late medieval cities: Technological innovation and tactical changes. In *Technology and resource use in medieval Europe: Cathedrals, mills, and mines,* ed. Elizabeth Bradford Smith and Michael Wolfe, 185–208. Aldershot: Ashgate.

Hand, Carl M., and Kent D. Van Liere. 1984. Religion, mastery-over-nature, and environmental concern. *Social Forces* 63:555–70.

Harrison, Peter. 1999. Subduing the earth: Genesis 1, early modern science, and the exploration of nature. *The Journal of Religion* 79: 86–109.

Henry, John. 1990. Magic and science in the sixteenth and seventeenth centuries. In *Companion to the history of modern science,* ed. R. C. Olby, G. N. Cantor, J. R. R. Christie, and M. J. S. Hodge, 583–96. London: Routledge.

Herron, John P., and Andrew G. Kirk. 1999. Introduction. In *Human/nature: Biology, culture, and environmental history,* ed. John P. Herron and Andrew G. Kirk, 1–10. Albuquerque: University of New Mexico Press.

Holt, Richard. 1996. Medieval technology and the historians: The evidence for the mill. In *Technological change: Methods and themes in the history of technology,* ed. Robert Fox, 103–21. Australia: Harwood Academic Press.

———. 1997. Mechanization and the medieval English economy. In *Technology and resource use in medieval Europe: Cathedrals, mills, and mines,* ed. Elizabeth Bradford Smith and Michael Wolfe, 139–57. Aldershot: Ashgate.

Hughes, J. Donald. 1994. *Pan's travail: Environmental problems of the ancient Greeks and Romans.* Baltimore: Johns Hopkins Press.

Jolly, Karen. 1993. Father God and Mother Earth: Nature-mysticism in the Anglo-Saxon world. In Salisbury 1993, 221–52.

Kinsley, David. 1995. *Ecology and religion: Ecological spirituality in cross-cultural perspective.* Englewood Cliffs, NJ: Prentice Hall.

Landes, David S. 1969. *The unbound Prometheus: Technological change and industrial development in western Europe from 1750 to the present.* Cambridge: Cambridge University Press.

Laslett, Peter. 1988. The European family and early industrialization. In *Europe and the rise of capitalism,* ed. Jean Baechler, John A. Hall, and Michael Mann, 234–41. Oxford: Basil Blackwell.

Le Goff, Jacques. 1980. *Time, work, and culture in the Middle Ages.* Trans. Arthur Goldhammer. Chicago: University of Chicago Press.

Little, Lester K. 1978. *Religious poverty and the profit economy in medieval Europe.* Ithaca, NY: Cornell University Press.

Long, Pamela O. 2001. *Openness, secrecy, authorship: Technical arts and the culture of knowledge from antiquity to the Renaissance.* Baltimore: The Johns Hopkins University Press.

Magnusson, Roberta J. 2001. *Water technology in the Middle Ages: Cities, monasteries, and waterworks after the Roman Empire.* Baltimore: The Johns Hopkins University Press.

Mann, Michael. 1988. European development: Approaching a historical explanation. In *Europe and the rise of capitalism,* ed. Jean Baechler, John A. Hall, and Michael Mann, 6–19. Oxford: Basil Blackwell.

Marangudakis, Manussos. 2001. The medieval roots of our ecological crisis. *Environmental Ethics* 23:243–60.

Mark, Robert. 1990. *Light, wind, and structure: The mystery of the master builders.* Cambridge, MA: MIT Press.

McKibben, Bill. 1990. *The end of nature.* New York: Alfred A. Knopf.

Merchant, Carolyn. 1980. *The death of nature: Women, ecology, and the Scientific Revolution.* San Francisco: Harper and Row.

———. 1995. *Earthcare: Women and the environment.* New York: Routledge.

Musgrave, Peter. 1999. *The early modern European economy.* New York: St. Martin's Press.

Nelson, Michael. 2001. Lynn White, Jr., 1907–87. In *Fifty key thinkers on the environment,* 200–205. London: Routledge.

Newman, William. 2000. Technology and alchemical debate in the late Middle Ages. In *The scientific enterprise in antiquity and the Middle Ages,* ed. Michael H. Shank, 271–94. Chicago: University of Chicago Press.

Osler, Margaret J., ed. 2000. *Rethinking the Scientific Revolution.* Cambridge: Cambridge University Press.

Ovitt, George, Jr. 1987. *The restoration of perfection: Labor and technology in medieval culture.* New Brunswick, NJ: Rutgers University Press.

Petroff, Elizabeth Alvilda. 1994. *Body and soul: Essays on medieval women and mysticism.* New York: Oxford University Press.

Roland, Alex. 2003. Once more into the stirrups: Lynn White jr., *Medieval technology and social change. Technology and Culture* 44:574–85.

Ruether, Rosemary Radford. 1994. *Gaia and God: An ecofeminist theology of earth healing.* New York: HarperCollins Publishers.

Salisbury, Joyce E. 1993. *The medieval world of nature: A book of essays.* New York: Garland Publishing, Inc.

Santmire, H. Paul. 1985. *The travail of nature: The ambiguous ecological promise of Christian theology.* Philadelphia: Fortress Press.

Sawyer, P. H., and R. H. Hilton. 1963. Technical determinism: The stirrup and the plough. *Past and Present* 24:90–100.

Schwarzschild, Steven S. 2003. The unnatural Jew. In *Worldviews, religion, and the environment: A global anthology,* ed. Richard C. Foltz, 296–306. Belmont, CA: Wadsworth/Thompson Learning.

Sessions, George. 1995. Ecocentrism and the anthropocentric detour. In *Deep ecology for the twenty-first century: Readings on the philosophy and practice of the new environmentalism,* ed. George Sessions, 156–82. Boston: Shambhala.

Squatriti, Paolo. 1997. "Advent and conquests" of the water mill in Italy. In *Technology and resource use in medieval Europe: Cathedrals, mills, and mines,* ed. Elizabeth Bradford Smith and Michael Wolfe, 125–38. Aldershot: Ashgate.

Toch, Michael. 1997. Agricultural progress and agricultural technology in medieval Germany: An alternative model. In *Technology and resource use in medieval Europe: Cathedrals, mills, and mines,* ed. Elizabeth Bradford Smith and Michael Wolfe, 158–69. Aldershot: Ashgate.

Toynbee, Arnold. 1973. The genesis of pollution. *Horizon* 15(3):4–9.

White, Lynn, Jr. 1962. *Medieval technology and social change.* London: Oxford University Press.

———. 1967. The historical roots of our ecologic crisis. *Science* 155:1203–7.

———. 1978a. The future of compassion. *The Ecumenical Review* 30:101–5.

———. 1978b. The iconography of *Temperantia* and the virtuousness of technology. In *Medieval religion and technology: Collected essays,* 181–204. Berkeley: University of California Press.

———. 1978c. *Medieval religion and technology: Collected essays.* Berkeley: University of California Press.

Whitney, Elspeth. 1990. *Paradise restored: The mechanical arts from antiquity through the thirteenth century.* Philadelphia: The American Philosophical Society.

———. 1993. Lynn White, ecotheology, and history. *Environmental Ethics* 15:151–69.

Winner, Langdon. 1977. *Autonomous technology: Technics-out-of-control as a theme in political thought.* Cambridge, MA: MIT Press.

CHAPTER 2

Creating Ecology: Protestants and the Moral Community of Creation

Mark Stoll

One of the most famous passages in American nature writing is Aldo Leopold's "Land Ethic," from his 1949 classic, *A Sand County Almanac*. In it, he used the ecological concept of plant and animal "communities" to argue that, just as ethics apply to humans living in an interdependent society, so too we should extend a "land ethic" to the broader land community of which we should see ourselves an interdependent member. Using such ecological ideas as the food pyramid and energy flow through the food chain, Leopold tied humans into the web of ecological interrelations. "In short," he wrote,

> a land ethic changes the role of Homo sapiens from conqueror of the land-community to plain member and citizen of it. It implies respect for his fellow-members, and also respect for the community as such. (Leopold 1966, 240)

Leopold's use of ecology to support the concept of the land ethic grew out of the model of "community." "Pyramids," energy "flows," food "chains," and "webs" have no ethical implications, but "community" certainly does. This is no accident. From the time the field of ecology coalesced in the 1890s, the vocabulary and conceptual framework of its theory was rife with moral implication. Ecology's creators repeatedly saw moral consequences in either the interrelationships of the natural world or the natural world as a model for human society. Furthermore, that moralistic view of nature took shape within the moralistic Protestant worldview that all the leading founders of the field shared.

Coined to make a scientific study out of the older concept of the "economy" of nature, "ecology" refers to investigation into nature's management of her "household" (Greek *oîkos*). However, the foundational ecological studies of the 1880s and 1890s conceived of nature not in terms of a "household," but of a "community," which as metaphors have rather different implications. Indeed, the biologists who began seeing grasses, shrubs, trees, insects, birds, reptiles, fish, and mammals as members of a "community" went beyond bare scientific analysis in their conclusions. A forest can be cleared or a prairie plowed, but if one views nature as individual organisms and species living together as a community, the forest or prairie community has been disrupted or destroyed. A *moral* act has occurred.

Community hence implies morality, and moral judgment implies religion. The simultaneous appearance in the United States of ecology, sociology, and the social gospel as organized movements in widely separated fields of life science, social science, and religion bespeaks common roots, as well as common concerns and perhaps common goals (McIntosh 1985, chap. 1, esp. 21–27). Indeed, early ecologists, as well as sociologists and social gospel advocates, shared a common religious heritage (Crunden 1982). They, along with virtually all founding ecologists, the theorists of the communities of nature, had Protestant backgrounds. Prior to the Second World War, American and European Protestants very nearly monopolized ecological theory: first German and Scandinavian Lutherans, then Swiss Reformed, English Anglicans, and American Protestants. American Protestants from only certain denominations participated in developing this new field: ecology as a science crystallized mainly out of the Calvinist Puritan tradition that planted Congregationalism and Presbyterianism in America. Within the general attitudes and doctrines of these and their daughter churches, and not within the much larger Catholic, Methodist, and Southern Baptist denominations, lay the taproot of modern American ecological science.

COMMUNITY AND ECOLOGY

"Community" was much on the minds of American Protestants in the last quarter of the nineteenth century and the first quarter of the twentieth. As Cittadino (chapter 3, this volume) suggests, the scientific study of natural and human communities, ecology and sociology, arose as self-conscious fields at the same moment—the early 1890s—in the same area of the country—the Midwest—and with the same university—the University of Chicago—playing a major role. In 1889 the University of Kansas created a department of history and sociology, but Albion Small founded the first department of sociology proper at the University of Chicago in 1892. One year later, Midwestern botanists at the Madison Botanical Congress were the first body of scientists to officially adopt the word "ecology." Participants in the congress included Charles Bessey, chair of botany of the University of Nebraska since 1884, and John Merle Coulter, at that moment organizing the new department of botany at the University of Chicago (Tobey 1981, 2).

A century later the close relationship between American ecological and social thought continued. To give a prominent case in point, the current popularity of the term "biodiversity" has its social counterpart in the idea of cultural, ethnic, and racial "diversity." The concept of animal and plant "diversity" first appeared in titles in library catalogues in the early 1960s, followed within a few years by "biological diversity." After 1965, as racial integration efforts made significant headway, social thinkers began to speak of ethnic and racial "diversity." Both expressions came suddenly into extraordinary vogue after the mid-1980s, presumably at least partially in response to the Reagan administration's conservative social and environmental policies. Ethnic "diversity" and its handmaiden "multiculturalism" became a political shibboleth at the very same moment that biologists coined "biodiversity," which in turn immediately turned environmental and ecological shibboleth. The few hundred books with references to either ethnic or biological diversity in their titles published in the 1980s exploded into thousands in the 1990s.[1] "Diversity" as a cultural value affected the development of two disparate areas of science by providing natural and human "communities" an ideal against which they should be measured.

The concept of "community," therefore, bridged ecological and social thought; both fields analyzed aggregates of individuals and their interrelationships (Mitman 1992, 1). Students of both ecology and sociology also believed firmly in the intrinsic *value* of the subjects they studied (the natural world and society, respectively)—as opposed to studying them solely for their economic or social utility—which surely also played a role in attracting scholars to these areas in the first place. In their works or autobiographies, ecologists, for example, often describe an ardent love of the outdoors and deep sympathy for the plants and animals they study. Belief in intrinsic value introduces subjective value judgment and lends itself to perception of injustice when the respective objects of study are abused, endangered, or seriously disrupted. Community therefore implies morality, which leads to moral judgments and thence to political activism, visible in the common social activism of social scientists and environmental activism of ecologists from Charles Bessey, active in numerous parks and conservation organizations, to E. O. Wilson, defender of biodiversity. The Odum family, father and sons, form a perfect example: the father, Howard, was a social scientist and defender of black rights in the segregated South, while the sons, H. T. and particularly Eugene, were prominent ecologists as well as environmental advocates.

ECOLOGY'S THEOLOGICAL ROOTS: NATURAL THEOLOGY AND NEOPLATONISM

Protestant theology and thought incorporated many strands that would later appear in the theoretical and moral framework of ecology and prepared the foundations of the new science by gradually developing in proto-ecological directions. Proto-ecological concepts developed within the traditions of Protestant natural theology and the closely related Protestant revival of Neoplatonism. An ancient Christian tradition, natural theology deals with the evidences in the natural world of God and his attributes. Within the English-speaking world and, later, Protestant Germany, it enjoyed a huge popularity in the two centuries before Darwin. Long influential in Christian theology, Neoplatonism emerged with particular energy in the late seventeenth century, notably among the so-called Cambridge Platonists, and flowered among nineteenth-century Protestant Romantics like Friedrich von Schelling, Samuel Taylor Coleridge, and Ralph Waldo Emerson. Intertwined with natural theology,

Neoplatonic thought pervaded nineteenth-century Protestant intellectual activity and continues to have its echoes today.

Natural theology lay much of the groundwork for European natural science in general and ecology in particular, and justified and encouraged the study of nature as a religious activity. Many passages of the Bible, most explicitly in St. Paul's Epistle to the Romans 1:20, describe how the knowledge of the Creator is available in Creation, which shows his existence, power, wisdom, and goodness. Since this knowledge complemented and logically must agree with knowledge of God given in the revealed Book of the Bible, churchmen and theologians referred to creation as a "Book of Nature" open to all to read and understand. In the seventeenth century, as a century of bloody religious warfare wound down, Europeans increasingly regarded the interpretation of the Book of Nature as much less contentious than interpretation of God's revealed Book, and indeed as grounds for universal religious belief. Because a basic principle of Protestantism was *sola Scriptura,* the Bible alone as the basis for religious truth, Protestants were already predisposed to view close study of a book as essential to religious knowledge and consequently lay particularly heavy emphasis on the importance of the Bible's complementary Book of Nature (Webb 1915; Glacken 1967; Harrison 1998).

The question of how the Spirit of God pervaded and created the natural world had found an answer in a Protestant revival of Christian Neoplatonism. Plotinus, the third-century founder of pagan Neoplatonism, taught that a tripartite World Soul animates and constantly creates the natural world, much as the human soul inhabits and animates the body. Creation emanates from the Spirit like light from a candle. Like the human body, the universe therefore exhibits a unity in its diversity, an organic holism, in that all parts of the world function together analogously to the various organs and limbs of the body. Plotinus's organic holism has clear ecological implications, if saturated with mysticism. Plotinus taught that meditation on the beauty of the natural world would lead the contemplative soul back first to the Spirit that created it; thence to the Divine Mind from which Spirit itself emanated, and wherein the Platonic idea of perfect beauty resided; and finally to mystical union with the divine One from which all ultimately emanated. Christianity incorporated Neoplatonism primarily through writings of many leaders of the early church who found it easy to adapt to Christian theology (the three-in-one of the Neoplatonic One-Mind-Spirit conveniently paralleled the Christian trinity). Indeed, a number of church fathers, St. Augustine among them, were themselves former Neoplatonists (Craig 1980; Glacken 1967; Harris 1976; Lovejoy 1936; Santmire 1985; Stoll 1997, 12–21).

Natural theology's long career took an abrupt turn after the Reformation. In its fight against the spread of Protestantism, the Catholic Church emphasized obedience to the religious authority of the Church. This emphasis worked against theologies based on sources outside the church, like nature, which might lead to independent, suspect, or heretical conclusions. (The rise of Deism in seventeenth-century England was but one instance that proved Catholic suspicions valid.) Moreover, the basis of the Church's religious authority in the operation of the Holy Spirit through the community of believers also effectively deflected discussion of the Holy Spirit's presence in nature. This operation of the Spirit in the body of the Church ensured inerrant doctrine and obviated need for the heavy stress on the Bible or the Book of Nature as sources of religious truth that was utterly foundational to Protestant theology (Stoll 2004).

For their part, having rejected the authority of the institutional Church for that of *sola Scriptura,* Protestant theologians and intellectuals proclaimed all the more loudly that the Book of Nature supported the authority of the Bible and hence the truth of Protestantism. Protestants of all social levels typically battled religious doubt by reasoning from the evidence of God in nature back to the truth of Protestantism (Stoll 1997). Similarly, the Westminster Confession of Faith, which Puritans and Presbyterians wrote in the 1640s, began with a paraphrase of Romans 1:20, the evidence of God in nature. In contrast, Catholics reasoned their way from doubt to orthodoxy on the basis of the Church's authority or such evidence as miracles. The Protestant tenet of *sola fide* further undermined the influence of institutional churches by making the Holy Spirit operate directly on individuals rather than through the mystical body of the faithful. Thus Protestantism fostered varieties of spiritual individualism and encouraged believers to search for the spirit of God in nature.

Calvinists above all found themselves theologically driven to put significant emphasis on the theological roles of nature and the human relation to it. Calvinism's distinctive tenets of the total sovereignty of God and each person's predestination to salvation or damnation had interesting implications for creation. While humans *deserved* damnation due to their innate sinfulness, Calvinists regarded nature as the pure, ongoing creation of God, whose innocence was a foil to human corruption. Thus they gave nature a sort of moral standing. As the Book of Nature, the natural world was also an appropriately pious subject for study. In addition, John Calvin first formulated the modern notion of stewardship of the earth (Stoll 1997, 25–26). Obsession with the fall of Adam, which forever cut humanity off from innocence, bliss, and harmony with creation, also focused nostalgic attention on Eden, lost forever due to human sin. Appropriately, the great Puritan epic was John Milton's *Paradise Lost,* whose hold on Protestant imagination did not begin to fade until the end of the nineteenth century (Abrams 1971). The great American Puritan divine Jonathan Edwards expressed these notions in his famous sermon, "Sinners in the Hands of an Angry God," in a passage that rolls together God's sovereignty, man's vile corruption, earth's goodness, and stewardship:

> Were it not that so is the sovereign pleasure of God, the earth would not bear you one moment. For you are a burden to it; the creation groans with you; the creation is made subject to the bondage of your corruption, not willingly; the sun don't willingly shine upon you, to give light to serve sin and Satan; the earth don't willingly yield her increase to satisfy your lusts. . . . God's creatures are good, and were made for men to serve God with, and don't willingly subserve to any other purpose, and groan when they are abused to purposes so directly contrary to their nature and end. And the world would spue you out, were it not for the sovereign hand of him who hath subjected it in hope.[2]

The astonishing celerity, destructiveness, and waste of American civilization's nineteenth-century advance into the last remnants of wild country worried the Puritans' descendants that humankind's sinful actions were destroying Eden once again.

Theology also had thoroughly mixed with science. As natural theology thrived on the one hand, natural science became a religious occupation on the other, and even clerics pursued scientific studies, among them American Puritans Cotton Mather and Edwards, the Calvinist and later Unitarian minister Joseph Priestly, and Anglican clergyman Gilbert White. Dissenters disproportionately filled the ranks of the Royal Society and of natural science generally. Cambridge Platonist and former Puritan Henry More thought that the evidences of the Divine in nature constituted *An Antidote against Atheism,* and his fellow Platonist and former Puritan Ralph Cudworth supported this point with his *True Intellectual*

System of the Universe. An admirer of More, Puritan naturalist John Ray published in 1691 the influential book *The Wisdom of God Manifested in the Works of the Creation,* while Anglican clergyman William Derham produced *Physico-Theology* in 1713. Edwards read the Cambridge Platonists at Yale University and later composed the heavily Neoplatonic "Dissertation Concerning the End for Which God Created the World." Emerson's *Nature* of 1836 was almost pure Neoplatonism, and in its first edition carried an epigraph by Plotinus. The great capstone works of natural theology were Anglican Archdeacon William Paley's *Natural Theology; or, Evidences of the Existence and Attributes of the Deity Collected from the Appearances of Nature of 1803,* and the *Bridgewater Treatises* of the 1830s. Paley, in fact, was required reading for many early-nineteenth-century undergraduate students, including Emerson at Harvard (Coslett 1984; Gillispie 1951; Howe 1989; Stoll 1997; Thomas 1983; Worster 1994).

God in Nature

The nineteenth century represented an important watershed as the modern scientific disciplines developed in an atmosphere redolent of pervasive Neoplatonic nature mysticism and its German counterpart, *Naturphilosophie.* Nature absolutely fascinated the nineteenth-century mind. Spiritually minded Romantics like William Wordsworth or Emerson or John Muir perceived the currents of Universal Being while walking through the woods. Landscape painting enjoyed an unprecedented vogue in Germany, Scandinavia, the Netherlands, Britain, and the United States. Protestant Romantic artists like Caspar David Friedrich or the painters of the Hudson River School or, later, photographer Ansel Adams depicted the spiritual aspects of wild nature (Adams 1992; Beierwaltes 1972; Novak 1980).

Scientific and mystical visions of the interconnection of the world continued to evolve in tandem. Scientific-minded Protestants from Alexander von Humboldt to Asa Gray investigated the interconnections of the natural world as a spiritual exercise to gain knowledge of the Creator. In his popular nature writings, John Muir, for example, frequently alluded to the Book of Nature and referred to his geological studies of the Sierra as reading "the glacial manuscripts of God" (Badè 1924, 1:358), and

John Coulter, first chair of the University of Chicago's Botany Department and son of Presbyterian missionaries, often wrote about the presence of God in nature and the harmony of science and religion. Romantic Neoplatonic ideas shaped the ecological holism of such early botanists and ecologists as Goethe, Humboldt, Ernst Haeckel, and Frederic Clements. Alfred North Whitehead's process philosophy is a form of Neoplatonism adapted to twentieth-century science; in the form of the process theology of Charles Hartshorne and John Cobb, Jr., in which God participates continuously in the evolution of an organically interrelated universe, Whitehead's philosophy keeps Neoplatonism relevant for contemporary environmentally minded Protestants. Moreover, there is more than a little of a secularized Plotinian system in James Lovelock's recent "Gaia hypothesis." Lovelock proposed that the living beings of earth worked together to make the earth suitable for life. Their organic interdependence so resembled a single living entity that he has given it the name of the ancient Greek earth goddess. However, humans had so disrupted the system that humanity resembled a global pathogen making Gaia ill—echoing Edwards's colorful personification that the nauseated world might "spue you out." While Lovelock as a scientist kept his system entirely secular, others adopted its concepts enthusiastically with the added spiritual element that pushes it closer to Plotinus's original conception (Barbour 1990; Harris 1976; Lovelock 1979; Tobey 1981, 88–98).

FROM RELIGION TO SCIENCE

Secularization of the study of the interrelationships of nature accelerated throughout the nineteenth century, and the explicit religious meanings of scientific endeavor grew ever more implicit. Archaeology, geology, and higher criticism eroded the authority of the Bible by raising troubling questions about the reliability, authorship, intent, and history of the text. As the authority of *sola Scriptura* ebbed, educated Protestants turned to a sort of *sola Natura,* God's other, less problematic "Book," and drifted out of orthodox churches and into Unitarianism, Transcendentalism, or agnosticism. Yet always the religious aspect remained, though often shorn of its explicit Christianity, and earth scientists in general and biologists in particular saw themselves as "priests" of Nature (Hovenkamp 1978; Mitman 1992, 12).

In the last decades of the nineteenth century, organic holism shaded ever more from religious mysticism into secular science. Ecology emerged and took shape first in Lutheran Germany and Denmark, where biologists originally began imagining animals and plants as "communities." In 1866 Ernst Haeckel, a religious youth but an adult advocate of secular holism, coined the word "*Oekologie,*" although a quarter century would pass before it acquired a specific scientific definition. Deeply influenced by Humboldt's vision of the phenomena of nature interconnected in a cosmic unity, German Karl Möbius was the first to popularize the community concept in his study of the biological "community" of an oyster bank. In 1877 he described this community by coining the term "biocoenosis" (or *Lebensgemeinde*), from the Greek roots for "life-sharing" but intriguingly close to the word "coenobios," the term for a religious community—literally "common life"—and source of the English "cenobite" (König 1981; Kölmel 1981). Building on Humboldt's pioneering insights into plant geography, German Oscar Drude focused on the geographical distribution of plants in his "phytogeography," which inspired Clements's first significant research project in Nebraska. Studies of plant "societies" led German botanists to conceptualize their ecological studies as plant "sociology." This line of study later culminated in the taxonomy of plant societies of Swiss Protestant botanist Josias Braun-Blanquet, whose important *Plant Sociology* of 1931 relied heavily on social metaphors. Braun-Blanquet worked in Montpellier, France, whose university under the Huguenots had become a center of botanical study in Europe contained Europe's oldest scientific botanical garden,[3] and had historical connections with Linnaeus in Sweden; Montpellier, Switzerland, and Sweden would become the European centers of the plant sociology model of ecological theory (Von Rath 1998; Van der Windt 1995, 80–84; Grove 1995; Matagne 1999). Son of a Danish Lutheran minister and closely related to four more, Eugenius Warming spoke of the coastal landscape of his youth with deep feeling and rather mystical reverence. His investigation of plant communities led in 1895 to the influential and oft-translated *Plantesamfund: Grundträk af den Ökologiska Plantegeografi* ("Plant Community: Introduction to Ecological Plant Geography"). As the first textbook with "ecological" in the title, Warming's book thus pointed from community[4] to ecological studies (Prytz 1984; reverence: e.g., 12, 102–3; ministers: 10, 188).[5]

ECOLOGY AS A PURITAN SCIENCE

Already in the 1890s Americans were assuming the leadership of the nascent science of ecology. Nearly all early American ecologists had roots in churches that descended from the Puritan tradition, which included, among others, the Congregational, Unitarian, American (Northern) Baptist, Presbyterian, and Quaker denominations, which in the Puritan diaspora of the nineteenth century had firmly established themselves in the upper Midwest. There the first American ecologists arose, inserting into their science the Puritan elements of organic holism and moralistic suspicion about what the sons of Adam were doing in the landscape. As a young Congregationalist, an admirer of Puritan Jonathan Edwards, and a Unitarian as an adult, Illinois professor Stephen Forbes introduced Möbius's idea of the biological community to America (Croker 2001, 15, 64, 105, 126). Forbes's holistic study of a lake, which he called a "microcosm," was a founding paper in the new science of ecology. To Forbes, if the environment was an organism, ecology was the equivalent to physiology, and his own practical role as a biologist was like a physician's in healing his "patient." "Human interference with the natural order of plant and animal life gives rise to reactions which correspond closely to those of bodily disease," he wrote (Croker 2001, 112), repeating the metaphor of humans as global disease. Warming inspired another Congregationalist, Henry Chandler Cowles, to study the plant communities in the extensive sand dunes near Chicago. Cowles developed a theory of plant succession that used organic analogies and terminology to describe the development of a dune plant community from an embryo to maturity to death (Hagen 1992, 16–20). Cowles's student, Presbyterian Victor Shelford, influentially developed the concept of animal communities (Croker 1991, 50, 103).

Frederic Clements of Lincoln, Nebraska, gave ecological organic holism its classic statement. A collaborator with Shelford and a student of Bessey, who was yet another Congregationalist, Clements had the demeanor of a dour, puritanical minister. He stopped going to his Methodist church in Lincoln because he felt "hypocritical" church members were not pure enough, and soon became an agnostic.[6] Clements produced internationally influential works on ecological methodology and theory of plant succession in which he portrayed the plant community as a literal organism. As he wrote in his most important book, *Plant Succession:*

> The developmental study of vegetation necessarily rests upon the assumption that the unit or climax formation is an organic entity. As an organism the formation arises, grows, matures, and dies. . . . The life-history of a formation is a complex but definitive process, comparable in its chief features with the life-history of an individual plant. (Clements 1916, 3)

Like Forbes, but moving much further than he, Clements saw little place for Western civilization in the American wilderness, as its arrival severely disrupted succession and crippled the organism. In later years Clements's interest turned from biological to philosophical holism. Continental plant sociologists resisted his ideas, but Clements had wide influence in Anglo-American ecology, even if most ecologists took the "organism" of a community as an analogy, not a literal reality (Hagen 1992, 21, 23, 37–38, 47–48; Tobey 1981, 79–80).[7]

In the 1920s and '30s, British ecologists developed new aspects to Clementsian organic holism, but in its sense as a general principle rather than as a literal organism. Britons Charles Elton and G. Evelyn Hutchinson (who worked at Yale University) developed the idea that plant and animal communities, like organisms, had "metabolisms" (Hagen 1992, chap. 4). (Elton, by the way, whom Humboldt and Shelford deeply influenced, developed the notions of "food chains," "food webs," and biotic "pyramids.") Then in 1936 Briton Arthur Tansley coined and defined the term "ecosystem," which he based on the organismic idea but without certain logical difficulties of it in boundary and definition. The word also was free of holism's objectionable political implications on both the left (communism) and right (fascism) in the 1930s (Hagen 1992, 79–87). Yet this simple change in terminology preceded a major opening of ecological theory to additions from outside the Reformed world of its birth. After 1945, Eugene Odum, brought up in a staunch Southern Methodist family far from Midwestern Puritan culture, was among those who continued to promote holism.[8] However, the term "eco*system*" had mechanical rather than organic implications, and, with the addition after World War II of cybernetic metaphors and concepts, a rising number of non-Protestants began making significant contributions to ecological theory (Bergandi 1998).[9]

Nature's Moral Implications and Environmentalism

The heavy preponderance of Midwesterners of New England or Presbyterian background among early ecologists suggests the application of Calvinistic notions of nature's innocence and human depravity to awareness of the last vanishing remnants of pristine prairie before the pioneer's plow. Ecologists at the University of Chicago (which essentially was an American Baptist college inflated with Rockefeller money) were for years more concerned than those of other universities with preserving the natural world. Many early ecologists seemed to be working to preserve the last bits of Paradise. This is evident in Forbes's remark, "Primeval nature . . . presents a settled harmony of interaction among organic groups which is in strong contrast with the many serious maladjustments of plants and animals found in countries occupied by man" (Forbes 1880, 5).[10] Cowles's idea of the climax community and Clements's theory of succession introduced a teleology that privileged the climax state as perfect, Edenic in fact, which man, especially capitalistic man, could only disturb. Clements's warnings about the "plow that broke the Plains" and the need to preserve the climax grassland ecology fit this paradigm.

Non-Calvinists would come at the same idea from other theological directions. Quaker by heritage with a Methodist preacher for a paternal grandfather, Shelford student Warder Clyde Allee's vision of nature seemed to be along the lines of the Peaceable Kingdom, either Edenic or millennial, like the Quaker painter Edward Hicks's famous series of paintings. As Clements's single-climax theory came under greater attack, Southern Methodists Eugene and H. T. Odum replaced it with a similar idea, ecosystem stability, which implicitly retained implications of the superiority of "natural" landscapes over those shaped by human presence.

There are few social implications in Romantic nature-Protestantism, based as it is on the individual mystical experience in nature, but it has strong moral consequences, particularly to highly moralistic and evangelical Puritans and Presbyterians. They and their descendants tended to view untouched nature as pure, whereas human economic activity there, and particularly in areas of natural beauty, was equivalent to Satan gaining entrance into Eden, another paradise lost. Concerned with rooting sin out of society and, as evangelicals, with converting society to a "right" view of nature's holiness, a significant wing of the American environmental movement consisted of descendants of Puritans and Presbyterians attempting to protect the remnants of Eden from commercial exploitation and destruction by preaching a gospel of nature. Many of them, and not a few of the ecologists, transformed the language and methods of evangelism into a message of repentance of modern man from his modernity and salvation in the purity of untouched wilderness. A former Unitarian minister, Emerson, with his friend and follower Thoreau, for example, decried the materialism of Jacksonian America and defended the spiritual value of nature (Stoll 1997, 101–8; Worster 1994, part 2). Son of a preacher, Muir saw himself as a John the Baptist preaching salvation in God's mountains to over-civilized Americans. Helping to create the American national park system, he saw the parks as cathedrals built by God himself and founded the Sierra Club in 1892 to defend them against the schemes of "Satan and company." Both David Brower—charismatic president of the Sierra Club in the 1960s, raised Presbyterian—and Dave Foreman—a founder of Earth First! who as a teenager aspired to be a Churches of Christ preacher—had notably evangelical speaking styles and intensely moralistic worldviews, and worked to save "pristine" natural areas from greedy, self-interested, shortsighted capitalists (Stoll 2001). Presbyterians Rachel Carson, Edward Abbey, and Gary Snyder each in his or her own way sought to defend vulnerable nature from self-seeking, thoughtless modern industrial society and to spread appreciation for nature's beauty and wonder (Stoll 2005).

However, despite the individualism of Romantic nature mysticism, Neoplatonic organic holism has deep implications for society. As nature's "priests," American Protestant botanists hoped to discover in nature guidelines for human society. Organicism therefore was a model for people (Mitman 1993, chap. 1). The social counterpart of Neoplatonism teaches that the World Spirit directs not just change and growth of the natural world but the development and progress of humanity as well. This philosophy of social idealism was developed by Germans, most famously by Hegel, and appeared in America for example in Lester Frank Ward's *Dynamic Sociology,* from which Clements probably drew his fundamental term, "dynamic ecology." Another Midwesterner of Puritan ancestry, and grandson of a minister, Ward was the nation's first and leading sociologist (Tobey 1981, 83–85; Chugerman 1939, 23–24). One of the most salient examples of the desire to apply lessons from nature to society is Quaker pacifist Allee's attempt (quickened by the experience of the First World War) to find nature to be a peaceful, nonhierarchical, cooperative world, with socially destructive individualistic competition controlled by concerns for the good of the whole (Mitman 1992, chaps. 2–4). Better known is Leopold's "land ethic." Forester and founder of the field of wildlife management, and of Midwestern German Lutheran heritage, Leopold used ecological concepts of the "community" literally to develop a basis for environmental ethics. To his mind, as members of the land "community," landowners have a responsibility to treat the plants and animals, who are our fellow "citizens," with ethical concern.[11] However, fear of totalitarianism led Americans to downplay organic metaphors after World War II, and cybernetic and mathematical models of ecosystems captured ecology (Mitman 1992, 5). The ecosystem idea represents an interesting shift from these Protestant ideas. Associated with "hard" science, mathematics, economics, and technology (Mitman 1992, 1; Hagen 1992, chap. 4), the concept of "system" lends itself much less readily to moral readings. A "system" is not a "community," much less an organism. No "ecosystem ethic" has achieved any influence. Because of the lack of moral implications, however, there are fears that the moral content of ecology will vanish completely, leaving none but practical or economic reasons to preserve species and ecosystems.

Protestant churches that were once established churches, such as the Episcopal and Methodist Churches (which share origins in the Church of England), the Congregational and Unitarian Churches (heirs of Puritan New England), the Presbyterian Church (Scotland), and the Lutheran Church (Germany and Scandinavia), also have a robust social ethic. Although probably weaker than that of the Roman Catholic Church, the paradigmatic established Western Christian church, this social ethic derives from an established church's responsibility for creating and maintaining a moral, just society based on religious principles. This may be the source of the idea of Protestant ecologists who expressed their holistic viewpoint in terms of "community," with all its religious and moral connotations. It is explicitly the root of the Odum brothers' environmental activism, particularly of the elder Eugene, who felt his father's moral beliefs most intensely. Biographers trace his moral views to his father's fight for a just Southern society in which the races would be treated fairly and work together in organic unity for the betterment of all. Through his popular textbook, *Fundamentals of Ecology,* which went through three editions between 1953 and 1971, and his classroom lectures, Eugene Odum sought to inspire students to see the social implications of ecology.

Like Allee, Odum saw the cooperative, mutualistic, interdependent aspects of natural communities. His textbook was the last major textbook to include a large section on the environmentalist responsibilities of the ecologist. All of part 3 was essentially a guidebook and call to environmental action for the ecologist: "Remember that what the world needs is more and better specialists who are knowledgeable about the ecological whole!" (Craige 2001, introduction, 2–9; E. Odum 1971, 407). Less successfully, H. T. Odum also attempted to apply ecosystem concepts to society, but in a less moralistic and more cybernetic way. His 1971 book *Environment, Power, and Society* generalized flowcharts that he developed for ecological systems to economics, politics, and even religion.

In a sense, ideas about nature have always mirrored ideas about society. The dominant premodern view of nature emphasized a hierarchy, the Great Chain of Being, which ranked all creatures from lowest to highest, very much as social thinkers ranked all humans as members of classes from the bottom to the top. All of this, the order of both nature and society, was ordained by God. Today a profoundly individualistic and democratic version of ecology holds sway, undermining old ideas of the harmony or balance of nature, a pristine climax state, or even of a stable ecosystem. In this every-species-for-itself ecology, moral implications may be difficult to infer. Nevertheless, former Southern Baptist E. O. Wilson, along with many others, implicitly build on the moral high ground that cultural and ethnic diversity currently commands to preach the moral imperative of preserving biodiversity (Stoll 2002). Very likely, the sharing of metaphor and paradigm between social and ecological sciences will continue hand-in-hand with moral critiques and political, social, and environmental activism.

NOTES

1. Based on the author's bibliographical searches.
2. Jonathan Edwards, "Sinners in the Hands of an Angry God," in *Jonathan Edwards: Representative selections with introduction, bibliography, and notes,* ed. Clarence H. Faust and Thomas H. Johnson, (New York: American Book Company, 1935), 162–63. Edwards alludes to Romans 8:19–22 and Leviticus 18:28.

3. That is, as opposed to botanical gardens for purely medicinal plants, as at Padua.

4. An interesting short history of the fate of "community theory" is in McIntosh (1985, 263–67).

5. It is extraordinarily difficult to discover the religious beliefs or backgrounds of European scientists; their biographers apparently believe that religion could not be of interest to a modern scientist in "secular" Europe. I have inferred Braun-Blanquet's religious background from his birth in the Protestant city of Chur and other details of his biography. His predecessors and co-workers in the so-called Zurich-Montpellier school of ecology include Carl Schröter, Charles Flahaut, and others, of whose religious backgrounds I have thus far found no hint in historical literature, although the former is probably Protestant and the latter almost certainly Catholic. The descriptive and taxonomic emphasis of their studies of plant communities has no strong correlation with any particular religious tradition, unlike the aspects of ecology I focus on in the text. (cf. Sutter 1981). On the influence of Schröter and Flahaut on British botany, see Sheail (1987, part 1).

6. I have discovered no record of Clements's religious upbringing. However, records indicate that his grandfather and two uncles were devout Methodists (Clements 2001; *Portrait and biographical album* 1889, 1152–54). I have inferred from this the denominational identity of the church he left.

7. One might also note the Calvinistic, predestinarian implications of Darwinism. In the survival of the fittest, heredity determines fitness. The individual is powerless to affect the destiny of its fit, or unfit, genetic material. Nature (as opposed to God) elects some for survival and condemns others to eternal extinction—"natural election," so to speak.

8. The twentieth-century debates between holism and reductionism are summarized in McIntosh (1985, 252–56).

9. Since the late nineteenth century, Russian ecologists have been active, but I do not have the information that would allow comparisons about their motivations or philosophical or moral assumptions with those of Western Protestant ecologists.

10. But, Croker writes, "Forbes took issue with those . . . who . . . considered human beings 'outside the natural system,' who considered primitive nature as an 'earthly paradise,' and civilized humans 'a kind of fiend,' whose entry into the ancient world 'had introduced . . . the germs of that fatal and frightfully contagious disease known as civilization'" (Croker 2001, 124).

11. Although *A Sand County almanac* appeared in 1948, Leopold first conceived "The Land Ethic" section during the depths of the Depression, when reaction against individualism and faith in the community was at its height, although his ideas did not take final shape until around 1947. See Stoll (1997, 183–88) and Worster (1994, 284–90).

WORKS CITED

Abrams, M. H. 1971. *Natural supernaturalism: Tradition and revolution in Romantic literature.* New York: W. W. Norton.

Adams, Ansel. 1992. The meaning of the national parks. In *Ansel Adams: Our national parks,* ed. Andrea G. Stillman and William A. Turnage. Boston: Little, Brown.

Badè, William Frederic. 1924. *The life and letters of John Muir.* 2 vols. Boston: Houghton-Mifflin.

Barbour, Ian G. 1990. *Religion in an age of science: The Gifford lectures, 1989–1991.* Vol. 1. San Francisco: Harper & Row.

Beierwaltes, Werner. 1972. *Platonismus und Idealismus.* Frankfurt: Vittorio Klostermann.

Bergandi, Donato. 1998. The geography of human societies. In *The European origins of scientific ecology (1800–1901),* ed. Pascal Acot, trans. B.P. Hamm. vol. 2, Amsterdam: Gordon and Breach.

Chugerman, Samuel. 1939. *Lester F. Ward: The American Aristotle.* Durham: Duke University Press

Clements, Frederic E. 1916. *Plant succession: An analysis of the development of vegetation.* Washington DC: Carnegie Institute of Washington.

Clements, Isaac. 2001. A Civil War memoir. *War, Literature and the Arts* 13:6–44.

Coslett, Tess, ed. 1984. *Science and religion in the nineteenth century.* Cambridge: Cambridge University Press.

Craig, William Lane. 1980. *The cosmological argument from Plato to Leibniz.* New York: Barnes & Noble.

Craige, Betty Jean. 2001. *Eugene Odum: Ecosystem ecologist and environmentalist.* Athens: University of Georgia Press.

Croker, Robert A. 1991. *Pioneer ecologist: The life and work of Victor Ernest Shelford, 1877–1968.* Washington DC: Smithsonian Institution Press.

———. 2001. *Stephen Forbes and the rise of American ecology.* Washington DC: Smithsonian Institution Press.

Crunden, Robert M. 1982. *Ministers of reform: The Progressives' achievement in American civilization, 1889–1920.* New York: Basic Books.

Forbes, Stephen A. 1880. On some interactions of organisms. *Illinois Laboratory of Natural History, Bulletin* 1:3–17.

Gillispie, Charles Coulston. 1951. *Genesis and geology: A study in the relations of scientific thought, natural theology, and social opinion in Great Britain, 1790–1850.* Cambridge, MA: Harvard University Press. Repr., New York: Harper & Brothers, 1959.

Glacken, Clarence J. 1967. *Traces on the Rhodian shore: Nature and culture in western thought from ancient times to the end of the eighteenth century.* Berkeley: University of California Press.

Grove, Richard H. 1995. *Green imperialism: Colonial expansion, tropical island Edens, and the origins of environmentalism, 1600–1860.* Cambridge: Cambridge University Press.

Hagen, Joel B. 1992. *An entangled bank: The origins of ecosystem ecology.* New Brunswick, NJ: Rutgers University Press.

Harris, R. Baine, ed. 1976. *The significance of Neoplatonism.* Norfolk, VA: International Society for Neoplatonic Studies.

Harrison, Peter. 1998. *The Bible, Protestantism, and the rise of natural science.* Cambridge: Cambridge University Press.

Hovenkamp, Herbert. 1978. *Science and religion in America, 1800–1860.* Philadelphia: University of Pennsylvania Press.

Howe, Daniel Walker. 1989. The Cambridge Platonists of old England and the Cambridge Platonists of New England. In *American Unitarianism, 1805–1865*, ed. Conrad Edick Wright. Boston: Northeastern University Press.

König, Rudolf. 1981. Karl Möbius, eine kurze biographie. *Karl Möbius: Beiträge zu Leben und Werk.* Krefeld, Germany: Kommissionsverlag Goecke & Evers.

Kölmel, Reinhard. 1981. Zwischen universalismus und empirie—die begründung der modernen ökologie- und biozönose-konzeption durch Karl Möbius. *Karl Möbius: Beiträge zu Leben und Werk.* Krefeld, Germany: Kommissionsverlag Goecke & Evers.

Leopold, Aldo. 1966. *A Sand County almanac: With essays on conservation from Round River.* New York: Ballantine Books.

Lovejoy, Arthur O. 1936. *The great chain of being: A study of the history of an idea.* Cambridge, MA: Harvard University Press. Repr., 1964.

Lovelock, J. E. 1979. *Gaia: A new look at life on earth.* Oxford: Oxford University Press.

Matagne, Patrick. 1999. *Aux origines de l'écologie: Les naturalists en France de 1800 à 1914.* Paris: Éditions du CTHS.

McIntosh, Robert P. 1985. *The background of ecology: Concept and theory.* Cambridge: Cambridge University Press.

Mitman, Gregg. 1992. *The state of nature: ecology, community, and American social thought, 1900–1950.* Chicago: University of Chicago Press.

Novak, Barbara. 1980. *Nature and culture: American landscape and painting, 1825–1875.* New York: Oxford University Press.

Odum, Eugene P. 1971. *Fundamentals of ecology.* 3rd ed. Philadelphia: W. B. Saunders.

Odum, Howard T. 1971. *Environment, power, and society.* New York: Wiley-Interscience.

Portrait and biographical album of Otoe and Cass Counties, Nebraska. 1889. Chicago: Chapman Brothers.

Prytz, Signe. 1984. *Warming: Botaniker og reisende.* Lynge, Denmark: Bogan.

Santmire, H. Paul. 1985. *The travail of nature: The ambiguous ecological promise of Christian theology.* Philadelphia: Fortress Press.

Sheail, John. 1987. *Seventy-five years in ecology: The British Ecological Society*. Oxford: Blackwell.

Stoll, Mark. 1997. *Protestantism, capitalism, and nature in America*. Albuquerque: University of New Mexico Press.

———. 2001. Green *versus* green: Religions, ethics, and the Bookchin-Foreman dispute. *Environmental History* 6:412–27.

———. 2002. Edward O. Wilson: The science of religion and the religion of science. Paper delivered at the conference "Science and Religion: The Religious Beliefs and Practices of Scientists: 20th Century," Göttingen, Germany.

———. 2004. The Catholic ethic and the spirit of environmentalism: Catholics in the American environmental movement. Paper delivered at the conference "Faith, Ethics, and the Environment: The Response of a Catholic University," University of Notre Dame, Notre Dame, Indiana.

———. Forthcoming. Religion and American wilderness. In *The American wilderness*, ed. Michael Lewis. New York: Oxford University Press.

Sutter, Ruben. 1981. Dr. Josias Braun-Blanquet—Eine Würdigung von Leben und Werk. *Botanica Helvetica* 91:17–33.

Thomas, Keith. 1983. *Man and the natural world: A history of the modern sensibility*. New York: Pantheon Books.

Tobey, Ronald C. 1981. *Saving the prairies: The life cycle of the founding school of American plant ecology, 1895–1955*. Berkeley: University of California Press.

Van der Windt, Henny. 1995. *En dan: Wat is natuur nog in dit land? Natuurbescherming in Nederland 1880–1990*. Amsterdam: Boom.

Von Rath, Ulrich. 1998. *Botanik und Pharmakologie in der Renaissance: Die Gründungsgeschichte des Botanischen Gartens Montpellier 1593 und seine Rezeption im nördlichen Mitteleuropa unter besonderer Berücksichtigung eines botanischen Frühdrucks der Lübecker Stadtbibliothek*. Lübeck: Bibliothek der Hansestadt Lübeck.

Webb, Clement C. J. 1915. *Studies in the history of natural theology*. Oxford: Clarendon Press.

Worster, Donald. 1994. *Nature's economy: A history of ecological ideas*. 2nd ed. Cambridge: Cambridge University Press.

CHAPTER 3

Ecology and American Social Thought

Eugene Cittadino

Ecology is a complex, multifaceted science. Its domain is all of nature, and its subject matter is not individual organisms but interrelationships. From its beginning, of necessity, it drew heavily upon concepts, models, and metaphors from other fields within and outside the sciences. That transfer of ideas, not at all uncommon in the sciences, has given ecologists valuable insights and aided them in organizing their empirical data. Ecology, then, is a highly derivative science, one that by its very nature relies upon language fraught with meaning beyond the science. Discussions of ecology and its history always emphasize the great diversity of its subject matter, the extreme differences in methods and approaches depending on the type of environment one is studying or the level of organization (from single-species populations to communities, ecosystems, and the biosphere itself), the lack of consensus on the meanings of terms, the proliferation of empirical generalizations of limited applicability, the paucity of broad general principles, and the prevalence of national and regional styles owing to both environmental and cultural differences. In the United States, where ecology has enjoyed perhaps its most consistent and extensive intellectual and institutional development, ecology has grown up within a peculiarly American set of social needs, institutional requirements, and cultural changes. Its early practitioners emphasized the potential practical applications of the new science to agriculture, fisheries, forestry, and conservation; sociologists, geographers, and regional planners saw it as a model for an integrated scientific approach to their disciplines; utopian visionaries have viewed it as the scientific underpinning for a new social order and an antidote to the excesses of modern civilization; and most recently ecologists and economists have made efforts to merge their two disciplines within a single system of rational planning. Throughout its history, the science of ecology could not always fulfill the needs and expectations of those who drew upon it for inspiration. Still, ecology has grown more sophisticated, rigorous, mathematical, and empirical over the century or so of its existence, and if it has not reached anything like consensus in the early twenty-first century, that situation is due as much to the complexity of its subject matter as to the limitations of its methods and concepts and the shortcomings of its practitioners.

THE SOCIAL AND INTELLECTUAL ROOTS OF ECOLOGY IN THE U.S.

References to a new science dealing with interrelationships in nature began to appear in Europe and America during the last decade of the nineteenth century. When a formal name was attached to this new field of research, the word "ecology" was the most frequent choice, although other contenders, such as "bionomics" or even "ethology," among certain zoologists, occasionally surfaced as well. The origin of the word is clear enough. It was coined in 1866 by Ernst Haeckel, a German zoologist who thought that there should be a name for the study of the relationships between organisms and what Charles Darwin loosely termed their "conditions of existence," that is, all of the factors, abiotic and biotic, that affect their survival. Haeckel chose the word *Ökologie* for this new field—literally, from its Greek roots, the study of households—and defined it more or less as we would define it now (Haeckel 1866, 2:234–36, 286–87; Stauffer 1957). A visionary with a comprehensive monist worldview in which nature and God are one, Haeckel shared with most of his contemporaries, including Herbert Spencer (an equally influential thinker in the early development of ecology), a progressive interpretation of evolution and a belief in the ultimate beneficence of nature. However, Haeckel himself made little use of his new word, and neither did anyone else until the 1890s, when it was quietly adopted by botanists in the U.S. and Europe. Ecology came to be accepted as the general term for the new science only after the turn of the century. The following is a brief attempt to highlight some of the intellectual and social factors surrounding the American emergence of the new science.

Ecology was born at a time of intense interest in social reform in America, a time during which the Christian spirit of reform was wedded closely to new efforts at studying social ills with the tools and within the framework of modern science. Ecology developed as a scientific discipline in America at the same time as sociology. The same influences that steered some dedicated researchers toward a scientific study of human society may have steered others toward a scientific study of organisms in society, as it were. Much of the impetus for urban reform had come from the Protestant ministry in the late nineteenth century, in which a missionary zeal fueled an urge to find meaningful work in an increasingly secularized world. The motivations for this "social gospel" movement, as it was sometimes called, were complex. The Protestant ministry had lost some of its social and economic status in the post–Civil War years and saw urban reform as an opportunity for gaining back at least some social, if not economic, respectability. In addition, however, America in the Gilded Age had become a place tarnished by worldly values; the nation had lost some of its antebellum innocence. The other side of rapid industrial and commercial expansion, urban growth, and increased affluence was fierce competition, political graft and corruption, urban squalor, labor unrest, and alternating economic booms and busts. The scientific approach to societal ills offered at least the promise of objectivity and a kind of moral purity in welcome contrast to the physical blight and moral decadence that characterized the urban and industrial environment of the late nineteenth and early twentieth centuries. It was a way to combine Christian charity with a rational, pragmatic approach to problem solving (Hofstadter 1955; Coser 1978; Ross 1991).

Although the conservation movement, concern for anthropogenic extinctions, and efforts to preserve natural areas represented expressions of this reform spirit, the origins of ecology in America were tied only indirectly to these early examples of environmental activism. Other immediate intellectual and institutional motivations led to the creation of a new discipline: exciting developments in the life sciences, including evolutionary theory, physiology, and biogeography; the expansion of the university system following the Civil War; extensive scientific explorations into the western regions of the continent; and the desire to emulate the European, particularly German, trend toward increased sophistication, specialization, and laboratory emphasis in the life sciences. The formal American adoption of the word "ecology," perhaps the earliest anywhere, took place in 1893 at a meeting in Madison, Wisconsin, attended by botanists concerned with the professional development of their discipline within the growing framework of academic and government-sponsored science. They officially adopted Haeckel's word, with its anglicized spelling, as part of the terminology of plant physiology, treating ecology as the study of the physiology, broadly conceived, of whole plants and groups of plants in their natural habitats. Their immediate motivation was to remedy what they perceived as a misuse among German-speaking scientists of the terms "biology" and "biological," applied narrowly to studies of the adaptations of organisms and interrelationships between organisms and their environments. However, the American botanists were also by this act acknowledging the growing interest in studies of adaptations and the geographical distribution of organisms, an interest that capped a century of explorations in this field opened up by Alexander von Humboldt and gradually refined and modified by numerous subsequent naturalists, mainly on the European continent (Madison Botanical Congress 1894; Cittadino 1980).

Attendees at the Madison conference included leaders in plant science whose work tapped into the peculiarly American version of this biogeographical tradition: the natural history survey, the compilation of a record of the geological, zoological, and botanical features of a region that served the dual function of providing useful information and bringing the natural productions of the new continent within the purview of western science. John Merle Coulter, then in the process of establishing botany as an academic department at the new University of Chicago, had earned his reputation in the 1870s as a member of the federally sponsored Hayden survey of the western territories. Charles Bessey, a taxonomist and pioneering botanical educator, established an exemplary botany department at the University of Nebraska in the 1880s and then set his students to work on a botanical survey of the state, conceived as part pure science and part aid to agriculture and commerce, as large tracts of the Nebraska prairie were coming under the plow. Under Bessey's tutelage, numerous students, most notably Frederic Clements, worked on the survey and incorporated into their work the ecological perspective already making its way into European plant geography in the late nineteenth century. Bessey himself even pursued a pet ecological project to restore forests to the Nebraska sand hills (Overfield 1993; Pound and

Clements 1900). Clements eventually found a research position with the Carnegie Institution in 1917 and became the premiere plant ecologist in the U.S., working out of several Carnegie research stations in the West. In Chicago, Henry Chandler Cowles, encouraged by Coulter, applied the ecological perspective to a study of the succession of plant communities on the sand dunes along the nearby Indiana shore of Lake Michigan, a region which Coulter had been among the first to explore botanically in the 1870s. When Cowles's research in the dunes earned him a doctoral degree and an invitation to remain at the University of Chicago, he became the first professor of plant ecology in the U.S. He introduced to American ecology the concept of the climax, the mature community that is the supposed endpoint of a successional sequence (Cowles 1899, 1901). Clements, by emphasizing the self-sustaining and rejuvenating qualities of the climax community, developed this idea into a powerfully influential doctrine that still resonates in environmental literature (Clements 1905, 1916).

Although they represented only two among a generation of young botanists drawn into the new science, Clements and Cowles, due to their pioneering work and their advantageous positions, continued to exert a strong influence on the field well into the twentieth century. The scientific views of both were influenced by the progressive reform movement. Henry Cowles spent his undergraduate years at Oberlin College, an institution with a reputation for tolerance and a strong dedication to public service. Liberal arts colleges like Oberlin often provided the necessary undergraduate training for ministers who would serve parishes in the nation's hinterlands. Cowles, as it were, chose a career in science and found himself a position in the nation's largest interior city, but it was a city whose educated elite was obsessed with social reform. Besides offering his services in numerous ways in various civic projects, Cowles focused his teaching program on studies of plant succession in the area surrounding Chicago, particularly on the Indiana dunes. His description of the process of succession, from the first plant life taking hold on the beach to the growth of a luxuriant forest, was a description of communities struggling against adversity, altering their environment in the process, and establishing permanent, prosperous settlements. This was a story that fit in well with the city of Chicago; it was a combination of Frederick Jackson Turner's frontier hypothesis and the urban reform program of the progressives who held sway in that city. The settlement-house workers and social reformers who numbered among Cowles's friends in the Hyde Park community where he lived and worked and his colleagues in the sociology department who focused their research on urban problems had imbibed the lessons of the social gospel very well. Cowles transferred the reform spirit to his plant communities struggling to establish a place for themselves on the shifting sands of the Lake Michigan shore (Engel 1983; Cittadino 1993b).

Frederic Clements pursued his organicist approach to plant communities with a passion born of a holistic social vision. Whereas Cowles focused his research and teaching program on the process of succession, a process that for him was never complete, at least not for very long, Clements focused on the endpoint of the process, the climax formation. Once the climax was achieved, it functioned as an organic whole, resisting perturbations and persisting indefinitely (barring major climate change) as long as human interference did not destroy its integrity. Clements had been influenced by the writings of Herbert Spencer, particularly his notion of the social organism and his discussion of the mitigating effects of the evolutionary process in dampening competition and creating conditions conducive to harmony and cooperation. Clements and his collaborator Roscoe Pound (later the dean of Harvard Law School) read Spencer at the University of Nebraska in the 1890s, particularly his *Principles of Biology* (1867). Since other popular sociological writers at this time, notably Lester Frank Ward, held similar notions of social units functioning as organic wholes, Spencer was not likely the sole source for Clements's organicist notions. Still, for Clements the process of succession led inevitably, in the absence of interference from humans, to the establishment of the stable and self-regenerating climax formation, which resembles in many respects the harmonious and stable endpoint of the evolutionary process for Spencer, the same endpoint for organisms in nature as for humans in civilized society (Spencer 1891; Pound 1954; Tobey 1981).

The idea of integrated communities of organisms interacting with each other and with the physical environment was not confined to botanical studies. A half dozen years before the 1893 Madison meeting, and about two hundred miles due south, Stephen Forbes delivered his now famous talk, "The Lake as a Microcosm" (see Forbes 1925), at a meeting of the Peoria Scientific Association. Forbes, a professor of zoology and entomology at the University of Illinois and director of the Illinois State Laboratory of Natural History, an institution he had founded in 1877, focused his research on the feeding habits and population fluctuations of birds, insects, and fish. Much of his field work was associated with lakes, streams, and rivers, particularly the Illinois River, which flows through the center of Peoria. The central message of his talk was that all of the components of an aquatic system, such as an inland lake, function as an integrated whole and that any effect on one part of the system will be felt in all the others. Although he was drawing on his own extensive field experiences, his debt to Darwin and Spencer is evident, as well as to Karl Möbius, author of a recent study of the depleted oyster bank off the coast of Schleswig-Holstein. Forbes's explanation of the natural balance found in lakes was thoroughly Spencerian. In *Principles of Biology* (1867) Spencer had argued that the evolutionary process results, ultimately, in an equilibrium condition, in which not only do births balance deaths but the different components of a biological community become adapted to one another, in habits and structure as well as in number, so that the entire community functions harmoniously. Over time, wild oscillations in the numbers of predators and prey, for example, gradually dampen as the organisms become adjusted to each other. Forbes, like Spencer, saw this process as evidence of the ultimate beneficence of nature (Forbes 1925; Croker 2001; Bocking 1990; Schneider 2000). He expressed this teleological viewpoint, and its implications for humans, in even clearer terms in an earlier article on interactions in nature in which he cited Spencer directly, as well as the pre-Darwinian classic, *Introduction to Entomology* by Kirby and Spence: "There is a general consent," he wrote, summarizing Kirby and Spence, "that primeval nature, as in the uninhabited forest or the untilled plain, presents a settled harmony of interaction among organic groups which is in strong contrast with the many serious maladjustments of plants and animals found in countries occupied by man." To avoid these problems, he argued, we need to discover how nature controls disturbances and then try to imitate these methods as best we can. "But far the most important general conclusion we have reached is a conviction of the general beneficence of Nature, a profound respect for the natural order, a belief that the part of wisdom is essentially that of practical conservation in dealing with the system of things by which we are surrounded" (Forbes 1880, 5, 15).

Forbes was to exert considerable influence on the science of ecology through his work with many students and colleagues, including Charles Kofoid, a pioneering limnologist and later marine biologist, and two University of Chicago trained zoologists: Charles C. Adams, who became a champion of conservation and applied ecology, and Victor Shelford, a budding animal ecologist who began his research by applying Henry

Cowles's approach toward ecological succession to the study of animal communities along the Lake Michigan shore. Adopting the strong Chicago sociological emphasis, Shelford viewed ecology as first and foremost the study of communities, by which he meant pristine "natural" communities unaffected by human civilization. He spent considerable effort throughout his career encouraging the preservation of natural areas in North America in which such communities could be found. In 1915 he and Cowles collaborated with others to launch the Ecological Society of America (ESA), an organization that from its outset tended to emphasize the professional development of a young science struggling for identity and respect among other disciplines (Shelford 1938). Sensing the potential overemphasis on "pure" research in pristine environments, Stephen Forbes took advantage of his presidency of the Ecological Society in 1921 to speak on "The Humanizing of Ecology." He made a strong appeal for practical applications of ecological knowledge and for incorporating within the body of ecology studies of immediate or potential economic significance, since ecology is the science that deals most directly with matters of interest to human welfare. Forbes objected strongly to the view "that applied biology is no part of ecology itself," adding: "I would humanize ecology, therefore, first by taking the actions and relations of civilized man as fully into account in its definitions, divisions, and coordinations as those of any other kind of organism" (Forbes 1922, 89). The previous president of the society, Barrington Moore (1920), had made a similar appeal, arguing that forestry, agriculture, and geography are all aspects of ecology. Moore, a forester by training, served as the first editor of *Ecology,* the journal of the Ecological Society, for twelve years, from 1920 through 1931. Despite individual ecologists expressing considerable sympathy for the views of Forbes and Moore, the Ecological Society and its journal, for the most part, emphasized academic science over practical applications and did not adopt positions on socially controversial issues, a situation that vexed certain members of the society and eventually came to a head after World War II (Croker 1991; Tjossem 1994).

ECOLOGY IN AMERICA TO THE 1970S:
A SELECTIVE OVERVIEW

As a brief preview of major trends in American ecology, the first paradigm—ecological succession leading to the climax community—received considerable attention among plant ecologists and inspired work on animal ecology through the first three decades of the twentieth century. Meanwhile, from the 1920s through the 1940s distinct research programs in animal ecology began to emerge, some emphasizing cooperation within groups and adopting a group selection approach to evolution, some focusing more on competition and predation, and many beginning to apply a variety of quantitative techniques to the study of animal populations. The ecosystem concept was introduced in the 1930s mainly in response to developments that had taken place within plant ecology, but ecosystem ecology did not come into its own until after the Second World War, as a result of seminal studies of aquatic systems and abundant funding from the Atomic Energy Commission, the latter perhaps providing the most important stimulus. From the 1950s on, various reductionist approaches to ecology, influenced by a stricter, individualistic interpretation of Darwinian natural selection theory and employing a growing array of mathematical and statistical tools and concepts, vied with various holistic approaches that recurred in different forms in ecosystem ecology and in other branches of the discipline. This section traces a few of the connecting threads within this increasingly diverse and complex science and suggests some of their broader social contexts.

One strand of influences links early plant and animal ecology to conservation and ecosystem ecology. In 1935, in a paper written as part of a tribute to the ailing Henry Cowles, the foremost plant ecologist in Britain, Arthur Tansley, uneasy with the underlying philosophical basis of the climax concept and other holistic conceptions of organic communities, suggested "ecosystem" as the proper unit of ecology, defining it as comprising all the organisms that interact together in a particular environment along with all of the inorganic features of that environment. Raymond Lindeman, a young American limnologist, introduced Tansley's concept to the world in 1942, in a paper based on a study of the energy budget of a Minnesota lake, although the paper did not receive much attention at the time it was published. In addition to Tansley's ecosystem concept Lindeman made use of British zoologist Charles Elton's concepts of food webs and pyramids of numbers, concepts that Elton did not originate but that, along with the ecological niche, had become part of the vocabulary of ecological science as a result of his work (Elton 1927; Cook 1977). Elton, in turn, had been strongly influenced early in his career by Victor Shelford's *Animal Communities of Temperate America* (1913), one of the first textbooks of animal ecology. Elton went on to develop his own approach to the subject and inaugurate a remarkably productive program of animal population studies whose influence extends down to the present in both Europe and the U.S., particularly now with studies of the effects of invasive species. Elton met American conservationist/wildlife biologist Aldo Leopold at a conference on population cycles in 1931, and as a result of that meeting Leopold's later writings adopted a distinct ecological perspective that was lacking in his earlier work (Crowcroft 1991; Meine 1988). Meanwhile, Shelford established a solid research and teaching program at the University of Illinois, where he numbered among his students Eugene P. Odum. In the 1930s Shelford and Frederic Clements sought to link animal and plant ecology, which had more or less gone their separate ways, into a comprehensive "bio-ecology," but the project was largely unsuccessful (Clements and Shelford 1939). A more successful effort at linking the various strands of ecological science was accomplished by Odum, who, through his research institute at the University of Georgia and especially through the three editions of his textbook, *Fundamentals of Ecology,* made the ecosystem concept one of the central features of ecology and introduced the concept to countless students from the 1950s on (Odum 1953; Croker 1991). There was an uninterrupted series of influences, then, from the early pioneering works on plant ecology, through developments in animal ecology, conservation, and wildlife biology in America and Britain, to the ecosystem studies that occupied much of the attention of American ecologists in the 1960s and 1970s.

Already home to one of the founding schools of plant ecology, the University of Chicago became a center of a school of animal ecology that linked studies of animals in groups to social theory. When Shelford left Chicago for the University of Illinois in 1914, his place was eventually filled by his former student W. C. Allee, whose work focused on animal populations as integral evolutionary units. Allee, a Quaker, an outspoken pacifist, and a critic of natural selection theory, self-consciously set about creating a program of research that focused on animal populations as cooperative social units, a viewpoint that paralleled the work of some of his contemporaries in anthropology and social psychology. Although worlds apart in some respects, Clements's climax community and Allee's single-species animal aggregations, as he called them, had in common the quality that they functioned as integral physiological wholes. Allee modified his views somewhat as he began to work with colleagues of different training and social orientation, but the notion of the population as a functional evolutionary unit persisted. The Chicago group became a dominant force in the Ecological Society in the 1930s and 1940s and produced a major textbook in 1949. However, both the textbook and the school of animal ecology that it represented held limited appeal after the early 1950s, as Allee's cooperative and group selectionist perspective gave way to revived Darwinian treatments of competition, on the one hand, and to ecosystem ecology, which focused on flows of energy and materials in complex multi-species systems, on the other hand (Allee 1931; Allee et al. 1949; Mitman 1992).

A more lasting influence came from an unexpected source outside the small but growing community of professional ecologists. In the mid-1920s, while Allee was working out his views on animal aggregations and Clements was refining his notion of the climax, amateur scientist Alfred Lotka published a curious book titled *Elements of Physical Biology* (1925). The book happily mixed ideas and information from chemistry, physics, biology, statistics, and demography, holding all this together within a broad philosophical framework that was Spencerian in scope and viewpoint. It was nothing less than a system of the world, including discussions of the carbon and nitrogen cycles, evolution, thermodynamics, chemical equilibria, population growth, food chains, and speculations on the origins of consciousness. The book influenced economists, political theorists, and industrial managers and anticipated the general systems perspective that would emerge after World War II, that is, the approach to understanding complex phenomena that assumes that systems behave as integrated wholes in ways not reducible to sums of mechanical interactions among their individual components. Lotka secured a fellowship to complete *Elements* with assistance from another scientist outside the mainstream of ecology, Raymond Pearl, a biometrician at the Johns Hopkins University who later independently rediscovered, and then set about actively promoting, the logistic (S-shaped) curve of population growth, first suggested in the nineteenth century (Kingsland 1995).

Despite their only marginal interest in ecology, Pearl and Lotka have had a profound influence on the subsequent development of the science. Both adopted a holistic view of animal and human communities, Lotka embracing the older Spencerian notion of the social organism, Pearl adopting the more contemporary homeostatic view promoted within biochemistry and physiology, that is, the notion that such functions as the regulation of temperature and blood chemistry in organisms are controlled by elaborate feedback mechanisms. Both saw as the ultimate goal of their work the extension of their scientific insights to a rational understanding of social and political processes. Organicist models of social systems, grounded in equilibrium theory derived from the life sciences, had been introduced by biochemist L. J. Henderson and his Harvard colleague, physiologist Walter B. Cannon. Henderson based his insights very deliberately on his reading in sociology. Cannon extended his groundbreaking revelations into the body's natural homeostatic processes to speculations about social homeostasis. Lotka and Pearl, steeped in these broad equilibrium approaches to biological and social theory current in the 1920s and 1930s, developed or helped promote several ideas that were then picked up on and extended by ecologists. Lotka had discovered mathematical regularities governing predator-prey oscillations independently of Italian mathematician Vito Volterra. The Lotka-Volterra equations, as they came to be called, had a considerable influence on animal ecologists, especially those interested in biological control of insect pests and others, like Charles Elton, interested in the causes of population cycles. Pearl influenced the work of Russian scientist G. F. Gause, who developed a mathematical demonstration of what came to be called the competitive exclusion principle, the idea that two species cannot occupy the same ecological niche. The Lotka-Volterra equations, Gause's competitive exclusion principle, and Pearl's logistic curve all eventually became central features of theoretical ecology, particularly in the postwar years, when mathematical approaches to the science came into their own (Kingsland 1995; Henderson 1913, 1917; Cannon 1932; Russet 1966).

The development of ecosystem ecology was also tied, in part, to ideas of social organization and control. Although the coiner of the term "ecosystem," Arthur Tansley, was a terrestrial plant ecologist, much of the initial impetus for the study of ecosystems came from aquatic biology. Perhaps the strongest influence on Raymond Lindeman had been his mentor as a graduate student at Yale, G. Evelyn Hutchinson, not himself an ecosystem ecologist, whose work in limnology reflected research that was being done in Europe on the biogeochemistry of aquatic systems. Hutchinson had come to Yale from England, by way of South Africa. Highly critical of the plodding, methodical work that was being done on this side of the Atlantic, Hutchinson was searching for larger, integrative themes. He initiated studies of nutrient cycling in a local Connecticut pond with his Yale students during the 1930s, and Lindeman took his cue from there. Utilizing Tansley's ecosystem concept as his organizing principle, Lindeman combined nutrient cycling with the idea of trophic levels (that is, food levels—producers, consumers, etc.) along with succession and the climax and Elton's food webs and pyramid of numbers. Although Lindeman's untimely death cut short a promising career, another of Hutchinson's students, Howard T. Odum, brother of Eugene, carried on ambitious ecosystem studies, also mainly on aquatic systems, after the war and provided much of the inspiration for his brother's turn toward ecosystem ecology. H. T. Odum, who read Lotka's *Elements*, had become enamored with the technocracy movement led by Howard Scott (1933), and he transferred the movement's optimistic view (that an enlightened engineering perspective offered the best, and perhaps only, solution to social problems) to the study of ecosystems. In Odum's hands the earlier organic metaphors that dominated ecology gave way to mechanical metaphors based on electrical circuitry and, eventually, cybernetics. Whereas Lindeman had grounded his ideas in the food relations of the organic components of the system and had retained the notion of the climax, H. T. Odum reduced everything to energy transfers, constructing complex energy-flow diagrams with input and output boxes resembling, quite deliberately, electrical circuitry (H. T. Odum 1960). Still, the sense of integral, self-sustaining units was not lost. Eugene Odum included Howard's circuit diagrams in the second and third editions of *Fundamentals of Ecology*, although he himself retained the older organicist perspective, treating ecosystems as organic units that respond to environmental perturbation as functional wholes (Taylor 1988; Slobodkin and Slack 1999; E. Odum 1969; Craige 2001).

Because of the valuable role played by radionuclides in tracing the flow of energy and materials in ecosystems, the new Atomic Energy Commission provided much of the funding for the postwar work of the Odum brothers and a very influential group of ecosystem ecologists at Oak Ridge National Laboratory in Tennessee. Ostensibly set up to study the health effects of radiation from nuclear weapons testing and nuclear reactors, this group soon turned its attention almost exclusively to ecosystem studies. Among others with ties to various Chicago ecology programs, the Oak Ridge group included botanist Jerry Olson, a University of Chicago graduate whose doctoral research tested some of the assumptions and conclusions of the successional studies of Henry Cowles and his colleagues at the Indiana dunes earlier in the century (Olson 1958). The resulting ecosystem work at Oak Ridge and elsewhere would have been unrecognizable to Cowles—highly quantified, filled with flow charts and abstruse calculations, and employing language and metaphors from the physical sciences and the industrial world. The Oak Ridge group, still in existence, became one of the major players in the systems approach to ecology that dominated the American faction of the International Biological Program (IBP) in the 1960s and 1970s. The IBP attracted unprecedented funds from the federal government, offered considerable opportunities for ecological researchers and their students, and quite simply put ecosystem ecology on the map. The program ran from 1968 to 1974, a period that coincided exactly with the rise of the environmental movement. At least part of its rationale was to provide an assessment of the natural conditions of the earth's major biomes as a prelude to developing informed environmental policies. Despite its mixed results, the program has had repercussions that are still being felt in terms of both the contents and methods of ecological science and the application of ecology to environmental policy (Bocking 1997; Golley 1993; Hagen 1992; Kwa 1987, 1993).

The predominance of mathematics and the physical sciences in war-related research spilled over into ecology in the postwar years in the form of greater emphasis on quantitative studies and on applications of engineering theory to understanding ecological systems, as in H. T. Odum's highly technical approach to ecosystem studies using models based on electrical circuitry. Wartime research into information theory also began to filter into ecological studies during the 1950s and '60s, with various conceptions of the diversity and stability of ecosystems formulated in terms of signal-noise ratios, the ability of a signal to maintain its content in long-distance transmission, and so on. Hutchinson, interested in applying information science and cybernetics to ecology, had also begun exploring applications of Gause's work to a mathematical understanding of the ecological niche. Another of his students, Robert MacArthur, extended this work and applied mathematical modeling techniques in ingenious ways to various problems grounded in natural history, such as the nature of competition, the partitioning of niche-space among closely related species, and the changing species composition of island populations. MacArthur, whose premature death probably added to his mystique, became the inspirational symbol for a new generation of ecologists better trained in mathematics than their predecessors and increasingly having access to computers. It was around the time of the height of MacArthur's popularity within ecology, the late 1960s and early 1970s, that the new environmental movement began drawing heavily upon the science of ecology for inspiration and on professional ecologists for practical advice and guidance. This was a role that some ecologists may have relished but for which most found themselves either unsuited or inadequately prepared. The science was itself incomplete, imprecise, and conceptually inconsistent. Whereas individual ecologists had been avid proponents of conservation and nature protection since the formal beginnings of their science, ecology could offer limited assistance toward solving environmental problems, not only because of the enormous complexity of the problems themselves, as well as the limitations of existing ecological knowledge, but also because the solutions required complex value choices involving political, economic, moral, and esthetic considerations that far transcended the boundaries of their science (Kingsland 1995; McIntosh 1985, chaps. 6–8; Nelkin 1977; Shrader-Frechette and McCoy 1993a).

THE INFLUENCE OF ECOLOGICAL SCIENCE ON SOCIAL THEORY

Although the discovery of ecology by the general public can be dated in the U.S. to the period between the publication of Rachel Carson's *Silent Spring*, 1962, and the first Earth Day, 1970, the science had a significant, if less dramatic, influence on social thought much earlier in the twentieth century. Both plant and animal ecologists drew upon language and concepts from social theory to express their ideas, as when they discussed community structure and organization, dominance hierarchies, division of labor, "pioneer" species, and so forth. It would not be surprising for social scientists to have adopted some of the terminology and concepts of ecology as the science developed formally. One direct adoption of ecological concepts came in the establishment of a school of human ecology among sociologists associated with the University of Chicago. The sociology program begun there in the 1890s had been inspired by the settlement-house movement and the spirit of Protestant social reform. Field work conducted in urban settings became the hallmark of Chicago sociology from its beginnings. The founder of the Chicago department, Albion Small, was a Baptist minister convinced that the purpose of the scientific study of society was to improve it, particularly to alleviate suffering and enhance the quality of life for the average city dweller. The faculty and students who gathered around Small in Chicago began conducting studies of the living and working conditions in the surrounding city, particularly those among the lower classes, including recent European immigrants as well as migrants from other regions in the U. S. (Coser 1978; Ross 1991). When former journalist and publicist Robert Ezra Park joined the department in the second decade of the twentieth century, he inaugurated a distinct school of urban sociology that called itself "human ecology" and came to dominate the Chicago program, which itself was the dominant sociology graduate program in the country. Chicago sociologists qua human ecologists, with considerable financial support from the Rockefeller Foundation, studied the distribution patterns of social classes and ethnic groups, the process of zonation from the city center outwards, and the interplay of cultural and economic forces within and between the various neighborhoods. Although these studies sometimes closely resembled Henry Cowles's studies of the successive replacement of plant communities from the Lake Michigan shore to the oldest established dunes, when they cited the work of plant ecologists the Chicago human ecologists usually cited Clements, whose work was systematized in readily accessible texts (Park, Burgess, and McKenzie 1925; Zorbaugh 1926; McKenzie 1924; Rauschenbush 1974; Turner and Turner 1990; Cittadino 1993a).

Although Chicago's human ecology program went into decline by the late 1930s, the term human ecology has persisted to the present, albeit more as a vague, general term with a variety of meanings than as a label denoting a particular research agenda. There were several aborted efforts to integrate human ecology into the framework of ecological science in the first half of the century. The second president of the Ecological Society, the geographer Ellsworth Huntington, attempted to make human ecology a more significant part of ecological science. Huntington had spent several seasons at the Carnegie Institution's Desert Botanical Laboratory at Tucson, Arizona, where he met plant ecologists and became impressed with the new science. When the Ecological Society was formed in 1915, he eagerly joined as a representative human ecologist. Huntington was a prolific writer whose special field was the relationship between climate and human society. He had just completed his major work, *Civilization and Climate* (1915), when the Ecological Society was founded. As the society's president in 1917 he tried unsuccessfully to recruit more members from the social sciences and to convince his colleagues of the importance of that goal. He continued to promote human ecology, managing to persuade the National Research Council to let him organize a Committee on Human Ecology to investigate environmental conditions in American cities, but the committee's work was reduced eventually to a single study of weather and mortality rates in New York City (Huntington 1915, 1927, 1930; Martin 1973; Cittadino 1993a). Among other efforts, Charles Adams and Paul Sears managed in 1939 to organize a symposium with the title "On the Relation of Ecology to Human Welfare" as a joint effort between the Ecological Society of America and the American Association for the Advancement of Science. Adams and Sears thought this symposium might become part of a larger effort to make human ecology an integral part of the Ecological Society. However, the war intervened, and after the war a request for the inclusion of more articles on human ecology in the journal *Ecology* brought about a sharp rebuke from the editorial board, indicating that the board and many members of the society did not think highly of either the scientific merit or the objective standards of most articles on human ecology (Adams et al. 1940; Lawrence and Park 1949).

Huntington was not alone among geographers drawn into ecology. Human geography had developed as a branch of geography in Europe in the last half of the nineteenth century, and, while early works in this field emphasized the causal effects of the earth on humans, as the field evolved the focus shifted to intensive regional studies that emphasized reciprocal effects between humans and their physical and biological surroundings. The major program granting advanced degrees in geography, at the University of Chicago, gradually changed its emphasis from physiography to human geography during the first two decades of the twentieth century. Carl O. Sauer, a product of the Chicago program who had studied under Cowles, among others, became one of the most influential geographers of the twentieth century, establishing a thriving research and teaching program at the University of California. Whereas geography as a discipline had moved away from its physical science origins, under Sauer it retained its connections to the physical earth. He utilized his background in plant ecology in various studies on the origins of agriculture, the uses of fire by primitive people, and the reconstruction of the environments of past civilizations. His work emphasized the destructive effects of humans on the earth's resources and natural environments, and he often referred to the nearly forgotten nineteenth century work, *Man and Nature,* by George Perkins Marsh (1864), which had influenced the early conservation movement in the U.S. Marsh, a native Vermonter whose attitude toward nature was firmly grounded in Christian stewardship, had focused his study on the devastating effects of several millenia of human occupation on the forests of the Mediterranean region, offering a poignant warning to his American countrymen. Sauer focused his attention on extinctions and the destruction of natural landscapes in the western U.S. and Mexico (Sauer 1967; Leighly 1967; Schulten 2001; Dickinson 1976).

Sauer considered himself a regional geographer. In the period between the world wars the concept of regionalism crept into a number of social sciences, and much of the work done by regionalists was tied directly or indirectly to ecology. The central idea behind the regionalist concept is essentially an ecological one. While one could define a region as any spatial unit that has social, economic, or political significance for whatever reason, as the term has been used in geography, sociology, and economics the spatial limits of the region are usually assumed to be "natural," that is, watersheds, valleys, deserts, mountain ranges, estuaries, and so on. Political or administrative boundaries do not always coincide with these natural divisions, but many regionalists have argued, and still argue, that we ignore these divisions at our peril. Pioneering American regionalists included Benton MacKaye, the originator, in 1921, of the idea of the Appalachian Trail and later one of the primary organizers of the Wilderness Society. MacKaye (1921, 1928), a forester by training, had eschewed the managerial ethos that pervaded conservationist thinking in the early twentieth century for a more integrated planning perspective that took into account natural ecological relationships. He had envisioned the Appalachian Trail as a way to bring people into contact with primeval nature and to acquaint them with the organic roots of culture, now lost in an industrial world bent on severing its ties to the landscape. Ultimately, he conceived the trail as a prelude to a plan for repopulating rural areas in a way that would respect and maintain natural interrelationships. MacKaye was influenced strongly by his friend and colleague Lewis Mumford, and by Mumford's mentor, Scottish regionalist Patrick Geddes. Mumford adopted an ecological approach to regional planning in *The Culture of Cities* (1938), perhaps his most influential book. In both this work and his earlier *Technics and Civilization* (1934), he adopted Geddes' terminology regarding technological epochs. The paleotechnic order, characterized by centralization and heavy industrial development based on iron and coal, was coming to a close and rapidly giving way to the neotechnic order, characterized by electrical energy and generally cleaner, less wasteful, and less polluting technologies, and a trend toward decentralization. Ultimately, so Mumford hoped, these trends would continue, and the neotechnic would give way to a biotechnic order, characterized by the stabilization of human population growth, the replacement of mechanistic with organic modes of organization, and adherence to ecological principles. Mumford shared with many ecologists of this period a critique of mechanistic reductionism and a belief in the integrity and stability of natural social units. He tended to take this organicist model of social organization for granted, but where he did cite sources for it he tended to cite authors of broad philosophical perspectives, such as Lloyd Morgan and Alfred North Whitehead (Luccarelli 1995; Mumford 1982).

In discussing his approach to regional planning, Mumford spoke often of balance. Like Carl Sauer, he cited George Perkins Marsh regarding the destructive effects of civilization, and he suggested that attitudes were beginning to change since Marsh wrote. Here is a typical passage from *Technics and Civilization* describing the changes that took place with the transition to the neotechnic order:

> In order to maintain the ecological balance of a region, one could no longer exploit and exterminate as recklessly as had been the wont of the pioneer colonist. The region, in short, had some of the characteristics of an individual organism: like the organism, it had various methods of meeting maladjustment and maintaining its balance: but to turn it into a specialized machine for producing a single kind of goods—wheat, trees, coal—and to forget its many-sided potentialities as a habitat for organic life was finally to unsettle and make precarious the single economic function that seemed so important. (Mumford 1934, 256–57)

The goal was to recreate in the human community the kind of balance and harmony found in nature, and, if possible, to improve on nature. In *The Culture of Cities* he stated bluntly (1938, 314): "Our task is to replace the primitive balance that exists in a region with organisms in a state of nature, by a richer environment, a more subtle and many-weighted balance, of human groups and communities in a state of high culture."

That concept of balance runs through the writings of another regionalist, the sociologist Howard W. Odum, father of Eugene and H. T. Odum. H. W. Odum got his training at the other major center of sociology in the early twentieth century, Columbia University, and he returned to the South to set up the Institute for Research in Social Science at the University of North Carolina, funded by a Rockefeller grant not quite as munificent as the one that financed Park and his group at Chicago. The focus of Odum's institute was southern regionalism, and he used his journal, *Social Forces,* to feature articles dealing with the resources, folkways, laws, agricultural practices, racial tensions, family structures, and so on in the South. Although his work centered on the South, Odum's ideal vision was for a nation of strong natural regions that functioned as integrated wholes, interacted in harmony with one another, and offered equal opportunities to all racial and ethnic groups. In this ideal vision there was balance within each region and among the different regions. Summarizing a quarter century's work at the institute, he wrote, "Now, we have learned a lot about this South of the United States but we have also learned a lot about the way of Nature and culture in a magnificent reality that knows no turning back and gives no special privilege to any culture and no special priorities to any region or race" (H. W. Odum 1945, 42–43). Odum freely used examples and analogies from ecological science in his work. He thought that the ecologists's studies of communities, biomes, zones of distribution, and so forth. offered fitting analogies for regional sociological studies. In a general text on *American Regionalism* he cited not only the work of Robert Park and Carl Sauer, but also various ecologists, including Elton, Clements, Shelford, Allee, and even an unpublished manuscript by his own son Eugene, then a graduate student at the University of Illinois (Odum and Moore 1938). The elder Odum seems to have transmitted to his sons not only his obvious interest in ecology but also his desire to change society for the better. His passion for social justice, which focused on the plight of the poor and minorities in the rural South, was tied to an ecological vision of vibrant self-sustaining regions. His sons concentrated their reform efforts on the latter, working for improved relationships between humans and natural environments (Turner and Turner 1990; Craige 2001). Eugene Odum (1963) later dedicated a small volume on ecology to his father, "whose life works on 'Southern Regionalism' and 'American Regionalism' early inspired me to seek more harmonious relationships between man and nature."

THE TRANSFORMATION OF ECOLOGY IN THE POSTWAR YEARS

Although an ecological perspective found its way into sociology, geography, and urban and regional planning during the first half of the twentieth century, the sense of ecology as a philosophy, a general worldview, or a holistic vision is absent from these examples. A general science of ecology did not exist at this time. There was no single, organized, coherent body of theory to which one could point. After World War II, as the general public became increasingly aware of ecological science, expectations were raised that ecology would provide the kind of synthetic vision that would help us through a series of crises. In the first quarter-century after the war, an educated elite, looking to science for an integrative and comprehensive worldview, gradually placed more and more hope and faith in a science that was becoming increasingly sophisticated, complex, quantitative, and, therefore, less accessible, and that was beginning to call into question some of its earlier cherished notions about balance, harmony, and stability in nature. A simple, uncomplicated ecological vision began to gain momentum outside of scientific ecology at a time when ecology, as science, was becoming anything but simple and uncomplicated.

Ironically, one of the early, and not well-publicized, challenges to traditional ecological theory and its implications came from outside the science. In a series of articles written mainly in the late 1940s and early 1950s, Kansas agricultural historian James C. Malin, a regionalist who focused nearly all his work on the people and environments of the plains states, criticized Frederic Clements's climax theory, which he believed had been imposed dogmatically and irresponsibly on the people of the plains through the agency of federal conservation laws and policies. Clements had convinced federal agencies to apply his theory of plant succession to problems of overgrazing in the arid West as early as 1917. During the devastating dust storms of the 1930s, Clements argued for a more general application of ecological theory to agriculture and expressed his view that agricultural practices that served to destroy the natural climax communities in the grasslands had brought on the recent disaster. Although he called for drastic changes in systems of land tenure, a more modest application of his climax theory to conservation practices was incorporated into federal policies in the U.S.D.A. and the Soil Conservation Service (Clements 1917, 1935; Sampson 1919; Clements and Chaney 1936).[1] Malin argued that dust storms had been a part of the plains experience long before modern agriculture had arrived in the region, citing the work of Carl Sauer, who argued that fires set by Native Americans had created the grasslands in the first place. Malin reasoned that these were not climax communities that should be left undisturbed but environments that had been disturbed regularly since humans occupied the land. Clements's ideas were not only unnecessarily critical of civilization and progress, they were also a threat to democratic values and the individualism that characterized American culture and had shaped the American landscape. Technological innovation and faith in progress, not blind worship of some mystical "climax" that probably never existed, would ultimately solve the problem of agriculture on the plains (Malin 1956b, 1984; Worster 1994, 242–49).

Malin's critique offered a preview of more recent challenges to ecological theory and its applications to environmental problems. Even as Malin wrote, a new generation of plant ecologists was supplanting the Clementsian view of integral, self-sustaining, discrete communities with one of vegetation as a continuum of plant groupings determined by environmental gradients and not by internal dynamics. Community ecology in general was moving away from the holistic models of the prewar period and toward individualistic models, that is, communities as collections of interacting individuals—a view more in keeping, as Malin might have argued, with the individualistic spirit of American democracy, with a period of economic growth and expansion, and perhaps with the general fragmentation of American culture during the 1950s. This view was lost on the nonscientist, however, until it was incorporated into popular treatments of the new ecological perspective at the end of the century (Whittaker 1953; McIntosh 1967, 1974; Simberloff 1980; Mitman 1995; Barbour 1995).

In the immediate postwar years, works that offered a simpler, and more holistic, view of ecology were beginning to have some impact on the reading public. Aldo Leopold's collection of essays, *A Sand County almanac,* was published posthumously in 1949. Leopold, never a sophisticated ecological theorist, offered readers the promise of a "land ethic," grounded in a belief in the integrity of natural systems. The more dire consequences of ignoring that integrity were spelled out clearly in two more pessimistic and consciousness-raising books published in 1948: *Road to Survival,* by ornithologist William Vogt, and *Our Plundered Planet,* by Fairfield Osborn, president of the New York Zoological Society and founder of the private Conservation Foundation. The message was simple and forceful: overpopulation, resource depletion, famine, and pollution were already serious problems and would only get worse unless we begin to take seriously the laws and limitations of natural interrelationships. Both books, Vogt's more explicitly, made references to ecological science and to the natural equilibrium conditions disrupted by over-crowding and by irresponsible agricultural, commercial, and industrial practices. The recent devastating effects of the war itself, from which the North American continent had been spared, served to fuel the sense of urgency in these messages. The examples of Hiroshima and Nagasaki made clear that the health of the entire planet was in jeopardy and that science and technology were now part of the problem. Recent incidents of fatal smog in London and Los Angeles only intensified that view (Fox 1981; Gottlieb 1993).

In recognition of these growing problems and concerns, the Wenner-Gren Foundation for Anthropolgical Research sponsored a week-long symposium at Princeton, New Jersey, in the summer of 1955 on the theme "Man's Role in Changing the Face of the Earth." The symposium included over seventy participants mainly from the U.S. and Europe, representing anthropology, geography, botany, zoology, earth sciences, history, economics, and a smattering of engineering fields. Dedicated to the memory of George Perkins Marsh, the symposium had been organized by Carl Sauer, Lewis Mumford, and Marston Bates, a zoologist who had worked on the eradication of malaria and yellow fever for the Rockefeller Foundation. Topics ranged from the destructive roles of ancient civilizations to recent land-tenure practices to waste removal to radiation from nuclear bomb tests, a kind of historical record of human effects on the natural world, a comparison of natural with human-caused changes, and some speculations regarding the future (Thomas 1956). There was a restrained atmosphere to the proceedings, not much hint of the apocalyptic prophecies of a decade or so later, and no general sense of ecology as philosophy. However, many of the participants were knowledgeable about ecological concepts and theories, and many of the panel discussions reproduced in the published volume reveal a tension between the simple equilibrium model of ecological balance accepted by nonscientists, or by scientists from other fields, and some of the more sophisticated nonequilibrium theories developing within ecology. The ecologists, mainly Frank Egler of the American Museum of Natural History in New York, F. Fraser Darling of Edinburgh University, and John T. Curtis of the University of Wisconsin, made clear to the other participants that contemporary ecological science was not based on a simplistic equilibrium model. At one point Egler, who got involved in every one of the discussions on this issue, gave his blunt eulogy to traditional ecology, paraphrased in the published work as follows:

Egler felt that much of traditional ecology is pretty well "on the skids"—going out—and it would be rather hard to find a strong and powerfully convinced, evangelistic ecologist, even though there are some who are thoroughly grounded in the old "plant succession to climax." There seem to be no good lines of evidence, for example, to indicate that the United States was in a state of virgin climax at the time of entry of the white man, who, in fact, arrived at an unstable moment. (Thomas 1956, 940)

In the ensuing discussion, geographer Clarence Glacken from the University of California pointed out that these ideas of constant change and disequilibrium were not to be found in the ecological literature. He was mistaken. The new ideas were there in the periodical literature but they had yet to find their way into the textbooks or in popular treatments of ecology. They would not for another two decades. Still, James Malin was present at the symposium and contributed a paper on the grasslands that supported Egler's position. Arguing for a long history of devastating dust storms and recovery predating the appearance of European descendants on the plains, he concluded: "No more brazen falsehood was ever perpetrated upon a gullible public than the allegation that the dust storms of the 1930s were caused by 'the plow that broke the Plains'" (Malin 1956a, 356).

In another of the discussions economist Kenneth Boulding of the University of Michigan perceived a tension among the participants between those who followed a biological-ecological point of view and those who adopted a socioeconomic point of view. The former assume equilibrium systems that are disturbed only at our peril, the latter assume directional change based on decreasing entropy and increasing information. Egler ignored Boulding's foray into thermodynamics and argued that since ecologists no longer assume equilibrium systems, it is wrong to attribute such ideas to them (Thomas 1956, 447): "Ecologists should not be be blamed for what is no longer ecology," he complained. Paul Sears—a student of both Cowles and Clements, author of the conservation classic *Deserts on the March* (1935), and chair of a new conservation program at Yale sponsored by Fairfield Osborn's Conservation Foundation— argued that although contemporary ecology recognizes constant change, at any given time "there is in the landscape a system of energy and material transformation whose trend—whether or not it is at climax—is very easily disrupted. Any landscape involves a multitude of organisms, all very closely integrated and interrelated, and each more or less helping to sustain the system" (Thomas 1956, 409). He added that over time the systems develop toward a more efficient use of energy and material and tend to resist external disturbances, but human intervention with these natural systems can lead to devastating results, as many of the contributions to the symposium revealed.

Sears framed his argument deliberately in the language of ecosystem ecology as it had developed through Lindeman to the Odum brothers and the Oak Ridge group, with the emphasis on transfers of energy and materials. A few other participants made use of this language, indicating that the ecosystem concept had become at least well enough known to discuss without having to define it. If before the war ecological theory was framed in the language of the organism, in terms of physiological processes, or the social unit as an organism, after the war ecological theory adopted the language of industry, commerce, and economics. One talked of systems rather than organisms, energy flows and efficiencies, consumers and producers, the processing and transmission of information. Ecosystem studies were just one part of ecology, but the ecosystem perspective caught the attention of nonscientists and began to have some effect on the social sciences. For example, the concept of the ecosystem was introduced to anthropologists by Marston Bates at another Wenner-Gren symposium, on current trends in anthropology, held three years earlier in New York (1953). The publication of the symposium papers coincided with the publication of the first edition of E. P. Odum's *Fundamentals of Ecology,* with its strong ecosystem perspective. Odum's book filled a void. It quickly became the standard textbook in general ecology and remained so until the mid-1970s. The combination of the Bates paper and the Odum book provided the impetus for the initiation of studies of human societies as integral components of ecosystems.

American anthropologists, led by Franz Boas, had long emphasized the primacy of culture and avoided any approach to their field that might hint of biological determinism. By the 1950s many anthropologists were beginning to think that the pendulum had swung too far. Julian Steward led this movement, introducing the term "cultural ecology" as a name for an approach to case studies that viewed individual examples of cultural adaptation as reciprocal products of culture and environment. Whether or not this was Steward's intention, new anthropological studies emerged by the 1960s utilizing the language and concepts of ecosystem ecology, particularly Clifford Geertz's work on subsistence agriculture in Indonesia, Roy Rappaport's study of ritual cycles among the people of New Guinea, and Marshall Sahlins very influential study of production and trade among hunter-gatherers (Steward 1955; Geertz 1963; Rappaport 1968; Sahlins 1972; Moran 1984). When environmentalism developed into a social movement in the 1960s, the idea of the ecologically noble savage emerged first in anthropology and then in American popular culture. Hunter-gatherers were now depicted as in tune with their natural environments and affluent rather than always on the verge of starvation. These were no longer the "primitives" studied only for the light they might shed on human evolution but knowledgeable citizens of planet earth with valuable lessons to share with their "civilized" observers (Bettinger 1991).[2] Partly due to guilt for our treatment of the original human occupants of this continent and partly due to increasing knowledge of the extent of our own wasteful and destructive practices, the myth of the ecologically noble savage persisted in the U.S. despite growing evidence of environmental alteration and destruction on the part of Native Americans. As one striking example, the ecologically astute speech attributed to Chief Seattle in the 1850s, but actually written by a television screenwriter in the 1970s, was quoted at length in Al Gore's *Earth in the Balance* (1992, 259), widely circulated (if not actually read) during the 1992 presidential campaign, although Gore's book was published five years after the revelation of the true authorship of the speech (Callicot 1989; Wilson 1992; Ellingson 2001, chap. 21). Exposure of the hoax, on the other hand, has served to fuel the arguments of anti-environmentalist critics.[3]

TOWARD A SOCIAL ECOLOGY?

The emergence of environmentalism as an active social movement in the late 1960s represented both continuity and a break with the past. On the one hand, the issues and arguments that had been raised at the 1955 Wenner-Gren symposium, despite lack of agreement, represented widespread concern among leaders in a variety of fields that a crisis was looming for which a better understanding of ecological relationships was going to prove crucial. On the other hand, there had been efforts on the part of scientists to spread this message beyond academia. Victor Shelford and others had organized the Ecologists' Union right after the war, renamed the Nature Conservancy in 1950, to obtain and preserve natural areas throughout the U.S. Despite its reluctance to publicly endorse environmental actions, the Ecological Society nevertheless had begun to sponsor symposia on pressing environmental problems, such as one on water pollution organized in 1951. Meanwhile, Fairfield Osborn's Conservation Foundation sponsored a series of films and lectures on ecological and conservation themes that received considerable attention and were often shown in schools and to interested adult groups (Croker 1991; Tjossem 1994; Gottlieb 1993; Mitman 1999). This attention among certain groups represented acknowledgement of an environmental crisis, but it was still a "quiet crisis," as Stewart Udall, John F. Kennedy's Secretary of the Interior, characterized it. In his book by that title, Udall (1963) recounted the views of Marsh and Leopold, among others; praised the policies of the two Roosevelts; and called for direct action by individuals, private organizations, and the federal government. He applauded efforts already being made by the Nature Conservancy, Conservation Foundation, Sierra Club, Audubon Society, and other groups. Even as Udall's book was published, however, the quiet crisis was about to become very noisy, largely due to the increasingly volatile political and social climate and the publication, the year before, of Rachel Carson's more confrontational *Silent Spring*. The success of her earlier book, *The Sea Around Us* (1951), which gave her the means to quit her job with the Fish and Wildlife Service and research and write *Silent Spring*, indicated a widespread public interest in the natural world, reflected also in the increased attendance at the national parks, a growing interest in camping and bird watching, and increased membership in conservation organizations. In the 1961 edition of the book Carson added a preface that warned about the dangers of using the sea as a dumpsite for nuclear wastes without adequate knowledge of effects on ocean life. *Silent Spring* delivered the same kind of message, although in more ominous terms, since Carson believed that the effects of widespread use of DDT and other pesticides were beginning to show themselves in dramatic fashion: decimating populations of birds, soil organisms, and beneficial insects; contaminating the soil and groundwater; and creating potential health problems. *Silent Spring* pointed out not only the unintended consequences of using invasive practices without adequate knowledge but also the effects of the greed and hubris of an affluent society that had forgotten its connection with nature, which in America has always been as important as the control of nature. Her book struck a chord: we had spoiled our home and were threatening the planet.

Carson's critics were quick to point out her naive belief in a "balance of nature," although she was careful to describe the balance as dynamic and changing rather than static. Conservationists had warned about DDT upsetting the balance of nature since 1945, when the new chemical, fresh from its wartime successes, was being promoted as a panacea for pest control. For Carson, the crucial equilibrium idea was that of "a complex, precise, and highly integrated system of relationships between living things which cannot safely be ignored" (Carson 1962, 246), a view similar to that defended by Paul Sears at the Wenner-Gren symposium in 1955. Still, she was viewed by her opponents as a luddite and a romantic promoting ideas that could only be an impediment to progress (Dunlap 1981; Fox 1981). Although radically different in personality and approach, Stanford ecologist Paul Ehrlich, author of the 1968 bestseller *The Population Bomb,* the other major popular work that exposed the general public to imminent environmental dangers, found himself similarly engaged in a succession of debates with economists over remarks that he had made in that work about the depletion of resources. His opponents, with economist Julian Simon leading the way, argued that scarcities inspire technological innovations that solve the problem by creating alternative sources of energy or materials, ultimately improving the human condition (Simon 1981; Simon and Kahn 1984). Both episodes illustrate that two deeply rooted tenets of American ideology—pious belief in the beneficence and restorative powers of nature and unbridled faith in people and technology—were clashing over a new set of environmental concerns.

By this time ecology had become "the subversive science," as Paul Sears and a popular anthology attested, and its message was beginning to resonate with a new wave of self-styled subversives, when the word "subversive" had for many people a positive connotation (Sears 1964; Shepard and McKinley 1969). Ecology came to be viewed during the 1960s as part of the critique of uncontrolled economic expansion, wasteful and exploitative industrial practices, mechanistic-reductionistic science, and economic imperialism, in short, the scientific underpinning for a new social order. Professional ecologists objected to this expanded role and to the proliferation of "ecologists" of questionable pedigree involved with policy making, litigation, consulting, and so forth in the wake of recent environmental legislation and the nation's heightened awareness of environmental issues. There was even a movement within the ESA to adopt a code of ethics and provide some sort of official certification for bona fide ecologists, but it proved not to be effective (Tjossem 1994, 95–103). By this time ecology had become more than a science. For those who turned to communal living, homesteading, organic food cooperatives, and other ecologically correct alternative lifestyles, ecology provided guidelines for living and conferred a sort of moral purity on their actions. There were parallels here with a longstanding American tradition of utopian communities, such as the Shakers, New Harmony, the Oneida community, and the original Mormons, including similarities in underlying philosophy, with elements of the older utopian societies—abandonment of private property, alternatives to traditional marital and family practices, a new work ethic—now given a scientific sanction. Historian and cultural critic Theodore Roszak, writing two years after the first Earth Day, made clear the debt of this countercultural vision to ecology with cryptic statements like the following: "The science we call ecology is the nearest approach that objective consciousness makes to the sacramental vision of nature which underlies the symbol of Oneness" (1972, 367). The adoption of ecology as philosophy for living, with a strongly implied, if not always stated, spiritual dimension, has echoed through various movements over the past three decades—deep ecology, varieties of green politics, ecofeminism, and so on (Merchant 1992).

For others of a more pragmatic bent, ecology offered a scientific basis for placing limits on traditional economic practices. Stewart Udall ended *The Quiet Crisis* with a note of optimism: "The creation of a life-giving environment can go hand-in-hand with material progress and higher standards of husbandry" (1963, 199). However, around the same time, Kenneth Boulding warned of the limits to economic growth, especially in developing nations, due to overpopulation and the scarcity of resources. He called for the abandonment of traditional ideologies of capitalism and socialism and their replacement with "scientific ideology itself applied to society" (1964, 179). Although Boulding did not frame his ideas explicitly within the language of ecological science at this time, ecologically oriented economic and political studies, based on scarcity rather than abundance, emerged within the next decade or so. Economists and political theorists began to probe into the question of what a sustainable

economy might look like and how it would alter existing political structures. Nicholas Georgescu-Roegen and Herman Daly led the way, ground-
ing their views in thermodynamic considerations based on limited supplies of nonrenewable resources. William Ophuls's *Ecology and the
Politics of Scarcity* (1977), based on his prize-winning 1973 thesis at
Yale, directly utilized ideas gleaned from current ecological science,
mainly holistic approaches to ecosystem ecology, to speculate on the emergence of a steady-state society characterized by greater state authority,
more modest living circumstances, diminished individual liberties, and a
generally higher level of morality due to "a real commitment to stewardship" (1977, 231; cf. Georgescu-Roegen 1971; Daly 1973, 1977). Economists and social theorists closer to the mainstream offered pessimistic
forecasts based more on social than physical limitations to growth, while
others continued to insist that environmental doomsayers were wrong
and that human resourcefulness and technological innovation would be
sufficient to deal with all the challenges (Thurow 1980; Hirsch 1976;
Myers and Simon 1994).

The more recent ecological economics movement, centered on concepts of sustainability and natural capital, is an outgrowth of the dialogue that has existed since the early 1970s, with some of the current
leaders, particularly Robert Costanza and Herman Daly, having direct
ties to the earlier developments (Costanza 1991, 1996).[4] While mainstream economists, such as Julian Simon until his death in 1998, continued to argue that an ecologically based approach to economics is both
unnecessary and counterproductive, a new spate of optimistic forecasts
has begun to emerge, some of which cast doubt on the entire environmentalist program (Simon 1995; Bailey 1993; Easterbrook 1995; Huber
1999). Since the 1980s, legal philosopher Mark Sagoff (1988) has made
a different kind of argument against the ecological economics movement.
To submit environmental issues to the calculus of cost-benefit analysis or
any other rational methodology within economic practice, he argues, is
to reduce environmental concerns to the level of commodities to be bar-
gained for in the marketplace. Then either ecological economics collapses
into mainstream economics or the methods so utilized reveal, on rational
analysis, that particular environmental goals are not economically feas-
ible and hence must be abandoned. Preserving biodiversity, maintaining
reasonably pristine nature reserves, and other goals must be based upon
moral judgments about their value and not on economic factors. Ultimately, he concludes, we must invoke notions of the intrinsic value of na-

ture: "The reasons to protect nature are moral, religious, and cultural far more than they are economic" (Sagoff 1995, 620; cf. Daly 1995).

Sagoff's tactic has been to point out the limitations of an environmental policy based purely on utilitarian concerns. Despite Sagoff's arguments, ecological economists are intent on pressing the utilitarian position, and most assume that an ecologically informed economics can be achieved by working within the mainstream, although more conventional economists might consider their views far from the mainstream. Considerably more radical attempts at economic and political reorganization have, of course, proliferated since the 1970s. Two examples reveal distinct links with the earlier regionalist movement. Murray Bookchin has been pursuing his ecologically informed approach to grassroots politics for more than four decades. Beginning with studies of public health concerns and a critique of the chemical industry, he developed his ideas into a full-blown "social ecology," as he calls it, arguing for regional political units defined by and integrated with the landscape and local resources, and making use of energy-efficient, non-polluting technologies and a thoroughly democratic, participatory social organization (Herber 1962; Bookchin 1971, 1980; Biehl and Bookchin 1998). Himself rooted in the old left, Bookchin had a select but enthusiastic audience among the new left in the early stages of the environmental movement, and more recently his ideas have had an effect on local politics in Burlington, Vermont, where he settled. Another program for radical social reorganization, that suggested by New York–based writer Kirkpatrick Sale, very deliberately adopted some of the regional planning perspectives of Lewis Mumford and Howard W. Odum. Sale called his approach to planning "bioregionalism," and he linked it backward to Frederick Jackson Turner and forward to current ecological science and James Lovelock's Gaia hypothesis. He drew upon a mixture of climax theory, ecosystem ecology, and system science as expressed in the writings of Edward Goldsmith, editor of the British periodical *The Ecologist*. He also utilized the ideas of Boulding, Bookchin, and E. F. Schumacher, the British advocate of small-scale economics. Sale imagined a future world of entirely self-sufficient regions, arguing that decentralism is a fundamental "ecological law" that ought to serve as the basis for bioregional politics (Sale 1985).

The more egalitarian regionalist models for an ecological social order proposed by Bookchin and Sale to some extent answer the charges of elitism leveled at environmentalists since the movement began. Critics have long claimed that the environmental movement deflected attention from more pressing social and political problems, neglected issues of social justice, and tended to serve the needs of its predominantly white, middle-class participants. Journalist William Tucker argued that position in detail during the 1970s and 1980s, citing particular examples wherein the desires of environmentalists for access to pristine nature conflicted directly with the interests of the vast majority of the less privileged (Tucker 1977, 1982). Taking a more neutral approach to the matter, historian Samuel Hays (1987) saw the debates over environmental policy as the natural result of a conflict between the needs of a growing middle class, which now desired environmental amenities as well as material wealth, and a pragmatic managerial and technical leadership, more than willing to point out the practical limits of such desires. Robert Gottlieb (1993) made the issue of social justice a major theme of his history of American environmentalism, presenting a case for a transformed egalitarian environmentalism that recognizes the needs of people while taking efforts to protect nature. Bookchin, sensitive to social justice issues, has criticized other environmentalists more for their aloofness than their elitism. Among his targets have been Sale, deep ecologists, and "Earth First!ers," that is, followers of organizer Dave Foreman who place the pristine natural world above the human and advocate strong preventative actions to protect the former from the latter, such as disabling road-building equipment or driving long spikes into the trunks of trees scheduled for logging. Bookchin singled out two related problems with these groups: their failure to face harsh social and economic realities and the residual Protestant evangelism evident in their approaches to environmental issues. Without doubt, there has been a tendency among environmentalists, as well as many ecologists, to assume a kind of moral purity, to worship pristine nature as both hallowed ground and source of salvation, and to treat its misuse and exploitation as sinful. Bookchin's social ecology, on the other hand, focuses on the human community, which uses its knowledge of ecological relationships to maintain a viable, responsive, and sustainable democratic society. However, it is not self-evident that Bookchin's social vision should necessarily exclude reverence for nature or that environmental idealism should necessarily prevent the working out of compromise solutions that recognize issues of social justice (S. Chase 1991; Bookchin 1988; Stoll 2001).

Such dichotomies may become irrelevant in the light of recent developments in ecology. As the science itself has moved away from its earlier emphasis on natural balance, harmony, and stability and toward a mana-

gerial ethos based on continual change and unavoidable human disturbance, social thought grounded in ecology will likely reflect the new
models. Whether or not there is at present a social model that will fit the
new ecology is difficult to say. The problem has been compounded by the
influence of postmodernism. In an intellectual culture in which all frameworks of knowledge, power, and authority have been eagerly decon-
structed, arguments for holding up pristine nature as a model of ecological correctness and claims about the inordinate destruction of "natural"
systems by the activities of modern humans sometimes meet with skepticism and doubt (Cronon 1995; Gare 1995; cf. Soulé and Lease 1995). The
skepticism and doubt may be unwarranted in some instances, but critics
of environmental policy have already begun to use the new ecological
models and the tools of postmodern critique to argue against the protection of natural areas and preservation of biodiversity. Ecologists now
sometimes find themselves in the position of having to justify the view
that human effects on the natural world can be devastating and irreversible.[5] Oak Ridge ecologist Robert O'Neill, first president of the U.S. Society for Ecological Economics, perhaps aided the critics' cause by con-
cluding in a paper on the merging of economics and ecology that ecologists
"must give up their favorite fiction: the 'natural world'" (1996, 1033).
O'Neill was arguing not so much that the natural world is a social construct as that there is no place on the globe free from human impact or
influence. Ecologists have been aware of the ubiquity of human influence
for decades, but their science through much of its history has rested,
sometimes uneasily and never without internal critics, on the notion of
an ideal, stable, self-rejuvenating, primal nature, existing outside human
influence, whose inner workings it is the ultimate goal of the science to
reveal. This is a notion that has been difficult to discard for scientists and
nonscientists alike, since it fit in so well with the earlier belief in a fundamentally beneficent and self-sustaining nature, with the aspirations and
hopes of utopian regional planners, with the evangelical Protestant idealism of many environmentalists, and even with the hopes and dreams of
more pragmatic, and secular, rational planners and managers. At the
same time, as this brief look at its history makes clear, the science of
ecology has received inspiration all along from the transfer of ideas—
including social, economic, and political concepts and technological
metaphors—from the human to the nonhuman world. In a sense, then,
ecology has always been social ecology, and the line drawn between the
human and the natural world has always been arbitrary. Ecological

science may not be able to tell us with certainty what is "natural," and ecological science alone surely cannot tell us what we should value in nature. However, one can hope that awareness of the continual dialogue between humans and nature that has brought the science to its present state could only help scientists, political leaders, and the lay public to define goals, consider possible courses of action, and make intelligent choices.

NOTES

1. Ronald Tobey (1981, chap. 7) discusses the fate of climax theory in the Dust Bowl era. Although Tobey argues that the severe 1930s drought called the climax theory into question among plant ecologists, the theory persisted as part of federal agricultural and grazing policy for decades after that episode. For example, it was not abandoned officially by the Society for Range Management until 1992 (Donahue 1999, 144).

2. The ecological reinterpretation of hunter-gatherers was first introduced broadly to anthropologists at yet another Wenner-Gren symposium, this one in Chicago in 1966. The published collection of papers from the symposium (Lee and DeVore 1968) became a standard text in anthropology courses and a standard reference work among environmentalists.

3. Stephen Budiansky gleefully recounts the Chief Seattle episode in his critique of contemporary environmentalism (1995, 32–34). A recent perusal of internet sources revealed this article posted on a Christian anti-evolution web site: John Woodmorappe, "The Anti-Biblical Noble Savage Hypothesis Refuted (Do Peoples Free of Biblical Influence ACTUALLY Live in Harmony with Nature and Each Other?)," http://www.rae.org/savage.html. (last accessed September 2005). The answer to the parenthetical question is a resounding "no," of course. To support his thesis, the author cites Alvard (1993), which is also cited by Ellingson (2001).

4. See the April 2000 issue of *Bioscience,* vol. 50, devoted to the integration of ecology and economics. Robert Costanza is the director of the Institute for Ecological Economics at the University of Maryland, established in 1991. A Ph.D. program in ecological economies was initiated at Rensselaer Polytechnic Institute in the 1990s. The U.S. Society for Ecological Economics was established in 2000.

5. For examples of critiques of environmentalism that make use of revisionist views of ecology, see Lewis (1992), Bailey (1993), A. Chase (1995), and Budiansky (1995). For ecologists' perspectives on the recent changes in the science

and their environmental implications, see Botkin (1990), but also the more restrained and thorough discussion in Pimm (1991). Paul and Anne Ehrlich (1996) offered a strident response to critics of environmentalism, including Bailey, Budiansky, Chase, and Easterbrook (1995). American ecologists have recently responded most vigorously to the controversial critique of environmentalism by Danish statistician Bjørn Lomborg (2001), which was apparently inspired by an article on Julian Simon by journalist Ed Regis (1997). Lomborg's account contrasts sharply with ecologist Stuart Pimm's contemporary assessment of the human impact on the earth's biotic resources (2001). See the reviews of Lomborg by Pimm and Harvey (2001), Simberloff (2002), and the several essays invited by the editors of *Scientific American* (Rennie et al. 2002).

WORKS CITED

Adams, Charles C., H. L. Shantz, C. W. Thornthwaite, Benton MacKaye, A. B. Hollingshead, and Eduard C. Lindeman. 1940. Symposium on relation of ecology to human welfare—the human situation. *Ecological Monographs* 10:307–72.

Allee, W. C. 1931. *Animal aggregations: A study in general sociology.* Chicago: University of Chicago Press.

Allee, W. C., Orlando Park, Thomas Park, Alfred E. Emerson, and Karl P. Schmidt. 1949. *Principles of animal ecology.* Philadelphia: Saunders.

Alvard, M. S. 1993. Testing the "ecologically noble savage" hypothesis: Interspecific prey choice by Piro hunters of Amazonian Peru. *Human ecology* 21:355–87.

Bailey, Ronald. 1993. *Ecoscam: The false prophets of environmental apocalypse.* New York: St. Martin's Press.

Barbour, Michael. 1995. Ecological fragmentation in the fifties. In Cronon 1995 233–55.

Bates, Marston. 1953. Human ecology. In *Anthropology today,* ed. A. L. Kroeber, 700–713. Chicago: University of Chicago Press.

Bettinger, Robert L. 1991. *Hunter-gatherers: Archaeological and evolutionary theory.* New York: Plenum Press.

Biehl, Janet, and Murray Bookchin. 1998. *The politics of social ecology: Libertarian municipalism.* Montreal: Black Rose Books.

Bocking, Stephen. 1990. Stephen Forbes, Jacob Reighard, and the emergence of aquatic ecology in the Great Lakes region. *Journal of the History of Biology* 23:171–98.

———. 1997. *Ecologists and environmental politics: A history of contemporary ecology.* New Haven: Yale University Press.

Bookchin, Murray. 1971. *Post-scarcity anarchism*. Montreal: Black Rose Books.
———. 1980. *Towards an ecological society*. Montreal: Black Rose Books.
———. 1988. Social ecology versus deep ecology. *Socialist Review* 18:11–29.
Botkin, Daniel B. 1990. *Discordant harmonies: A new ecology for the twenty-first century*. New York: Oxford University Press.
Boulding, Kenneth. 1964. *The meaning of the twentieth century: The grand transition*. New York: Harper and Row.
Budiansky, Stephen. 1995. *Nature's keepers: The new science of nature management*. New York: Free Press.
Callicot, J. Baird. 1989. American Indian land wisdom? Sorting out the issues. *Journal of Forest History* 33:35–42.
Cannon, Walter B. 1932. *The wisdom of the body*. New York: Norton.
Carson, Rachel. 1951. *The sea around us*. New York: Oxford University Press.
———. 1962. *Silent spring*. Boston: Houghton Mifflin.
Chase, Alston. 1995. *In a dark wood: The fight over forests and the rising tyranny of ecology*. New York: Houghton Mifflin.
Chase, Steve, ed. 1991. *Defending the earth: A dialogue between Murray Bookchin and Dave Foreman*. Boston: South End Press.
Cittadino, Eugene. 1980. Ecology and the professionalization of botany in America, 1880–1905. *Studies in History of Biology* 4:171–98.
———. 1993a. The failed promise of human ecology. In *Science and nature: Essays in the history of the environmental sciences,* ed. Michael Shortland, 251–83. Oxford: British Society for the History of Science.
———. 1993b. A "marvelous cosmopolitan preserve": The dunes, Chicago, and the dynamic ecology of Henry Cowles. *Perspectives on Science* 1:520–59.
Clements, Frederic E. 1905. *Research methods in ecology*. Lincoln, NE: University Publishing Co.
———. 1916. *Plant succession*. Washington DC: Carnegie Institution.
———. 1917. Ecology. *Carnegie Institution Yearbook* 16:303.
———. 1935. Experimental ecology in the public service. Ecology 16:342–63.
Clements, Frederic E., and Ralph W. Chaney. 1936. *Environment and life in the Great Plains*. Washington DC: Carnegie Institution.
Clements, Frederic E., and Victor E. Shelford. 1939. *Bio-ecology*. New York: John Wiley and Sons.
Cook, Robert E. 1977. Raymond Lindeman and the trophic-dynamic concept of ecology. *Science* 198:22–26.
Coser, Lewis. 1978. American trends. In *A history of sociological analysis,* ed. Tom Bottomore and Robert Nisbet, 287–320. New York: Basic Books.
Costanza, Robert, ed. 1991. *Ecological economics: The science and management of sustainability*. New York: Columbia University Press.
———. 1996. Ecological economics: reintegrating the study of humans and nature. *Ecological Applications* 6:978–90.

Cowles, Henry Chandler. 1899. Ecological relations of the vegetation on the sand dunes of Lake Michigan. *Botanical Gazette* 27:95–117, 167–202, 281–308, 361–91.

———. 1901. The physiographic ecology of Chicago and vicinity. *Botanical Gazette* 31:73–108, 145–82.

Craige, Betty Jean. 2001. *Eugene Odum: Ecosystem ecologist and environmentalist.* Athens: University of Georgia Press.

Croker, Robert A. 1991. *Pioneer ecologist: The life and work of Victor Ernest Shelford, 1877–1968.* Washington DC: Smithsonian Institution Press.

———. 2001. *Stephen Forbes and the rise of American ecology.* Washington DC: Smithsonian Institution Press.

Cronon, William, ed. 1995. *Uncommon ground: Toward reinventing nature.* New York: W. W. Norton.

Crowcroft, Peter. 1991. *Elton's ecologists: A history of the Bureau of Animal Population.* Chicago: University of Chicago Press.

Daly, Herman E., ed. 1973. *Toward a steady-state economics.* San Francisco: W. H. Freeman.

———. 1977. *Steady-state economics.* San Francisco: W. H. Freeman.

———. 1995. Reply to Mark Sagoff's "Carrying capacity and ecological economics." *Bioscience* 45:621–24.

Dickinson, Robert E. 1976. *Regional concept: The Anglo-American leaders.* London: Routledge and K. Paul.

Donahue, Debra L. 1999. *The western range revisited: Removing livestock from public lands to conserve natural biodiversity.* Norman: University of Oklahoma Press.

Dunlap, Thomas R. 1981. *DDT: Scientists, citizens, and public policy.* Princeton, NJ: Princeton University Press.

Easterbrook, Gregg. 1995. *A moment on the earth: The coming age of ecological optimism.* New York: Viking.

Ehrlich, Paul R. 1968. *The population bomb.* New York: Ballantine.

Ehrlich, Paul R., and Anne H. Ehrlich. 1996. *Betrayal of science and reason: How anti-environmental rhetoric threatens our future.* Washington DC: Island Press.

Ellingson, Terry Jay. 2001. *The myth of the noble savage.* Berkeley: University of California Press.

Elton, Charles. 1927. *Animal ecology.* London: Sidgwick and Jackson.

Engel, J. Ronald. 1983. *Sacred sands: The struggle for community in the Indiana dunes.* Middletown, CT: Wesleyan University Press.

Forbes, Stephen A. 1880. On some interactions of organisms. *Illinois Laboratory of Natural History, Bulletin* 1:3–17.

———. 1922. The humanizing of ecology. *Ecology* 3:89–92.

———. 1925. The lake as a microcosm. *Illinois Natural History Survey, Bulletin* 15:537–50. (Orig. pub. 1887.)

Fox, Stephen. 1981. *The American conservation movement: John Muir and his legacy.* Madison: University of Wisconsin Press.

Gare, Arran E. 1995. *Postmodernism and the environmental crisis.* London: Routledge.

Geertz, Clifford. 1963. *Agricultural involution: The processes of ecological change in Indonesia.* Berkeley: University of California Press.

Georgescu-Roegen, Nicholas. 1971. *The entropy law and the economic process.* Cambridge, MA: Harvard University Press.

Golley, Frank B. 1993. *A history of the ecosystem concept in ecology: More than the sum of the parts.* New Haven: Yale University Press.

Gore, Al. 1992. *Earth in the balance: Ecology and the human spirit.* New York: Houghton Mifflin.

Gottlieb, Robert. 1993. *Forcing the spring: The transformation of the American environmental movement.* Washington DC: Island Press.

Haeckel, Ernst. 1866. *Generelle morphologie der organismen.* 2 vols. Berlin: Reimer.

Hagen, Joel B. 1992. *An entangled bank: The origins of ecosystem ecology.* New Brunswick, NJ: Rutgers University Press.

Hays, Samuel P. 1987. *Beauty, health, and permanence: Environmental politics in the United States, 1955–1985.* Cambridge: Cambridge University Press.

Henderson, Lawrence J. 1913. *The fitness of the environment.* New York: Macmillan.

———. 1917. *The order of nature.* Cambridge, MA: Harvard University Press.

Herber, Lewis [Murray Bookchin]. 1962. *Our synthetic environment.* New York: Knopf.

Hirsch, Fred. 1976. *Social limits to growth.* Cambridge, MA: Harvard University Press.

Hofstadter, Richard. 1955. *The age of reform: From Bryan to F.D.R.* New York: Vintage.

Huber, Peter. 1999. *Hard green: Saving the environment from the environmentalists; A conservative manifesto.* New York: Basic Books.

Huntington, Ellsworth. 1915. *Civilization and climate.* New Haven: Yale University Press.

———. 1927. *The human habitat.* New York: Van Nostrand.

———. 1930. Weather and health: A study of daily mortality in New York City. *Bulletin of the National Research Council, no. 75.* Washington DC: Government Printing Office.

Kingsland, Sharon E. 1995. *Modeling nature: Episodes in the history of population ecology.* 2nd ed. Chicago: University of Chicago Press.

Kwa, Chunglin. 1987. Representations of nature mediating between ecology and science policy: The case of the International Biological Programme. *Social Studies of Science* 17:413–42.

———. 1993. Modeling the grasslands. *Historical Studies in the Physical and Biological Sciences* 24:125–55.

Lawrence, D. B., and T. Park. 1949. Report of the editors of *Ecology*. *Bulletin of the Ecological Society of America* 20:10.

Lee, Richard B., and Irven DeVore. 1968. *Man the hunter.* Chicago: Aldine.

Leighly, John. 1967. Introduction. In Sauer 1967, 1–8. Berkeley: University of California Press.

Leopold, Aldo. 1949. *A Sand County almanac and sketches here and there.* Oxford: Oxford University Press.

Lewis, Martin W. 1992. *Green delusions: An environmentalist critique of radical environmentalism.* Durham, NC: Duke University Press.

Lindeman, Raymond L. 1942. The trophic-dynamic aspect of ecology. *Ecology* 23: 399–418.

Lomborg, Bjørn. 2001. *The skeptical environmentalist: Measuring the real state of the world.* Cambridge: Cambridge University Press.

Lotka, Alfred J. 1925. *Elements of physical biology.* Baltimore: Williams and Wilkins. Repr. as *Elements of mathematical biology.* New York: Dover, 1956.

Luccarelli, Mark. 1995. *Lewis Mumford and the ecological region: The politics of planning.* New York: Guilford Press.

MacKaye, Benton. 1921. An Appalachian trail. *AIA Journal* 9:325–30.

———. 1928. *The new exploration: A philosophy of regional planning.* New York: Harcourt, Brace.

Madison Botanical Congress. 1894. *Proceedings of the Madison Botanical Congress.* Madison, WI.

Malin, James C. 1956a. The grassland of North America: Its occupance and the challenge of continuous reappraisals. In *Man's role in changing the face of the earth,* ed. William L. Thomas, Jr., with collaboration of Carl O. Sauer, Marston Bates, and Lewis Mumford, 350–366. Chicago: University of Chicago Press.

———. 1956c. *The grassland of North America: Prolegomena to its history.* Lawrence, KS: James C. Malin.

———. 1984. *History and ecology: Studies of the grassland.* Ed. Robert P. Swierenga. Lincoln: University of Nebraska Press.

Marsh, George Perkins. 1864. *Man and nature, or physical geography as modified by human action.* New York: Charles Scribner. Repr., Cambridge, MA: Harvard University Press, 1965.

Martin, Geoffrey J. 1973. *Ellsworth Huntington: His life and thought.* Hamden, CT: Archon Books.

McIntosh, Robert P. 1967. The continuum concept of vegetation. *Botanical Review* 33:130–87.

———. 1974. Plant ecology, 1947–1972. *Annals of the Missouri Botanical Garden* 61:132–65.

———. 1985. *The background of ecology: Concept and theory.* Cambridge, MA: Cambridge University Press.

McKenzie, Roderick D. 1924. The ecological approach to the study of the human community. *American Journal of Sociology* 30:287–301.

Meine, Curt. 1988. *Aldo Leopold: His life and work.* Madison: University of Wisconsin Press.

Merchant, Carolyn. 1992. *Radical ecology: The search for a livable world.* New York: Routledge.

Mitman, Gregg. 1992. *The state of nature: Ecology, community, and American social thought, 1900–1950.* Chicago: University of Chicago Press.

———. 1995. Defining the organism in the welfare state: The politics of individuality in American culture, 1890–1950. In *Biology as society, society as biology: Metaphors,* ed. Sabine Maasen et al., 249–78. Dordrecht: Kluwer Academic Publishers.

———. 1999. *Reel nature: America's romance with wildlife on film.* Cambridge, MA: Harvard University Press.

Moore, Barrington. 1920. The scope of ecology. *Ecology* 1:3–5.

Moran, Emilio F. 1984. Ecosystem ecology in biology and anthropology: A critical assessment. In *The ecosystem concept in anthropology,* ed. E. F. Moran, 3–40. Boulder, CO: Westview Press.

Myers, Norman, and Julian Simon. 1994. *Scarcity or abundance? A debate on the environment.* New York: Basic Books.

Mumford, Lewis. 1934. *Technics and civilization.* New York: Harcourt, Brace.

———. 1938. *The culture of cities.* New York: Harcourt, Brace.

———. 1982. *Sketches from life.* New York: Dial Press.

Nelkin, Dorothy. 1977. Scientists and professional responsibility: The experience of American ecologists. *Social Studies of Science* 7:75–95.

Odum, Eugene P. 1953. *Fundamentals of ecology.* Philadelphia: Saunders. 2nd ed. 1959. 3rd ed. 1971.

———. 1963. *Ecology.* New York: Holt, Rinehart, and Winston.

———. 1969. The strategy of ecosystem development. *Science* 164:262–70.

Odum, Howard T. 1960. Ecological potential and analogue circuits for the ecosystem. *American Scientist* 48:1–8.

Odum, Howard W. 1945. The regional quality and balance of America. In *In search of the regional balance of America,* ed. H. W. Odum and K. Jocher, 27–43. Chapel Hill: University of North Carolina Press.

Odum, Howard W., and Harry Estill Moore. 1938. *American regionalism: A cultural-historical approach to national integration.* New York: Henry Holt.

Olson, Jerry S. 1958. Rates of succession and soil changes on southern Lake Michigan sand dunes. *Botanical Gazette* 119:125–70.

O'Neill, R. V. 1996. Perspectives on economics and ecology. *Ecological Applications* 6:1031–33.

Ophuls, William. 1977. *Ecology and the politics of scarcity: Prologue to a theory of the steady state.* San Francisco: W. H. Freeman.

Osborn, Fairfield. 1948. *Our plundered planet.* Boston: Little Brown.

Overfield, Richard A. 1993. *Science with practice: Charles E. Bessey and the maturing of American botany.* Ames: Iowa State University Press.

Park, Robert E., Ernest W. Burgess, and Roderick D. McKenzie. 1925. *The city.* Chicago: University of Chicago Press.

Pimm, Stuart L. 1991. *The balance of nature? Ecological issues in the conservation of species and communities.* Chicago: University of Chicago Press.

———. 2001. *The world according to Pimm: A scientist audits the earth.* New York: McGraw-Hill.

Pimm, Stuart L., and Jeff Harvey. 2001. No need to worry about the future: Environmentally, we are told, "things are getting better." *Nature* 414: 149–50.

Pound, Roscoe. 1954. Frederic E. Clements as I knew him. *Ecology* 35:112–13.

Pound, Roscoe, and Frederic E. Clements. 1900. *The phytogeography of Nebraska.* 2nd ed. Lincoln, NE: Botanical Seminar.

Rappaport, Roy. 1968. *Pigs for the ancestors: Ritual in the ecology of a New Guinea people.* New Haven: Yale University Press.

Rauschenbush, Winifred. 1974. *Robert E. Park: Biography of a sociologist.* Durham, NC: Duke University Press.

Regis, Ed. 1997. The environment is going to hell, and human life is doomed to only get worse, right? Wrong? Conventional wisdom, meet Julian Simon. *Wired* 5(2):136–40, 193–98.

Rennie, John, Stephen Schneider, John P. Holdren, John Bongaarts, and Thomas Lovejoy. 2002. Misleading math about the earth. *Scientific American* 286 (Jan.): 61–71.

Ross, Dorothy. 1991. *The origins of American social science.* Cambridge: Cambridge University Press.

Roszak, Theodore. 1972. *Where the wasteland ends: Politics and transcendence in postindustrial society.* Garden City, NY: Doubleday.

Russett, Cynthia Eagle. 1966. *The concept of equilibrium in American social thought.* New Haven: Yale University Press.

Sagoff, Mark. 1988. *The economy of the earth: Philosophy, law, and the environment.* Cambridge: Cambridge University Press.

———. 1995. Carrying capacity and ecological economics. *Bioscience* 45: 610–20.

Sahlins, Marshall. 1972. *Stone age economics.* New York: Aldine.

Sale, Kirkpatrick. 1985. *Dwellers in the land: The bioregional vision.* San Francisco: Sierra Club Books.

Sampson, A. W. 1919. *Plant succession in relation to range management.* U.S.D.A. Bulletin 791. Washington DC: Government Printing Office.

Sauer, Carl O. 1967. *Land and life: A selection from the writings of Carl Ortwin Sauer,* ed. John Leighly. Berkeley: University of California Press.

Schneider, Daniel W. 2000. Local knowledge, environmental politics, and the founding of ecology in the United States: Stephen Forbes and "The lake as a microcosm" (1887). *Isis* 91:681–705.

Schulten, Susan. 2001. *The geographical imagination in America, 1880–1950.* Chicago: University of Chicago Press.

Scott, Howard. 1933. *Introduction to technocracy.* New York: The John Day Company.

Sears, Paul. 1935. *Deserts on the march.* Norman: University of Oklahoma Press.

———. 1964. Ecology—a subversive subject. *Bioscience* 14:11–13.

Shelford, Victor E. 1913. *Animal communities in temperate America as illustrated in the Chicago region: A study in animal ecology.* Chicago: University of Chicago Press.

———. 1938. The organization of the Ecological Society of America, 1914–19. *Ecology* 19:164–66.

Shepard, Paul, and David McKinley, eds. 1969. *The subversive science: Essays toward an ecology of man.* Boston: Houghton Mifflin.

Shrader-Frechette, K. S., and E. D. McCoy. *Method in ecology: Strategies for conservation.* Cambridge: Cambridge University Press.

Simberloff, Daniel. 1980. A succession of paradigms in ecology: Essentialism to materialism and probabilism. *Synthese* 43:3–39.

———. 2002. Skewed skepticism. *American Scientist* 90 (March–April): 184–86.

Simon, Julian. 1981. *The ultimate resource.* Princeton, NJ: Princeton University Press

Simon, Julian, ed. 1995. *The state of humanity.* Oxford: Blackwell.

Simon, Julian, and Herman Kahn, eds. 1984. *The resourceful earth: A response to Global 2000.* Oxford: Blackwell.

Slobodkin, Lawrence B., and Nancy G. Slack. 1999. George Evelyn Hutchinson: 20th-century ecologist. *Endeavor* 23:24–30.

Soulé, Michael E., and Gary Lease, eds. 1995. *Reinventing nature? Responses to postmodern deconstruction.* Washington DC: Island Press.

Spencer, Herbert. 1867. *Principles of biology.* 2 vols. New York: Appleton.

———. 1891. The social organism. In *Essays: Scientific, Political, and Speculative* 1:265–307. New York: Appleton. (Orig. pub. 1860.)

Stauffer, Robert C. 1957. Haeckel, Darwin, and ecology. *Quarterly Review of Biology* 32:138–44.

Steward, Julian. 1955. *Theory of cultural change: The methodology of multilinear evolution.* Urbana: University of Illinois Press.

Stoll, Mark. 2001. Green versus green: Religions, ethics, and the Bookchin-Foreman dispute. *Environmental History* 6:412–27.

Tansley, A. G. 1935. The use and abuse of vegetational concepts and terms. *Ecology* 16:284–307.

Taylor, Peter J. 1988. Technocratic optimism, H. T. Odum, and the partial transformation of ecological metaphor after World War II. *Journal of the History of Biology* 21:213–44.

Thomas, William L., Jr., ed. 1956. *Man's role in changing the face of the earth.* With collaboration of Carl O. Sauer, Marston Bates, and Lewis Mumford. Chicago: University of Chicago Press.

Thurow, Lester C. 1980. *The zero-sum society: Distribution and the possibilities for economic change.* New York: Basic Books.

Tjossem, Sara. 1994. Preservation of nature and academic respectability: Tensions in the Ecological Society of America, 1915–1979. Ph.D. diss., Cornell University.

Tobey, Ronald. 1981. *Saving the prairies: The life cycle of the founding school of American plant ecology, 1895–1955.* Berkeley: University of California Press.

Tucker, William. 1977. Environmentalism and the leisure class. *Harpers* (Dec.): 49–56, 73–80.

———. 1982. *Progress and privilege: America in the age of environmentalism.* New York: Doubleday.

Turner, Stephen P., and Jonathan H. Turner. 1990. *The impossible science: An institutional analysis of American sociology.* London: Sage Publications.

Udall, Stewart. 1963. *The quiet crisis.* New York: Holt, Rinehart, and Winston.

Vogt, William. 1948. *Road to survival.* New York: William Sloane Associates.

Whittaker, R. H. 1953. A consideration of the climax theory: The climax as a population and pattern. *Ecological monographs* 23:41–78.

Wilson, Paul S. 1992. What Chief Seattle said. *Environmental Law* 22: 1451–68.

Worster, Donald. 1994. *Nature's economy: A history of ecological ideas.* 2nd ed. Cambridge: Cambridge University Press.

Zorbaugh, Harvey W. 1926. The natural areas of the city. *Publications of the American Sociological Society* 20:188–97.

CHAPTER 4

The Various Christian Ethics of Species Conservation

Kyle S. Van Houtan and Stuart L. Pimm

We tend to take a connection between religion and ethics for granted; one's faith ought to help shape one's moral values. For much of human history, however, worship meant making the proper sacrifices and following the proper ritual; it might have very little to do with morality.

William Placher (1983, 22)

Typology does not make scriptural contents into metaphors for extra-scriptural realities, but the other way around. . . . It is the text, so to speak, which absorbs the world, rather than the world the text.

George Lindbeck (1984, 118)

TENSIONS AND BARRIERS

The setting is High Table at Balliol College, Oxford University, early in the twentieth century. The characters are the cleric and Master of the college, Benjamin Jowett, and renowned Darwinist and atheist J. B. S. Haldane. The set up is Jowett's question: "What could one conclude as to the nature of the Creator from a study of His creation?" "An inordinate fondness for beetles," is Haldane's reply. Since there are more kinds of insects than anything else, and almost half of all insects are beetles, Haldane's quip is apt. As it turns out, however, this tale is a fabrication (May 1989; Williamson 1989). Nonetheless, it was a popular story at Oxford thirty-five years ago when one of us (Pimm) was an undergraduate there. To scientists who study biodiversity—the variety of life on Earth—and its evolution, the temptation to cock a snoot at Christians is sometimes hard to resist.

The story has the feel of gallows humor though for it reveals the sometimes strain between science and religion. While close historical and ideological ties exist between Christianity, ecology, and conservation (Stoll, chapter 2, this volume; Cittadino, chapter 3, this volume), the tension today in the United States between some scientists and conservative Christians is pronounced (Miller 1999; Eldredge 2000; Mooney 2005, 164–85). The threat of Christian-inspired litigation against the teaching of evolution is particularly significant here. In this battle, both sides expend considerable resources, resulting in a remarkable cultural stalemate. As an example, a recent USA TODAY/CNN/Gallup poll shows that 53 percent of Americans reject the Darwinian notion of evolution (*USA Today* 2005).

Maybe it is presumptuous in light of the current political climate to ask ecologists and Christians to find common ground in conservation. Yet, that is exactly what we propose. We recognize that some, mostly politically conservative, Christians in the United States likely put "environmentalism" and evolution in the same box. Of course, this association is legitimate. Evolution is an important aspect of ecology. Scientists studying extinction owe large debts to Wallace and Darwin—the founders of evolutionary theory. While the birth of species aids an understanding of the death of species, origins and demises are in many ways different topics. Yet some Christians may still view this affiliation suspiciously and therefore disregard ecologists and their science.

Even with different positions about evolution, common ground between ecologists and Christians seems possible, if not straightforward. If a biblical basis exists for environmental stewardship, and ecologists have shown ecological peril, then the two groups seem destined coworkers in conservation. However, this consensus is not as common as one may think. As we show in this chapter, for various reasons many Christians in the United States do not support environmental protection. In some ways this situation recalls the role the church played in the civil rights movement of the 1960's. Martin Luther King then observed that, "the contemporary church is a weak, ineffectual voice with an uncertain sound"

118 Kyle S. Van Houtan & Stuart L. Pimm

(King 1999, 359). King's remarks could also be said of the role Christians play in the United States today with environmental protection. Although disagreements between Christians and ecologists regarding evolution are common, tension also exists over the ethics of conservation.

For ecologists, there are three basic ways that biodiversity has value, namely, the three "e's": ethics, esthetics, and economics (Ehrlich and Ehrlich 1981; National Research Council 1999). That is, biodiversity has inherent value, may inspire, and provides for our practical human needs, respectively. Although each criterion provides its own case for preserving biodiversity, economic arguments are the most common. This comes as little surprise, and the numbers are astronomic. In one estimate, the environment and the services it provides were valued at twice the global GNP, or US$33 trillion (Constanza et al. 1997). This figure includes tangible goods (like food and medicines) but also "ecosystem services" such as crop pollination, clean water, and climate stability (Daily 1997). Despite their figures, however, Constanza et al. (1997) do not believe economic arguments are enough for environmental protection. If this is true, then the other forms of valuation—esthetic and ethical—deserve further exploration.

For many Christians, economic arguments, like those Constanza and his colleagues present, may miss the mark. A strictly logical approach to Church doctrine or ethics has received much insightful criticism from theological scholars in the past decades (MacIntyre 1981; Lindbeck 1984; Northcott 1996; Placher 1996). Logical reasoning plays a role in religious faith for certain, but it is a more complicated matter. Such scholars pay attention to the scriptures, the church, ritual practices, and the linguistic nature of thought—in addition to rationality. Along this line, Stanley Hauerwas (1983; 18) adds that, "if what is said theologically is but a confirmation of what can be known on other grounds or can be said more clearly in nontheological language, then why bother saying it theologically?" Here Hauerwas identifies that ethics in nontheological language will be worse than unattractive to Christians—such ethics will be incoherent. Theological language is what gives *Christian* ethics intelligibility. As a result, casually using "nature" or "biodiversity" in place of "creation" is incredibly significant when considering Christian environmental ethics.

On the other side of the aisle, ecologists are increasingly seeing conservation as an ethical issue (Wilson and Perlman 2000). Scientists are allowed moral convictions, too. At times this places ecologists in the ironic position of expressing their ethical concerns *to* the church. "Scientists are bad enough when they promote science," one imagines some churchgoers thinking, "now they are trying to define our moral agendas!" Indeed, we believe that the conviction for environmental conservation ought to come from the church—through its inspiration and leadership.[1] As we mention, the problem seems that the church does not articulate a consistent vision of environmental ethics (Haught, chapter 8, this volume).

Although we can debate how species are born for another century we do not have that long to contemplate extinctions. There is nothing normal with our current planet. The trends of ecological degradation that we discuss are singular in the Earth's history. They are the direct result of human mismanagement and negligence. For those who prefer using "creation" in the place of "biodiversity," perhaps the ethical position ought to be even clearer. Creation is God's gift to humanity; poor stewardship of this blessing is an explicit sin (Bartholomew I 1997). Unless we change our current actions, we will likely commit a third of all creation to an inevitable path to extinction during this century (Pimm 2002, 201–16). Common ground between ecologists and Christians is urgent.

The rest of this chapter is divided into three sections. In the first, we report on the ecological state of the planet. Science is crucial to a proper conservation ethic; what we present is the consensus of ecologists. We focus on the evidence for massive ecological change to forests, drylands, and oceans, and discuss their impacts to biodiversity. In the section that follows, we propose a typology of Christian environmental ethics. Christian groups do not agree on what a "Christian" environmental ethic is: there are deep expressions of concern, certainly, but many doubt the problem exists, others deem the problem irrelevant, and some are even indifferent to the issue. The final section is an assessment of the four typologies we propose.

Science's Worldview: The Planetary Audit

At the start of the new century, there are 6 billion humans. Some models predict this number to be 9 billion by 2050, but most projections consider that estimate optimistically low (United Nations 2003, 9). Currently, roughly 1.5 billion people live comfortable lives, while another billion are on the verge of starvation. Of the remaining 4 billion, a quarter will become major consumers (owning cars and refrigerators) within a few decades (Myers and Kent 2003). Population statistics are well known. Their environmental consequences are not.

Land covers roughly a third of the Earth's surface but generates 97 percent of our food (Pimm 2002). Our diverse uses of the land are easily visible where we convert natural systems to agriculture and cities. One all-encompassing single measure to summarize human impacts on the earth is to weigh the amount of material plants produce each year, and then ask how much of it we consume. The answer is "not much." About 4 percent of the annual plant production is used for our food; for our domestic animals; and by the wood we use for building, paper, cooking, and heating (Pimm 2002, 27–31). But that answer is misleading, because it does not include how much green stuff we waste while we directly consume the other parts. Add those numbers in and the total human use of plant production comes to about 40 percent of the global production (Vitousek et al. 1986; Rojstaczer et al. 2001). In other words, humans consume almost half of what plants produce every year, and 90 percent of what we consume is wasted.

Most of the stuff we use is from the warmer, wetter half of the planet where plants grow best. What remains in dry or cold areas is much less suitable for our use. The warm, wet places are where forests grow most easily. The warmest and wettest of those are the tropical forests. These forests once covered 15 percent of the Earth's land surface, yet they contain an astounding 80 percent of the world's tree species (Vitousek et al. 1986). Despite this great ecological importance, we do not use tropical forests sustainably. To the contrary, we are continuously harvesting them and reducing their total area. The result is that tropical forests shrink by 10 percent of their original area every decade (Myers 1992; Skole and Tucker 1993). Unlike temperate forests, however, tropical forests do not regenerate nearly as easily (Pimm and Askins 1995).

The drier half of the land surface offers less plant production. It is harder to grow crops there. Yet, paradoxically, we use these areas in less efficient ways. Drylands are harder to use, they provide less food, and they are easier to abuse. Because they contain few resources, those resources are easier to exhaust. Dryland misuse has led to wind and water erosion and has depleted the fertility of the soils on over half of these areas. As an example, massive plumes of eroded African soil stretch across the Atlantic Ocean. Not only does this demonstrate dryland abuse, the effect to the oceans is significant. These dust plumes destroy corals throughout the Caribbean (Garrison et al. 2003). Grazing animals (mostly cows and sheep) are largely to blame for this mismanagement (Pimm 2002). Grazing has changed the vegetation of these areas, often irreversibly (Dregne 1983, 1986; Dregne and Chou 1992). The effects of dryland abuse are serious and far-reaching.

Next to vegetation and soils, freshwater is another universal currency that we spend freely and without much consideration for the future. Of the rain that falls over land surfaces, the land soaks up two-thirds. The remaining third runs off the land into rivers, mostly in remote places, or as floodwater. We consume a remarkable 60 percent of the accessible runoff each year (Postel et al. 1996).

Shifting our attention from terrestrial ecosystems, we look at the marine environments. Despite its vastness, about 90 percent of the ocean is a biological desert. We use a third of the ocean's annual production in the remaining area—from which comes 99 percent of the global fish catch. Surprisingly, however, our increasing ability to harvest these fisheries is not yielding a larger catch. In spite of advances in harvesting technologies, overwhelming evidence points to the opposite: fisheries are declining, and dramatically so. Our activities are destroying the ocean's ability to supply even what we take today (Food and Agricultural Organization of the United Nations 1995; Pauly et al. 1998; National Marine Fisheries Service 1999).

Now, to our focus: biodiversity. Probably 10 million types of animals and plants inhabit this Earth. Their loss poses the greatest environmental concern, because species extinction is irreversible. The scientific position asks, is there anything special about the present loss of species, compared to half a billion years of change? Haven't species always gone extinct? Isn't nature always in flux? Isn't humanity a part of natural ecosystems? If so, are our impacts allowable? The overwhelming scientific consensus is that human impacts are driving species to extinction hundreds to thousands of times faster than is expected from the natural, or background, rate (Pimm, Russell, et al. 1995; Pimm 2002, 201–16).

A relevant question then is to ask how often life has disappeared at the rate we project. The answer is only five times in life's history. This is potentially the sixth great extinction. For a measuring stick, the last comparable event in the Earth's history (65 million years ago) eliminated the dinosaurs. We know from the last major extinction that it took about 5 million years to regain a comparable variety of species and an additional 15 million years to restore the variety of families to their previous value (Raup and Sepkoski 1984). To place these numbers in perspective, consider that 5 million years is twenty times longer than the entirety of human existence. Based on stable population growth, 500 *trillion* people will be affected during this period, which is 10,000 times all the humans that have ever lived (Myers and Knoll 2001)! Clearly, even if just for anthropocentric reasons, our present course of action deserves consideration.

Scientists use the term "biodiversity" to represent the entire variety of life—ecosystems, species, populations, and genes. Human actions toward land, freshwater, and oceans have already caused biodiversity to decline. Even greater losses will occur if humanity continues its present unsustainable use of natural resources. In documenting this decline scientifically, there has been a focus on species extinctions. Species losses are also the aspect of biodiversity loss most often considered, for example, by the United Nations Convention on Biological Diversity. This chapter too focuses on species extinctions, as species are a proven and effective unit to measure conservation.[2]

Within our own species, we can apply language as a measure of biological diversity and distinctiveness. All totaled, there are roughly 6,500 distinct languages. An ecologist's first question might be to ask, "What is the minimum number of speakers required to ensure the survival of a language?" That is to say, how many speakers are required so that the language passes on to the next generation, in the face of challenges from the major international languages? History suggests that the cut off is somewhere between 100,000 and a million speakers (Pimm 2000). Above this threshold, languages are resilient to even determined efforts to eliminate them. Below it, and few languages survive. Only about 500 languages are spoken by more than a million people. This suggests that about 90 percent of the linguistic—and so likely cultural—diversity will disappear within a generation. While this is often narrated as the advancement of modern civilization, the reality of this loss is stark.

The greater part of biodiversity is in the world's tropical wilderness forests. These forests are distributed in three major regions: the Amazon, the Congo, and in and around New Guinea. When these forests disappear, the indigenous peoples inhabiting them do as well. This formula for genocide has culled languages and peoples throughout history. In recent history, the lessons from destroying the prairies and forests in North

America, South America, and Australia are clear. The fate of ecosystems and native peoples are linked. When the ecosystems disappear, so do the indigenous cultures.

Finally, there is the concomitant threat of global climate change. The planet has already warmed and done so at a geologically unprecedented rate. This is a direct result of increasing greenhouse gases from human activity.[3] The projections are that the Earth will warm more, and perhaps much more, in the next fifty years. The ecological consequences of these changes are not easy to predict, but they are already frightening. Other things being equal, species with small geographical ranges will suffer proportionately greater than species with larger ranges (Thomas et al. 2004). Species with small ranges are already disproportionately vulnerable to extinction (Pimm and Lawton 1998). These species simply do not have as many places to survive.

The Christian Worldviews

An interesting tension arises when people sharing the same religion disagree on ethical issues. Even though common traditions unite Christian groups, theological unity is regrettably infrequent. This is certainly true in the case of environmental issues, especially those associated with biodiversity conservation. The remainder of this chapter asks how the major Christian groups in the United States approach the conservation of species. How do they respond to what scientists say about the state of biodiversity? What are the different positions and patterns of thinking? In addition, on what bases do these views disagree? For right now, we focus on dissecting the different positions, and not on adjudicating them.

To answer these questions, we conducted a survey of Christian ethics on the environment. We researched the official policies of different Christian groups toward biodiversity conservation and extinction. We investigated the resolutions, publications, and public statements of various Christian groups—and their leaders—to see how Christians are responding to this environmental issue. Having discovered several interesting paradigms at the organizational level, we recognize that a truly comprehensive survey is beyond this study. Certainly, the environment-religion connection has received much scholarly attention, even within the context of Judeo-Christian theology. But whereas previous works focus on theological interpretation, we provide a typology of the most common Christian responses to the call for environmental conservation.

The attitudes that we discuss comprise powerfully held worldviews, offering insight to forging a more faithful and unified Christian ethic among Christians. Such worldviews are not unique to the Christian community (secular groups may hold such views), yet they reveal interesting disagreements between Christian groups. We recognize that the everyday practice of Christians may not correspond to the official teachings of their organizations. Such disagreements are not without historical precedent (the abolition of slavery and the civil rights movement are other examples).[4] Nevertheless, we surveyed official statements and group leaders to gauge their views, acknowledging that churchgoers do not always do what their leaders teach.

Our first hypothesis was that there would be a clear acceptance or rejection of environmental concerns. We assumed that Christians would either support some sort of species conservation or simply dismiss it. Rather than finding a simple dichotomy of positions, we encountered a more nuanced scheme of worldviews. We document four unique worldviews that reflect the dominant teachings in the Christian Church toward biodiversity: Earthkeeping, Skeptic, Priority, and Indifferent (see appendix).

The Earthkeeping worldview engages biodiversity conservation and embraces it as an ethical issue with a biblical origin. The Skeptic worldview recognizes biodiversity issues, but disagrees with the scientific community that there is a biodiversity crisis. The reasons for this are several and we discuss them below. The Priority worldview focuses not on scientific credibility but on a sort of practical urgency. Simply put, other moral issues trump conservation concerns. The Indifferent worldview does not address biodiversity, endangered species, or extinction whatsoever. Either consciously or unconsciously, the topic is unattended.

We limited our research to three different categories of Christian entities to provide a proper cross-section of Christianity. Our study focuses on official denominations, nonprofit organizations, and prominent individuals. We restricted our analyses to exclude smaller groups so this study would represent the major Christian groups in America. We only survey denominations with greater than one million members nationally, organizations with an annual budget of at least one million dollars, and individuals who play an important role in church polity, politics, or culture.[5]

Some may contend with our methodologies. Our decision to survey individuals may seem counterintuitive to accurately representing Christian groups, for example. However, we thought it was important to recognize the significant role of group authority structures and the media in communicating and promoting beliefs. Those who lead their denominations, write books, host radio shows, and appear on television have a loud voice and reach a great audience. Additionally, we do not survey nondenominational churches. The many Church of Christ and "evangelical" congregations, for example, are not centrally organized. Although they are numerous and influential, these groups defy simple characterization, and therefore we cannot survey them as a whole. Additionally, some groups we surveyed may express opinions in more than one worldview. Where this is the case, we categorized the entities by their more dominant ethic. In other words, a worldview may represent a group without encompassing it.

The idea for this section is not to judge the fidelity or merit of Christian groups based on their ecological theology or their political views. Although we hold strong convictions that the Bible calls for environmental stewardship, we impose no blanket judgments based on our findings. Rather, we discuss the rationale and the theology behind the different environmental ethics. If the ecological evidence is correct, this is both necessary and pressing.

Earthkeeping Worldview

The Earthkeeping worldview recognizes the biodiversity crisis and responds to it from a biblically based ethical conviction. Patriarch Bartholomew I, the spiritual leader of the Orthodox Church, summarizes this worldview well. In compelling tones, he declared, "For humans to cause species to become extinct and to destroy the biological diversity of God's creation . . . to degrade the integrity of the Earth by causing changes in its climate, stripping the earth of its natural forests, or destroying its wetlands . . . to contaminate the earth's waters, its land, its air, and its life with poisonous substances—these are sins" (Bartholomew I 1997).

The United Methodist Church (UMC) expresses similar sentiments, clearly articulating their doctrine in several official statements. Beginning with a reference to Psalm 24, one UMC statement reads, "All creation is the Lord's, and we are responsible for the ways we use and abuse it. Water, air, soil, minerals, energy resources, plants, animal life, and space are to be valued and conserved because they are God's creation and not solely because they are useful to human beings. . . . Therefore, let us recognize the responsibility of the church and its members to place a high priority on changes in economic, political, social, and technological lifestyles to support a more ecologically equitable and sustainable world leading to a higher quality of life for all of God's creation."[6]

From the Jewish tradition, Rabbi David Saperstein offers us insight from the book of Genesis. In a lecture to the National Press Club in May 2001, Saperstein equated our current situation with that of the Old Testament patriarch, Noah. He cited Noah's faithfulness as what saved species on the verge of extinction from the Great Flood. This resulted in a covenant that God gave *all* of creation. Saperstein declared, "[W]e are experiencing an extinction crisis. During the time of this press conference, at least three plant and animal species will be lost forever—species that might have produced medicines to save lives, or species that work to purify our air and water, creatures that are links in the food chain—all parts of God's interconnected creation. . . . So now we must ask ourselves: will we, at this moment when so many species are vulnerable, be partners in God's covenant with creation?" (Saperstein 2001).

The Christian conservation writer Wendell Berry captures this worldview well when he wrote, "to live we must daily break the body and shed the blood of Creation. When we do this lovingly, knowingly, skillfully, reverently, it is a sacrament. When we do it greedily, clumsily, ignorantly, destructively, it is a desecration" (Berry 1982, 272). Paraphrasing Berry: a proper Christian environmental stewardship is the biblically informed interaction of mankind's authority and creation's multivalent value. Here the intent of creation is realized through humility, protection, and use. This intricate balance forms a responsibility that comes together in the biblical teachings of environmental stewardship. To those in the Earth-keeping worldview preserving biodiversity may have several rationales, but all draw inspiration from the biblical text.

Skeptic Worldview

The Skeptic worldview enters the dialogue by disagreeing with the scientists who claim that serious environmental problems exist. This worldview may acknowledge that extinction is occurring, but it asserts that it is not at rates that warrant alarm. Attention here is primarily on the validity of conservation science. By this worldview, we mean something far more pointed than the guarded language of the United States Conference of Catholic Bishops (the italics are ours): "*Opinions vary* about the causes and seriousness of environmental problems. Still, we can experience their effects in polluted air and water; in oil and wastes on our beaches; in the loss of farmland, wetlands, and forests; and in the decline of rivers and lakes. Scientists identify several other less visible but particularly urgent problems currently *being debated* by the scientific community, including depletion of the ozone layer, deforestation, the extinction of species, the generation and disposal of toxic and nuclear waste, and global warming" (1991, section 1).

The Catholic bishops are not themselves skeptics, they merely point to the disunity on the nature and extent of threats to the environment. The Skeptic worldview emphasizes such observations and uses them to deny the need for environmental protection. It is clear from many Vatican publications affirming ecology—from both the Roman Catholic leadership and the Pontifical Academy of Sciences (e.g., Raven 2001)—that the Roman Catholic Church does not doubt that ecological problems exist. We use this quotation merely to articulate the Skeptic view.

The Southern Baptist Convention (SBC) gives a prominent example of skepticism in environmental science. One of the most visible denominations on contemporary political issues, the SBC has historically approved denominational resolutions *favoring* environmental stewardship. In these particular resolutions, Southern Baptists agreed that (a) God has called humans to be environmental stewards, (b) environmental crises abound, and (c) action to abate these crises is ethical (Southern Baptist Convention 1970, 1974, 1990). Recent actions have strayed from this message, however. The Ethics and Religious Liberty Commission (ERLC)—the public policy arm for Southern Baptists—claims that environmentalists often mount "unfounded" campaigns of gloom and doom (2004b). In a message disseminated nationally to Southern Baptists as church bulletin inserts, the ERLC emphasized that "The challenge is separating reality from myth when it comes to determining a proper response to environmental issues" (ERLC 2004b, 1). In another ERLC tract, the scientific status of several endangered species and their inherent value was disputed (2004a). In the view of the ERLC, environmental regulations such as the Endangered Species Act "have been allowed to spiral out of control" (2004a, 4).

Other groups express similar stances. Several articles from the Focus on the Family media group are revealing. In one, catastrophic global warming is referred to as "a grotesque distortion of science" (Shepard 2004). In another, we are warned that, "Too many environmental decisions and practices are based on incomplete or faulty science" (Howden 2001). George Weigel, a senior fellow at the Ethics and Public Policy Center (a think tank dedicated to Judeo-Christian moral values) added that, "Fears of chemicals poisoning the land are vastly exaggerated. Species aren't disappearing at a precipitous rate. . . . Cooking the books so that Chicken Little always wins is, in a word, sinful" (2002). Another example comes from the Institute on Religion and Democracy (IRD). Criticizing the National Council of Churches' advocacy of energy policy reform, the IRD casts doubts on the link between fossil fuels and global warming (Nelson 2002). In another article, the IRD labeled climate change science as "silly," "offensive," and "one more left-wing cause *du jour*," (Tooley 2002). To Skeptics, ecologists are either wrong in their calculations, or far worse, they are deliberately passing off junk science.

Priority Worldview

The Priority worldview maintains that biodiversity conservation takes the focus away from issues with greater moral importance. John Howard Yoder portrayed this worldview as affirming that "man's true need is the initial commitment of faith, so that the church should limit herself to this priority concern and not confuse things by speaking to society at large about all sorts of moral issues" (2002, 21). Whatever ecology research shows, preserving *our* species and our activities has greater relevance. Even if extinction is happening, it does not warrant the church's attention. This is a subtle, but likely prevalent, anti-conservation paradigm.

The Assemblies of God (AOG) church illustrates the Priority position. On their website, the AOG presents their beliefs on several popular contemporary issues (a practice becoming common with many denominations).[7] In this case, they present a seemingly contradictory stance on biodiversity preservation. While the AOG acknowledges biblical environmental stewardship, their position seems more concerned with combating New Age spirituality, paganism, and other forms of earth worship. The AOG states, "A major concern for Christians is the overemphasis of the environment at the expense of spiritual issues effecting life and eternity. The Bible's message declares that spiritual matters (those affecting the hearts of humankind) are the priority issues with God. These and *not the environment* are the reason He sent His own Son Jesus as a sacrifice to save people. For God did not send His Son to save the earth in a physical sense but to save the people who inhabit it. We believe this must be the main focus and concern for all Christians today" (Assemblies of God 2004; italics ours). According to the AOG, because the Earth will be destroyed in the end times, environmental stewardship takes a back seat to concerns directly related to human welfare.

A separate, although prevalent, attitude in the Priority worldview is that environmental protection stymies economic progress and is overly suspicious of technology. For some in this worldview, human ingenuity will evolve and overcome any environmental problems we encounter, and technology will outpace our ability to create environmental hazards. In short, every environmental problem has, or will have, a technological solution. This worldview has become so widespread that theologians began using the phrases "Christian humanism" and "techno-messianism" to describe the attitude (Ehrenfeld 1978; Derr 1997; Wingfield 1999).

Gary Bauer, in his unsuccessful runs for the presidency in 1996 and 2000 also championed the Priority worldview. Outlining his environmental platform, Bauer wrote, "The generation that produced the environmental movement and the anti-technology Unabomber is attempting to indoctrinate the next generation in its anti-technological and anti-progressive creed" (1996, 120). For Bauer, economic freedom and individual property rights have been eroded by federal environmental regulations. "What's missing in today's radical environmentalism is balance. Book after book and tract after tract [on the environment] ignores the benefits derived from expanding human dominion over nature" (123). This argument sets up a conflict between human dominion and ecological stewardship.

The Acton Institute for the Study of Religion and Liberty is a strong force on this specific position. This group boasts an impressive collection of academic and religious figures promoting economic and political issues. To summarize a consistent argument: economic growth generates clean environments, environmental regulations stymie growth, and property rights promote conservation voluntarily, obviating government interference (Beisner et al. 2000). Much of what the Acton Institute produces advocates that "richer is cleaner." In other words, properly implemented free market economics produces wealth and stewards creation. Akin to this reasoning, the Acton Institute also implores human subjugation of nature as a moral imperative. "When man does not exercise dominion over nature, nature will exercise dominion over man and cause tremendous suffering for the human family" (Beers et al. 2000). Beers and colleagues argue the Puritanical environmental position that human "creativity can bring nature to a higher degree of perfection."[8]

Taken wholly, this worldview affirms that the value of nature is determined through human use and that prioritizing environmental ethics ahead of economics shuns our God-given responsibilities. At the core, however, this worldview emphasizes humanity's superiority over all other species. Our concerns should not be pointed at creation, but at concerns directly affecting human beings. Any impediment of economic activity prevents this because it "ignores the full scale of human values that a free economy otherwise allows" (Beisner et al. 2000).

Indifferent Worldview

For various reasons, the *Indifferent* worldview does not address biodiversity, endangered species, or extinction whatsoever. Biodiversity is simply not a topic that registers in these groups' resolutions, policies, or publications.

Several groups in this worldview have a self-identified "pro-family" agenda. Pro-family Christian political action groups are common in Washington DC. Their purpose is to remind legislators of the issues that are important to Christian families. The Family Research Council (FRC) is among the most active and notable of these lobbying groups. According to their mission, the "FRC shapes public debate and formulates public policy that values human life and . . . promotes the Judeo-Christian worldview as the basis for a just, free, and stable society."[9] Not surprisingly therefore, the FRC focuses on legislative issues related to abortion, marriage, pornography, and education. Engaging issues seemingly less directly related to families—gambling, foreign affairs, or even tattoos (Parshall 2002)—the FRC does not address environmental policies whatsoever. This is curious considering the clear remarks from the FRC's former president who said, "conservation and stewardship of the environment are profoundly pro-family concepts" (Bauer 1996).

The American Center for Law and Justice (ACLJ) and the influential James Dobson also represent this view. Dedicated to preserving religious and constitutional freedoms,[10] the ACLJ is a frequent litigator of high profile cases in the federal courts. In these activities, the ACLJ argues a definitive political philosophy on specific issues. To date, however, the ACLJ has not taken any stance on issues or cases related to the environment. Dobson, director of the Christian media giant Focus on the Family—and founding board member of the FRC—represents this worldview. While the organization Dobson now runs is associated with statements we classify elsewhere, Dobson himself avoids issues directly related to the environment. In spite of making daily radio broadcasts that address national political issues, Dobson does not consider biodiversity.[11]

Several historically African-American denominations also maintain this worldview. The African Methodist Episcopal Church, the African Methodist Episcopal Zion Church, the National Baptist Convention U.S.A., Inc., and the National Baptist Convention of America, Inc. all do not engage environmental issues. The lack of official policies, teachings, or published material addressing environmental stewardship here reveals broader organizational and doctrinal issues that go beyond the scope of this essay (Washington 1986; Lincoln and Mamiya 1990).

ASSESSING THE SCIENTIFIC AND CHRISTIAN POSITIONS

The Earthkeeping Hermeneutic

Experience teaches that, when participants in two different fields of knowledge meet, they will have symmetrical views. For example, when economists meet ecologists, the former have a detailed drawing of the economy and a single, simple box for "ecology," whereas ecologists have a detailed drawing of environmental processes and a single, simple box for "the economy." This seems the case for religion and the environment. Those concerned with the practical issues of protecting the environment are likely to see the multifaceted problems of their trade, but view religion, ethics, and the church as single and monolithic. The reverse is also common.

Lynn White, Jr. illustrated this in a *Science* article, citing Christians and their theology as "bearing a great burden" of responsibility for the current ecological crisis (1967). Because White linked Christianity with negative environmental attitudes, his paper had a significant impact with ecologists. Many ecologists—and the scientific community in general— received White's thesis with open arms, and the Ecological Society of

America responded by awarding him their prestigious Mercer prize. Not everyone was as enthusiastic, however. His ideas raised concern with many Christians who saw the Bible as advocating a distinct environmental ethic (Whitney, chapter 2, this volume).

The select ecologists who dig deeper than White may read eco-theology or the eloquent writings of Wendell Berry. They might feel reassured that Christians view extinction as an ethical problem. More often, it seems, they will summarily dismiss Christians, either pointing to White's thesis or citing Genesis as a charter for nature domination. As our chapter documents, White's position is a simplistic abstraction. Christian environmental worldviews cannot be placed in one simple box. Rather, they represent a multitude of sometimes conflicting ideas. As Christians may have different opinions on the environment, we ask, what does the Bible say? As ecologists, we recognize the work of theologians who interpret Genesis as a guide to protect the Earth.

A central issue in the theology of ecology is the relative position of humanity within the rest of creation. This has been a flashpoint for disagreement. In the Priority worldview, opinions often stem from a theology that humans, as a species, have a unique relationship with God. This privileged relationship leads to a belief that only humans are redeemable. This view focuses on humanity being set apart from the rest of creation, having a special likeness and future with God. The first chapter of Genesis supports this: "Let us make man in our image, in our likeness. . . . So God created man in his own image, in the image of God he created him" (Genesis 1:26–27). Significant portions of Christians have taken this passage as an entitlement to subjugate creation. However, as Richard Hays writes of the literalist's slogan "God said it, I believe it, that settles it," "bumper-sticker hermeneutics will not do" (Hays 1996, 3).

Calvin DeWitt (1998) sheds light on the dominion issue. In *Caring for Creation: Responsible Stewardship of God's Handiwork*, DeWitt recognizes three essential biblical ideas for conservation. Paradoxically, it is Genesis—the same text often used to confront ecologists—that provides DeWitt inspiration. He outlines a biblical concept for stewardship in three ways: (a) earthkeeping, (b) fruitfulness, and (c) the Sabbath.[12]

The concept of earthkeeping comes from Genesis 2:15, where God instructs Adam about his vocation in the garden of Eden. Looking at the Genesis text in its original Hebrew language, DeWitt discusses two crucial words, referencing how they are used elsewhere in the Old Testament. He reads the words *abad* and *shamar* collectively to mean, "to serve and keep nature in dynamic integrity." Expanding the notion of environmental stewardship, DeWitt derives the fruitfulness principle from Genesis 1. Here God speaks to Adam—as well as to all the birds and fish—instructing them to "be fruitful, increase in number and fill [the earth]." DeWitt points out that God gives this charge to both humanity *and* creation. Humans are not alone with the inherent right to be bountiful and fill their habitat.

Lastly, DeWitt points to the Sabbath principle as a significant "means of assuring fruitfulness." As it is generically known, the Sabbath is where people rest from their work one day each week. However, it is a profound rule with deep spiritual implications. As a Hebrew tradition in the Old Testament scriptures, the Sabbath informed agriculture practices (e.g., Exodus 23, Leviticus 25–26). At all times one-seventh of all the farmed land was kept fallow, and every seven years all the land was to rest from cultivation. Every seventh Sabbath year, or the 50th year, was the Jubilee. During the Jubilee, monetary debts were forgiven and all slaves were freed (Leviticus 25). From the New Testament scriptures, the Christian tradition teaches that Jesus Christ, himself, embodies the Sabbath and the Jubilee. The fourth chapter of Luke chronicles Jesus recitation of the prophet Isaiah: "The Spirit of the Lord is on me, because he has anointed me to bring good news to the poor. He has sent me to proclaim release to the captives and recovery of sight to the blind, to the oppressed go free, to proclaim the year of the Lord's favor" (Luke 4:18–19, NRSV). Therefore, in both the Hebrew and Christian traditions, the Sabbath represents the rejuvenation and restoration of life. As DeWitt emphasizes, this is integral to earthkeeping.

Earthkeeping, fruitfulness, and Sabbath form a rich theological tapestry that defines biblical environmental stewardship. Those few scientists who got past Lynn White might well ask where such Christian teachings of stewardship are today. Those Christians who consider DeWitt's perspectives might ask, how does the Christian understanding of Sabbath inform an environmental ethic today? Answers are not always easy to find.

Baptizing Secular Conservatism

Despite well-reasoned arguments like DeWitt's, a strong and organized force interprets the Bible towards a decidedly different environmental ethic. A prominent example is *The Cornwall Declaration*, published by the Interfaith Council for Environmental Stewardship and signed by a broad selection of Christian and Jewish figures (Interfaith Council for Environmental Stewardship 1999). Underlying *The Cornwall Declaration* is an acute optimism in human reason and economic progress, complemented by pessimism in government-mediated science policy. Oddly, *The Cornwall Declaration* resembles conservative political rhetoric more than it does biblical language.

The signers of *The Cornwall Declaration* believe that God calls humankind to a "serious commitment" to free-market capitalism, where individual liberty is valued above government interference. Wary of government, the document hails private property rights and widespread economic freedom as the means to "sound environmental stewardship." As a result, science becomes the path to realize economic prosperity, not a way to assay economic activity itself. Consider three key common environmental issues: human population growth, resource exploitation, and biodiversity extinction. In *The Cornwall Declaration,* each of these predicaments has a technological solution. For example, overpopulation is not a serious problem because agricultural engineering continues to generate greater crop yields. Overexploitation is not a concern because the ability to extract natural resources increases with technological advances. One assumes that even biodiversity loss can be mitigated through biotechnology. If species drift close to extinction, surely their populations can be bolstered through *Jurassic Park*–like efforts (Taggart 2002). Are we to believe these arguments? More important, is there a biblical cause to do so?

Aside from *The Cornwall Declaration,* the collusion of the political right and the religious right is more than linguistic. For Christians who are skeptical that environmental problems exist, Michael Sanera and Jane Shaw's *Facts, Not Fear* (1999) is a frequent reference (Ethics and Religious Liberty Commission 2004b). Sanera is neither a theologian nor a scientist of any repute but the former Director of Environmental Education Research of the politically conservative Claremont Institute. However, Sanera is not the only secular conservative cited by anti-environmental Christians. The Southern Baptist church quoted a writer for The Brookings Institution to dismiss ecological science as a false and "assiduous" liberal campaign (Ethics and Religious Liberty Commission 2004a). In another example, a recent article published by Focus on the Family cites a senior fellow at the reactionary Lexington Institute to debunk climate change science (Howden 2001). Probably, one expects some liaison between such groups, but how much is too much? Where do we draw the line between theology and secular politics?

An examination of the financial reports of several of the groups we surveyed revealed deeper connections between Christian and politically conservative think-tanks. In many cases, the ties were financial as well as ideological. Such nominally distinct groups were not merely promoting similar environmental agendas; the same politically conservative foundations funded them. Some religious organizations we surveyed—the Ethics and Public Policy Center, the Acton Institute for Study of Religion and Liberty, the Institute on Religion and Democracy, and the Institute on Religion and Public Life, for example—all received major contributions from powerful right-wing political foundations, such as the Lynde and Harry Bradley, the John M. Olin, and the Sarah Scaife foundations, (Goodstein and Kirkpatrick 2004; Philanthropic Research Inc. 2005). This finding is revealing in itself, but even more so given that these same foundations also funded extremely conservative political organizations such as the American Enterprise Institute for Public Policy Research, the Claremont Institute, the Heritage Foundation, and the Pacific Research Institute for Public Policy, among others (Philanthropic Research Inc. 2005). Liaisons of this nature are the rule and not the exception.

Although one expects some cooperation between faith-based and political think tanks, these relationships should not transform the meaning of the biblical scriptures. As George Lindbeck reminds us, the Bible does not present us with a "figurative representation" of how life should be, subject to our own political leanings or preferred interpretations (1984, 118). Rather, a faithful theology is "intratextual" as it redescribes the world to fit the scriptural story. Applying Lindbeck to our situation, an environmental ethic that is faithful to the scriptures does not consist of a secular political ideology "baptized" with certain biblical passages. Rather, it is an inherently biblical ethic, of course, having political ramifications—not the reverse. The collusion of the political and religious conservatism casts doubt on the ethics these partnerships produce.

A Better Way

Tertullian observed that, in the first centuries of the Roman Empire, conventional wisdom blamed early Christians for society's perils. He wrote, "If the Tiber floods or the Nile fails to flood, if the skies darken, if the earth trembles, if famine, war or plague occurs, then immediately the shout goes up: 'The Christians to the lions'" (Bainton 1964, 44). Although accusing Christianity for our ecological crisis may have appealed to Roman senators, or Lynn White, the view that the Christian faith is summarily anti-environmental is a misconception.

As this chapter has demonstrated, Christian worldviews differ greatly in reference to the value of biodiversity and its conservation. Here we noted four distinct worldviews that encompass typical Christian responses to biodiversity preservation. The patterns we observed were more complex than a straightforward acceptance or rejection of environmental stewardship. Indeed, expressions of support for species preservation were the most enduring worldview we surveyed. This worldview had a strong tradition that frequently employed biblical teachings for its justification. Also represented in our study was a strong attitude of distrust toward the scientific community that sounds the alarm for conservation. Largely separate from debates over scriptural meaning, this view calls scientific research into question and recommends conservation efforts be postponed until there is more convincing evidence. Another response we discovered was a prioritization of other issues ahead of environmental concerns. This worldview provided a sort of conservation "lip service" without any demonstrated effect. Amidst passionate beliefs, there was still ample room for indifference. The remaining worldview we identified did not give significant attention to biodiversity issues or conservation whatsoever.

While the majority of Christian groups officially support conservation, Christians ought not gloat on their group's environmental theology. A large confusion remains in churches on how to mesh theology and ecology. Concerns over economic prosperity, New Age spirituality, scientism, and liberal ideologies abound. As a result, many Christians may believe the Bible commands some sort of environmental protection, they just will never *do* anything about it. A 2004 survey by *Christianity Today* is revealing. According to their poll, over half of those "uncomfortable with environmentalism" are so because they believe other concerns are more important. Among these concerns, a strong economy and preventing earth-worship were prominent. Of the remaining, a quarter did not think there were any environmental problems; the rest doubted the Bible's call for stewardship.

Certainly, there are paths of environmental ethics that are secular, some of which are certainly unfaithful to both the Hebrew and Christian portions of the Bible. For those of faith, though, the primary concern is not nature itself nor humanity, but obedience to the scriptures. The remaining challenge then, requires theologians to teach the scriptures, ecologists to measure the state of the environment, and both to work in concert.

This sort of vision requires both the work of ecologists and the work of the Church—the secular and the Christian. We conclude with another remark for the Conference of Catholic Bishops: "These important issues are being explored by scientists, and they require urgent attention and action." They continue: "We are not scientists, but as pastors we call on experts, citizens, and policy makers to continue to explore the serious environmental, ethical, and human dimensions of these ecological challenges" (1992). We do not call for a baptizing of secular agendas—either liberal or conservative—but rather obedience to God's word.

APPENDIX

Dominant Christian Teachings toward Biodiversity

SOURCES

The following lists the sources from which we have drawn information in order to classify the worldviews of denominations, organizations, and individuals in the table above. The references are self-authored and published unless otherwise noted. All URLs current as of September 2005.

Denominations

African Methodist Episcopal Church: http://www.amecnet.org/; C. E. Lincoln and L. H. Mamiya, *The Black Church in the African American Experience* (Durham, NC: Duke University, 1990).

African Methodist Episcopal Zion Church: http://www.theamezionchurch. org/; C. E. Lincoln and L. H. Mamiya, *The Black Church in the African American Experience* (Durham, NC: Duke University, 1990).

American Baptist Churches U.S.A.: "Policy Statement on Ecology: An Ecological Situational Analysis," res. 7040 (1989, available at http://www.abc-usa. org/resources/resol/ecology.htm).

Table 4.1 Worldviews of Major Denominations, Organizations, and Individuals

	Earthkeeping	Skeptic	Priority	Indifferent
Denomination (10⁶ members)	Roman Catholic Church (59.2) United Methodist Church (8.7) Evangelical Lutheran Church in America (5.2) Presbyterian Church, U.S.A. (3.2) Lutheran Church, The Missouri Synod (2.6) Greek Orthodox Archdiocese of America (2.5) Episcopal Church (2.5) United Church of Christ (1.6) American Baptist Churches U.S.A. (1.6) Russian Orthodox Church (1.1) Christian Church, Disciples of Christ (1.0)	Southern Baptist Convention (15.4)	Assemblies of God (2.3)	National Baptist Convention U.S.A., Inc. (7.5) National Baptist Convention of America, Inc. (3.5) African Methodist Episcopal Church (3.3) African Methodist Episcopal Zion Church (1.2)
Organizations	Au Sable Institute Christianity Today International National Council of Churches of Christ in the U.S.A. National Religious Partnership for the Environment Sojourners Target Earth International	Ethics and Public Policy Center Focus on the Family Institute on Religion and Democracy Institute on Religion and Public Life Toward Tradition	Acton Institute for Study of Religion and Liberty	American Center for Law and Justice Christian Coalition of America Family Research Council
Individuals	Patriarch Bartholomew I Tony Campolo Cal DeWitt Ted Haggard Pope John Paul II Francis Schaeffer Ron Sider Archbishop Rowan Williams	Richard Baer, Jr. Charles Colson Thomas Sieger Derr Richard Land Richard John Neuhaus Pat Robertson	Gary Bauer Jerry Falwell Robert A. Sirico	James Dobson

Assemblies of God: http://ag.org/top/beliefs/contemporary_issues/issues_02_ environment.cfm

Christian Church, Disciples of Christ: "The Alverna Covenant on Christian Lifestyle and Ecology" (Indianapolis, IN, 1991, available at http://www.webofcreation.org/education/policystatements/disciples.htm).

Episcopal Church: http://www.eenonline.org/; The Anglican Communion, *The Official Report of the Lambeth Conference 1998* (Harrisburg, PA: Morehouse, 1999); J. M. Golliher, "This Fragile Earth, Our Island Home," in *Beyond Colonial Anglicanism: The Anglican Communion in the 21st Century*, ed. I. T. Douglas and K. Pui-Lan, 139–64 (New York: Church Publishing Inc., 1999); The Global Anglican Congress on the Stewardship of Creation, "Declaration to the Anglican Communion," Johannesburg, South Africa (2002).

Evangelical Lutheran Church in America: *Caring for Creation: Vision, Hope, Justice* (Kansas City, MO, 2000).

Greek Orthodox Archdiocese of America: A. Belopopsky and D. Oikonomou, eds., *The Orthodoxy and Ecology Resource Book* (Bialystok, Poland: Syndesmos, 1996).

Lutheran Church, The Missouri Synod: *Stewardship of Creation* (St. Louis, MO, 2000).

National Baptist Convention of America, Inc.: http://www.nbcamerica.net/; J. M. Washington, *Frustrated Fellowship: The Black Baptist Quest for Social Power* (Macon, GA: Mercer University Press, 1986); C. E. Lincoln and L. H. Mamiya, *The Black Church in the African American Experience* (Durham, NC: Duke University, 1990).

National Baptist Convention U.S.A., Inc.: http://www.nationalbaptist.com/; J. M. Washington, *Frustrated Fellowship: The Black Baptist Quest for Social Power* (Macon, GA: Mercer University Press, 1986); C. E. Lincoln and L. H. Mamiya, *The Black Church in the African American Experience* (Durham, NC: Duke University, 1990).

Presbyterian Church, U.S.A.: http://pcusa.org/environment; 213th General Assembly of the PCUSA, "Preserving Biodiversity and Halting Mass Extinction," overture 01-60 (Louisville, KY, 2001).

Roman Catholic Church: N. Cabibbo and W. Arber, *The Challenges of Sciences: A Tribute to the Memory of Carlos Chagas* (Vatican City: The Pontifical Academy of Sciences, 2001); The Pontifical Academy of Sciences, *Science and the Future of Mankind: Science for Man and Man for Science* (Vatican City: The Pontifical Academy of Sciences, 2001).

Russian Orthodox Church: Moscow Patriarch, "The Church and Ecological Problems," section 13 of *Basic Social Concept of the Russian Orthodox Church*.

Southern Baptist Convention: "Resolution on the Environment" (Denver, CO, 1970); "Resolution on Stewardship of God's Creation" (Dallas, TX, 1974);

"Resolution on Environmental Stewardship" (New Orleans, LA, 1990); Ethics and Religious Liberty Commission, *The Facts, Environmental Stewardship* (Nashville, TN, 2004); Ethics and Religious Liberty Commission, *Faith and Family: Focus on Environmental Issues* (Carol Stream, IL: Tyndale House Publishers, 2004).

United Methodist Church: General Board of Church and Society of the United Methodist Church, *Our Social Principles (The Natural World)* (2000); "Environmental Justice for a Sustainable Future" (1992, available at http://dev. umc.org/interior.asp?ptid=4&mid=959).

United Church of Christ: http://www.ucc.org/justice/environment.htm.

Organizations

Acton Institute for Study of Religion and Liberty: www.acton.org/ppolicy/ environment; M. B. Barkey, ed., *Environmental Stewardship in the Judeo-Christian Tradition: Jewish, Catholic, and Protestant Wisdom on the Environment* (Grand Rapids, MI, 2000).

American Center for Law and Justice: http://www.aclj.org/Issues/Default. aspx.

Au Sable Institute: http://ausable.org/.

Christian Coalition of America: http://www.cc.org/issues.cfm.

Christianity Today International: Carl H. Reidel, "Christianity and the Environmental Crisis," *Christianity Today*, p. 5, April 23, 1971; R. Sider, "Redeeming the Environmentalists," *Christianity Today*, pp 26–29, June 21, 1993; H. A. Snyder, "Why We Love the Earth," *Christianity Today*, p. 15, May 15, 1995; Staff editorial, "Heat Stroke," *Christianity Today*, p. 26, October 2004.

Ethics and Public Policy Center: M. Cromartie, *Creation at Risk? Religion, Science, and Environmentalism* (Grand Rapids, MI: Eerdmans, 1995); G. Weigel, "The Sky Is Not Falling," *The Catholic Difference*, January 31, 2002.

Family Research Council: http://www.frc.org.

Focus on the Family: M. Hartwig, "Who's Afraid of Earth Day?" *Teachers in Focus* (2000); M. Howden, "Confusion vs. Facts," (Attorneys Ministry, 2001); C. R. MiVille, "Textbooks Distort History, Critics Say," *Family News in Focus*, October 31, 2001; S. Shepard, "Left-Wing Groups Champion 'Day After Tomorrow,' " *Family News in Focus*, May 26, 2004.

Interfaith Coalition for Environmental Stewardship (ICES): *The Cornwall Declaration* (Washington DC, 1999, available at http://www.stewards.net/CornwallDeclaration.htm).

Institute on Religion and Democracy: M. Tooley, "Ecumenical Partnership Seeks to 'Green' America's Churches," *National Liberty Journal*, October 1999; E. Nelson, "Religious Leaders Call for Energy Conservation and Climate Justice" (Washington DC: The Institute on Religion and Democracy, 2002); M. Tooley, *What Would Jesus Drive?* (Washington DC: The Institute on Religion and Democracy, 2002).

Institute on Religion and Public Life: http://www.firstthings.com/.

National Council of Churches: http://www.nccecojustice.org; V. K. White, *It's God's World: Christians, the Environment, and Climate Change* (New York: National Council of the Churches of Christ in the USA, 2003).

National Religious Partnership for the Environment: http://www.nrpe.org/.

Sojourners: http://www.sojo.net; T. M. Barnett, "Eco-Theology Gems, The Best Reading on Christianity and the Environment. *Sojourners* 33 (2004): 41–44.

Target Earth International: http://www.targetearth.org.

Toward Tradition: http://www.towardtradition.org; D. Klinghoffer, "The Gospel of the Trees: The Strange Rise of Eco-faith," *National Review On-Line*, August 1, 2001 (available at http://www.nationalreview.com/comment/comment-klinghoffer080101.shtml.

Individuals

Richard Baer, Jr.: "Environmental Realism," in *Caring for Creation: Responsible Stewardship of God's Handiwork*, ed. J. W. Skillen and L. Lugo, 61–70 (Grand Rapids: Baker Books, 1998).

Patriarch Bartholomew I: Opening address to the Environmental Symposium of the Greek Orthodox Church, Santa Barbara, CA (1997).

Gary Bauer: *Our Hopes, Our Dreams: A Vision for America* (Colorado Springs: Focus on the Family Publishing, 1996).

Tony Campolo: *How to Rescue the Earth Without Worshiping Nature: A Christian's Call to Save Creation* (Nashville, TN: Thomas Nelson, 1992).

Charles Colson: Interfaith Coalition for Environmental Stewardship (ICES), *The Cornwall Declaration* (Washington DC: ICES, 1999, available at http://www.stewards.net/CornwallDeclaration.htm); *Worldview for Parents, Christians and the Environment* (Reston, VA: Prison Fellowship Ministries, 2003).

Thomas Sieger Derr: "The Complexity and Ambiguity of Environmental Stewardship," in *Caring for Creation: Responsible Stewardship of God's Handiwork*, ed. J. W. Skillen and L. Lugo, 71–84 (Grand Rapids: Baker Books, 1998); Interfaith Coalition for Environmental Stewardship (ICES), *The Cornwall Declaration* (Washington DC: ICES, 1999, available at http://www.stewards.net/CornwallDeclaration.htm).

Calvin DeWitt: "Religion and the Environment," in *Caring for Creation: Responsible Stewardship of God's Handiwork*, ed. J. W. Skillen and L. Lugo, 15–59 (Grand Rapids: Baker Books, 1998); D. N. Livingstone, C. B. DeWitt, et al., "Eco-Myths," *Christianity Today*, June 25, 2001.

James Dobson: http://www.family.org/.

Jerry Falwell: M. Tooley, "Ecumenical Partnership Seeks to 'Green' America's Churches," *National Liberty Journal*, October 1999; D. Kupelian, "The Year 2000's 10 Most Underreported Stories," *National Liberty Journal*, February 2001.

Billy Graham: C. Greer, "Change Will Come When Our Hearts Change," *Parade*, pp. 4–6, October 20, 1996.

Ted Haggard: http://www.nae.net; "Sandy Cove Covenant and Invitation" at the Creation Care Conference, Sandy Cove, MD (2004); L. Goodstein, "Evangelical Leaders Swing Influence Behind Effort to Combat Global Warming," *New York Times*, March 10, 2005.

Pope John Paul II: *The Ecological Crisis: A Common Responsibility*, articles 1 and 15 (1998); *Centesimus Annus* (1991); available at http://bav.vatican.va/en/v_home_bav/home_bav.shtml.

Father Richard John Neuhaus: *In Defense of People: Ecology and the Seduction of Radicalism* (New York: Macmillan, 1971); "Christ and Creation's Longing," *First Things* 78 (1997): 20–25.

Pat Robertson: *Bring It On*, p. 128 (Nashville: W Publishing Group, 2002).

Francis Schaeffer: *Pollution and the Death of Man: The Christian View of Ecology* (Wheaton, IL: Tyndale House, 1970).

Ron Sider: "Redeeming the Environmentalists," *Christianity Today*, pp. 45–47, June 21, 1993.

Father Robert A. Sirico: Interfaith Coalition for Environmental Stewardship (ICES), *The Cornwall Declaration* (Washington DC: ICES, 1999, available at http://www.stewards.net/CornwallDeclaration.htm); T. Strode, "Religious Leaders Issue Calls for Biblical View of Ecology," *Baptist Press*, April 19, 2000.

Archbishop Rowan Williams: *Changing The Myths We Live By* (Lambeth: Anglican Communion, 2004).

NOTES

1. As both Chappell (2004) and Marsh (2005) argue, led by Martin Luther King, Jr., an explicit vision from the Christian church is what propelled the civil rights movement to success in overthrowing Jim Crow.

2. Naturally, the subject is broader and more complex than our simplification. For example, a species may survive in a given area yet lose much of its genetic diversity (Hughes, Daily, and Ehrlich 1997, 1998). Furthermore, an ecosystem may survive yet shrink enough in area and thus lose its historical function, or even most of its constituent species.

3. National Research Council (2001). Additionally, a good and succinct summary of the causes and effects of global warming is available at http://yosemite.epa.gov/oar/global warming.nsf/content/Climate.html.

4. Comparing the current discussion with the role Christianity played in the abolition of slavery and Civil rights movement in the United States is illuminating. Dew (2002) provides a worthy account of pro-slavery, secessionist dialogue among white Christians before the Civil War. Chappell (2004) gives a particularly thoughtful counterexample of the role of prophetic Christianity with southern black activists against Jim Crow.

5. Accounting information for all not-for-profit organizations is available on the Internet through the research database, GuideStar, available at www.guidestar.org. Membership statistics for denominations were taken from Mead et al. (2001).

6. See the UMC's www.umc.org, for policy statements regarding the environment and the natural world.

7. See the AOG web site for statements on their environmenatal beliefs.

8. Full text of this book chapter is available online at http://www.acton.org/ppolicy/environment/theology/m_catholic.html.

9. See the FRC's web site, www.frc.org, to view their legislative concerns.

10. The ACLJ's full mission statement is available at http://www.aclj.org

11. Dr. Dobson's radio broadcasts are archived and available on his organization's web site, at www.family.org/fmedia/broadcast

12. De Witt's description of biblical environmental stewardship—earthkeeping, fruitfulness, Sabbath—bears remarkable similarity to Henri Nouwen's description of the Christian life. Citing a passage in the epistle of John, Nouwen argues that intimacy, fecundity, and ecstasy are vital elements of the Christian who takes the Gospel seriously (1986). A Roman Catholic priest, Nouwen wrote his book from the experiences he had during a Sabbatical year he spent in a community of handicapped Christians.

WORKS CITED

Assemblies of God. 2004. Environmental protection. Available at the Assemblies of God web site (last accessed Sept. 2005).

Bainton, R. H. 1964. *The Horizon history of Christianity*. New York: American Heritage.

Bartholomew I, Patriarch. 1997. Opening address. The Environmental Symposium of the Greek Orthodox Church, Santa Barbara, CA.

Bauer, G. 1996. *Our hopes, our dreams: A vision for America*. Colorado Springs: Focus on the Family Publishing.

Beers, J. M., R. Hittinger, et al. 2000. The Catholic Church and stewardship of creation. In *Environmental stewardship in the Judeo-Christian tradition: Jewish, Catholic, and Protestant wisdom on the environment*, ed. M. B. Barkey. Grand Rapids, MI: Acton Institute for the Study of Religion and Liberty.

Beisner, E. C., et al. 2000. A biblical perspective on environmental stewardship. In *Environmental stewardship in the Judeo-Christian tradition: Jewish, Catholic, and Protestant wisdom on the environment*, ed. M. B. Barkey. Grand Rapids, MI: Acton Institute for the Study of Religion and Liberty.

Berry, W. 1982. *The Gift of Good Land*. San Francisco: Northpoint Press.

Chappell, D. L. 2004. *A stone of hope: Prophetic religion and the death of Jim Crow*. Chapel Hill: University of North Carolina Press.

Constanza, R., et al. 1997. The value of the world's ecosystem services and natural capital. *Nature* 387:253–60.

Daily, G. C., ed. 1997. *Nature's services: Societal dependence on natural ecosystems*. Washington DC: Island Press.

Derr, T. S. 1997. *Environmental ethics and Christian humanism*. Nashville, TN: Abingdon.

Dew, C. B. 2002. *Apostles of disunion*. Charlottesville: University Press of Virginia.

DeWitt, C. B. 1998. *Caring for creation: Responsible stewardship of God's handiwork*. Grand Rapids: Baker Books.

Dregne, H. E. 1983. *Desertification of arid lands*. New York: Hardwood Academic.

———. 1986. Desertification of arid lands. In *Physics of desertification*, ed. F. El-Bax and M. H. A. Hassan. Dordrecht: Kluwer Academic Publishers.

Dregne, H. E., and N. T. Chou. 1992. Global desertification dimensions and costs. In *Degradation and Restoration of Arid Lands*, ed. H. E. Dregne. Lubbock: Texas Tech University.

Ehrenfeld, D. W. 1978. *The arrogance of humanism*. New York: Oxford University Press.

Ehrlich, P. R. and A. H. Ehrlich. 1981. *Extinction: The causes and consequences of the disappearance of species*. New York: Random House.

Eldredge, N. 2000. *The triumph of evolution: And the failure of creationism*. New York: W H Freeman.

Ethics and Religious Liberty Commission. 2004a. *The facts, environmental stewardship*. Nashville, TN: Ethics and Religious Liberty Commission.

———. 2004b. Faith and family: Focus on environmental issues. Carol Stream, IL: Tyndale House Publishers.

Food and Agricultural Organization of the United Nations. 1995. *The state of the world fisheries and aquaculture*. Rome: United Nations. (Available at www.fao.org, last accessed Sept. 2005).

Garrison, V. H., et al. 2003. African and Asian dust: From desert soils to coral reefs. *Bioscience* 53 (5): 469.

Goodstein, L. and D. D. Kirkpatrick. 2004. Conservative group amplifies voice of Protestant orthodoxy. *New York Times*, May 22, A1.

Hauerwas, S. 1983. On keeping theological ethics theological. In *Revisions: Changing perspectives in moral philosophy*, ed. S. Hauerwas and A. MacIntyre. Notre Dame, IN: University of Notre Dame Press.

Hays, R. 1996. *The moral vision of the New Testament*. San Francisco: Harper-SanFrancisco.

Howden, M. 2001. Confusion vs. facts. Available at the Focus on the Family web site (last accessed Sept. 2005).

Hughes, J. B., G. C. Daily, P. R. Ehrlich. 1997. Population diversity: Its extent and extinction. *Science* 278:689–92.

———. 1998. The loss of population diversity and why it matters. In *Nature and Human Society: The quest for a sustainable world,* ed. P. H. Raven, 71–83. Washington DC: National Academy Press.

Interfaith Council for Environmental Stewardship. 1999. *The Cornwall Declaration.* Washington DC: The Interfaith Council for Environmental Stewardship. (Available at http://www.stewards.net/CornwallDeclaration.htm, last accessed Sept. 2005).

King, M. L., Jr. 1999. Letter from a Birmingham jail. In *Baptist Roots*, ed. C. W. Freeman, J. W. McClendon, Jr., and C. R. Velloso da Silva. Valley Forge, PA: Judson Press.

Lincoln, C. E. and L. H. Mamiya. 1990. *The black church in the African American experience*. Durham, NC: Duke University.

Lindbeck, G. 1984. *The nature of doctrine*. Philadelphia: The Westminster Press.

MacIntyre, A. 1981. *After virtue*. Notre Dame, IN: University of Notre Dame Press.

Marsh, C. 2005. *The beloved community: How faith shapes social justice, from the civil rights movement to today*. New York: Basic Books.

May, R. M. 1989. An inordinate fondness for ants. *Nature* 341:386–87.

Mead, F. S., et al. 2001. *Handbook of denominations in the United States*. Nashville, TN: Abingdon Press.

Miller, K. R. 1999. *Finding Darwin's God*. New York: Cliff Street Books.

Mooney, C. 2005. *The Republican war on science*. New York: Basic Books.

Myers, N. 1992. *The primary source*. New York: W. W. Norton and Co.

Myers, N., and J. Kent. 2003. New consumers: The influence of affluence on the environment. *Proceedings of the National Academy of Science, U.S.A.* 100: 4963–68.

Myers, N., and A. H. Knoll. 2001. The biotic crisis and the future of evolution. *Proceedings of the National Academy of Science, U.S.A.* 98 (10): 5389–92.

National Research Council. 1999. *Perspectives on biodiversity: Valuing its role in an everchanging world*. Washington DC: National Academy of Sciences.

National Research Council. 2001. *Climate change science: An analysis of some key questions*. Washington DC: National Academy of Sciences.

National Marine Fisheries Service. 1999. *Status of the fisheries of the United States.* Washington DC: National Marine Fisheries Service. (Available at http://www.nmfs.noaa.gov, last accessed Sept. 2005).

Nelson, E. 2002. Religious leaders call for energy conservation and climate justice. Available at the Institute on Religion and Democracy web site (last accessed Sept. 2005).

Northcott, M. 1996. *The environment and Christian ethics.* Cambridge: Cambridge University Press.

Nouwen, H. J. M. 1986. *Lifesigns.* New York: Doubleday.

Parshall, J. 2002. Washington watch, January 16. Washington DC: Family Research Council.

Pauly, D., et al. 1998. "Fishing down marine food webs." *Science* 279:860–63.

Philanthropic Research Inc. 2005. GuideStar. Available at http://www.guidestar.org (last accessed Sept. 2005).

Pimm, S. L. 2000. Biodiversity is us. *Oikos* 90:3–6.

———. 2002. *The world according to Pimm.* New York: McGraw Hill.

Pimm, S. L., and R. Askins. 1995. Forest losses predict bird extinctions in eastern North America. *Proceedings of the National Academy of Sciences, U.S.A.* 92:9343–47.

Pimm, S. L., and J. H. Lawton. 1998. Planning for biodiversity. *Science* 279:2068–69.

Pimm, S. L., G. J. Russell, et al. 1995. The future of biodiversity. *Science* 269: 347–50.

Placher, W. 1983. *A history of Christian theology.* Philadelphia: The Westminster Press.

Placher, W. 1996. *The domestication of transcendence.* Louisville, KY: Westminster John Knox Press.

Postel, S. L., et al. 1996. Human appropriation of renewable freshwater. *Science* 271:785–88.

Raup, D. M., and J. J. Sepkoski. 1984. Periodicity of extinctions in the geologic past. *Proceedings of the National Academy of Science, U.S.A.* 81:801–5.

Raven, P. 2001. Biodiversity and the human prospect. In *The challenges of sciences: A tribute to the memory of Carlos Chagas,* ed. N. Cabibbo and W. Arber, 71–77. Scripta Varia 103. Vatican City: The Pontifical Academy of Sciences.

Rojstaczer, S., et al. 2001. Human appropriation of photosynthesis products. *Science* 294:2549–52.

Sanera, M., and J. Shaw. 1999. *Facts not fear: Teaching children about the environment.* Federalsburg, MD: Regnery Publishing.

Saperstein, D. 2001. Enforcement and full funding of the endangered species act. Lecture to the National Press Club, Washington DC.

Shepard, S. 2004. Left-wing groups champion "Day After Tomorrow." *Family News in Focus,* May 26.

Skole, D., and C. J. Tucker. 1993. Tropical deforestation and habitat fragmentation in the Amazon: Satellite data from 1978 to 1988. *Science* 260:1905–10.

Southern Baptist Convention. 1970. Resolution on the environment. Denver, CO.

———. 1974. Resolution on stewardship of God's creation. Dallas TX.

———. 1990. Resolution on environmental stewardship. New Orleans, LA.

Taggart, S. 2002. Will the Tasmanian tiger clone work? *Wired*, June 10.

Thomas, C. D., et al. 2004. Extinction risk from climate change. *Nature* 427:145–48.

Tooley, M. 2002. *What would Jesus drive?* Washington DC: The Institute on Religion and Democracy.

United Nations. 2003. *World population monitoring 2001: Population, environment, development.* New York: United Nations.

United States Conference of Catholic Bishops. 1991. Renewing the earth: An invitation to reflection and action on environment in light of Catholic social teaching. Available at http://www.nccbuscc.org/sdwp/ejp/bishopsstatement.htm (last accessed Sept. 2005).

USA Today, 2005 The whole world, from whose hands? October 11, 6D.

Vitousek, P. M., et al. 1986. Human appropriation of the products of Photosynthesis. *Bioscience* 36: 368–373.

Washington, J. M. 1986. *Frustrated fellowship: The black Baptist quest for social power.* Macon, GA: Mercer University Press.

White, L. 1967. The historical roots of our ecological crisis. *Science* 155: 1203–07.

Weigel, G. 2002. The sky is not falling. *The Catholic Difference,* January 31.

Williamson, M. 1989. High table tales. *Nature* 341:691.

Wilson, E. O., and D. L. Perlman. 2000. *Conserving earth's biodiversity.* Washington DC: Island Press.

Wingfield, D. 1999. There are no technological solutions for environment. *The Baptist Standard,* October 20.

Yoder, J. H. 2002. *The Christian witness to the state.* Scottdale, PA: Herald Press.

CHAPTER 5

Judeo-Christian Perceptions of Nature and Its Variability: A Foundation for Environmental Awareness?

Gary E. Belovsky

In light of ever-increasing environmental degradation, concerned individuals are seeking ways in which environmental awareness can be fostered among citizens to help turn the tide. Because the development of a new ethic and its adoption through education takes considerable time and could meet with uncertain success, some individuals propose that preexisting beliefs with which people are already comfortable might be employed to foster environmental stewardship. Because religious beliefs are pervasive in many societies, they might serve this goal. To reach the same goal, others would foster environmental stewardship using preexisting beliefs of hunter/gatherer and subsistence agricultural/pastoral societies, because these people must possess an uncanny knowledge of nature simply to persist given nature's vicissitudes (Diamond 1993), and a "new" environmental ethic might be based on this knowledge (Nabhan and St. Antoine 1993).

Employing preexisting belief systems to foster environmental awareness assumes that these systems as a whole are consistent with environmental stewardship. These beliefs must not provide hollow justification for environmental stewardship based on selected references that can be countered by other references to the tradition. A belief system's failure to consistently support environmental awareness has no relationship to its value in areas other than environmental awareness, such as spirituality, morality, and cultural heritage, but it does undermine its ability to counter the arguments made by forces fostering environmental degradation in the political and economic marketplaces.

Judeo-Christian traditions constitute a convenient foundation for environmental awareness in Western societies, given their pervasive influences through history and today. This tradition not only reflects a strong religious perspective, but many of its tenets are based upon ancestral Hebrew oral traditions, preserved in the book of Genesis, passed down by people who practiced subsistence agriculture and pastoralism. Therefore, at least for Western society, Judeo-Christian traditions may unite religion and subsistence knowledge as a foundation for environmental stewardship (see MacKinnon and McIntyre 1995; Carroll and Warner 1993; Fern 2002).

Adoption of the Judeo-Christian tradition as a foundation for environmental awareness, however, brings its own problems. Lynn White, Jr., (1967) claimed that this tradition is the major cause of environmental degradation in Western civilization because of its devotion to technology. White further argued that devotion to technology stems from biblical passages, especially in Genesis, that convey the tenets that humans have dominion over nature and that nature exists to benefit humans. Therefore, White's thesis has been adopted by some who argue that Judeo-Christian traditions cannot provide a foundation for environmental ethics.

White's thesis concerning the unique environmental destructiveness of the Judeo-Christian tradition can be questioned. First, as Whitney (chapter 1, this volume) points out, his historical interpretations may not be correct. Second, as Haught (chapter 8, this volume) and Rasmussen (chapter 9, this volume) suggest, his use of the common attribution of human dominion over nature in the Bible may be due to selective reading and mistranslation. However, a more basic rationale for refuting White's thesis emerges from the observation that degradation of the environment over the past tens of thousands of years is not restricted to Western civilization or peoples adopting the Judeo-Christian tradition. Whether it was Paleolithic hunters overkilling large mammals (Martin 1973; Mosimann and Martin 1975; Martin and Klein 1984; Belovsky 1988; Alroy 2001) or Mayans farming in unsustainable ways (Deevey et al. 1979), people have an uncanny ability to despoil the environment. Therefore, environmental degradation brought about by people is not restricted to particular cultural traditions, but may be a human proclivity to over-exploit their environment; this casts doubt on employing any preexisting tradition as a foundation for environmental ethics. Nevertheless, pre-existing traditions may still be useful, if viewed from a "behave as I say, rather than I do" perspective.

In this chapter, the Judeo-Christian view of Nature is examined in several ways. First, what is the tradition's attitude towards nature (e.g., balance versus dynamic), and is this supported by environmental science? Second, does the tradition recognize the role of nature in its historical development? Third, were ancient Hebrews limited in their ability to understand how nature influenced them and would this have colored their perspective on nature? Finally, by reflecting on these questions, the Judeo-Christian tradition is examined to determine whether it might serve as a sound foundation for enhancing environmental awareness and stewardship.

WHAT IS THE SCRIPTURAL VIEW OF NATURE?

In a comparison of Judaic, Christian, and Islamic theological writings, Nasr (1996) argues that these traditions hold that the natural world is inherently in a state of benign order or harmony, which is unchanging ("balance of nature"). Furthermore, disruption of this harmony is due to human transgressions against God. This is a common literalist, scripturally based interpretation of nature (Cartmill 1993; Richardson 1998), which differs from White's (1967) interpretation of the Judeo-Christian role in history. Even so, Nasr, like White, claims that part of our transgression may be our faith in secular technology and science, and both would have us solve our ecological crisis by going back to medieval mysticism.

In the "balance of nature" perspective, nature would have been benign for human existence if we had been faithful to God's will (Cartmill 1993). Ultimate disruption of the "balance" occurred when Adam and Eve ate from the forbidden Tree of Knowledge and were driven out of Eden (Genesis 3), while the massive calamity of the Diluvium was God's punishment for sinfulness (Genesis 6:2—11). The book of Isaiah, which is so influential to Christian thought, claims that basic characteristics of nature (e.g., predation, competition, death, etc.) are due to sin (Isaiah 11:6, 65:25), did not exist in the Garden of Eden, and would disappear again if we were faithful to God's will (Cartmill 1993; Richardson 1998; Fern 2002). Extended to uniquely Christian thought, Paul and Augustine adopt this position and further argue that mankind need not be concerned with nature, because all will become right if we just eliminate sin (Cartmill 1993). Therefore, a scriptural notion of a "balance of nature" is an extension of the essential tenet that God acts through history (Redmount 1998), where nature is but one aspect of history and "balance" is a baseline condition against which God's displeasure can be assessed.

This is not to say that scripture does not refer to flux in nature. Reference is made to the natural rhythm of seasonal change and the passing of life (Ecclesiastes 3:1–2; Daniel 2:20–21). People are cautioned to be prepared for periodic drought (Genesis 41:33–36), rain storms (Ecclesiastes 11:3), and devastation by locusts (Joel 1:4). However, flux is not the norm, but a disruption of the expected harmony ("balance of nature") due to sinfulness and God's displeasure (e.g., drought: Deuteronomy 11:17, 28:23–24 and Amos 4:7; rain: James 5:17 and Psalms 38:22; locusts: Deuteronomy 28:38–42). A striking example of this disruption is when the people of Israel suffer drought and plague, not due to general sinfulness, but due to the sins of their kings, such as Saul (2 Samuel 21:1–14) and David (2 Samuel 24:1–25).

In a philosophical review of the "balance of nature" concept, Egerton (1973) argues that it can be found in many traditions throughout the world, and moreover is a very strong element of ancient Hellenistic teachings, which exerted substantial influence on scripture, and which are much more recent than the oral traditions of the ancient Hebrews who lived in a subsistence economy. This raises the question: how much of the portrayal of nature in scripture may reflect uncanny knowledge of nature that is possibly possessed by hunter/gatherer and subsistence agricultural/pastoral people (Diamond 1993)?

The scripturally based idea of the "balance of nature" should not be confused with science's view of balance, where the interplay of conflicting natural forces or processes produce patterns in nature, such as planetary motion, trajectories of falling bodies, and the structure of ecological systems (Levin 1999; Botkin 2001; Pimm 1991). Scientists adopting a more static (equilibrium) or transient (non-equilibrium) perspective still agree that interacting processes produce regularities in nature that can be understood at least after the fact, if not always predicted beforehand.

The above points raise questions about the Judeo-Christian tradition's utility as a foundation for environmental awareness. First, if later Hellenistic perspectives obscure the "uncanny" knowledge of nature that ancient Hebrew hunter/gatherers and subsistence farmer/pastoralists may have possessed, then how much environmental knowledge is relayed in scripture? Second, if a literalist reading of scripture is inconsistent with how we scientifically know that nature operates, then can it provide logical arguments against the forces fostering nature's destruction? A non-literalist reading may claim that human-nature relationships in scripture are parables for how people should follow God's laws, but unless these parables relate explicitly to environmental stewardship, what is the foundation for environmental awareness?

What Is the Role of Nature in Producing the Judeo-Christian Tradition?

Two recent scientific treatises by Diamond (1997) and Fagan (1999) have argued that we are just beginning to understand how environmental changes have influenced and continue to influence various human cultures. These treatises have their foundation in environmental archaeology, which examines how humans interact with environments (Butzer 1971, 1982). In particular, Fagan (1999) has created what is termed historical climatology, which combines new insights from climate studies and ecology with human history. Fagan argues that ecologists, archaeologists, and anthropologists need to pay greater attention to historical climatology in order to understand the past and future of human societies, and how people influence and are influenced by their environment.

I examine three Biblical events that are fundamental to the Judeo-Christian tradition in light of historical climatology: Noah and the Diluvium, Abraham and his wanderings, and the early emergence of Israel. These environmental scenarios are plausible given archaeological and climatological findings. To examine them, one superimposes chronologies from Biblical archaeology and historical climatology, which immediately raises the treacherous issue of the Bible's historical accuracy. Some archaeologists argue that the Bible is a precise historical document, even claiming that most Biblical characters were real (e.g., Dever 2001). While some archaeologists argue that the Bible has little historical validity, most concede that it contains kernels of tradition about real events that have become obscured over time (Redmount 1998; Stager 1998; Isserlin 2001). Consequently, gleaning historical fact from the literary epic of the Hebrew people and their relationship with God is a challenge, but not an insurmountable one.[1]

The goal of this exercise is to demonstrate how environmental changes in the Near East may have influenced the people responsible for the oral traditions that are the foundation for the Bible and Judeo-Christian tradition. This in turn may cast additional light upon the suitability of this tradition as a foundation for a new environmental awareness.

Noah and the Diluvium

Fagan (1999) relates how paleoclimatological and archaeological findings indicate that an onset of cool, dry conditions reduced the carrying capacity of the land to support early agriculturalists and pastoralists in Asia Minor around 6200 BC. This forced people to seek out lake margins, such as the then freshwater Black Sea, for habitation. Warmer, moister conditions returned around 5800 BC, and the Mediterranean's sea level again began to rise as glaciers continued to recede at the end of the last ice age. At this time, a narrow barrier separated the Mediterranean from the freshwater Black Sea, which was 150 meters lower than the Mediterranean. Approximately 5500 BC, the barrier between the Mediterranean and Black Sea gave way and waters from the Mediterranean rushed into the Black Sea. This made the Black Sea saline and flooded extensive low-lying areas in which most people lived and on which they depended for their subsistence. Thus both long-term and gradual climatic fluctuations that repeatedly occurred with each glacial period during the Pleistocene had profound impacts on the biota used by people in their subsistence pastoral and agricultural economies, leading to a rapid and unexpected natural catastrophe. All of these events are today scientifically explainable, but would not have been understood in the same way by the people at the time.

Ryan and Pitman (1998) argue that the above documented environmental changes and catastrophe are the basis for the Biblical story of Noah and the Diluvium, though Fagan (1999) cautions against trying to relate this or any Biblical story to real events. Nonetheless, it is tantalizing that Noah's Ark comes to rest on the mountains of Ararat (Genesis 8:4), a region in present Armenia to the southeast of the Black Sea. Furthermore, it is interesting that the Diluvium story is common to a number of ancient Mesopotamian cultures (e.g., the Gilgamesh epic of Sumer), but not elsewhere, including Egypt (Coogan 1998).

If this environmental scenario is the historical basis for the Noah and Diluvium tradition, it is interesting because it refers to a sudden environmental catastrophe, but not the long-term environmental changes that concentrated people around lake margins and resulted in rising sea waters that led to catastrophe. Perhaps Noah's ancestors and neighbors were only impressed by relatively benign and constant conditions around a lake margin, not drought conditions that had forced them to migrate to and concentrate around lake margins over centuries. Nor do these people seem concerned with a rising nearby sea, probably because their subsistence may not have depended on the Mediterranean. This may reflect an inability to grasp long-term and gradual changes, especially those that did not immediately influence daily existence.

Abraham and His Wanderings

Many archeologists believe that the Amorites of northwest Mesopotamia were the ancestors of the Arameans, the people of Abraham (Isserlin 2001), and the Bible states that Abraham's ancestral home was Haran in this region (Genesis 11:31) (May and Metzger 1965). Haran lies south of the mountains of Ararat, which provides some geographical link to the Diluvium tradition (see above). However, when the Bible first mentions Abraham, he is dwelling in southern Mesopotamia near the city of Ur in the Akkadian empire (Genesis 12:31). Abraham leaves Ur and returns to his ancestral home of Haran before moving to Canaan, the dwelling place promised to him by God (Genesis 11:31). Throughout Genesis, Abraham's son, Isaac, and grandson, Jacob, are referred to as coming from Haran (Genesis 24:10 and 29:4). Many Biblical scholars place the Abraham tradition as arising from the end of the third and early second millennia BC (Isserlin 2001; Pitard 1998). Archaeology and historical climatology provide some interesting associations for Mesopotamia during this period.

At the end of the third millennium BC, there appears to have been extensive drought throughout the Near East, India, and Africa (Fagan 1999; Hassan 1997; Rosen 1997; Hole 1997; Wilkinson 1997; Courty and Weiss 1997; Weiss 1997; Weiss et al. 1993; Butzer 1976). We know that this drought led to the abandonment of villages in northwest Mesopotamia such as Abraham's ancestral home (Haran), where agricultural and pastoral economies relied upon rainfall (c. 2200 B.C.) (Weiss et al. 1993; Wilkinson 1997; Courty and Weiss 1997). We know that the Amorites (ancestors to the Arameans, Abraham's people) migrated into southern Mesopotamia where agriculture and pastoralism would have been less affected by drought, because the Tigris and Euphrates Rivers provided water for livestock and irrigation (Weiss et al. 1993). The drought in northwest Mesopotamia was so severe that villages were not resettled for hundreds of years until c. 1900–1728 BC, when climatic conditions became wetter (Weiss et al. 1993; Wilkinson 1997; Courty and Weiss 1997).

The Akkadian empire in southern Mesopotamia constructed a wall of fortresses called the "Repeller of the Amorites" attempting to accomplish what the name implies (c. 2054–2030 BC) (Weiss et al. 1993). Nonetheless, people from the northwest moved into southern Mesopotamia and settled around major urban centers in Akkad and Sumer. This is where Biblical tradition finds Abraham, near Ur in Sumer. However, the drought also reduced carrying capacity in southern Mesopotamia, and these migrants further strained the ability of the land to support sufficient agricultural and pastoral production (Weiss et al. 1993). As a result, political turmoil developed, and by the nineteenth century BC the Akkadian empire collapsed. One can imagine that Abraham returned to his ancestral home of Haran from Ur because of the social collapse in southern Mesopotamia; in fact, the Bible states that Abraham's life was threatened while in Ur, because he was an outsider. On returning to Haran, Abraham would find a landscape still plagued by drought and unfit for agriculture or pastoralism, which may explain his departure for Canaan.

The link between environmental change and social collapse in the late third and early second millennia BC occurs throughout the Near East, Egypt (Butzer 1976; Hassan 1997; Rosen 1997; see Butzer 1997 for refutation), and the civilizations in India (Possehl 1997). In Egypt, the fall of the Old Kingdom after 2160 BC occurred when agriculture, which depended on the flooding of the Nile, failed as floods annually peaked too early and were too small. Famine resulted and political unrest developed (Butzer 1976; Hassan 1997; Fagan 1999). The Old Kingdom pharaohs claimed to be divine and in control of the Nile's waters; when the pharaohs failed to provide the necessary water, the Old Kingdom fell. Pharaohs in subsequent dynasties still claimed divinity, but never again claimed control of the Nile; rather they became the earthly embodiment of the proper lifestyle (Fagan 1999). Fagan (1999) argues that other societies through history, when based on divine rulers claiming control of the environment, have failed when major environmental changes occurred.

No divine human ruler controls the environment in the Judeo-Christian tradition; only the God of Abraham has this power. In the covenant between God and Abraham, God protects and cares for His people, if they do not transgress. One way that God cares for His people is by maintaining a benign and constant environment. Such a covenant would be attractive to people who have experienced long-term displacement and social upheaval. However, the Bible does not mention the wide-ranging and long-term drought behind the upheaval and displacement. Abraham's people may not have comprehended the long-term and gradual increase in aridity that led to migration to new environs, because it did not immediately influence day to day existence. They may only have understood that they could no longer subsist in southern Mesopotamia with the turmoil or in their ancestral home upon return.

The Early Emergence of Israel

During the thirteenth to tenth centuries BC, there again is evidence of decadal droughts, although less intense and not as widespread as in the third millennium BC (Wilkinson 1997; Maley 1997; Fairbridge et al. 1997; Bryson and Bryson 1997; Lozek 1997; Starkel 1997; Magri 1997; Kayan 1997). These environmental changes again may have taxed the carrying capacity of the land to support agricultural/pastoral economies, and concurrently there was widespread disruption of late Bronze Age societies (Pitard 1998). This was the time of Joshua and Judges when the Hebrews finally gained control of Canaan as promised by God to Abraham, and the nation of Israel formed (Isserlin 2001; Stager 1998; Hackett 1998).

The Hebrews were not the only people moving into Canaan at this time; large-scale movements of other people also threatened the Canaanite status quo, as well as the Egyptian, Assyrian, and Hittite empires (Isserlin 2001; Stager 1998; Hackett 1998). One group of people referred to as the Sea Peoples were probably migrants from the Homeric Mycenaean culture, which collapsed at this time and led to a dark age in Greece (Wood 1985). Biblical Philistines were Sea People moving into Canaan from the west, while the Hebrews moved in from the east; eventually the two met and came into conflict. During this period, Canaanite rulers were nominal vassals of the Egyptian pharaohs and regularly requested military assistance to hold back these migrants. The Canaanite rulers refer to one group of wandering rural people, the Apiru, who are thought by some to be the Hebrews (Pitard 1998; Stager 1998; Isserlin 2001).

This crucial time for the Judeo-Christian tradition may have been a period of turmoil initiated by environmental change. The Bible, however, does not relate these geopolitical events to the environment. Again, these environmental changes were widespread, long-term, and gradual, not sudden, so that people may not have correlated them with societal changes.

Therefore, all of the above Biblical events may have been triggered by known environmental conditions. In fact, these environmental events may not have been unusual, but typical of long-term climatic patterns in the Near East—patterns that science is just beginning to decipher by understanding current climatic processes and by using these to reconstruct past climates.

Short-term Climatological Processes in the Near East

Only recently have we started to gain an understanding of how oceanic water temperatures and salinity create changing patterns in ocean currents and how one wide-ranging pattern (El Nino/Southern Oscillation or ENSO) created by these currents may operate (Fagan 1999). A few years ago, ENSO was recognized for its ability to create droughts and floods on the Indian subcontinent and to cause the collapse of Peruvian fisheries, but now its influence on wet, dry and warm, cool conditions in many regions has been documented. Today, one can hardly view an issue of *Science* or *Nature* without finding something new about ENSO or how oceanic currents influence climate. The ecological effects of these climatic fluctuations is only beginning to be realized (Stenseth et al. 2002).

Our growing understanding of ENSO has led to a realization that it creates self-enhancing conditions so that a combination of particular temperature and salinity conditions persists for a period of time before "jumping" to an alternate combination of conditions, and then "jumping" back again. This creates a pattern of oscillations in the associated climatic conditions for the landmasses influenced by ENSO. In the Near East, periods of drier and wetter conditions appear with a four to ten year frequency and with dramatically varying intensity (Fagan 1999).

ENSO's periodic climatic shifts were in part recognized in Biblical times, because mariners of the Arabian Sea commented on them, as they influenced winds and thereby the ability to sail to and trade with the Indian subcontinent (Fagan 1999). Nonetheless, these people did not recognize that periodic droughts (Genesis 41:33–36) that created famine and accompanying disease outbreaks (Deuteronomy 11:17, 28:23–24; Amos 4:7; Leviticus: 26:26; James 5:17), periodic severe rain storms (Ecclesiastes 11:3; Psalms 38:22, 135:7; Job 37; James 5:17), and periodic locust plagues (Deuteronomy 28:38–42) might be a consequence of the climatic fluctuations that we today call ENSO. However, these are not the long-term or massive climate changes associated above with pivotal Biblical events.

Long-term Climatological Patterns in the Near East

The ENSO climatic pattern is observed in Near Eastern geological deposits (von Rad et al. 1999; Bar-Matthews et al. 1999; Bajjali and Abu-Jaber 2001). However, self-enhancing processes, like ENSO, not only produce basic oscillations between alternate states, but can also produce longer-term emergent oscillations. Paleoclimatological studies in the Near East indicate emergent oscillations occurring with 750–, 250–, 125–, 96–, 56–, 45–, 39–, 30–, 26–, and 14–year periodicity that lead to ENSO being wetter or drier than average (von Rad et al. 1999).

While ENSO is the underlying climatic "machine" in the Near East, it also is modified by other long-term environmental events. For example, large amounts of cold freshwater from melting continental ice sheets were added to the oceans starting at the end of the last period of glaciation (c. 13,000 BC). This influx of cold freshwater changed the oceans' salinity and temperature, and thereby modified ENSO and the climatic patterns that it produced.

Observed long term wet/dry cycles in the Near East have been questioned by some scientists (Butzer 1997; Bottema 1997), but most believe that they are real (Weiss 1997). These changes were not instantaneous but required decades or centuries to be manifested on the biota and cultures. It is the protracted effects of these environmental changes that lead to the confusion over their importance to human societies (Weiss 1997). This may also explain why biblical authors did not recognize them or comment on their importance.

How Much Did Biblical Authors Understand about Environmental Change?

People during the times and in the environs in which Judeo-Christian traditions first developed were able to associate short-term environmental changes with the land's ability to support them (i.e., carrying capacity). Egyptians during the third millennium BC erected columns along the Nile to mark flood levels, which were used to predict the availability of water and thereby the amount of land that should be farmed (Butzer 1976). This was an early application of statistical forecasting, because flood levels affected agricultural production. Amounts of food to be stored had to be based on past shortfalls in production (Genesis 41: 33–36); while taboos on the harvesting of adult wild birds and fruit had to be related to the next year's production (Leviticus 19:23–25, 25:4; Deuteronomy 22:6–7). These actions manage risk for short-term phenomena, where cause and effect could be established with minimal data or synthesis.

The massive environmental changes associated with biblical events are different from short-term associations made by biblical people. Long-term and gradual changes do not provide immediate associations between the environment and events: the Diluvium must be an act of God because of its suddenness. The breakdown of the land separating the Mediterranean from the Black Sea could not have been anticipated through the slow increase of the Mediterranean sea level. Reduction in carrying capacity due to the droughts of 8200–7800 BC, the third millennium BC, and again in the thirteenth to tenth centuries BC occurred slowly, but when carrying capacity failed, it was conflict between resident and displaced people that was the problem, and this consequence must be God's will.

We have begun to understand long-term climatic patterns in the Near East and elsewhere, because weather records have been accumulated and sophisticated methods have been used to analyze them. ENSO was not identified until the late nineteenth century when British bureaucrats in India had to deal with recurrent famines. They began to correlate weather patterns with crop production and establish a system of weather stations (Fagan 1999). Later, scientists began to investigate ENSO's underlying processes, which required long-term data of greater precision and improved computational capabilities (Fagan 1999). However, we still cannot precisely forecast ENSO, because its self-enhancing character is chaotic (i.e., deterministic, but unpredictable without knowledge of initial conditions) (Fagan 1999). Chaotic dynamics were not identified until the 1960's (Gleick 1987). None of this was available to biblical people.

Without prior knowledge of long-term climatic oscillations, like ENSO, it is even more daunting to identify how climate might influence human populations. A simple mathematical model that is commonly used to portray populations (Hutchinson 1948, 1978; May 1973; Renshaw 1991) can be employed to illustrate how people would have difficulty associating annual weather conditions with the environment's ability to sustain them if there are long-term climatic oscillations. The basic model has a population growing asymptotically to an environmentally determined maximum number (i.e., carrying capacity) (fig. 5.1a). This is called density dependent population growth, because growth diminishes as the population approaches carrying capacity. However, the diminished population growth as carrying capacity is approached may not be due to current population numbers, but past numbers (i.e., time-lagged response), if population members respond to the conditions they experienced while maturing (e.g., past stresses on growth or reproduction) or carrying capacity is temporarily reduced by large populations (e.g., recovery of overexploited resources is inhibited). In this case, the asymptotic approach to carrying capacity becomes oscillatory, with the oscillations increasing in severity and becoming cyclic as the time-lag increases (fig. 5.1b). Furthermore, these oscillations tend to become even more severe and cyclic if birth and death processes occur at particular times, such as seasonally or at specific ages (i.e., discrete dynamics). This can produce oscillations that regularly repeat over time or become chaotic (fig. 5.1c). All of the above traits are typical of human populations. Finally, a varying carrying capacity can be imposed on the population, such as that produced by an environment driven by short-term ENSO cycles and its emergent longer-term cycles.

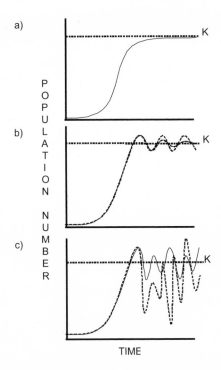

Figure 5.1. Possible population dynamics emerging from the model are plotted. With simple density dependence (a), the population smoothly approaches carrying capacity (K). With time-lagged density dependence (b), the population either approaches K with damped oscillations (solid line) or cyclically overshoots and undershoots K (dashed line), as time lag increases. With discrete growth and density dependence (c), the population can exhibit cycles of varying periodicity (solid line) or can appear to randomly oscillate (chaos: dashed line) as growth rate increases.

To illustrate what the scenario described above would mean for the ability of people to predict how the environment influenced their population, a population model (Hutchinson 1948, 1978; May 1973; Renshaw 1991) with the following parameters was used:

1. Maximum human population growth measured for subsistence agriculture/pastoralism (~0.04% per annum; Hassan 1981; Angel 1975; Deevey 1960).

2. Environmental cyclicity for the strongest cycles observed in the Middle East (250, 125, 56, 26, 14 and 4 years; von Rad et al. 1999).
3. Time lags dependent on subsistence mode. (For pastoralism or harvesting of wild plants there is no time lag, because livestock or wild plant production is directly linked to current precipitation. However, as agriculture becomes more sophisticated, time lags increase. Storage of crop surpluses produce approximately five-year lags given technologies in the third through first millennia BC. Fallowing and irrigation ameliorate drought effects but diminish long term agricultural production by soil degradation and salination, which produce ten- to one hundred–year time lags).

What might biblical people conclude? A simple intuitive approach, like the ancient Egyptian logic of measuring Nile flood levels to predict agricultural production, plots the current environmentally determined carrying capacity with current population number (fig. 5.2). A positive relationship with little scatter indicates strong environmental control of population. This is not observed except perhaps for environments of long periodicity (about 250 year) and small lag times (less than 20 years). Therefore, simple intuition might lead biblical people to conclude that some unperceivable force, rather than the environment, controls their population or fate as a people. However, the population model generating the relationship between carrying capacity and population numbers (as seen in fig. 5.2) is driven by environmental changes, so simple intuition fails.

With a long-term database and more sophisticated computations, the failure of simple intuition can be overcome. First, a population's density dependent response is more important than total numbers, so annual population growth rate should be examined (current population less last year's population divided by last year's population). Second, annual population growth rate is not a reflection of current carrying capacity but past carrying capacity set by the time lag. A plot of the above values would produce a negative relationship with little scatter if the environment exerts a strong influence on the population. This is observed for all time lags and cycles (fig. 5.3). This simple analysis can be conducted, because the population model, time lags, and cycles are known. Without this knowledge, sophisticated computer analyses are necessary to identify the underlying environmental causes. Is it any wonder that biblical people might not associate pivotal events with environmental changes that are now known to have occurred?

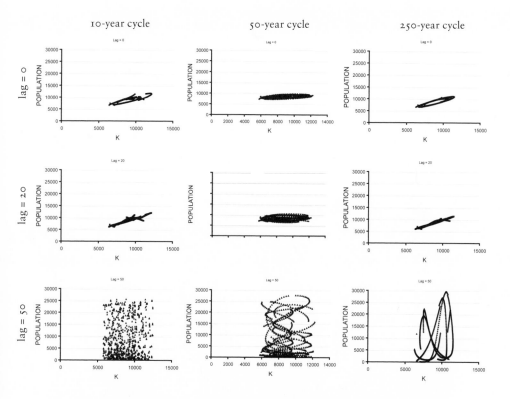

Figure 5.2. The simple relationship between carrying capacity and population number from the data generated by the model are plotted. Carrying capacity is varied with environmental cycles of 10-, 50-, and 250-year periodicity and the population is allowed to exhibit time lags in density dependence of 0, 20 and 50 years.

The environment of pastoralists and agriculturalists in the third to first millennia BC in the Near East was far more complicated than portrayed in the above population model. First, different climate cycles interacted to amplify the wet, dry conditions (Fagan 1999; von Rad et al. 1999). This was not identified until paleoclimates over tens of thousands of years were reconstructed. Second, the economies of people in the Near East during this period influenced population dynamics in more complex ways than the model portrays (Wilkinson 1997). Nonetheless, the model illustrates how environmental influences can be obscured.

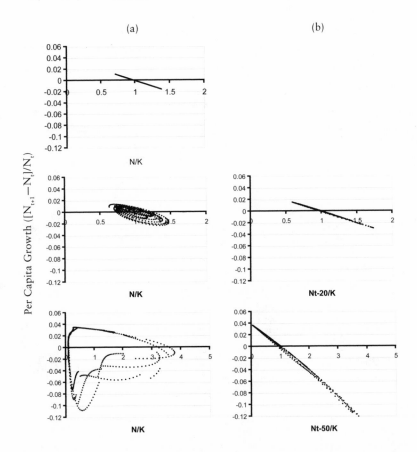

Figure 5.3. Using the data generated from the model with carrying capacity (K) cycling with 50 year periodicity and 0-, 20-, and 50-year time lags in density dependence (L), (a) the relationship between population number relative to carrying capacity (N/K) and per capita population growth rate $([N_{t+1}-N_t]/N_t)$ is plotted; (b) the same data are plotted when the population number relative to carrying capacity is time lagged by the appropriate value (N_{t-L}/K) in the model.

WHAT CAN WE LEARN FROM THE BIBLICAL DEPICTION OF NATURE?

Pivotal events were almost certainly influenced by environmental changes that were not recognized by biblical people. They did recognize short-term environmental influences from drought, floods, and locusts. Yet they persisted in attributing constant harmony or "balance" to nature. The biblical "balance" may not be literal, but a parable to portray God's influence. However, there may be another explanation based on a nomadic pastoral heritage. The ancient Greeks' ancestors were also nomadic pastoralists, and Hellenistic thought held the same view of nature (Egerton 1973, 2001a, 2001b). Perhaps, rather than the Biblical view arising from Hellenistic thought, a common perspective was fostered by nomadic pastoralism.

Subsistence pastoralists should be aware of environmental fluctuations, because animal forage and resulting animal production will respond to environmental factors like rainfall. A nomadic lifestyle can ameliorate environmental variation, if movement between different habitat types and regions leads to more constant environmental conditions. For example, the proximity of hill and plain habitats in Canaan and migration between these areas ameliorated the impact of variable rainfall for pastoralists (Isserlin 2001), as did the Greek landscape. Therefore, a sense of environmental "balance" or constancy could emerge with a nomadic lifestyle.

A nomadic lifestyle and resulting environmental constancy disappear as population increases and movements are restricted because other people are already resident and bar access. In such cases, environmental change leads to social conflict, and the latter is blamed for disruptions, rather than environmental change. Populations grow and conflict increases as agriculture is adopted and becomes more sophisticated. Recognition of the environment's influence becomes even more obscured, because time lags increase. Therefore, a past with a smaller population becomes idyllic, a Garden of Eden, because stresses were less pronounced in a more constant environment due to mobility. Perhaps, the "balance of nature" is a collective memory of these conditions.

To this point, environment has referred to natural events such as drought; however, as human population increases, environmental degradation can emerge. Therefore, the environment not only affects people, but people affect the environment. Today, human impacts are evident: global climate change, ozone depletion, desertification, deforestation, lost soil fertility, and lost biodiversity. Human impacts have occurred for millennia, but the Bible reflects very little on this, as it does not with environmental impacts on people. Again, anthropogenic impacts are presented as a departure from "balance" due to God's displeasure.

Desertification, loss of soil fertility, and deforestation were recognized in ancient Mesopotamian official records (Olson 1981), but were merely referenced and not associated with drought, irrigation, or overexploitation. In the Bible, natural reforestation, something we consider beneficial, is viewed as a punishment from God, because productive fields were lost (Isaiah 29:17, 32:15, 32:19). Loss of soil fertility is not understood as arising from human overexploitation but as punishment from God for sins such as murder, rape, and sexual improprieties (Deuteronomy 11: 16–17, 28:15–19, 29:22–28; Jeremiah 4:23–28; Hosea 4:2–3; Leviticus 18:24–28). While there are protestations against people fouling land and water (Ezekiel 32:2, 34:18–19), in other passages, it is viewed as a punishment for sin (Revelations 8:8–10, 16:3–4).

Large losses of biodiversity occurred in the Near East over the millennia in which biblical tradition developed. In Syria, gazelles went extinct from hunting by agriculturalists as early as the fourth millennium BC (Legge and Rowley-Conwy 1987). Lions, wolves, and bears were common in biblical times (2 Kings 17:25–26). However, the Bible makes no mention of these losses occurring well before Christ, even though a medieval pilgrim commented on the novelty of hearing a lion near Haifa (Isserlin 2001). Biblical cautions against overexploiting game and fruit (Deuteronomy 22:6–7; Leviticus 19:23–25), even against the destruction of an enemy's fruit trees during warfare (Numbers 13:20; Deuteronomy 20:19–20), refer to the immediate impact on subsistence, not any long-term notion of conservation and sustained productivity.

Biodiversity losses, as well as other environmental degradations, caused by people can require a long time to reach a critical threshold before those degradations (e.g., extinction) become rapid (Gilpin and Soulé 1986). Therefore, Biblical people may not have been able to associate their actions with the effects they produced, just as they were unable to do for long-term natural changes.

The Bible and Environmental Awareness

In summary, the Bible may present environmental attitudes of a people unable to identify how environmental changes affected their lives, and a view of "nature's balance" emerging from a lifestyle heritage (nomadic pastoralism) that no longer applied to their circumstances. All traditions reflect the ability of its founders to define their world and a collective cultural memory; therefore, any tradition's utility to increase awareness about modern technical problems may be limited. This assessment applies to the Judeo-Christian tradition as well as to hunter/gatherer traditions of indigenous peoples.

With increasing environmental destruction by growing human populations, more demanding technologies, and accumulating impacts, some individuals are calling for a new environmental ethic to stave off projected environmental disasters (e.g., Leopold 1966). Judeo-Christian traditions with roots in the Bible are an attractive foundation for environmental ethics because of the tradition's pervasiveness in Western civilization. Lynn White (1967) and E. O. Wilson (2002), who attribute environmental degradation in part to Judeo-Christian attitudes, admit this utility. However, aside from expediency, the Judeo-Christian tradition may not be appropriate given its unscientific portrayal of nature and frequent disregard for environmental influences. This raises questions about using biblical tradition to foster environmental awareness.

First, a literal reading of scripture most often portrays nature as hostile towards people, because it is God's instrument for punishment (Nasr 1996; Richardson 1998). Furthermore, scripture treats nature strictly as a source of human sustenance. This is not surprising since the Bible is the epic saga of a heroic people and their covenant with God as told by third to first millennia BC shepherds and farmers. How can this tradition foster environmental "friendliness," when nature is viewed as either hostile or simply utilitarian?

Second, an ethical tenet ("reasonableness") starting with Plato and employed by most subsequent philosophers is that moral schemes cannot be based on premises that are false, because this would discard reason (Fern 2002). The stricture of "reasonableness" does not require ethical schemes to be based on science (i.e., faith is allowed); however, schemes must be consistent with existing knowledge. This questions whether Judeo-Christian traditions, or any traditions, that cannot correctly define the role of environment on people or the role of people on the environment can serve as a rational foundation for environmental awareness. How can this tradition foster environmental awareness, when it does not correctly identify the interplay between people and the environment (cf. Fleming, chapter 7, this volume)?

Many individuals overlook the above difficulties in adopting past traditions as a foundation for environmental awareness and ethics. Whether traditional religious perspectives like Judaism, Christianity, and Islam (e.g., Nasr 1996; Richardson 1998) or more radical perspectives of eco-logical theology and deep ecology (e.g., Zimmerman 1987; King 1989; Hinsdale 1991; Himes and Himes 1990; Clifford 1992; Cobb 1988; Swimme 1988; Macy 1988; Fern 2002) are advocated, modern science is de-emphasized, because it defines nature too narrowly. The unifying theme of these perspectives is that science through a materialistic quest for mechanistic explanations demystifies nature, makes it inanimate, and perceives it as having no purpose. In addition, scientific knowledge is viewed as partial truths that do not justify rejection of belief systems that are counter to it. Ultimately, a higher plane of perception about nature that mandates moral protection of the environment is sought, and science is viewed as counter to this goal. Higher planes might include the notion that nature reflects God's beneficence so that its destruction is an affront to God, or that animals are sentient and thus have rights like humans, or that ecosystems have purpose and evolution is directed, reflecting God's will and requiring protection (Fern 2002).

Issues of nature's sentience, purposefulness, and directedness, how-ever, are counter to scientific evidence (Simpson 1967), and thus violate the stricture of "reasonableness." Furthermore, the claim that nature re-flects God's beneficence, so that its destruction is an affront to God, is faith-based and cannot be scientifically tested, which makes it no more than a personal belief.

Final cautions in applying any tradition to foster environmental aware-ness need to be set forth. First, traditions must be invoked carefully and consistently. For example, Luke 12:41—48 is cited by some environmen-tal ethicists as justification for stewardship of the earth; however, this passage, which calls for the care of one's master's property and to be pre-pared for the master's return, is usually interpreted by theologians as being prepared to answer to God upon death or the second coming. Sec-ond, many Judeo-Christian writings that refer to nature are not accepted as canonical by many who believe in the tradition (e.g., the New Testa-ment by Jews, the Apocrypha by many Protestants, or the writings of Christian hermit mystics; Nasr 1996). Third, more environmentally friendly retranslations may be self-serving or lose their relevance to past thought. For example, if human dominion over nature in Genesis is rein-terpreted as human care of nature (e.g., Cobb 1988; Himes and Himes 1990), this must be carefully researched and even so may not reflect how the tradition was practiced for millennia. Fourth, one must deal with ele-ments of traditions that are not environmentally "friendly." For example, while increasing human populations ultimately underlie most environmental problems, the Bible repeatedly advocates human fertility (e.g., Genesis: 1:28, 9:1, 9:7). Finally, because environmental degradation is worldwide and faced by all cultures, an environmental ethic suitable for all people, not just a single culture, is desirable.

All of the difficulties listed for basing environmental ethics on preexisting traditions, as well as the fact that all cultures have produced environmental destruction, lead some to seek new paradigms. Suggestions include our innate love of nature, our dependence on nature, and our evolutionary heritage with nature (biophilia: Wilson 1984, 1996, 1998; Kellert and Wilson 1993). Most are based on a premise that there is a scientific basis for environmental protection, especially an evolutionary imperative. For example, the noted environmental ethicist, Holmes Rolston III (1993) goes so far as to claim that evolutionary science mandates conservation of other species because all species share a large proportion of genes. These paradigms are termed natural philosophy or religious naturalism (Wilson 1998; Fern 2002).

The new paradigms focus solely on the well-being of nature, which is contrary to anthropocentric perspectives of religious-based environmental ethics, like the Judeo-Christian tradition, that stress justice, health and safety, goods and property, and economic development for people (American Baptist Churches 1989; Interfaith Council for Environmental Stewardship 1999; John Paul II 1990; United States Conference of Catholic Bishops 1991). Religious-based environmental ethicists also criticize the new paradigms because they do not provide an ultimate moral imperative—one can justify destroying something that is loved under appropriate conditions, but not if its destruction is forbidden by God—the Socratic dilemma of ethics based on reason alone versus faith (Fern 2002).

The new paradigms are revolutionary, but they are akin to some religious-based environmental ethics. St. Francis of Assisi advocated concern for all living things as our brothers and sisters, a oneness with nature (Himes and Himes 1990). St. Francis's view is contrary to traditional Judeo-Christian perspectives presented by St. Paul and Augustine in which worldly concerns are sinful and nature is of no matter (Cartmill 1993). While Lynn White (1967) lays blame for environmental degradation on the Judeo-Christian tradition, he endorses the revolutionary religious-based environmental ethics of St. Francis. John Paul II (1990) named St. Francis the patron saint of ecology. However, St. Francis's teachings are not the mainstream Judeo-Christian tradition upon which others would base environmental ethics (see MacKinnon and McIntyre 1995; Carroll and Warner 1993; Fern 2002).

Perhaps the ethics needed to address current environmental problems must be revolutionary. Nearly nine hundred years before St. Francis, St. Basil the Great (AD 329–379) was instrumental in developing theology on the Trinity, the divinity of Christ, and the importance of the Holy Spirit, and he advocated an even more revolutionary environmental attitude:

> O God, enlarge within us the sense of fellowship with all living things, our brothers, the animals, to whom thou gavest the earth as their home in common with us. We remember with shame that in the past we have exercised the high dominion of man with ruthless cruelty, so that the voice of the earth, which should have gone up to thee in song, has been a groan of travail. May we realize that they live not for us alone but for themselves and for thee and that they love the sweetness of life. (as cited in Fern 2002, 241)

NOTE

1. For example, one might view biblical patriarchs as lineages or tribes, not as individuals (Isserlin 2001). The challenge of assessing Biblical historicity is no more or less controversial than attempts to document other ancient tales, such as the *Iliad* and *Odyssey* (Wood 1985).

WORKS CITED

Alroy, J. 2001. A multispecies overkill simulation of the end-Pleistocene mega-faunal mass extinction. *Science* 292:1893–96.
American Baptist Churches. 1989. Policy statement on ecology: An ecological situational analysis. General Board of the American Baptist Churches.
Angel, J. L. 1975. Paleoecology, paleodemography and health. In *Population, ecology, and social evolution*, ed. S. Polgar, 167–90. The Hague: Mouton.

Bajjali,W., and N. Abu-Jaber. 2001. Climatological signals of the paleoground-water in Jordan. *Journal of Hydrology* 243:133–47.

Bar-Matthews, M., A. Ayalon, A. Kaufman, and G. J. Wasserburg. 1999. The eastern Mediterranean paleoclimate as a reflection of regional events: Soreq cave, Israel. *Earth and Planetary Science Letters* 166:85–95.

Belovsky, G. E. 1988. An optimal foraging-based model of population growth in hunter-gatherers. *Journal of Anthropological Archaeology* 7:329–72.

Botkin, D. B. 2001. *No man's garden: Thoreau and a new vision for civilization and nature.* Washington DC: Island Press.

Bottema, S. 1997. Third millennium climate in the Near East based upon pollen evidence. In Dalfes, Kukla, and Weiss 1997, 489–515.

Bryson, R. A., and R. U. Bryson. 1997. High resolution simulations of regional Holocene climate: North Africa and the Near East. In Dalfes, Kukla, and Weiss 1997, 565–93.

Butzer, K. W. 1971. *Environment and archeology: An ecological approach to prehistory.* 2nd ed. Chicago: Aldine Publishing Company.

———. 1976. *Early hydraulic civilization in Egypt: A study in cultural ecology.* Chicago: University of Chicago Press.

———. 1982. *Archaeology as human ecology.* Cambridge: Cambridge University Press.

———. 1997. Sociopolitical discontinuity in the Near East c. 2200 B. C. E.: Scenarios from Palestine and Egypt. In Dalfes, Kukla, and Weiss 1997, 245–96.

Carroll, J. E., and K. Warner. 1993. *Ecology and religion: Scientists speak.* Quincy, IL: Franciscan Press.

Cartmill, M. 1993. *A view to death in the morning: Hunting and nature through history.* Cambridge, MA: Harvard University Press.

Clifford, A. M. 1992. Feminist perspectives on science: Implications for an ecological theology of creation. *Journal of Feminist Studies in Religion* 8:65–90.

Cobb, J. B., Jr. 1988. Ecology, science, and religion: toward a postmodern world-view. In *The reenchantment of science: Postmodern proposals,* ed. D. R. Griffin, 132–64. Albany: State University of New York Press.

Coogan, M. D. 1998. In the beginning: the earliest history. In *The Oxford history of the biblical world,* ed. M. D. Coogan, 3–24. New York: Oxford University Press.

Courty, M. A., and H. Weiss. 1997. The scenario of environmental degradation in the Tell Leilan Region, NE Syria, during the late third millennium abrupt climate change. In Dalfes, Kukla, and Weiss 1997, 107–47.

Dalfes, H. N., G. Kukla, and H. Weiss, eds. 1997. *Third millenium BC climate change and old world collapse.* NATO ASI series, vol. 149. Berlin: Springer-Verlag.

172   Gary E. Belovsky

Dever, W. G. 2001. *What did the biblical writers know and when did they know it? What archeology can tell us about the reality of ancient Isreal.* Grand Rapids, MI: Eerdemans Publishing Co.

Deevey, E. S., Jr. 1960. The human population. *Scientific American* 203: 195–204.

Deevey, E. S., Jr., D. S. Rice, P. M. Rice, H. H. Vaughan, M. Brenner, and M. S. Flannery. 1979. Maya urbanism: Impact on a tropical karst environment. *Science* 206:298–306.

Diamond, J. 1993. New Guineans and their natural world. In Kellert and Wilson 1993, 251–71.

———. 1997. *Guns, germs, and steel.* New York: W. W. Norton & Company.

Egerton, F. N. 1973. Changing concepts of the balance of nature. *Quarterly Review of Biology* 48:322–50.

———. 2001a. A history of the ecological sciences: Early Greek origins. *Bulletin of the Ecological Society of America* 82:93–97.

———. 2001b. A history of the ecological sciences, part 3: Hellenistic natural history. *Bulletin of the Ecological Society of America* 82:201–5.

Fagan, B. 1999. *Floods, famines, and emperors: El Niño and the fate of civilizations.* New York: Basic Books.

Fairbridge, R., O. Erol, M. Karaca, and Y. Yilmaz. 1997. Background to Mid-Holocene climatic change in Anatolia and adjacent regions. In Dalfes, Kukla, and Weiss 1997, 595–610.

Fern, R. L. 2002. *Nature, god, and humanity: Envisioning an ethics of nature.* Cambridge: Cambridge University Press.

Gilpin, M. E., and M. E. Soulé. 1986. Minimum viable populations: Processes of species extinction. In *Conservation biology: The science of scarcity and diversity,* ed. M. E. Soulé, 19–34. Sunderland, MA: Sinauer Associates, Inc.

Gleick, J. 1987. *Chaos: Making a new science.* New York: Viking Press.

Hackett, J. A. 1998. "There was no king in Israel": The era of the judges. In *The Oxford history of the biblical world,* ed. M. D. Coogan, 132–64. New York: Oxford University Press.

Hassan, F. A. 1981. Food production and population density. In *Demographic archaeology,* ed. F. A. Hassan, 39–50. New York: Academic Press.

———. 1997. Nile floods and political disorder in early Egypt. In Dalfes, Kukla, and Weiss 1997, 1–23.

Himes, M. J., and K. R. Himes. 1990. The sacrament of creation: Toward an environmental theology. *Commonweal* 117 (2): 42–49.

Hinsdale, M. A. 1991. Ecology, Feminism, and Theology. *Word and World* 11 (2): 156–64.

Hole, F. 1997. Evidence for Mid-Holocene environmental change in the Western Khabur drainage, Northeastern Syria. In Dalfes, Kukla, and Weiss 1997, 39–66.

Hutchinson, G. E. 1948. Circular causal systems in ecology. *Annals of the New York Academy of Sciences.* 50:221–46.

———. 1978. *An introduction to population biology.* London: Yale University Press.

Interfaith Council for Environmental Stewardship. 1999. *The Cornwall Declaration on Environmental Stewardship.* Available at http://www.stewards. net/CornwallDeclaration.htm (last accessed Sept. 2005).

Isserlin, B. S. J. 2001. *The Israelites.* Minneapolis: Fortress Press.

John Paul II, Pope. 1990. Peace with God the creator, peace with all of creation. Message for the celebration of the World Day of Peace, available at http:// www.vatican.va (last accessed September 2005).

Kayan, I. 1997. Bronze Age regression and change of sedimentation on the Aegean Coastal Plains of Anatolia (Turkey). In Dalfes, Kukla, and Weiss 1997, 431–50.

Kellert, S. R., and E. O. Wilson. 1993. *The biophilia hypothesis.* Washington DC: Island Press.

King, Y. 1989. The ecology of feminism and the feminism of ecology. In *Healing the wounds: The promise of ecofeminism,* ed. J. Pant, 132–64. Toronto: Between the Lines.

Legge, A. J., and P. A. Rowley-Conwy. 1987. Gazelle killing in stone age Syria. *Scientific American* 257:88–95.

Leopold, A. 1966. The land ethic. In *A Sand County almanac: With essays on conservation from Round River,* 237–64. New York: Ballantine Books.

Levin, S. 1999. *Fragile dominion: Complexity and the commons.* Cambridge, MA: Perseus Publishing.

Lozek, V. 1997. Development of sediments, soils, erosional events, molluscan and vertebrate assemblages in connection with human impact in Central Europe during the time span 3,000–5,000 BP. In Dalfes, Kukla, and Weiss 1997, 551–64.

MacKinnon, M. H., and M. McIntyre, eds. 1995. *Readings in ecology and feminist theology.* Kansas City: Sheed & Ward.

Macy, J. 1988. The ecological self: Postmodern ground for right action. In *Readings in Ecology and Feminist Theology,* ed. M. H. MacKinnon and M. McIntyre, 259–69. Kansas City: Sheed and Ward.

Magri, D. 1997. Middle and late Holocene vegetation and climate changes in peninsular Italy. In Dalfes, Kukla, and Weiss 1997, 517–30.

Maley, J. 1997. Middle to late Holocene changes in tropical Africa and other continents: Paleomonsoon and sea surface temperature variations. In Dalfes, Kukla, and Weiss 1997, 611–40.

Martin, P. S. 1973. The discovery of America. *Science* 179:969–74.

Martin, P. S., and R. G. Klein, eds. 1984. *Quaternary extinctions: A prehistoric revolution.* Tucson: The University of Arizona Press.

May, H. G., and B. M. Metzger, eds. 1965. *The Oxford annotated Bible with the Apocrypha*. New York: Oxford University Press.

May, R. M. 1973. *Stability and complexity in model ecosystems*. Monographs in Population Biology 6. Princeton, NJ: Princeton University Press.

Mosimann, J. E., and P. S. Martin. 1975. Simulating overkill by Paleoindians. *American Scientist*. 63:304–13.

Nabhan, G. P., and S. St. Antoine. 1993. The loss of floral and faunal story: The extinction of experience. In Kellert and Wilson 1993, 229–50.

Nasr, S. H. 1996. *Religion and the order of nature: The 1994 Cadbury Lectures at the University of Birmingham*. New York: Oxford University Press.

Olson, G. W. 1981. *Soils and the environment: A guide to soil surveys and the applications*. New York: Chapman and Hall.

Pimm, S. L. 1991. *The balance of nature: Ecological issues in the conservation of species and communities*. Chicago: University of Chicago Press.

Pitard, W. T. 1998. Before Israel: Syria-Palestine in the Bronze Age. In *The Oxford history of the biblical world*, ed. M. D. Coogan, 25–57. New York: Oxford University Press.

Possehl, G. L. 1997. Climate and the eclipse of the ancient cities of the Indus. In Dalfes, Kukla, and Weiss 1997, 193–243.

Redmount, C. A. 1998. Bitter lives: Israel in and out of Egypt. In *The Oxford history of the biblical world*, ed. M. D. Coogan, 58–89. New York: Oxford University Press.

Renshaw, E. 1991. *Modelling biological populations in space and time*. Cambridge Studies in Mathematical Biology 11. Cambridge: Cambridge University Press.

Richardson, J. 1998. *The spiritual roots of our ecological crisis—was Lynn White right?* Available at http://www.btinternet.com/j.p.richardson/lynnwhite.html (last accessed September 2005).

Rolston, H, III. 1993. Biophilia, selfish genes, shared values. In Kellert, and Wilson 1993, 381–414.

Rosen, A. M. 1997. Environmental change and human adaptational failure at the end of the Early Bronze Age in the Southern Levant. In Dalfes, Kukla, and Weiss 1997, 25–38.

Ryan, W., and W. Pitman. 1998. *Noah's flood: The new scientific discoveries about the event that changed history*. New York: Simon & Schuster.

Simpson, G. G. 1967. *The meaning of evolution: A study of the history of life and its significance for man*. New Haven, CT: Yale University Press.

Stager, L. E. 1998. Forging an identity: The emergence of Ancient Israel. In *The Oxford history of the biblical world*, ed. M. D. Coogan, 90–131. New York: Oxford University Press.

Starkel, L. 1997. Environmental changes in Central Europe 5000–3000 BP. In Dalfes, Kukla, and Weiss 1997, 531–50.

Stenseth, N. C., A. Mysterud, G. Ottersen, J. W. Hurrell, K. S. Chan, and M. Lima. 2002. Ecological effects of climate fluctuations. *Science* 297: 1292–96.

Swimme, B. 1988. The cosmic creation story. In *The reenchantment of science: Postmodern proposals,* ed. D. R. Griffin. Albany: State University of New York Press. 47–56.

United States Conference of Catholic Bishops. 1991. Renewing the earth: An invitation to reflection and action on environment in light of Catholic social teaching. Available at http://www.nccbuscc.org/sdwp/ejp/bishopsstatement. htm (last accessed Sept. 2005).

von Rad, U., M. Schaaf, K. H. Michels, H. Schulz, W. H. Berger, and F. Sirocko. 1999. A 5000-yr record of climate change in varved sediments from the oxygen minimum zone off Pakistan, northeastern Arabian Sea. *Quarternary Research* 51:39–53.

Weiss, H. 1997. Late third millennium abrupt climate change and social collapse in West Asia and Egypt. In Dalfes, Kukla, and Weiss 1997, 711–23.

Weiss, H., M. Courty, W. Wetterstrom, F. Guichard, L. Senior, R. Meadow, and A. Curnow. 1993. The genesis and collapse of third millennium north Mesopotamian civilization. *Science* 261:995–1004.

White, L. 1967. The historical roots of our ecological crisis. *Science* 155: 1203–7.

Wilkinson, T. J. 1997. Environmental fluctuations, agricultural production and collapse: A view from Bronze Age Upper Mesopotamia. In Dalfes, Kukla, and Weiss 1997, 67–106.

Wilson, E. O. 1984. *Biophilia*. Cambridge, MA: Harvard University Press.

———. 1996. *In Search of Nature*. Washington DC: Island Press.

———. 1998. The return to natural philosophy. In *Ecology and religion: Scientists speak,* ed. J. E. Carroll and K. Warner, 39–51.Quincy, IL: Franciscan Press.

———. 2002. *The future of life*. New York: Alfred A. Knopf.

Wood, M. 1985. *In search of the Trojan War*. New York: Facts on File Publications.

Zimmerman, M. E. 1987. Feminism, deep ecology, and environmental ethics. *Environmental Ethics* 9:21–44.

CHAPTER 6

Disturbance, the Flux of Nature, and Environmental Ethics at the Multipatch Scale

Peter S. White

The earth's environments and ecosystems are not fixed but vary over a wide range of space and time scales (Delcourt, Delcourt, and Webb 1982; see also fig. 6.1). At the scale of tens of thousands of years, the wobble of the Earth on its axis causes variation in the solar radiation received at the earth's surface, driving variation in climate. On shorter time scales, the Southern Oscillation of sea surface temperature in the eastern Pacific influences precipitation over large areas, causing floods at some locations and droughts at others. Change can be as gradual as the movement of continents and the uplift of mountain ranges and as abrupt as hurricanes and earthquakes. Because change is characteristic, present-day ecosystems must be understood in the context of their histories (Foster, Knight, and Franklin 1998), for example, in the context of ancient ice ages (Davis and Shaw 2001) and recent fires (Covington et al. 1999). The ubiquity of change raises the issues that are the subject of this chapter—the relationship of ecosystem dynamics, conservation management, and environmental ethics.

Among the most important sources of change at middle scales of space and time are natural disturbances (White and Jentsch 2001). These disturbances operate within the scales of our own lifespans and management choices, and a representative list of such events immediately suggests their relevance to humans, as well as to natural ecosystems: hurricane, fire, flood, drought, avalanche, and volcanic eruption. While it is easy to view such disturbances as destructive (and they certainly have been viewed as punishments inflicted on the human race, as Belovsky points out in chapter 5 of this volume), these events are also part of the natural order—they have been recurrent, and many species are adapted to them. Natural disturbances can play a rejuvenating role in ecosystems, often increasing soil resources, plant growth, and reproduction of disturbance-dependent species. Many ecosystems depend on a pattern of disturbance for their composition, structure, and species diversity (White and Harrod 1997).

The importance of disturbance as a natural process in ecosystems has helped bring about the shift from the "balance of nature" paradigm to

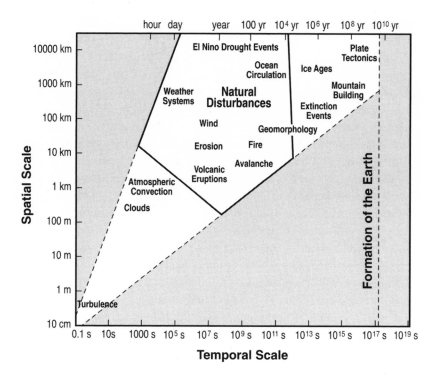

Figure 6.1. Variability in ecosystems occurs at a wide range of spatial and temporal scales. Natural disturbances occur over a broad area at middle space and time scales (from http://www.env.leeds.ac.uk/envi2150/oldnotes/lecture5/lecture5.html).

the "flux of nature" paradigm (Pickett, Parker, and Fiedler 1992; Callicott 2002). The balance of nature paradigm holds that ecosystems progress toward equilibrium states when free of human influence, that
disturbances are external and rare, that integrated communities composed of the most adapted species occur in undisturbed conditions, and
that such communities are self-perpetuating. The flux of nature paradigm holds that ecosystems are frequently disturbed in relation to the
lifespans of the organisms present and thus are always in a state of response to previous disturbances, that disturbances are caused by factors
both external and internal to the ecosystem, that species of early succession are just as "adapted" as species of late succession (albeit to different
conditions), that communities are not tightly integrated, and that some
communities are regenerated only through disturbance. The flux of nature paradigm suggests that we cannot find the basis for conservation
management and environmental ethics in an eternal, equilibrium, unchanging, and prehuman natural condition. Where, then, can we find
this basis?

   In this essay, I present the basic concepts of disturbance ecology and
an overview of recent findings in this field. I illustrate these concepts and
findings through fire ecology in Great Smoky Mountains National Park,
North Carolina and Tennessee, a landscape my collaborators and I have
studied for over twenty years. I then return to questions about the flux of
nature. The flux of nature is a nonequilibrium view, but the persistence
of repeated dynamic sequences has, interestingly, suggested the possibility of larger scale, if locally dynamic, stability (White, Harrod, et al.
1999). The disturbance literature also raises questions about the human-
nature relationship. How similar are human disturbances to natural dynamics? How do human and natural disturbances interact? How do
humans affect the ability of ecosystems to respond to natural disturbances and climate change?

   Throughout this essay, my assumption is that the conservation of biological diversity is a fundamental goal underlying environmental ethics.
The premise of this assumption is that biological diversity supports
human well-being, that species have rights to exist, or both (Callicott
1994). Nature supports human well-being by providing "ecosystem services" such as clean water, resistance to soil erosion, and pollination, and
by providing direct benefits, both tangible (e.g., medicinal plants, fish
and wildlife, and timber) and intangible (e.g., beauty and the sense of
awe). In contrast, species-rights arguments justify conservation without

regard to human benefit. This approach is represented by the U.S. Endangered Species Act which, in theory, protects all species regardless of value to humans (although the act now also requires consideration of the costs of protection in human economic terms).

Biological diversity has been defined in two ways (White and Nekola 1992). The narrow definition of biological diversity is simply the number of species present. The broader definition recognizes that species diversity itself depends on genetic diversity within species, interactions between species, and the diversity of habitats and environments at larger spatial scales (Noss 1990). In this discussion, I have biological diversity in the broadest sense in mind. A fundamental proposition about diversity is that the resilience of nature—the ability to respond to future changes—is dependent on diversity. Genes, species, and habitat diversity all depend on a diverse array of conditions, some of them created by disturbance, and broaden the range of possible responses to future change. In the largest sense, diversity provides yet another ecosystem service—the ability to respond to a world in flux.

Basic Concepts of Natural Disturbance

Definition

Disturbance has been defined in relative and absolute senses (White and Pickett 1985; White and Jentsch 2001). The relative definition defines disturbance relative to the normal dynamic domain of an ecosystem; thus some ecologists have reached the conclusion that "fire is not a disturbance in the prairie, absence of fire is the disturbance." The problem with this definition is that it assumes normal conditions can be defined. In fact, prairie fires are not all alike (there is considerable year to year and seasonal difference) and a single fire leaves behind a patchwork of varying effects. Given climatic variation, normalcy depends on the temporal scale on which it is assessed. Finally, the relative definition diverts attention from the measurable and absolute impacts of a given disturbance and hence is a poor starting point for studies of the mechanisms of disturbance response.

A widely used absolute definition is that disturbance is a "discrete event in time that disrupts ecosystem, community, or population structure and changes resources, substrate, or the physical environment" (White and Pickett 1985, 7). The emphasis here is on the changes caused, although the degree of disturbance is relative to two characteristics: discreteness relative to the ecosystem under study and amount of change relative to the conditions of the pre-disturbance ecosystem. An easily grasped subset of the White and Pickett (1985) definition is that of Grime (1979): disturbance is a destruction of biomass. The destruction of biomass often opens space for new colonization, releases resources formerly contained in biomass, and creates new structures (e.g., arrangements of organic matter in the ecosystem). This definition applies to disturbance, whether natural, human, or the result of an interaction of human and natural factors.

Disturbance Regime

Disturbances vary tremendously—both within and between kinds of disturbance. This variation is described by the parameters of the disturbance regime under six categories: kind (for example, wind, fire, flood), spatial characteristics (for example, the size of the area affected and its position on the landscape), temporal characteristics (for example, frequency and season), specificity (for example, affecting larger plants, as wind does, or smaller ones, as ground fires do), magnitude (the amount of biomass affected), and synergisms (the interactions between disturbances, as when one disturbance, like wind damage, influences the occurrence of another disturbance, like fire) (White, Harrod, et al. 1999). Some characteristics are correlated: frequency is often inversely correlated with magnitude. Some authors have asked whether the highest magnitude disturbances (large, infrequent disturbances or LIDs) are a special disturbance case (Foster, Knight, and Franklin 1998; Romme et al. 1998) (see fig. 6.2).

Recent Disturbance Findings

Since the 1970s, there has been a burst of ecological interest in disturbance. This has resulted in the development of rich empirical detail about the way disturbances work. In the following paragraphs, I describe eight exciting areas of recent disturbance research.

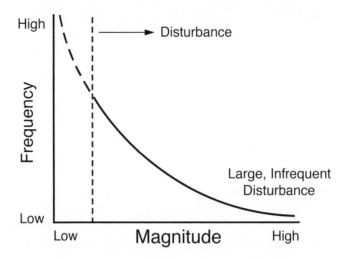

Figure 6.2. The inverse relationship of disturbance frequency and magnitude can be used to define "disturbance" and "Large, Infrequent Disturbances" (from White and Jentsch 2001).

Disturbance and succession. Ecologists at first saw disturbance as a mechanism for setting succession back to earlier stages. However, it is now clear that disturbance can have all possible effects on succession, depending on disturbance specificity—that is, whether disturbances affect all plants equally or have different effects depending on the disturbance property called specificity, namely, the size, age, or species affected (White, Harrod, et al. 1999). Disturbances that prevent the establishment of new or smaller individuals, like frequent fires in grasslands, hold succession in check. Disturbances that remove early successional dominants and release late successional species, such as wind disturbance in stands dominated by light-demanding trees, advance succession. Disturbances that remove dominant species and open up space for colonization of early successional species, such as crown fires in old stands, set succession back to earlier stages.

Some disturbances increase resource availability because they remove dominant competitors, thus reducing use of soil resources and light, and result in the mineralization of nutrients held in living biomass (Vitousek 1984). Succession in these situations is termed secondary succession because soil remains as a substrate. In contrast, the erosional zone of debris avalanche scars may be left with no soil and low nutrient availability controlled only by the very slow process of rock weathering. Where no soil remains, succession is termed primary succession. Secondary successions are, of course, faster than primary successions because of the soils and resources present. Differences in successional starting point are differences in the legacy of the predisturbance ecosystem (see below) and are the result of differences in disturbance magnitude.

Disturbance-climate relations and regional synchronicity. Variation in climate causes variation in the incidence of disturbance (Clark 1988; Johnson and Larsen 1991; Swetnam 1993). For example, Swetnam and Betancourt (1990) showed that the total area burned in Arizona and New Mexico was approximately ten times higher in La Niña years than in El Niño years, with severe fire years approximately at six-year intervals. What is particularly important about this finding is that climate systems synchronize dynamics over large spatial regions—a bad fire year in one area of the Southwest is a bad fire year in all areas of the Southwest. This regional synchronicity causes stress to management agencies.

Ecosystem legacy. Disturbances vary in magnitude and thus in the kinds, amounts, and arrangement of organic matter and living organisms that are present and respond after the disturbance. The impact of the previous ecosystem on subsequent response is called ecosystem legacy (Swanson and Franklin 1992). Legacy consists not only of the organic matter, soil resources, and living organisms and their propagules, but also creates new structures, like pits and mounds from treefall, that influence response. Legacy is one key to ecosystem response to disturbance. The influence of legacy typically decreases with time since disturbance.

Synergisms. Disturbances interact. In many cases, repeat disturbances are likely, as when wind damage allows insect or fungal attack, or when insect damage increases the risk of severe fire (White, Harrod, et al. 1999). Sometimes one disturbance diminishes the chance of another, as when avalanche scars become fire breaks in mountain lodgepole pine forests or when a severe fire consumes so much organic matter that subsequent fire is unlikely (Veblen et al. 1994). Sometimes, the age and state of the ecosystem determine its vulnerability to disturbance such that disturbance probability is initially low but increases with time. A feedback to time-since-disturbance would exert an ecosystem effect to make disturbances more regular in occurrence.

Natural disturbance and human influences. Where once we conceived of presettlement North America as wilderness with minimal human influence, we now are discovering that Native Americans had substantial influence in many areas (Samuels and Betancourt 1982). Particularly with regard to fire, past human influence blurs the distinction between natural and human disturbances.

Landscape effects, pattern, and process. Disturbance creates pattern in ecosystems (e.g., the distribution of disturbed and undisturbed patches), but the pattern of ecosystems also alters the process of disturbance (Turner, Gardner, et al. 1989). This effect can be either to increase or decrease disturbance rate. For example, an ecosystem that is fire prone but surrounded by fire breaks is less likely to burn (Veblen et al. 1994), but an ecosystem that is fire resistant may nonetheless burn if surrounded by ecosystems that allow intense fires to develop. In a particularly well-developed example, Bergeron and Brisson (1990) have shown that islands in boreal forest lakes have different fire regimes than the surrounding mainland—they escape the infrequent but large and intense boreal forest fires but, particularly if they are high and attract lightning, have more frequent but lower intensity fires. As a result, red pine can only survive on the islands and not on the mainland.

Mechanisms of disturbance action and response. The last several decades have produced a wealth of empirical details about species response to disturbance. Fire effects vary with the heat generated, flame height, and the speed of movement—thus we have to study fire in terms of specific and variable effects rather than as a single phenomenon (Ryan 2002). In terms of species response, Vogl (1974) suggested classifying species not as early or late successional, but rather, with reference to specific disturbance events, as increasers, decreasers, invaders, retreaters, and neutrals. In this sense, no single disturbance event (and no particular human management action) is good for all species. Too much disturbance can be as bad for biological diversity as too little; maintaining all species will require a mix of conditions.

Nonindigenous species. Recent research has shown that disturbances can increase the rate of invasion of alien pest species by opening
up space and increasing resources. Because alien species invasion is one
of the key threats to biological diversity, this complicates the job of managers seeking to reintroduce disturbance for native species. Some exotic
species invaders can greatly change the disturbance regime. For example,
alien trees in the Florida everglades can transpire more water into the atmosphere than the native plants, thus lowering the water table, drying
organic matter, and making subsequent fires hotter (Bodle, Ferriter, and
Thayer 1994). Introduced grasses in the American Southwest have altered the fire regime there (Billings 1990).

DISTURBANCE, FIRE, AND PINE ECOSYSTEMS
IN GREAT SMOKY MOUNTAINS NATIONAL PARK

Great Smoky Mountains National Park illustrates these concepts and
the attendant questions for conservation management and environmental
ethics. The park is about two thousand square kilometers and protects
about five percent of the high mountain region along the border of North
Carolina and Tennessee. Unlike western national parks, Great Smoky
Mountains National Park was established through state purchases of private land. About one third of the park consists of forests not directly disturbed by people, and thus the park protects some of the finest old growth
in the eastern United States. The remainder had been disturbed by farming or logging when the park was established in 1934.

Although the Smokies are famous for their old-growth forests, natural
disturbances were always important, including wind, fire, flood, avalanche, and insect attack (Harmon, Bratton, and White 1983). Even old-
growth forests are maintained as a diverse mix of species with different
strategies through gap phase dynamics, that is, the dynamics that occur
on individual patches after the death of a canopy tree (Busing and White
1993; White, MacKenzie, and Busing 1985).

Disturbances play many ecological roles in the Smokies. Some plant
species cannot reproduce in the undisturbed forest, while at the same
time other species depend on undisturbed areas. High species diversity
requires both conditions. Second, some animal species move between
and depend upon both disturbed and undisturbed patches. Black bears
often den in the hollow parts of old-growth trees, yet also depend on

areas in which recent fires have stimulated berry production. Third, disturbances serve to connect terrestrial and aquatic ecosystems. Fire and wind disturbances in the forest influence the many characteristics of stream habitats: amount of woody debris, light availability, temperature, and nutrient status. These characteristics, in turn, influence stream organisms.

Fire was historically important in the national park, and its reduction, through fire suppression beginning about 1940, has resulted in changes to ecosystems (Harmon 1982; Harrod et al. 2000). The most fire-prone ecosystems, originally dominated by pine, have increased size and abundance of trees, shifted composition, and reduced diversity. Whereas managers have little influence on such disturbances as wind, flood, and avalanche, managers have had a large influence on fire. In the late 1990s, managers began the experimental reintroduction of fire to restore native species and ecosystems.

Historically, fire frequency varied with topography, increasing from moist valleys and lower slopes to ridges, but also decreasing from low to high elevations (Harmon, Bratton, and White 1983). Fires were thus most important on low and mid-elevation ridges. On these sites, fires ranged from frequent low intensity ground fires at 5–12 year intervals that killed understory seedlings and saplings but not overstory trees, to rare intense fires at 80–150 year intervals that caused high mortality and removed leaf litter and organic matter from the soil surface (fig. 6.3). Pine stands depended on both kinds of fire: the frequent ground fires kept out invading hardwoods but did not kill the overstory pine, and the intense fires allowed pine seedling establishment (which requires both light and open mineral soil without a covering of leaf litter) (White 1987). With fire suppression, size and abundance have increased in pine stands, and composition is shifting to hardwood dominance, with a gradual decline in fire-tolerant species (Harrod, Harmon, and White 2000).

Disturbance interactions are evident in pine stands—intense fires are more likely in drought years (and thus in La Niña years) and on high woody fuel levels after southern pine beetle attack (White 1987). The beetle is a native insect that targets mature trees, so as postfire stands age they also become more vulnerable to beetle attack. Overstory trees die in a relatively short period of time and, as they drop branches and needles, produce high fuel loads.

Disturbances in pine stands also illustrate the many ways disturbances influence succession. Frequent ground fires killed hardwood seedlings

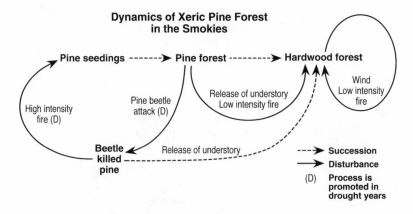

Figure 6.3. Pine and fire interactions on low and midelevation ridges in Great Smoky Mountains National Park (modified from White 1987).

and saplings invading pine stands from less fire-prone (moister) habitats, thereby holding succession in check. In the absence of fire, wind and the southern pine beetle are disturbances that advance succession because they kill the older pines and release understory hardwoods. Intense fires in older or beetle-killed pine stands set succession to an early stage and initiate pine regeneration.

Landscape pattern also probably influenced fire occurrence. Lower elevation pine stands are larger and closer together in the landscape. We can conjecture that one fire can spread from stand to stand and that many pine stands will have their origin from a single fire. At higher elevations, pine stands become more restricted to ridges. Isolated pine stands may each require a separate lightning strike, and such stands may burn in separate fires. However, regional droughts may cause all ridges to have high probability of burning in the same years.

Reduced fire frequency in the park has changed stand composition and structure, thereby altering legacy and response to management fires. For example, as the invading hardwoods age, they develop a thicker bark and become tolerant of fires that would have killed them in an earlier period (Harmon 1984). Thus, fire no longer decreases hardwood density and does not initiate pine regeneration. We may also be losing fire legacy in the form of the dormant seed bank of fire-dependent species. While the jury is still out (only a few fires have been set in the Smokies, and only in the last few years), reintroducing fire alone may not restore diversity because suppression has altered forest structure.

As elsewhere, fire in the Smokies encourages invasion by invasive exotics, most noticeably the Japanese princess tree, *Paulownia tomentosa*. Managers seek to develop a fire-management plan that doesn't also promote invasive species. Research is now underway to see if the season or intensity of the fire affects how much princess tree invasion occurs.

Finally is the issue of naturalness (White and Bratton 1980; Sprugel 1991): is fire a natural process in the park and should the National Park Service reintroduce fire? Both Native Americans and European settlers burned the forest in the period before park establishment in 1934. The problem with treating fire as a purely human disturbance, however, is that human-set fires would also change the occurrence of natural fire. In some cases, human-set fires may have simply replaced natural fires that would have burned. However, human-set fires may have differed from natural fires in season and intensity. We do know that many plant species depend on fire (for reproduction and establishment), that these species have decreased during fire suppression, and that these species certainly predate the arrival of Native Americans some twelve thousand years ago, thus suggesting the importance of fire in the prehuman era. While our view of the past is qualitative and clouded, managers have proceeded to reintroduce fire to the park.

SCALE, DISTURBANCE, AND DYNAMIC EQUILIBRIUM

One of the issues raised by disturbance ecology and fire ecology in the Smokies is the issue of spatial scale. Let's start by defining two scales (White and Jentsch 2001): the patch scale (the area affected by the particular disturbance event) and the multipatch scale (the landscape scale, which consists of many patches with various histories and times since disturbance) (see fig. 6.4). Patches that differ in age and disturbance history also differ in the species present, resource levels, and environmental factors. The multipatch scale thus contains many different species, resource levels, and environments. Indeed, disturbance is important because it creates an array of different age states and thus adds to the diversity of habitats present across a landscape. The multipatch scale is

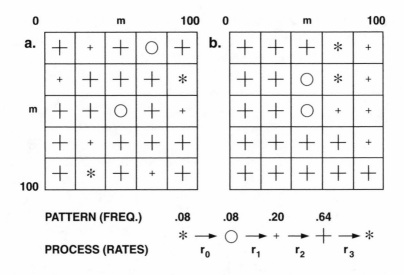

Figure 6.4. Diagrammatic representation of the patch and multipatch scales. Each square in the checkerboard represents one patch. Each patch can be in one of four states which are connected by a successional pathway (labeled r_0 to r_3). The patch states are as follows: * (dead trees), O (seed colonization stage), + (young trees), + (mature trees). The two diagrams represent (a) patch types randomly distributed in space, and (b) patch types spatially clustered because the patch size of disturbance is larger than in (a).

critical to the maintenance of species diversity and to thinking about the role of disturbance—and, I will argue, is also critical to human ethical choice. In the Smokies, the multipatch scale encompasses many pine stands and the intervening stands of hardwoods on less fire-prone sites.

Recognizing the patch and multipatch scales allows us to ask not only about the dynamics of individual patches but also the properties of larger spatial scales. Consider the average biomass at the multipatch scale as an average across all patches (Shugart 1984). Younger patches have lower biomass than older patches. Though younger patches mature into older patches, thereby increasing biomass, older patches can be converted to younger patches through disturbance, decreasing biomass. The average across many independent patches will vary less through time than the values at the patch scale. As I describe below, the average through time need not be constant—it can exhibit what I will term bounded variation, that is, a characteristic but ultimately limited variation about the average. The notion of dynamic stability is appealing because it suggests at large scales all species and successional ages are persistent despite great change at the patch scale. That persistence is obviously a characteristic conservation managers desire.

Even the early disturbance literature recognized the possibility of large-scale dynamic equilibrium (Watt 1947). For example, Heinselman's (1973) shifting mosaic concept was one in which the locus of disturbance shifts continually in space, but the total amount of land in any one successional age class remains constant. The term "patch dynamics" (Thompson 1978) was coined for the class of dynamics that included those within patches and the interaction among patches. Within patch dynamics, we distinguish two forms of potential equilibrium: quantitative and qualitative equilibrium (see fig. 6.5). Quantitative equilibrium (also called shifting mosaic or steady-state equilibrium) is a stricter form of equilibrium in which the distribution of age states at the multipatch scale is constant. Qualitative equilibrium (also called persistence equilibrium) is less stringent in that all species and stages are always present but may fluctuate considerably in abundance.

While studies of large spatial and time scales are not frequent, nature supplies examples of both quantitative (e.g., gap dynamics in old-growth forests of the Great Smoky Mountains) and qualitative (e.g., fire regime in the Yellowstone National Park) equilibrium (Turner, Romme, et al. 1993). However, superimposed on these dynamics, climate variation and human influence alters the underlying disturbance regimes. Hence, qualitative equilibrium is generally more likely than quantitative equilibrium and even qualitative equilibrium may be absent at time scales in excess of five hundred or several thousands of years.

Pickett and Thompson (1978) provided another conservation perspective on dynamic stability: spatial scale needed to support that stability. They argued that nature reserves had to be large enough to include a minimum dynamic area—if they were too small relative to the scale of disturbance, then the natural dynamic pattern would be lost. The nature reserve would be dominated by one or only a few age states, and species of other states would be eliminated (Baker 1992). If a preserve is too small for natural dynamics, managers must attempt to manage disturbance in a way that all species and age states would survive. Since there is a cost to management, nature reserves ought to be large enough for minimal management intervention.

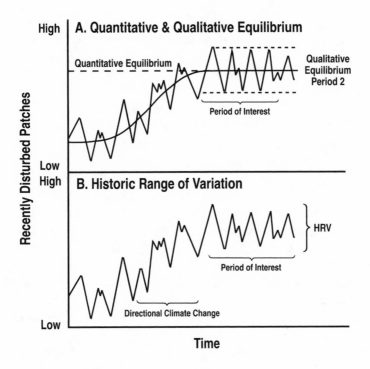

Figure 6.5. Patch dynamic equilibrium: (A) quantitative equilibrium and qualitative equilibrium, and (B) the historic range of variation or range of natural variability (from White and Walker 1997).

In order to develop targets for ecosystem management, ecologists have sought to define the "historic range of variation" or the "natural range of variability" for particular ecosystems (fig. 6.5; see also Landres, Morgan, and Swanson 1999; White and Walker 1997). This corresponds to the concept of the qualitative equilibrium for particular landscapes—the range of conditions (spatial and temporal variability) that they would have possessed under historic disturbance regimes. Like the concept of qualitative equilibrium, this suggests that nature exhibits bounded rather than unconstrained flux, at least when disturbance regimes and climate do not themselves vary greatly.

In the Smokies, we know that the pine ridges are now outside the bounds of historic variation. Fire frequency is lower, tree size and abundance are higher, composition is shifting, and fire-dependent species are declining (Harrod, Harmon, and White 2000). However, we have neither a long temporal record nor a very detailed picture of the spatial pattern and incidence of fire. In the absence of this information, managers are more likely to manage for species and habitat diversity than for natural process or historic range of variation. This becomes management for persistence of species and successional states and thus is implicitly a form of management for qualitative or persistence equilibrium. However, minimum dynamic area is certainly met in the Smokies. The park is large enough to contain many age states of the pine ecosystem at any one time.

THE CHALLENGE TO ENVIRONMENTAL ETHICS FROM THE FLUX OF NATURE AND MULTIPATCH SCALES

Flux causes two paradoxes in nature preservation: we seek to preserve ecosystems that must change and we often must extend the human hand, in the form of management, into ecosystems we want to see free of human influence (White and Bratton 1980). Fire management in the Smokies is an example of these paradoxes in that park establishment brought fire suppression and thus ongoing loss of pine stands. Fire management involves human-set fires, but what kind of fire (e.g., season and intensity) do we use? These paradoxes represent one of the challenges that the flux of nature brings to environmental ethics.

A related challenge is that, since nature is in flux, there appears to be no reference state by which to evaluate human-caused change. If ecosystems are dynamic and long-term climatic instability causes continual change, it is easy to view human-caused changes as just another and analogous source of change. A final challenge is represented by the multipatch scale: while a property of interest (biological diversity, in this case) has a behavior at the patch scale, it also has a behavior at the multipatch scale. Dynamic changes at the patch scale may not be correlated with dynamic patches at the multipatch scale. This makes observations at the patch scale potentially misleading and conclusions based on small-scale, short-term observations potentially wrong. Indeed, the behavior at the patch scale may, itself, be a function of patch dynamics at larger scales. How do we think about ethics at this scale, particularly when individual actions at the patch scale cannot be judged on their own terms without reference to their contribution to the whole?

The Dilemma of Flux

Given my assumption that environmental ethics seeks behavior that conserves biological diversity, biological diversity itself becomes the metric for evaluating human and natural changes. Some human-caused changes may, in fact, mimic natural disturbances and support biological diversity. Ecologists have proposed that logging be based on natural disturbance patterns (Franklin and Forman 1987; Hansen et al. 1991; Bergeron et al. 2002). We also know that diversity depends on low intensity human cultural influence in some landscapes (e.g., the southern Appalachian grassy balds; see White and Sutter 1998; White 1984). At the other end of the spectrum, some natural changes may be so outside the adaptations of species that diversity is lost (e.g., the asteroid impacts that have caused mass extinctions in the past). In this regard, the intensity and scale of disturbance is more important than whether its cause can be unambiguously found in humans or nature. Unfortunately, the scale and intensity of human disturbances often does indeed lie outside the bounds of natural variability and the evolved range of responses of the biota. Fire in the Smokies is a good example: fire in the 1920s developed on huge pre-park clearcuts and, in this high rainfall region, resulted in so much post-fire soil erosion that some sites are still unforested seventy-five years after the fires. Clearly those fires were outside the natural range of variability in the park in terms of size and intensity. The general conclusion is this: we must not accept the analogy between natural and human disturbance uncritically but must ask about the absolute nature of that change.

The idea of qualitative equilibrium implies the recurrence of disturbance in space and time in a way that allows continued, though shifting, presence of all species and successional states in a patch dynamic state. Human action can result in a destabilization of this patch dynamic, by increasing or decreasing the frequency of disturbance (affecting which species can reproduce) and by increasing or decreasing the distance among patches (affecting which species are able to disperse among patches). If humans increase homogeneity (of age states) and decrease diversity, the range of possible species responses is reduced and the resilience at larger scales decreases. In this sense, humans cause not just change, but, potentially, a reduced capacity of the ecosystem to respond to change, as well.

Multipatch Ethics

Because individual patches experience drastic changes even without human influence, the important outcomes of flux (e.g., diversity) cannot reside at the patch scale but are, rather, properties of the multipatch scale. Death and destruction at the patch scale can be part of birth and renewal at the multipatch scale. If we have an egalitarian view of species, then because different species require different patch conditions, we need a collection of patches in different states for all species to persist. The challenge to environmental ethics is that the ethical value does not reside at the patch scale, but at the multipatch scale.

Multipatch ethics can be illustrated in this way. Suppose that a student picks a native wildflower, for example an aster, and brings it to one of my classes. Was this a right or wrong action? At the patch scale, it can be argued the action was wrong because it deprives the plant of potential reproduction and robs the pollinator of a potential food source. However, asters, after long selection under various disturbances, often produce new flowering heads after loss. The reproductive contribution of a single group of flowers to the future of the population is low in this species. One could also argue that the aster improved the indoor environment—and enlivened the class. Given the premise that we want to maintain biodiversity, the more important question of rightness or wrongness is at the larger scales—if one student picks one plant out of a large population on a single day, the effect is small, but if thousands of students picked plants every day, the loss of reproduction, as well as the trampling of the soil, would lower future reproduction and the population would decline, ultimately until the species was extinct from campus. Clearly, the rightness and wrongness of the action can only be judged by sustainability at the multipatch scale.

We can extend this reasoning to an even larger scale. Suppose asters are eliminated from campus. This becomes less significant to biological diversity if asters still persist in wilder habitats beyond campus. The campus population might have a small impact on the future of the species.

Also, the campus once had more populations than it does now—my classroom facility itself replaced some native habitat and many species with it, yet classrooms are clearly needed if we are going to train conservation biologists. The answer to these dilemmas lies at broader scales: a balance must always be struck between human effects at the patch scale and the persistence of biological diversity at larger scales. There are biological constraints, determined by the tolerance of the species present to habitat loss and fragmentation, as well as tolerance to direct impacts on the quality of remaining habitats (e.g., pollution). Further, it is clear that the greater the number of populations (e.g., of asters) the more resistant the species is to extinction. It is also clear that humans rarely have considered the patch versus multipatch balance until populations have been so reduced that the species is on the verge of extinction. So, what is the right scale and the right balance? The answers to these questions are likely to be different for different species and different ecosystems and different if we consider long-term climate change versus short-term persistence. We simply need to collect the information needed to answer the questions in different circumstances.

Multipatch ethics suggests that ethics of individual, patch-scale action is less important than the ethics of collective action at the multipatch scale. It is possible for an action at the patch scale to be judged on its own terms—whether the intensity of disturbance at the patch scale exceeds the tolerance and response of species that respond to disturbance—but it is at the multipatch scale that this evaluation is most critical. Because the species have a finite range of tolerances as the result of their evolutionary history, there is likely to be a strong historic or "precedence" component to response. Thus, from an ethical point of view, we must also ask questions such as: Are human actions inside or outside the historic range of variation? Are they inside or outside the tolerances of species present?

SYNTHESIS: SOCIETY AND THE FLUX OF NATURE

What principles should we take away from this discussion? I propose three. First, we should accept natural disturbances as important forces and support their restoration where needed. Second, we should not put human life and property in disturbance's way—we should avoid building on earth's shifting sands, eroding and migrating coastlines, steep unstable slopes, floodplains, and fire-prone sites. Third, we should conserve the ability to respond to dynamics itself by conserving diversity. Ultimately this is based on the proposition that resilience derives from diversity.

The management of nature for dynamics may seem a daunting task. What if we can't conserve nature in a way that supports a dynamic equilibrium? Can we substitute human disturbances? How right do you have to get the disturbance regime (White and Walker 1997)? How tolerant are species and ecosystems to some variation in disturbance and dynamics? What scale of conservation is critical? These are important questions and, although I suspect that species and ecosystems are moderately tolerant, we do not have good answers to these questions in a quantitative sense. Our job, however, is not to complete the job for all time—indeed, future climatic change is inevitable. Rather, our job is more like the passing of a baton rather than the completion of a race. Even when we can't solve all conservation problems for all time, we must remember that our job is to pass ecosystems along in the best state we can. One fundamental goal is expressed by Leopold's First Law of Tinkering—we must save all the pieces. This translates to saving variation in species and habitats and thus the processes, such as disturbance, that create the conditions for that variety. This rests on the dictum that diversity itself is a resource for future adaptation and future response to change.

Works Cited

Baker, W. L. 1992. The landscape ecology of large disturbances in the design and management of nature reserves. *Landscape Ecology* 7:181–94.

Bergeron, Y., and J. Brisson. 1990. Fire regime in red pine stands at the northern limit of the species' range. *Ecology* 71:1352–64.

Bergeron, Y., A. Leduc, B. Harvey, and S. Gauthiere. 2002. Natural fire regime: A guide for sustainable management of the Canadian boreal forest. *Silva Fennica* 36:81–96.

Billings, W. D. 1990. *Bromus tectorum*, a biotic cause of ecosystem impoverishment in the Great Basin. In *The earth in transition*, ed. G. M. Woodwell, 301–22. Cambridge: Cambridge University Press.

Bodle, M. J., A. P. Ferriter, and D. D. Thayer. 1994. The biology, distribution, and ecological consequences of *Melaleuca quinquenervia* in the Everglades.

In *Everglades: The ecosystem and its restoration,* ed. S. Davis and J. Ogden, 341–55. Delray Beach FL: St. Lucie Press.

Busing, R. T., and P. S. White. 1993. Effects of area on old-growth forest attributes: implications for the equilibrium landscape concept. *Landscape Ecology* 8:119–26.

Callicott, J. B. 1994. Conservation values and ethics. In *Principles of Conservation Biology,* ed. G. K. Meffe and C. R. Carroll, 24–49. Sunderland, MA: Sinauer Associates.

———. 2002. From the balance of nature to the flux of nature: The land ethic in a time of change. In *Aldo Leopold and the Ecological Conscience,* ed. R. L. Knight and S. Riedel, pp. 91–105. Oxford: Oxford University Press.

Clark, J. S. 1988. Effect of climate change on fire regimes in northwestern Minnesota. *Nature* 334:233–35.

Covington, W., W. A. Niering, E. Starkey, and J. L. Walker. 1999. Ecological restoration and management: Scientific principles and concepts. In *Ecological stewardship: A common reference for ecosystem management,* ed. N. C. Johnson, A. J. Malk, W. T. Sexton, and R. Szaro, 2:599–617. Kidlington: Elvesier Science.

Davis, M. B., and R. G. Shaw. 2001. Range shifts and adaptive responses to quaternary climate change. *Science* 292:673–79.

Delcourt, H. R., P. A. Delcourt, and T. Webb III. 1982. Dynamic plant ecology: The spectrum of vegetation change in space and time. *Quaternary Science Reviews* 1:153–76.

Foster, D. R., D. H. Knight, and J. F. Franklin. 1998. Landscape patterns and legacies resulting from large, infrequent forest disturbances. *Ecosystems* 1:497–510.

Franklin, J. F., and R. T. Forman. 1987. Creating landscape patterns by forest cutting: Ecological consequences and principles. *Landscape Ecology* 1: 5–16.

Grime, J. P. 1979. *Plant strategies and vegetation processes.* Chichester: Wiley and Sons.

Hansen, A. J., T. A. Spies, F. J. Swanson, and J. L. Ohman. 1991. Conserving biodiversity in managed forests: Lessons from natural forests. *Bioscience* 41:382–92.

Harmon, M. E. 1982. The fire history of the westernsmost portion of Great Smoky Mountains National Park. *Bulletin of the Torrey Botanical Club* 109:74–79.

———. 1984. Survival of trees after low-intensity surface fires in Great Smoky Mountains National Park. *Ecology* 65:796–802.

Harmon, M. E., S. P. Bratton, and P. S. White. 1983. Disturbance and vegetation response in relation to environmental gradients in the Great Smoky Mountains. *Vegetation* 55:129–39.

Harrod, J., M. E. Harmon, and P. S. White. 2000. Post-fire succession and twentieth century reduction in fire frequency on xeric southern Appalachian sites. *Journal of Vegetation Science* 11:465–72.

Heinselman, M. L. 1973. Fire in the virgin forests of the Boundary Waters Canoe Area, Minnesota. *Quaternary Research* 3:329–82.

Johnson, E. A., and C. P. S. Larsen. 1991. Climatically induced change in fire frequency in the southern Canadian Rockies. *Ecology* 72:194–201.

Landres, P. B., P. Morgan, and F. J. Swanson. 1999. Overview of the use of natural variability concepts in managing ecological systems. *Ecological Applications* 9:1179–88.

Noss, R. 1990. Indicators for monitoring biodiversity: A hierarchical model. *Conservation Biology* 4:355–64.

Pickett, S. T. A., V. T. Parker, and P. L. Fiedler. 1992. The new paradigm in ecology: Implications for conservation biology above the species level. In *Conservation Biology,* ed. P. L. Fiedler and S. K. Jain, 66–88. New York: Chapman Hall.

Pickett, S. T. A., and J. N. Thompson. 1978. Patch dynamics and the design of nature reserves. *Biological Conservation* 13:27–37.

Romme, W. H., E. H. Everham, L. E. Frelich, M. A. Moritz, and R. E. Sparks. 1998. Are large, infrequent disturbances qualitatively different from small, frequent disturbances? *Ecosystems* 1:524–34.

Ryan, K. C. 2002. Dynamic interactions between forest structure and fire behavior in boreal ecosystems. *Silva Fennica* 36:13–39.

Shugart, H. H. 1984. *A theory of forest dynamics.* New York: Springer.

Sprugel, D. G. 1991. Disturbance, equilibrium, and environmental variability: What is "natural" vegetation in a changing environment? *Biological Conservation* 58:1–18.

Samuels, M., and J. L. Betancourt. 1982. Modeling the long-term effects of fuelwood harvests on pinyon-juniper woodlands. *Environmental Management* 6:505–15.

Swanson, F. J., and J. F. Franklin. 1992. New forestry principles from ecosystem analysis of Pacific Northwest forests. *Ecological Applications* 2:262–74.

Swetnam, T. W. 1993. Fire history and climate change in giant *Sequoia* groves. *Science* 262:885–89.

Swetnam, T. W., and J. L. Betancourt. 1990. Fire-Southern Oscillation relations in the southwestern United States. *Science* 249:1017–20.

Thompson, J. N. 1978. Within-patch structure and dynamics in *Pastinaca sativa* and resource availability to a specialized herbivore. *Ecology* 59:443–48.

Turner, G. M., R. H. Gardner, V. H. Dale, and R. V. O'Neill. 1989. Predicting the spread of disturbance across heterogeneous landscapes. *Oikos* 55:121–29.

Turner, G. M., W. H. Romme, R. H. Gardner, R. V. O'Neill, and T. K. Kratz. 1993. A revised concept of landscape equilibrium: Disturbance and stability on scaled landscapes. *Landscape Ecology* 8:213–27.

Veblen, T. T., K. S. Hadley, E. M. Nel, T. Kitzenberger, M. Reid, and R. Villalba. 1994. Disturbance regime and disturbance interactions in a Rocky Mountain subalpine forest. *Journal of Ecology* 82:125–35.

Vitousek, P. M. 1984. A general theory of forest nutrient dynamics. In *State and change of forest ecosystems, indicators in current research,* ed. G. I. Agren, 121–35 Swedish University of Agriculture Scientific Report 13.

Vogl, R. J. 1974. Effects of fire on grasslands. In *Fire and ecosystems,* ed. T. T. Kozlowski and C. E. Ahlgren, 139–94. New York: Academic Press.

Watt, A. S. 1947. Pattern and process in the plant community. *Journal of Ecology* 35:1–22.

White, P. S. 1984. Impacts of cultural and historic resources on natural diversity: Lessons from Great Smoky Mountains National Park, North Carolina and Tennessee. In *Natural diversity in forest ecosystems,* ed. J. L. Cooley and J. H. Cooley, 120–32. Athens: Institute of Ecology, University of Georgia.

———. 1987. Natural disturbance, patch dynamics, and landscape pattern in natural areas. *Natural Areas Journal.* 7(1): 14–22.

White, P. S., and S. P. Bratton. 1980. After preservation: The philosophical and practical problems of change. *Biological Conservation.* 18:241–55.

White, P. S., and J. Harrod. 1997. Disturbance and diversity in a landscape context. In *Wildlife and landscapes,* ed. J. Bissonette, 128–59. New York: Springer-Verlag.

White, P. S., J. Harrod, W. H. Romme, and J. Betancourt. 1999. Disturbance and temporal dynamics. In *Ecological stewardship: A common reference for ecosystem management,* eds. N. C. Johnson, A. J. Malk, W. T. Sexton, and R. Szaro, 2:281–305. Kidlington: Elvesier Science.

White, P. S., and A. Jentsch. 2001. The search for generality in studies of disturbance and ecosystem dynamics. *Progress in Botany* 62:399–450.

White, P. S., M. D. MacKenzie, and R. T. Busing. 1985. A critique of the overstory/understory comparisons based on transition probability analysis of an old growth spruce-fir stand in the Appalachians. *Vegetatio* 64:37–45.

White, P. S., and J. C. Nekola. 1992. Biological diversity in an ecological context. In *Air pollution effects on biodiversity,* ed. J. R. Barker and D. T. Tingey, 10–27. New York: Van Nostrand.

White, P. S., and S. T. A. Pickett. 1985. Natural disturbance and patch dynamics, an introduction. In *The ecology of natural disturbance and patch dynamics,* ed. S. T. A. Pickett and P. S. White, 3–13. New York: Academic Press.

White, P. S., and R. D. Sutter. 1998. Southern Appalachian grassy balds: Lessons for management and regional conservation. In *Ecosystem management for sustainablity: Principles and practices illustrated by a regional biosphere cooperative,* ed. J. D. Peine, 375–395. Delray, FL: St. Lucie Press.

White, P. S., and J. L. Walker. 1997. Approximating nature's variation: Selecting and using reference sites and reference information in restoration ecology. *Restoration Ecology* 5:338–49.

CHAPTER 7

Can Nature (Legitimately) Be Our Guide?

Patricia Ann Fleming

In the introduction to this volume, editors Chris Hamlin and David Lodge ask "What is to guide us in the use of nature?" We were formerly advised in the Judeo-Christian tradition by our belief in harmonious nature about how to act in relation to our environment. Dominion over nature, interchanged with stewardship of nature, were operative metaphors meant to inform us of our right relationship *in* nature or *with* our environment. These relations depended, in part, on stability in nature. We are now confronted by recent advances in the sciences, notably ecology and biology, regarding our perspective on nature. Nature, we are told, is in constant flux. Nicolis and Prigogine (1989) capture this change in the preface to their work on complexity when they say,

> Our physical world is no longer symbolized by the stable and periodic planetary motions that are at the heart of classical mechanics. It is a world of instability and fluctuations, which are ultimately responsible for the amazing variety and richness of forms and structures we see in nature around us. New concepts and new tools are clearly necessary to describe nature, in which evolution and pluralism become the key words.

Kevin Kelly, author of *Out of Control* (1994), expresses this change as he reports a conversation with Stuart Pimm:

"In the beginning, ecologists built simple mathematical models and simple laboratory microcosms. They were a mess. They lost species like crazy" Stuart Pimm told me. Later ecologists built more complex systems in the computer and the aquarium. They thought these complex ones would be good. They were wrong. They were an even worse mess. Complexity just makes things very difficult—the parameters have to be just right. So build a model at random and, unless it's really simple (a one-prey-one-resource population model) it won't work. Add diversity, interactions, or increase the food chain lengths and soon these get to the point where they will fall apart. (94)

The current science of ecology has taken our referent of nature and destabilized it. We, in turn, have become disoriented, losing any belief in our ability to control or master nature. Chaos theory is an illustrative example of this changed perspective. As Carolyn Merchant puts it, "Chaos is the reemergence of nature as power over humans, nature as active, dark, wild, turbulent, and uncontrollable" (Merchant 1995, 54). Unpredictability, nonlinearity, interdependence, irreversibility, bifurcations, fluctuation, complexity, and diversity are all aspects of a new paradigm for understanding nature. This new paradigm led our editors, Hamlin and Lodge, to remark that "If the 'is' and 'ought' were ever comfortably joined, the new paradigm rips them apart as choices and trade-offs abound" (introduction, this volume, 8). They are fully aware of the impact of a fluctuating nature when they say, "In this milieu of radical uncertainty in the trajectory of nature, one may argue that the new paradigm fosters a more honest ecology by ceasing to disguise those moral problems as somehow resolved in the natural order of things" (introduction this volume, 9). And they are particularly attuned to the negative impact such an extension of nature's new paradigm to ethics might produce when they assert, "Certainly a recognition of nature as flux should not be taken to imply that all states of nature are equally good, or that human actions are inconsequential because it is all a muddle anyway " (introduction this volume, 7).

Where now can we turn? As a philosopher of science and ethicist contributing to this volume, I am interested in exploring some provisional answers my discipline can offer to this important question. My goal in this chapter is to assure the reader that, even without a linear, mechanistic nature to guide us, all is not lost. I examine with the reader a new way of imaging the connection between nature and value, one that allows nature to legitimately be our moral guide. I will confess that my intention is to lead the reader to a realization of how deeply metaphorical our understanding is of our relations between nature and the moral life.

To do this, we will look closely at the "nature-value" pair. In the first section, I start with the left side of the pair, *nature,* and ask about how we arrive at our scientific descriptions and explanations of nature. I also explore some concerns about our belief in the truth-value of those descriptions. The insights I offer are informed by both classic and recent work in philosophy of science. In the second section, I move to the right side of the pair, *value.* I explore challenges to a view of science that relegates any legitimate role for values, including moral values, to the arenas that lie outside the heart of scientific inquiry. Taking these challenges seriously helps us develop a more complex understanding of the epistemology that underlies our claims about nature.

I digress in the third section so as to refocus on the question at hand: "What is to guide us in the use of nature?" Implicit in our concern about nature is the potential answer: "These new views of the natural world should be our ethical guide." But, can these views legitimately do this without falling prey to serious philosophical difficulties, to say nothing of leading us into a morass of confusion reflected in the irregularities reported in nature? I examine some of the philosophical difficulties with this answer, notably a vicious circularity wherein the appeal to nature to help guide our relations with it merely begs the question.

In the fourth section, I return to the nature-value pair. I demonstrate how the philosophical difficulties described in the third section can be overcome by recognizing the potential metaphorical connection between descriptive nature and prescriptive ethics. We are relieved of the philosophical difficulty in literally using nature as our moral guide. A *virtuous circularity* can exist between nature as described and the moral life as prescribed. Finally, in the fifth section, I sketch the outlines of the metaphorical extension of chaos theory to environmental ethics.

The Left Side of the Pair: Nature

Mary Hesse reminds us in *Models and Analogies in Science* (1966), now a classic in the philosophy of science, of the key role that models, understood as metaphoric redescriptions, play in our scientific descriptions and explanations. She disabuses us of the view that a simple deductive model of explanation suffices to capture the underlying epistemology of scientific explanation. She relies heavily on the interaction theory of Max Black, who also saw the parallelism between metaphor and model in science.

Hesse wrote at a time when a cognitive view of metaphor was emerging among thinkers, that is, the idea that metaphors and hence models have *meaning* and are not merely emotive or psychological devices meant to evoke responses. While she did not create an elaborate theory of meaning (or theory of truth) for scientific models, her work has been significant in drawing our attention to features of our descriptions and explanations of nature that function as metaphors rather than straightforward deductive-nomological explanations. Her appeal to scientific models as an important source for making sense of the natural world is driven by at least two things: (1) by positivism's failure to find a perfect empirical fit between nature and our description of it—instead, science yields approximate fits, some of which are more acceptable than others because of greater accuracy, coherence, and so on; and (2) by scientists' recognition that (our present description of) nature and our specific explanations of it are mutually modified. This is the "kernel" of Max Black's interaction theory of metaphor represented by the now classic statement "Man is a wolf" in which both our understanding of man and our understanding of wolf are transformed by their metaphorical connection. Or, using Hesse's example, "Nature becomes more like a machine in the mechanical philosophy, and actual, concrete machines themselves are seen as if stripped down to their essential qualities of mass in motion" (Hesse 1966, 163).

This awareness is grounds for understanding science's use of models as metaphoric redescriptions of nature. The connection between nature and our understanding of it is no longer viewed as simply governed by correspondence rules (which could not do their job in any case). Speaking to the tradition of positivism, Hesse points out,

> In the metaphoric view, however, these problems are evaded, because here there are no correspondence rules, and this view is primarily designed to give its own account of the meaning of the language of the explanans. There is *one* language, the observation language, which like all natural languages is continually being extended by metaphoric uses

and hence yields the terminology of the explanans. There is no problem about connecting explanans and explanandum other than the general problem of understanding how metaphors are introduced and applied and exploited in their primary systems. (1966, 175)

This same capacity in science for its propensity to redescribe also makes predictions possible. On this view, Hesse points out that predictions might not be true but we can expect them to be rational insofar as "rationality consists just in the continuous adaptation of our language to our continually expanding world, and metaphor is one of the chief means by which this is accomplished" (1966, 177).

My point in introducing this section on nature with a discussion of the early and influential work of Mary Hesse is to suggest to (or simply remind) the reader that our newly emerging scientific views of nature are not, in many instances, straightforward literal descriptions of nature. We build our scientific theories in great part from metaphors. Hesse's interest in metaphor helps her (and positivism) out of difficulties in understanding the epistemological foundations of theoretical terms in science. As positivism began to face other difficulties, such as the underdetermination of hypotheses by their evidence, more legitimacy has been given the role of models in science.

Models of evolution, complexity, chaos, and flux function as metaphors. Recent observations in physio-chemical and biological systems and in climatic change in the environment give rise to concepts that mutually interact and refine each other, producing such theoretical terms as flux. Flux is one aspect of a model in ecology that functions metaphorically to "redescribe" nature. It is an enormously helpful model, but it provides an approximate, not a perfect fit with nature. We forget that our epistemic relation in nature is not a simple literal one, in other words, that our descriptions and explanations do not merely mirror or correspond with the way nature is. We shall see that this is an important insight, if not a reminder, as we move forward in determining if and how nature, as such, can legitimately provide us with a moral guide.

As we dislodge early positivism's hold on our understanding of how science proceeds in its inquiry of nature, there has been a shift in beliefs about science's capacity to *truly* capture nature. This becomes important to us because we tend to think that the truth-value of our descriptions of nature should play a major role in determining how we should act toward it. At this point, I transition to my second issue in this section, one that has shaken philosophy of science at its foundation: questioning the truth-value of scientific claims about nature.

For many ecologists, their main difficulty lies in getting true descriptions of nature. In what appears as a straightforward appeal to scientific realism, some ecologists herald the ability of chaotic dynamics to provide the science of ecology with a truer explanation of nature. Not content to follow Dostoevsky who might have advised ecologists to keep secret this explanation for fear of upsetting the security found in harmonious nature, our editors, like many of us, "prefer to embrace the new ecology of flux as a *description with a closer correspondence to reality*" (introduction, this volume, 9; emphasis added).

For examples of this realism we need only turn to the ecologists writing in this volume. Belovsky (chapter 5), for example, claims that environmental change in the Near East could never have been accurately understood until an interest in forecasting led to quantitative observations of cyclic climatic patterns. Although he admits that ENSO cannot be precisely forecasted, because the feedbacks between underlying processes create a chaotic or nonlinear dynamics, still Belovsky is one among many scientists who would claim that the science of ecology today yields better descriptions and predictions of environmental processes of nature than the Judeo-Christian tradition.

These statements, or ones like them, assume scientific realism. What is implied is that environmental explanations, based in theories of chaotic dynamics and supported by tools for the analysis of quantifiable aspects of nature, provide us with a far more accurate picture of nature. While the paradigm of chaos or flux may be disquieting in general, the many ecologists who have assumed scientific realism and have shifted their explanations of nature under this powerful explanatory framework believe they are moving closer to the truth about nature.

Realism appears to make sense of science's explanatory power. However, it is a view of our epistemic relation to nature that can only be had by its support from an inference to best explanation (Harman 1965). Simply put, this is the assumption that an explanation would not be as effective, would not yield the results it does in scientific inquiry, if it were not capturing the *truth* about nature. While ecological science might have formerly thought that nature was "truly" explained by appeals to harmony, balance, and wholism, the best explanation, that is, the true explanation, is the one that is more powerful, the one that makes greater sense of empirical facts (Putnam 1978; Boyd 1973). A realist must shift his view of the truth about nature when the explanatory power of a scientific theory changes. Currently, the view that nature fluctuates, indeterminacy reigns, and the smallest interaction in nature may lead to vast and unpredictable consequences is truer than the belief that nature seeks constant harmony with itself.

The antirealist does not affirm the connection between explanatory power and truth. She is content to withhold the additional inference that effective explanations, in other words, explanations that work well in scientific inquiry, entail the conclusion that these explanations capture the truth about nature. All antirealists, contrary to what some might believe, do not necessarily deny the possibility of truth; nor do they disavow the existence of nature. Rather, they are reluctant to jump so quickly to the truth claim about nature in the face of changing views of nature found in the history of science, most which have been claimed to be true at one time or another (Fine 1984; Laudan 1981).

As an engaged scientist, an antirealist will function quite similarly to a realist. She will seek empirical or theoretical support to confirm or disconfirm hypotheses; she will be pleased with the explanatory power of the theoretical frameworks to which she appeals and in support of which her own work functions. But, when pressed about epistemic commitments, she will be unwilling to utter the connecting statements between the truth of nature and the explanatory power of scientific theories and models, whether they are chaotic dynamics or ecological harmony. Antirealists will not even be seduced by the largess of the paradigm of chaotic dynamics which seems to put smaller-scale scientific views of nature in a more coherent and cohesive framework.

Antirealists are reluctant to say, on the basis of explanatory power, that ecology is getting closer to the truth. Whether or not truth is *entirely* abandoned by the antirealist is the feature that places antirealism on a continuum. For some antirealists, truth is a phenomenon resulting from complex epistemological (knowledge-producing) and axiological (value-oriented) activity. For others, truth is best described as asymptotic, something we might think we approximate but which we never, in principle, achieve. Some realists come close to this view in their belief that we are producing "better" science all the time. But the antirealist refuses the conclusion that this "better science" produces scientific truth at any point in time. For the antirealist, one never touches down on the truth axis but is always and only in asymptotic relation to it. Other antirealists are simply silent about truth as a discoverable epistemological trait.

For our current purposes, the reader need not decide if he or she is a scientific realist or antirealist. If these views prove to be based on some faulty distinctions or assumptions, as polarizing debates tend to be, one should avoid such a decision but continue to engage in the dialogue. If interested in this controversy, I would recommend careful and continued exploration on the reader's part. One question to explore is: "Is it possible that one's position about scientific realism may be driven by the adoption of certain values?" One could argue that the epistemic values of explanatory power, along with simplicity and predictability, may derive from the influence of a simple deterministic view of nature. Further, expecting a moral guide to result from a simple connection between nature and ethics may itself be the result of the influence of a leading, if outdated, dominant metaphor in science, namely mechanism. This could be equally said of antirealism: that it may be driven by the adoption of certain other values leading to moral skepticism of ever using nature as a moral guide.

The "realist vs. antirealist" debate is no small philosophical controversy, but one that I believe is working its way toward a transformed understanding of truth. With this perspective, I believe we must ask, "Should the relation between nature and ethics be conceived differently, neither as a pseudo-deterministic relation between 'is' and 'ought' nor as having no connection whatsoever?" We will see more on this below when we explore a virtuously circular connection between nature and value.

I raise both this concern and the reminder of the role of scientific modeling *as a corrective* for the discourse at hand. It is a significant realization that, in our concern about morally defensible action in relation to nature, we *need not unwittingly commit ourselves* to the idea that the ethical, in having ties to the natural, relies on a science that provides us simple, direct, and literal correspondence with nature itself and, thereby, produces the truth about nature.

Instead, the "nature" side of the "nature-value" pair rests on a far more complex epistemic relation. No matter how powerful the paradigms of chaotic dynamics or flux are, the belief that they provide the truest picture of nature rests on an often unrecognized inferential judgment. Insofar as this is the case, to further think that one can derive certainty regarding guiding moral values from the scientific explanatory power of these paradigms is fallacious. At most, one gets something like ethical probability: one's ethical views are held with the same degree of certainty as one's belief about the truth of a particular scientific perspective. Minimally, this needs to be acknowledged, since the expectation that current science produces epistemic certainty tends to also be transferred to ethics, leading one to expect that moral certainty, without degree, is achievable in an ethics with scientific truth as our guide. Beyond this minimalist view, I will show below that there is a more creative and productive way of understanding the "nature-value" connection. But, first, let us look more closely at the right side of the "nature-value" pair.

The Right Side of the Pair: Value

Another recent challenge to our view of science involves beliefs about the role of values in scientific inquiry. Positivism espouses science as a value-free activity. Science's self-understanding proudly demarcates science from nonscience according to the inquirer's ability to control unwarranted influences such as religious belief systems, political agendas, and economic incentives. Admitting that such influences exist has not been problematic for positivism (often referred to as the "received view") insofar as these things do not affect the heart of scientific inquiry, that is, the justification of hypotheses or the creation of theories.

Harmony, balance, and constancy no longer adequately explain natural phenomena. One hears scientists and philosophers whispering about the tenacity of these metaphors. Perhaps their embeddedness in ecological theories can be explained by a *circularity* wherein the perceptions that supported these discarded views were empirically justified by the values deeply rooted in the frameworks themselves. But good science must avoid this value-ladenness, says the positivist.

However, those living in post-positivist times have rejected such a simple dismissal of a complex epistemological task of hypothesis justification and theory confirmation. A first move toward admitting a role of values in science was made by Richard Rudner, positivist par excellence, in his now-classic position that "the scientist qua scientist makes value judgments" (Rudner 1962). Regarding the epistemic choices the scientist must make, Rudner argued that values, constitutive of science and without which it could not function, play a key role. Systematicity, simplicity, and coherence are a few scientific virtues valued by science. If chaotic dynamics is preferable to former views of nature, this is true because of certain constitutive values scientists have adopted.

Once down this road, it was not long before those who study science began to wonder if non-epistemic values insert themselves into scientific inquiry. Initially, this curiosity led nowhere of significance. Although critics of science were excited by discoveries of ties to political agendas, economic incentives, and religious worldviews (White 1967, Whitney, chapter 1, this volume), these ties only loosely bound the hands of science. Choice of hypotheses studied or problems chosen may have been affected by scientists' (or the scientific community's) non-epistemic values. However, the actual justification of scientific hypotheses or the choice of theories was confidently understood to be firmly rooted in contextually value-free empirical investigations or coherent theoretical proof.

But more recently, persistent post-positivists have suggested that scientific justification, those additional steps scientists must take after the discovery of a hypothesis or the formation and choice of a problem to be studied, may indeed be mired in contextual, non-epistemic values. Helen Longino's work illustrates this position. She makes the initial distinction between constitutive and contextual values and then asks about the plausibility of this distinction:

> For the sake of clarity I will call the values generated from an understanding of the goals of science *constitutive* values to indicate that they are the source of the rules determining what constitutes acceptable scientific practice or scientific method. The personal social and cultural values, those group or individual preferences about what ought to be, I will call *contextual* values to indicate that they belong to the social and cultural environment in which science is done. The traditional interpretation of the value freedom of modern natural science amounts to a claim that its constitutive and contextual features are clearly distinct from and independent of one another. Can this distinction, as commonly conceived, be maintained? (Longino 1990, 4)

Longino argues that scientific practice is in dynamic interaction with social needs and values and that "the logical and cognitive structures of scientific inquiry require such interaction" (Longino 1990, 5). She analyzes this interaction in great detail, demonstrating how scientific inquiry survives as a credible, albeit social activity, while still admitting the possibility of engaging both contextual and constitutive values. This interaction involves the effect of contextual values on practices in science, on questions asked, on the collection and description of data, or on the background assumptions facilitating inferences. Contextual values can also motivate the acceptance of global, framework-like assumptions to determine the character of research in an entire field. To illustrate this claim, she uses as an example the emergence of the mechanical notion of nature during the fifteenth and sixteenth centuries in congruence with the needs of technical trades for causal explanations (Longino 1990, 86).

For our purposes I am interested in this interaction. In exploring the nature of the interaction of the constitutive norms of science and the contextual values of the culture or society in which it thrives Longino uses expressions as various as "congruence" and "determine." She is cautious in defining this interaction as causal, logical, synchronistic, or simple correlation. As you will see below, I would like us to consider the metaphorical character of this connection.

Of course, Longino is *describing* ways in which we might find the values found in a culture in many aspects of scientific inquiry from practices to paradigms; she is not suggesting that these values *should be normative* for scientific inquiry. Neither does she complete the circle in her analysis by suggesting that the results of scientific inquiry, that is, the frameworks themselves, might be used to establish normative behavior toward nature. Nevertheless, these are the sorts of things I believe we need to think deeply about. We must consider the possibility that the values we adopt, which emerge from human needs, influence the assumptions made in scientific theories, and that these assumptions, in turn, might double back so as to help guide us in our behavior toward nature.

This analysis above may well sound nothing short of either vicious circularity or a relativistic endeavor that is hopelessly futile in ever achieving a distance that permits creativity, critique, and production of new and better guides for acting in and toward nature. It's time to refocus on the question at hand and the problem that certain answers beget.

REFOCUSING THE QUESTION: WHAT IS TO GUIDE US IN THE USE OF NATURE?

What is to guide us in the use of nature? Can it (legitimately) be nature itself? Why not simply say, "Human actions regarding nature, including environmental policies, ought to preserve what is found in nature"? For example, why shouldn't radiation protection limits merely reflect the levels of background radiation to which the human is naturally exposed? More radically, since radiation exposure differs by location (e.g., some natural formations yield greater exposure, such as uranium rich geology) why not set those limits to the protection that nature *locally* provides? While we know it is possible, with interventions, to provide greater protection, why should we? Why can't we use nature (legitimately) as our guide?

Philosophically, we have difficulty using nature in this way to establish our moral duties. We have called this "the naturalistic fallacy." That expression has its roots in the work of the philosopher G. E. Moore who sought to define the "good" by an appeal to nonnatural qualities. Moore, however, was reacting to a certain utilitarian tradition that reduced "the good" to "pleasure." In the broadest interpretation of Moore's views, he is troubled by the use of an empirical state of affairs (what he means by "natural") to define the goal of the moral life.

Eventually, the expression "naturalistic fallacy" came to be applied to another difficulty. Noted initially by David Hume, this difficulty emphasizes the logical problem of deducing an "ought" from an "is." The deduction does not hold, unless a missing premise is supplied: "What is, ought to be." But now we've merely begged the question. We haven't answered why nature should be our moral guide; for example, we have not answered *why* background radiation should set ethical limits on environmental policies.

Associated with this later "logical take" on the naturalistic fallacy is a plethora of solutions, including some attempts by environmental philosophers to resolve this difficulty in their desire to give nature its due. It is not the purview of this chapter to review these attempts. One can easily be sympathetic to both the Moorean and Humean strains of this intellectual history. What should guide us in our use of nature? On the one hand, a la Moore, having looked at the complexity of the left side of the nature-value pair, perhaps it shouldn't be nature itself, in some "literal" appeal to current scientific theory about nature. Perhaps, we should appeal to nonnatural qualities in determining the foundation of our environmental ethics. On the other hand, a la Hume, what looks like begging the question fails to note what we saw above in examining the right side of the nature-value pair—that sentiments *already* play a role in a complex circularity with nature.

The point at which I diverge from these views is where insufficient attention is paid to the inextricable connection between values and our view of nature. The recognition that values thrive in science in a number of ways prompts the questions: "How illicit is the move from *is* to *ought*? How problematic can the naturalistic fallacy be if the "is" (or, more accurately, the epistemic relation we have with the "is") is necessarily *already* laced with values?"

In his article, "Environmental Philosophy After the End of Nature" (2002) Stephen Vogel makes a similar point. Vogel argues that the deep problem for any environmental philosophy is the naturalistic fallacy. "This is not a problem because there is nothing ethical in nature . . . but rather exactly because nature is always already ethically interpreted" (Vogel 2002, 34). He contends that nature is above all a political danger insofar as, qua a complex of value-laden claims, it has been used against blacks, women, and homosexuals to establish their inferiority. Vogel seeks an end to this naïve, positivist understanding and use of nature.

Thinkers like Vogel would prefer to put an end altogether to *any* concept of nature and its subsequent use for guiding the moral life. I suggest that we press on toward a more fruitful approach wherein nature could function as a guide, but without the political dangers Vogel aptly characterizes. So, if a circularity of sorts between nature and value is unavoidable, rather than attempt to erase this circularity with philosophical argument, it might prove to be worthwhile to distinguish *virtuous* from *vicious* forms of this circularity, that is, preferable from less preferable relations between what we understand nature to be like and how we ought to act in relation to it. Since our views of nature are subject to change, to simply instantiate our understanding of nature, for example as either harmoniously linear, chaotically non-linear, or in flux, may only reduce any confidence we have of a connection that produces right action. Perhaps there is another way of seeking insight from a connection between nature and value (ethics) that we've overlooked or, more accurately, forgotten? In the next section, as I discuss a virtuous way of gaining insight from nature, I intentionally shift from an examination of the "nature-value" pair to the "nature-ethics" pair.

THE METAPHORICAL CONNECTION BETWEEN NATURE AND VALUE: A VIRTUOUS CIRCULARITY?

In this effort to determine if nature can be a legitimate guide for how we ought to act in the natural world, we return to metaphor. What we easily forget is the significant role metaphor plays not only in science through modeling but in our moral lives, particularly in our relations with our environment. Recent works drawn from perspectives including critical theory, deep ecology, and ecofeminism remind us of the metaphors that have guided our thinking about nature. For example, attempts have been made to replace metaphors of dominion or subservience with organic ones, like Gaia, giving all of nature a life of its own with which we must contend.

The intentional and explicit attempt at creating replacement metaphors is well worth exploring. The sources of these attempts are various and not necessarily from science per se. For example, ecofeminists are motivated by their experiences of connectedness. Critical theorists find their source in beliefs about preferable economic relations. Some deep ecologists rely on experiences in nature, others on science.

I wish to look closely at the latter. What would result if we used scientific models, such as "flux" or "chaos" as a source, a starting place for the production of newly influencing metaphors? And how do we get from those ideas to normative or prescriptive claims that can withstand the criticism of vicious circularity? To answer these questions, we must first look at the "rule of metaphor." By what dynamics is metaphor ruled?

I alluded briefly to the work of Max Black above insofar as it influenced Mary Hesse's thinking on models in science. Many theories abound that seek to explain the dynamics of metaphorical production, from Aristotle's substitution theory of metaphor and its emphasis on the word and nomination, to I. A. Richard and Max Black's interaction theory and its emphasis on the sentence and predication, to recent hermeneutic theories with their emphases on the larger work (the text) and its double interest in sense and reference. Each theory places different emphasis on the dynamics of a metaphor.

My discussion here is influenced by the work of Paul Ricoeur in *The Rule of Metaphor* (1977). In typical Ricoeurian fashion, this philosopher not only synthesizes all major thinking on metaphor, but also presents a theory of metaphor which, while in a kinship with this thinking, differs in two important respects: he focuses on an explication of a metaphor's ability to produce new meaning or semantic innovation, and he moves the explication of metaphor to the level of discourse, in other words, asking about a metaphor's power in redescribing reality through its referential function.

Recall that a metaphor is comprised of entities variously referred to as the principal subject and the secondary subject, the tenor and the vehicle, the focus and the frame. For example, we speak of "the fringes of society." "Fringes" is the secondary subject, vehicle, or frame. Its meaning is what comes to mind immediately, that is, the tail-ends (itself a metaphor!) of a weaving that form boundaries around cloth, mats, or rugs and that, while they have a fragile appearance as compared to the strength of the weaving itself, they keep the weaving from unraveling. The primary subject, tenor, or focus is an aspect of society. It is insufficient to say that the relation between them in the expression "fringes of society" is mere substitution or association of the name of one thing (or its sense) for another. The relation is more complex. Max Black recognized that metaphor is a function of a sentence, the interaction between a subject and a predicate. Ricouer brings to this recognition a sophisticated theory that explains more completely the way in which a metaphor produces new meaning.

There exists a tension discoverable in the *predicative* statement. This tension is between the predicates "is" and "is not." The boundaries of society are not real fringes in the physical sense; yet the expression "fringes of society" predicates the meaning of fringe onto society, producing a new meaning. In this case, the metaphor enlarges our understanding of society. Society is comprised of not only a tightly woven complex of interactions; it is bounded by fragile, independent, sometimes loosely connected groupings at its boundaries and without which society could unravel.

Ricouer describes this movement succinctly in this excerpt:

The maker of metaphors is (a) craftsman with verbal skill who, from an inconsistent utterance for a literal interpretation, draws a significant utterance for a new interpretation which deserves to be called metaphorical because it generates the metaphor not only as deviant but as acceptable. In other words, metaphorical meaning does not merely consist of a semantic clash but of a *new* predicative meaning which emerges from the collapse of the literal meaning, that is, from the collapse of the meaning which obtains if we rely only on the common or usual lexical values of our words. The metaphor is not the enigma, but the solution to the enigma. (1978, 144)

Because he adopts Frege's distinction between sense and reference, Ricoeur has remaining the task of describing what happens to the referent of a metaphor. The same tension that lies in the semantic predicative function of a metaphor applies also to the way in which it refers. Ricoeur describes this as a split reference between the ostensive reference of the secondary subject (that which has existence) and the non-ostensive referent of the primary subject (that which is brought into being, so to speak, with the utterance of the metaphor). The tension at the heart of this split produces not only a new meaning but a new reality. Metaphors have the capacity to create new realities, understood as new references in our experience.

What drives the split is the human imagination, that is, the human ability to extend or push features of the secondary subject in a variety of directions so as to produce new meaning for the principal subject. While retaining the "literal" meaning of "fringes," the metaphor "fringes of society" calls into being a reality not yet seen. Here, we have its non-ostensive referent.

Let us now return to the subject at hand. Is it possible to connect nature and value, in other words, ethics, in such a way that we avoid the vicious circularity described above? The answer to this question is resoundingly "yes" when we seek a metaphorical connection between nature and ethics. As we use the *is of nature* to guide us in the creation of the *ought of an environmental ethic,* we must not do so in the simplistic way described by "the naturalistic fallacy." This fallacious move does not allow for the production of new knowledge, new meaning, even new truth about our relationship with nature. Exploring a metaphorical connection acknowledges that the relation between nature and an environmental ethic can be both far more complex and creative. The analogical imagination explores the possible new meanings a description of nature might have for the moral life. These new metaphorical meanings can function as initial moral hypotheses that might withstand critical analyses to be able to function as powerful action guides.

Nature as Our Moral Guide

Discarded ecological descriptions of nature that emphasize hierarchy and dominion brought with themselves moral metaphors of stewardship and domination, placing humans at the center of ethical concern. This anthropocentric approach does not leave nature out. It places the human either high in the hierarchy or outside nature altogether. Concern with nature is not for its own sake; it is for the sake of human interests, albeit altruistic ones. A newer view of nature that emphasizes the harmonious and ordered character of nature has metaphorically produced different challenges regarding moral duties to nature. A holistic ethic has emerged that has emphasized the duty of maintenance of equilibrium in nature based on a linear causality in nature. Metaphors of health of the whole organism and the moral duty of therapeutic preservation of such health to all of nature transplanted dominion and stewardship.

In our newest descriptions of nature, some of these former views of nature have been retained. At the micro-level, we haven't given up on linear causality or hierarchy. But, in many respects, our newest descriptions of nature and the explanations that accompany them have abandoned or transformed the underlying assumptions of the above views. We talk now about the probability of causality; hierarchy becomes a function of biology rather than a preordained status. Complexity, chaos, and flux are the abiding scientific model replacements. Edward Lorenz's work, *The Essence of Chaos* (1993), introduces us to expressions which have specific, technical meaning within the theoretical framework of chaos theory. To reap the creative benefits of these new views we must ask: what is the metaphorical effect on the moral life of such things as non-linearity, a strange attractor, or the butterfly effect? How might complexity, fractality, unpredictability, and uncertainty metaphorically and creatively inform the moral life and an environmental ethic?

Once we feel we have a grasp of the essence of chaos, should we not also explore its ubiquity? (Krasner 1990). Should we also account for work in science on the taming of chaos, since, as Garnet P. Williams notes, "studying chaos has revealed circumstances in which we might want to avoid chaos, guide a system out of it, design a product or system to lead into or against it, stabilize or control it, encourage or enhance it, or even exploit it" (1997, 16)? The metaphorical extension of any one of these theoretical terms could take up pages.

The richness of the results of a metaphorical extension of a specific scientific view of nature for the creation of a new environmental ethic depends on the depth of our understanding of the view beyond its mere outlines. The ecologist well-versed in ethics or the ethician well-schooled in current ecological theory may be the best craftsman of some new moral metaphors to guide our relations in the environment. In the conference proceedings of the Society for Chaos Theory in Psychology and the Life Sciences, Jeffrey Goldstein titles his contribution "The Tower of Babel in Nonlinear Dynamics: Toward the Clarification of Terms" (1995). In doing so, he warns social scientists who hope to apply chaos theory either metaphorically or literally to their study of human action of the possibility that they might be using the fundamental terms so differently that they really "talk past each other." Not only do expressions such as "chaos," "attractor," "complexity," "energy," and "equilibrium" carry popular connotations from culture as well as from the cultural popularity of the new sciences, they also differ in definition among different schools of chaos theory. Additionally, he concedes that among the meanings of these terms are their metaphorical ones. He agrees that the metaphorical use of these terms is not erroneous but he suggests that "we give each other cues when we may be using a term in its more metaphorical meaning than in some kind of scientifically tested way" (Goldstein 1995, 42).

Sally Goerner provides the untutored in chaos theory with an excellent introduction in her work "Chaos, Evolution and Deep Ecology" (1995). The "utterly simple" key concept of chaos is nonlinearity. Three things are noteworthy in an understanding of this concept: (1) in a nonlinear system, input is not equal to output (as in treating a headache with increasing amounts of aspirin); (2) nonlinearity initially appears paradoxical but actually provides a richer model for understanding complex behavior (as in engineers seeing how adding a new road sometimes increases traffic congestion); and (3) the effects of nonlinearity are impossible to pin down, i.e. they can be positive (amplifying) or negative (dampening), producing stability or instability, coherence or divergence and explosion. "The key to understanding non-linearity is that, quite unlike linear systems, opposing tendencies may be built into a single system. This means a non-linear world is extremely versatile" (Goerner 1995, 20). Failure to recognize the large role of nonlinearity in nature has meant failure to recognize the subtlety of nature.

A second key concept of chaos theory is "interdependence." Goerner argues that popular literature confuses interdependence with nonlinearity. Interdependence concerns the reciprocating mutual effect system. Discourse is an example: both parties to a conversation are affected. The combination of nonlinearity and interdependence become the cornerstone of chaos theory. Goerner proceeds to claim, much like a realist, that chaos theory more accurately describes the world in its ability to account for phenomena normally labeled as accidental, anomalous, or mysterious. She claims that chaos has two messages about the environment: first, an evolving ecological universe is lawful and physical but not completely predictable, controllable, or knowable; and, second, most world systems are nonlinear interdependent ones.

On the basis of this simple introduction to chaos theory, Goerner concludes the following lessons: Order is hidden in chaos. It is a result of interdependent variables coeffecting each other. The dynamics of nonlinear interdependence tends to create wholes out of parts (e.g., self-synchronizing cuckoo clocks). And a single system may exhibit different forms (bifurcations) of behavior (e.g., a horse's gaits).

As chaos theory develops, recognition of unpredictability is coupled with a belief that order can emerge from chaos through *self-organization* (Prigogine and Stengers 1984). Self-organization theory furthers our understanding of chaos. The classical view of energy flow maintaining equilibrium in a system is replaced with Ilya Prigogine's insight that far-from-equilibrium systems do self-organize. As such, self-organization can be metaphorically extended to living and supra-living (e.g., cities) systems to help understand the spontaneous emergence of boundaries, or "self" (e.g., tornadoes, whirlpools). One cannot anticipate all the forms of organization that might emerge in the process of order through fluctuation, or whether they will happen and what they will look like. "Self" is used as a metaphor meant to articulate the bounded, ordered activity of a system.

There are many more aspects of chaos theory to examine prior to arriving with confidence at moral hypotheses about our right relations in and with the environment through an explicit metaphorical extension of chaos theory's meaning for the moral life. However the reader whose analogical imagination has been stimulated may already be at work with just these few concepts. At this point, we have sufficiently dabbled in chaos theory to suggest some moral hypotheses.

Fortunately, some of the craftsmanship needed to make moral metaphorical sense has already begun. For example, Carolyn Merchant recommends a partnership ethics between humans and nature, in part as a result of the discovery of chaos in nature. Arguing that we must leave room in our environmental planning for nature's unpredictable events, she asks us to recognize nature as a nearly equal subject, not an object to be controlled. She suggests that "a partnership ethic means that a human community is in a sustainable ecological relationship with its surrounding natural community. Human beings are neither inferior to nature and dominated by it, as in premodern societies, nor superior to it through their science and technology, as in modern societies. Rather human beings and nonhuman nature are equal partners in survival" (Merchant 1995, 20). As a consequence of this partnership, Merchant recommends an ethic of restraint, restoration, and reparation in our relations with nature. Not all her metaphors derive from chaos theory, but it has had some influence on her thinking about our right relations with the environment. An ethic of reciprocating mutual effect is suggested by a partnership ethics.

In *Complexity* (1998), Nicholas Reshcer contributes to the craftsmanship of this new relation, although he might not recognize his work as such. Taking the complexity of nature seriously, Rescher ask what this complexity means for the moral dimension of life, since a right action is unavoidably difficult in a complex world. He gives us helpful insights into how certain moral traditions might analyze duties in light of complexity:

> The answer here will depend on the sorts of moralists we are. If we are rigid utilitarians who estimate an act's rightness by its causal consequences, then heaven help us, since complex interactions will all too often be impossible to forsee. If we are statistical consequentialists who evaluate the rightness of actions via their foreseeably probable causal consequences, then matters become more manageable. Complexity is still an obstacle to overcome but not an insuperable one—a troublesome nuisance rather than a decisive obstacle. Finally if we are deontologists who prioritize motive and intentions in the evaluation of action, then the world's complexity becomes irrelevant; it is now the inner turmoil of personality that matters. But in any case and in any event, the cultivation of a moral life remains—as it must—a difficult project in this complex world of ours. (Reshcer 1998, 202)

Clearly, in this passage Rescher does not reject the traditional deontological or teleological approaches to determining our moral duties. Here, he simply argues that, as our world becomes increasingly more complex because of the future possibilities opened out to us by virtue of recognition of complexity, the moral life will become more difficult. For him, the complexity associated with our epistemic relation to nature transforms into challenges in the moral life "as the range of what we actually can do—be it for good or for evil—itself becomes enlarged in the course of scientific progress" (Rescher 1998, 202).

Earlier in his work he rejects the ideal of creating a *perfect* science, in other words, a science that gives us a definitive understanding of a complex world. He does not reject the possibility of science ever *improving* on our understanding of nature. Metaphorically extended to the moral life, we might ask: "What would an ethic that improves our relation to nature, while not insisting on perfect relations with nature, be like?" If he were speaking to the question of moral duties to the environment, Rescher would most likely claim that, as in both imperfect inquiry and imperfect technological advances, the prospect of error and risk of failure is inherent in the moral life. Bringing all these parts of our experience together he suggests, "the answer to how to conduct life in a complex world is—very carefully. Caution, and if possible, pre-caution should be the order of the day" (Rescher 1998, 195).

Restraint, restoration, reparation, caution, and *pre*-caution may indeed be some of the ways to describe new relations with the environment in the light of nature's complexity. These virtues might be considered the results of the metaphorical extension of the key concepts of nonlinearity and interdependence. Yet, this type of virtuous or principled moral life may limit us in aggressively tackling persistent environmental concerns. We could add other virtues or moral principles which are suggested by chaos and complexity in nature: the *surprise* found in a chaotic nature suggests the virtue of *resilience* in its wake, or the *secrecy* embedded in complexity as a function of time recommends being aggressively *patient* in our relations with and actions on the environment. These still suggest restrained relations and do not carry the metaphorical power that creates a new understanding of our relationship with and in the environment. Does chaos theory contain a key concept that creatively recommends more positive action in the environment?

Perhaps we can look for such relations in the emerging sense that, amidst the chaos, complexity, and flux, we find order through self-organization, Rescher describes this as the self-generation of order in a universe of chance (1998, 206). He points to stochastic phenomena in physics, evolutionary self-development in biology, collective self-organization in sociology, and fuzzy logic as examples of epistemic projects that are detecting a complex but highly ordered lawful universe. He says:

We do indeed inhabit a chaotic universe of chance. But the mathematical and conceptual instruments of modern science enable us to make it possible to see such a world as a stage for the self-generation of order. In such a world, order and the coheren[t] rational intelligibility that go with it are by no means lost altogether. It only requires more powerful cognitive instrumentalities to find them. The pathway to understanding is not blocked, it only becomes more challenging to pursue. (1998, 207)

This capacity for self-generation of order or self-organization is described above in literal terms, that is, insofar as nature is complex, we need complex, powerful means to detect its high-ordered lawfulness. But if we extend this feature metaphorically to the moral life to help us in the creation of an environmental ethic, what might a *self-organizing or self-generating moral order* mean and what actions might function as its referents?

We saw earlier that thinkers like Vogel (2002) prefer to place emphasis on the autonomous self as a moral agent, rather than a moral self that uses nature as its guide. Vogel has rejected nature as a moral guide because, as such, it has not provided practical, positive solutions for the individual or society trying to decide on how to act in relation to nature. Vogel is also disturbed by an environmental ethic that appears to have ignored in great part the value-ladenness of the concept of nature. According to him, we would be better off acknowledging that nature is always already interpreted and "directly asserting the political and social character of environmental debates" (2002, 35). Instead, an environmental ethic *without nature* finds its normative foundation in an appeal to self-knowledge and self-recognition (Vogel 2002). This involves acknowledging that the environment we inhabit has emerged as constituted by our actions and will continue to do so. While we cannot reverse past action, we can correct future actions by recognizing that our actions and practices need not be "hidden" from us under the guise of the natural outcomes of free market forces. Rather,

The practices we engage in are social practices, on the one hand, which means that they are made possible by and get their meaning from the social context in which they arise; while, on the other hand, they are always transformative practices, which means that they change the real environment we inhabit. Those practices that know themselves as such, that acknowledge their own social and transformative character, are to be preferred, it seems to me, over those that do not. (Vogel 2002, 35)

This rightly placed emphasis on social context need not mean we must reject nature as a legitimate moral guide. While nature is not a social practice, certainly our understanding of it is. Rather than the heterono- mous nature that Vogel has in mind, I would like to suggest the concept of a "guiding nature." By this, I mean nature, as constituted by our thor- oughly social epistemic activity of value-laden scientific inquiry, is a source for transformative moral metaphors, such as the "self-generation or self-organization of moral order." This metaphor suggests a relation to the environment which comes close to what Vogel suggests above. We ar- rive at this metaphor by extending the secondary subject matter of self- organization emerging from complexity to the moral life. However, the concept of self-organization found in chaos theory that we are trying to extend to the moral life has a peculiar twist. The self, if it emerges, is an ordering entity *resulting from complexity*.

In my view, this is one of the most important concepts that chaos theory bequeaths to the moral life: a moral self or agent that emerges from complexity. Several things can be said about this metaphor. First, it is difficult to imagine right relations to and with the environment with- out the possibility of order. It would be extraordinarily difficult to see how chaos theory could provide a positive and productive basis for an en- vironmental ethic without the possibility of order. However, the order which is detectable is not a guaranteed effect of complexity. This pro- duces a sobering sense of how tenuous moral order is.

Second, order in chaos theory involves organization of what appears to be disparate, random phenomena. Chaos theory uses "self" to explain this type of organization that might result in nature at a complex level. Chaos theory actually borrows a concept from philosophy, namely, the self. Philosophy is replete with conceptions of the human self, including the self as human essence in the Aristotelian tradition to the self as merely the thread that ties together a bundle of perceptions in the Humean tra- dition. The self is also described in various traditions (from Kantian to existentialist) as an intentional organizing entity. For postmoderns, much like Vogel, the self is socially constructed.

The ideal moral self that is illuminated through a metaphorical extension of chaos theory is one that emerges from complexity. This ideal moral agent grows out of complexity, that is, opposing tendencies as well as a mutually reciprocating effect system. To view this self as an unconnected moral agent does not do justice to the full metaphorical impact of chaos as a moral guide. True, this self should understand, know, and respect complexity. One that does not is inappropriately placed in the moral scene. He or she may indeed be present, acting in and on the environment. But ideally, such moral agents, because they have emerged from the conditions that produce the ability to recognize mutual reciprocating effects of their actions, also recognize the social character of their individual actions. They understand with humility the metaphorical counterpart of nonlinearity: the moral effects of their actions are not guaranteed, and those effects are the result of complex interactions with other humans' actions. Failure to recognize this fundamental social character, the single moral agent will often act with moral immaturity. Admittedly, this is a comment about moral psychology and the development of the ideal moral self, but it is also a key to understanding more accurately the actions that would be promoted by these moral metaphors.

In some ways, this moral actor harkens back to the prudential moral agent, replete with phronesis or moral wisdom, capable of making a moral decision with recognition of the complex and interdependent world in which that decision needs to be made. This moral agent does not shy away from the complexity and does not seek to favor simple answers to complex moral environmental dilemmas. She recognizes the imperfection of her decisions but makes them anyway, with thorough awareness of the chance that the actions that follow upon her decisions may not result in her expectations or predictions. She acts to the best of her knowledge and then lets go. She recognizes her actions are among many that contribute to a sometimes indeterminate result. Chaos, fluctuation, complexity—none of this discourages this new moral agent from pursuing an environmentally ethical way of life; instead, in living that life, it produces insight into the need for moral versatility and subtlety. This moral agent is more like Vogel's self than one would think, insofar as that self took account of the complex factors, including both the actions of many other actors and the social context that contributes to our relation to the environment in seeking to transform it. One could argue that chaos theory, metaphorically extended to the moral life, actually provides the basis for an ethic of hope rather than despair.

MORAL METAPHORS

In this chapter, I have used most of the space *to frame* the answer to the question, "Can nature (legitimately) be our moral guide?" Rather than answering the question in great detail, I've spent some time looking at what "nature" has to offer us in this regard through contemporary views of it that are captured by the models of complexity and chaos. I have hinted above at the possibilities for a new understanding of a relationship with our environment, inspired by these current views of nature. This understanding is fueled by the human imagination which, in the production of guiding metaphors, circles back to these views, having freed themselves to produce new meanings for our new moral understanding.

In demonstrating that the derivation of ethics from nature, or ought from is, need not always be fallacious (insofar as that derivation is not merely literal, with no additive value imparted by the analogical imagination), I offer a caution: we would be foolish to think that only contemporary scientific models of nature *should* be the metaphorical foundation of the moral life. The human imagination, when used to create a better way to live with nature, should not be so curtailed in its moral hypotheses. Additionally, proposals for how to relate in nature must still withstand critical moral discourse.

What I have proposed above is very much like a scientific hypothesis not yet justified by the combination of empirical test, theoretical support, and peer review. These "moral hypotheses" do not receive legitimacy from any one place and especially not simply because they are metaphorical extensions of current science. I am not suggesting (although others might) that chaos theory more accurately explains nature and hence, its moral metaphors more accurately guide the moral life. Like scientific hypotheses, moral metaphors earn their legitimacy in the discourse of the world community of serious inquirers whose interests (even nonhuman ones) have been equally empowered through having a "voice." Just as the human community of scientific inquirers reject some scientific hypotheses because they fail to meet standards valued by this community (e.g., explanatory power, systematicity, simplicity), moral actors may reject some moral metaphors. They might, for example, fall short in providing the breadth and depth required of a systematic understanding of the moral life. Subjecting the moral metaphors of chaos theory to the critical discourses of the human community of inquirers is also a fundamental hermeneutic principle that provides standards that help us to decide between equally competing interpretations or, in this case, competing moral metaphors.

With this caution in mind, I recommend that we pay serious attention to our changing views of nature. Our consciousness of some of the unpleasant consequences of living through the metaphors of domination and subservience bequeaths to us an understanding of the need to critique the powerful effect of metaphors. As we enter an age wherein our scientific view of nature is shifting, the metaphorical impact of the nonostensive referents of this new view's key concepts should be approached both creatively and critically.

WORKS CITED

Boyd, Richard. 1973. Realism, underdetermination, and a causal theory of evidence. *Nous* 7:1–12.

Fine, Arthur. 1984. The natural ontological attitude. In *Scientific realism*, ed. Jarrett Leplin, 83–107. Berkeley: University of California Press.

Goerner, Sally. 1995. Chaos, evolution and deep ecology. In Robertson and Coombs 1995, 17–38.

Goldstein, Jeffrey. 1995. The Tower of Babel in nonlinear dynamics: Toward the clarification of terms. In Robertson and Coombs, 1995, 39–47.

Harman, Gilbert. 1965. The inference to the best explanation. *Philosophical Review* 74:88–95.

Hesse, Mary. 1966. *Models and analogies in science*. Notre Dame, IN: University of Notre Dame Press.

Kelly, Kevin. 1994. *Out of control: The new biology of machines, social systems, and the economic world*. Cambridge, MA: Perseus Books.

Krasner, Saul, ed. 1990. *The ubiquity of chaos*. Publication No. 89-15S. Washington DC: The American Association for the Advancement of Science.

Laudan, Lawrence. 1981. A confutation of convergent realism. *Philosophy of Science* 48(1):19–49.

Longino, Helen E. 1990. *Science as social knowledge: Values and objectivity in scientific inquiry*. Princeton, NJ: Princeton University Press.

Lorenz, Edward N. 1993. *The essence of chaos*. Seattle: University of Washington Press.

Merchant, Carolyn. 1995. *Earthcare: Women and the environment*. New York: Routledge.

Nicolis, Gregoire, and Ilya Prigogine. 1989. *Exploring complexity: An introduction.* New York: W. H. Freeman and Company.

Prigogine, Ilya, 1988. The rediscovery of time: Science in a world of limited predictability. Paper read to the International Congress on "Geist and Nature," Hanover.

Prigogine, Ilya, and Isabella Stengers. 1980. *Order out of chaos: Man's new dialogue with nature.* New York: Bantam.

Putnam, Hilary. 1978. *Meaning and the moral sciences.* London: Routledge and Kegan Paul.

Rescher, Nicholas. 1998. *Complexity: Science and technology studies*, ed. Mario Bunge. New Brunswick: Transaction Publishers.

Ricoeur, Paul. 1977. *The rule of metaphor.* Toronto: The University of Toronto Press.

———. 1978. The metaphorical process. In *On Metaphor*, ed. Sheldon Sacks, 141–57. Chicago: The University of Chicago Press.

Robertson, Robin and Allan Coombs, eds. 1995. *Chaos theory in psychology and the life sciences.* Mahwah, NJ: Lawrence Erlbaum.

Rudner, Richard. 1962. The scientist *qua* scientist makes value judgments. Philosophy of Science 20:1–6.

Vogel, Steven. 2002. Environmental philosophy after the end of nature. *Environmental Ethics* 24(1): 23–39.

White, L. 1967. The historical roots of our ecological crisis. *Science* 155: 1203–07.

Williams, Garnet P. 1997. *Chaos theory tamed.* Washington DC: Joseph Henry Press.

CHAPTER 8

Theology and Ecology in an Unfinished Universe

John F. Haught

Holmes Rolston III, one of America's most renowned environmental ethicists, has written that because of human factors and failings

nature is more at peril than at any time in the last two and a half billion years. The sun will rise tomorrow, because it rose yesterday and the day before; but nature may no longer be there. Unless in the next millennium, indeed in the next century, we can regulate and control the escalating human devastation of our planet, we may face the end of nature as it has hitherto been known. Several billion years worth of creative toil, several million species of teeming life, have now been handed over to the care of this late-coming species in which mind has flowered and morals have emerged. Science has revealed to us this glorious natural history; and religion invites us to be stewards of it. That could be a glorious future story. But the sole moral and allegedly wise species has so far been able to do little more than use this science to convert whatever we can into resources for our own self-interested and escalating consumption, and we have done even that with great inequity between persons. (Rolston 1996, 79)

Our species, Rolston and other environmentalists agree, is ruining the natural world. We humans are destroying rain forests, allowing the soil to erode, poisoning the air, and polluting rivers, lakes, and oceans. We have created a dangerous greenhouse atmosphere and reduced the protective ozone layer. And we are daily destroying many irreplaceable living species. Common sense demands that we change our ways, but apparently we need much more than common sense to fire our ethical responsibility for the earth. What we need is a *vision,* one that can move us to a firm and permanent commitment to ecological responsibility within the context of natural flux and cosmic evolution.

Can Christian faith provide such a vision? And can theological reflection discover in tradition or scripture a groundwork for dedicated ecological action? It seems to me, writing as a Christian theologian, that this is one of theology's most important contemporary challenges, especially in view of well-known accusations that Christianity is itself in some way responsible for our environmental neglect. Such a serious indictment forces us to ask whether theology can demonstrate an *essential* connection between Christian faith and ecological concern. Can Christian faith provide truly motivating reasons for taking care of the nonhuman natural world (Haught, 1993)?

The Australian philosopher John Passmore, for one, doubts that it can. Belief in God and the "next world," he says, softens our sense of obligation to *this* world. Otherworldly piety even gives rise to an implicit hostility toward nature. The only substantial basis for environmental concern, therefore, is a radical naturalism, a belief system that sees nothing beyond the existence of the physical universe. According to Passmore, only if humans accept the fact that we are situated here on this planet in a universe barren of any transcendent governance, will we begin to take full responsibility for our terrestrial home (Passmore 1974, 184).

Passmore is right in characterizing much traditional Christianity as otherworldly to the point of neglecting the earth's wellbeing. His complaint is justifiable, given his understanding of what Christianity essentially is. Moreover, he compels us to acknowledge that Christian theology must do a much better job of displaying whatever ecological relevance it might have than it has done so far.

So, precisely how can Christian theology respond? It may begin by emphasizing that according to biblical faith the natural world is inherently good and that God has even become incarnate in the cosmos. It can point to exceptional exemplars of love of nature such as St. Francis, Hildegard of Bingen, Meister Eckhart, or Gerard Manley Hopkins. It must in all candor acknowledge that most of our saints, poets and theologians have had little formal concern about the well-being of nature. But at the same time it may point to the fact that several distinct kinds of "ecological theology" are now emerging. For convenience's sake I shall call these respectively the *tradition-centered* (or "apologetic") approach, the *sacramental* approach, and the *cosmic promise* approach. The latter weaves the biblical theme of promise into the new scientific awareness of a universe still in the making.

Each of these three proposals is insufficient when taken alone, but taken together they constitute a substantial beginning for a Christian ecological theology. Cumulatively they are capable not only of responding to accusations that Christian faith is indifferent to the welfare of nature, but they can provide the underpinning of a new vision of religiously inspired responsibility to the earth. Each of the three approaches relies on points made by the others but adds its own emphasis. There is a good deal of overlap, but each has an accent not visible in the others. The three types are complementary in an additive sense: each is a piece of a whole puzzle.

As we shall see, the *cosmic promise* (or, more technically, the "cosmological-eschatological") approach becomes especially significant once we situate our reflections in the context of what science has demonstrated to be the *unfinished* condition of the physical universe and what the editors of this volume refer to as ecological flux. Cosmology has recently undergone a radical transformation, one that allows theology now to link up with ecological understanding in a way that would not have been available to our religious ancestors. Today it is imperative that theologians who address the contemporary ecological predicament attend very closely to what geology, evolutionary biology, genetics, and especially scientific cosmology are telling us about the natural world. We shall find, I believe, that theological reflection on what science has shown to be a world still in the making can reconfigure the meaning of stewardship in an entirely fresh manner, one that may bring about a new appreciation of the close connection between biblical faith and our obligations to nature in process. But first let us see what we can say about Christian responsibility to nature even independently of any encounter with the world of contemporary natural science.

A Tradition-centered (Apologetic) Approach

The first and probably most familiar approach to ecological theology is one that finds in scripture and tradition adequate resources for a Christian response to the ecological predicament. We may call this approach "apologetic" because, as the Latin world *apologia* suggests, it "defends" biblical faith against the charge that it is ecologically hazardous or inconsequential. Examples of the apologetic approach include recent statements on environmental issues by the pope, Catholic bishops, the World Council of Churches, and a growing number of theologians.[1] Their common message is that we have ignored the wealth of ecologically relevant material in the Bible and Christian tradition. Accordingly, what theology should be doing now is to retrieve this lost wisdom and allow it to address the present crisis. Theology will find numerous, often previously ignored, biblical passages and many other texts from the great teachers in the Church's history that proclaim the goodness and beauty of creation. It will come upon numerous ecologically relevant texts that it had barely noticed before we began recently to become aware of the fragility of life on this planet. How many of us, for example, had thought very much about the words in the Noah story in Genesis, where after the flood God made a covenant not only with human beings but with "every living creature"? And we should reflect on the profound significance that the familiar words in Genesis 1:31 may have today: "And God looked at everything he had made, and he found it very good."

The backbone of the "apologetic" approach, of course, is God's giving humans the task of "caring for" the garden in which they are situated (Genesis 2:15). Responsible stewardship, however, entails the practice of ecologically appropriate virtues: compassion, humility, moderation, detachment, and gratitude. Since the immediate "causes" of our ecological crisis are commonly said to be human arrogance, greed, violence, and the crude exercise of power, a renewed commitment to a biblically inspired ethic should lead directly to the repair of nature. Indeed, it is tempting to say that the solution to our ecological crisis lies simply in a serious return on the part of human beings to the practice of fundamental biblical values and classic religious virtues. Contrary to what critics of Christianity maintain, therefore, the apologetic approach insists that this tradition by no means lacks the basis for ecological conscientiousness. The fact is, we have not attended to its ethical directives. Environmental abuse is not the fault of Christianity, as Passmore and other secular thinkers have argued. Rather, it is the result of our failure to take seriously the imperatives embedded in Christian faith.

What could be more fundamental in restoring our relationship to the natural world, for example, than earnestly practicing compassion? Would we be stretching Christian faith beyond its boundaries were we to extend its emphasis on sisterly and brotherly love toward all of creation? Is St. Francis's compassion toward animals or his discourse about brother sun and sister moon an unnecessarily revisionist straining of the meaning of love? For Christians the paradigm of such widening of compassion for, and deeper relationship to, all of creation is revealed in the picture of Jesus as the Christ. The Gospels picture Jesus as one who constantly sought out deeper connections than those required by the customs of his time. They see him as passionately desirous of relating to those who were by all ordinary standards relationless: the sinners, the religiously despised, the sick, and even the dead. Perhaps the central motif of his life was the embracing of what did not belong. Is it not conceivable then that the contemporary movement to include all of life and all of nature within the circle of our own compassionate care is a justifiable extension of the spirit of Christ in our own time? An ecological theology may extend the circumference of Jesus's inclusive compassion for the unincluded to embrace the totality of nature.

Finally, there is an even more fundamental way in which theology may ground ecological concern in Christian tradition, while at the same time defending itself (apologetically) against the claim that radical secularism or pure naturalism provides a more favorable climate for ecological solicitude than does theistic belief. Numerous classic texts of Christian tradition echo St. Augustine's oft-repeated observation that each of us is restless until we rest in God (Augustine of Hippo 1960, 44). According to many religious traditions, in fact, we are each born with an insatiable desire for the infinite. From the Jewish, Christian, and Islamic perspectives, only the inexhaustible mystery of God can ultimately satisfy us. But when the modern world formally abandoned the idea of God it did not eliminate the infinity of our native longing. We remain *capax infiniti* (open to the infinite). Our unquenchable thirst for "more and more" stays with us as an anthropological constant. Having lost sight of its ultimate objective—the infinite God—this longing does not go away but instead turns itself toward devouring our proximate environment, the planet we live on. The restless human search for satisfaction is now engaged in the hollow project of squeezing the infinite out of what is increasingly exposing itself as utterly finite. Our tiny planet is unable to deliver the boundlessness that renders the human heart forever restless. We have not found in the earth a transcendent plenitude proportionate to the abysmal emptiness of our hearts. Thus, many of the earth's resources are now being used up with disproportionate rapidity, all in the senseless enterprise of milking infinity from a conspicuously bounded resource. Logically speaking, then, the solution to our disastrous exploitation of the planetary environment is not to deny the existence of the infinite mystery of God, but in conformity with our great religious traditions to direct our longing toward it once again.

Evaluation of the Tradition-centered Approach

Over the past fifteen years or so, I have witnessed at close hand the emergence of ecological theology, and I would say that most theologians, along with many other Christians, have made the tradition-centered or apologetic approach the substantial core of their response to our present ecological situation. There is much to recommend this approach, and its retrieval of the tradition must surely be part of any adequate ecological theology today. However, I fear that it does not adequately address all dimensions of the current situation. On the positive side, it has made us read the Bible and traditional theology with new eyes, and helped us peer more deeply into the ethical significance of the venerable teachings about creation, incarnation, divine wisdom, and so on. But, as I shall argue below, it needs to be supplemented by the sacramental and cosmic promise approaches. It is not enough by itself to deal with what this book is calling ecological flux.

Before taking up the alternatives, however, I should first emphasize that the apologetic stance is entirely justified in opposing the simplistic allegations made by Passmore, Lynn White, Jr., and others that Christianity is the main cause of our environmental ills. The fact is that the secularist and scientist assumptions of modern intellectual culture have led to a radical desacralizing of nature, which in turn has permitted us to treat the earth as though it were merely instrumentally good rather than a value in itself (Sheldrake 1991). In addition, the modern secularist outlook has generated a materialist philosophy of nature according to which life is reducible to lifeless chemicals and in which insensate "matter" is elevated to the status of ultimate reality (Daly and Cobb 1989; Haught 1993). It is hard to imagine how such a picture of things could ever lead people toward the reverencing of nature that ecological ethics now requires. Barry Commoner points out that if we consistently followed the materialist creed that life is reducible to lifeless matter *in principle*, sooner or later this reduction will take place *in fact* as well (Commoner 1971, 44). Moreover, as Herman Daly and John Cobb have shown at length, the causes of nature's present distress include runaway industrialization and naive economic assumptions about the unlimited resourcefulness of the earth, both of which are rooted in the materialist assumptions of modernity (Daly and Cobb 1989). Christians, like others, bear much of the blame, but Christianity's and other religions' antimaterialism is inherently a restraining influence, and their cultivation of virtues of moderation and humility, were we to take them seriously, would lead us to accept our finitude and temper our will to exploit and destroy the natural world.

However, after acknowledging all of this, there is room to doubt whether it is enough for Christian ecological theology simply to restore the most familiar elements of the tradition. I strongly suspect that the present crisis calls for something more from theology than simply pointing us to relevant and often forgotten texts and teachings. Today we may need a more animating and far-reaching articulation of what it means to be Christian in an ecological age. In view of the unprecedented modern and contemporary devastation of nature, perhaps we should not place too protective a shield around our traditions, but instead allow them also to be creatively transformed, as indeed nature itself is being transformed in its own evolution. Religious faith, after all, springs to life most floridly during those periods of history when it faces radically new challenges. Can we be certain that Christian tradition in its purely classical formulations is fully adequate to the dimensions of the current environmental crisis? Is it conceivable that faith and theology are now being summoned by radically new circumstances, and especially by developments in scientific cosmology, to undergo a more sweeping metamorphosis than the apologetic approach alone would permit?

There seems to me to be something utterly interruptive about our current ecological situation, and so our religions are now being challenged to a much more thoroughgoing self-renewal than an exclusively apologetic approach would allow. For Christianity, as for all other traditions, innovative responses may be needed. Consequently, I shall now outline two alternative routes—not completely separable from each other or from our first approach—that theology may take in our time as it looks toward the future of humanity's relationship with the natural world.

THE SACRAMENTAL APPROACH

For Christians the theological resources for an ecological renewal of faith can be found not only in biblical texts and doctrinal tradition, but also, and no less fundamentally, in the "sacramental" character of nature itself. To say that nature is sacramental simply means that, even apart from biblical revelation, nature in all of its beauty and diversity reveals the divine mystery—not just to Christians, of course, but to people of many traditions. A sacrament is anything through which we are gifted with a sense of the sacred, and it is especially nature's beauty and vitality that have communicated to humans an impression of the divine. In fact, it takes only a moment's reflection to realize that we really could not say very much about God at all apart from the richness and variety present in nature. Nature's sunlight, oceanic depths, fresh air, water, storms, rocks, trees, soil, growth, fertility, life, abundance, power, just to name several obvious examples, are perennially essential to religious metaphor. Even apart from traditional religious texts, therefore, nature's sacramental character gives us a deeply religious reason for taking care of it.

By acknowledging nature's inherent transparency to the divine, sacramentalism keeps us from turning our world into nothing more than raw material for our own human projects. Its sacramental capacity, therefore, should shield nature from diminishment at our hands. Without pantheistically identifying nature with God, as some traditionalists fear, the sacramental approach sees that the natural world is at heart a symbolic disclosure of God (Himes and Himes 1990, 45). This gives nature a "sacral" quality that should divert our manipulative tendencies. And today, after Darwin and Einstein, we are in a position to envisage all natural sacraments as embedded in an even more encompassing sacrament, that of an entire evolving universe gradually revealing the divine to us in a dramatic way that previous theological ages could never have imagined. For ecological theology not to notice and profit from this magnificent revelation would be a most appalling oversight.

Sacramental ecology argues that apologetics, with its emphasis on classic texts, is not enough to ground an ethically motivating ecological theology. If we want a theology capable of responding to the full dimensions of the ecological crisis we must learn once more to revere the natural world itself for showing forth to us the sacred reality that underlies it (Berry 1988). And as I shall argue below, we cannot do this without the help of contemporary science and cosmology. Our spirituality has become so acosmic, so obsessed with themes of history and human freedom, so concerned with interpreting written texts, that it has lost touch with the sacramentality of nature. It is now time to resacramentalize theology.

For Christians this means especially that they place fresh emphasis on the biblical theme of creation. Western religious tradition has unnecessarily subordinated creation—and by implication sacramentalism—to the theme of redemption (Berry 1988; Fox 1983). An exclusive emphasis on redemption has led Christian theology to exaggerate the "fallenness" not only of ourselves but also of the natural world. The assumption has been that redemption would be a momentous event only in proportion to the abysmal depths of a primordial Fall. By overemphasizing the fallenness of both humanity and nature "in the beginning," nature has been made at times to seem perverse and therefore undeserving of our care. By exaggerating the fallenness of nature we have too easily lost sight of the original goodness of the entire creation that God declared to be "good." At the same time, an undue focus on the human need for redemption from evil has distracted us from the travail of the entire creation, which, in St. Paul's words, also "groans" for radical renewal (Romans 8:22). The renewal of nature to which Christian faith alludes need not be postponed until the "last day," but it can begin to become a reality here and now—no less so than the renewal of our personal lives can begin in the present.

The sacramental approach emphasizes the present renewal of nature when it interprets "sin" to mean more than just our human separation from God or from each other. Sin also signifies the current alienation of nature from humanity, its estrangement from God and from its own creative possibilities envisaged by God from the outset of creation. Accordingly "redemption" and "reconciliation" must mean not only the restoring of the divine-human relationship, but also the healing of the entire earth-community and indeed the renewal of the whole creation, beginning right now.

Likewise, for a sacramental-ecological theology, the redeeming "Christ" is no longer exclusively a personal, historical savior but, even more fundamentally, a cosmic presence—indeed the rejuvenating heart of an entire universe—as represented in the writings of Paul, John, Irenaeus, and Teilhard de Chardin. We may even say that the whole cosmos is in some sense the "body of Christ." Concentrated and epitomized in the flesh and blood of Christ, the entire evolution of the universe becomes the corporeal expression of the very being of God.

A sacramentally shaped ecological vision also gives a cosmic dimensionality to eucharistic celebration. Eucharist symbolizes the healing not only of damaged human relationships but of our broken connection with the natural world as well. At the same time, a sacramental ecology gives fresh relevance to the doctrine of the Holy Spirit, the creative power that the Psalmist implores God to "pour out" so as to "renew the face of the earth."

This sacramental face-lift of theology calls in turn for new directions in Christian spirituality. It encourages, for example, a wholesome new sense of our intricate relationship to the natural world. In the past, the spiritual sensitivities of Christians have often been shaped by an anti-incarnational dualism that separates spirit from matter and thus distances us humans from nature. This dualism suppresses our natural intuition of being connected to an incalculably rich cosmic diversity and to a bodily existence completely continuous with the rest of the story of life on earth. The same dualism, incidentally, has also undergirded patriarchal exclusivism with its sinful oppression of women (Berry 1988, 138–62; Sheldrake 1991, 43, 56, 74f). Sacramentalism, in alliance with prophetic themes of biblical faith, links respect for the earth very closely to the social and religious liberation of women; and it argues that our religious institutions will not seriously accept ecological responsibility until they have begun to treat women with justice, both socially and ecclesially.

The sacramental approach is typically allied with a sense of the interrelationship of all forms of life. For this reason a renewed sacramental realization of the intricate way in which human life is woven into the natural world should lead us to see how inseparable ecological concern is from the demands of economic justice. Much of our mistreatment of this planet's life-systems, after all, stems from the inequitable way in which the world's goods are distributed from region to region, or from nation to nation. Impoverished places on earth are often the most ecologically spoiled simply because their inhabitants must strip them bare for the sake of mere subsistence. Hence we cannot hope to restore the ecological integrity of such locales without also addressing the extreme poverty that exists there. At the same time, those of us who live in areas of material bounty and wealth must realize that our own extravagant use of the world's resources contributes disproportionately to the global perpetuation of ecological disarray. The Christian tradition is powerfully relevant and often effective on issues of social justice, but social justice must now become allied closely—and everywhere—with a more sacramentally oriented focus on *eco-justice*.

Evaluation of the Sacramental Approach

Along with the tradition-centered approach, a sacramental vision adds indispensable ingredients to the larger project of formulating an ecological theology. Today Christian theology in particular needs to retrieve a sacramental sense of the cosmos. Our ancient intuition of the revelatory character of the universe, now brought up to date by scientific cosmology, is perhaps the most significant theological and ecological contribution our second approach has to make. More explicitly than the traditional apologetics, a sacramental theology allows us to recognize the *intrinsic* relation between religious faith and contemporary ecological concern. It helps us to realize, for example, that without the freshness of air, the purity of water, and the fertility of soil, the power of our most enduring symbols of God is diminished or lost. The integrity of nature is inseparable from the flourishing of religion. If we lose nature, as Thomas Berry puts it, we will also lose God.

Nevertheless, the sacramental approach is unable to give us a fully biblical or a distinctively Christian ecological theology. It can easily allow us to overlook the pivotal motif of biblical religion, namely, the theme of promise for the future. By emphasizing the theme of the "promise of nature," I am attempting to take the biblical substance of Christian tradition much more seriously than other ecological theologies, especially that of Thomas Berry, have done.

In its justifiable longing to recapture the sense of our connectedness to the natural world the sacramental approach does not always pay enough attention to the Bible's fundamental orientation toward *future* fulfillment. That is, it is often inclined to ignore what theology refers to as "eschatology," the biblical concern for future fulfilment. A biblically informed sense of what we may call "the *promise* of nature" must become central, I believe, to any explicitly Christian reflections on ecology. Moreover, when eschatology is conjoined with contemporary scientific cosmology the theme of "nature as promise" can preserve the best of both the classical and sacramental contributions to ecological theology while extending them into fresh territory.

The "Cosmic Promise" Approach

Biblical scholars over the last century or so have gradually rediscovered eschatology as the core of biblical religion. Promise of future fulfillment is the central message of the Hebraic scriptures and of the teachings of Jesus, and it is the driving force of the Christian vision of the world (Moltman 1967, 1975). But theology has also come to realize that eschatology—concern for future fulfillment—means not simply a hope for human survival in the "next world," but a conviction that *everything that happens* in the present world (or the present age) occurs within the context of a divine promise of future fulfillment (Haught 2000, 159–64). Although "what happens in the world" has usually meant primarily the affairs of human history, neither the doctrine of creation nor contemporary scientific cosmology permits us to leave the natural world out of the compass of Christian hope. An integral theology, one attuned to the biblical spirit of promise as well as to astrophysics, geology, evolutionary biology, and ecology, demands that we now view the entire universe, from its earliest beginnings to whatever end awaits it, as sharing in the same promise that the evangelist Luke, for example, beheld in the events associated with the birth of the Messiah.

An expansive and inclusive eschatological faith is convinced that the same divine promise that brought Israel and the church into being has in fact always encompassed the totality of the cosmos. Eschatology, in its deepest and widest meaning, therefore, implies that a resplendent fulfillment awaits the *entire universe*. The divine promise first announced to Abraham pertains not only to the "people of God" but also, if we listen attentively to St. Paul in Romans 8:22, to the "whole of creation."

However, the question immediately arises as to whether Christianity's eschatological orientation is ecologically helpful. Doesn't future expectation actually uproot us from nature instead of reconciling us to it? Some ecologists fear that religious concern for a future fulfillment will allow us to tolerate ecological indifference in the present. Hope for a future new creation, the argument goes, causes us to dream so extravagantly of the age to come that we will lose interest in this one, and even let it slip toward catastrophe. We cannot ignore this concern. After all, some kinds of biblical expectation, if taken in isolation, are ecologically dangerous. For example, apocalyptic visions, when interpreted too literally and independently of other biblical forms of anticipation, may even take consolation in the prospect of this world's imminent dissolution. Additionally, those individualistic earth-despising brands of supernaturalist optimism—more a heritage of the Greek than the biblical world— that seek an acosmic "spiritual" world as our final destiny seem to consign our present natural abode to final insignificance. Certain versions of eschatological fervor, in other words, do indeed appear to be ecologically problematic whenever they make "this world" only instrumental to the human religious journey.

Secular environmental ethicists characteristically charge that Christianity's futurist preoccupations make it inescapably indifferent to the present well-being of the nonhuman natural world. Western religious doctrine and spirituality appear so otherworldly that the conservation of this world cannot easily become a priority for believers. Christianity, after all, has often taught that "we have here no lasting home" and that our true abode lies elsewhere. But ecological responsibility demands that we think of the earth, and the entire cosmos for that matter, as our *home*. If we are going to have any lasting incentive to save the beauties of creation we need to feel deeply that we belong to nature here and now. Much of the enthusiasm that ecological ethicists now have for native peoples and non-Christian religions can be explained by the impression that alternative faith systems seem to nest us more comfortably within nature than do the dominant Western religious traditions. In the religions of many indigenous groups, for example, nature and humanity together formed a much more organic unity than they do in the classic Christian view of the world. Perhaps, then, the emergence of eschatology in religious history is more a problem than a solution to the ecological question.

Biblical eschatology, in fact, seems to partake of a general religious restlessness that emerged in several places around the world in the first millennium BC. During a historical period that philosopher Karl Jaspers has called the Axial Age, Indian mystics and Greek philosophers at times began to portray human destiny in terms of a withdrawal from "this world." Plato, for example, interpreted the natural world "here below" as a pale reflection of an ideal world that exists beyond time. The goal of our lives, from this perspective, is to find our way out of temporal existence into an eternity beyond time. Thus a sense of "cosmic homelessness" drifted into Western religion, and it became easier for us ever since to think of ourselves as strangers to nature. Christian spirituality has inherited much of this sense of cosmic homelessness; and so for that reason its eschatology often gives the impression of contradicting the ecological requirement that we experience ourselves as belonging to the wider world of nature.

How, then, is an ecological theology to address this troubling impression? It is undeniable, after all, that many influential religious teachings instruct us that excessive attachment to things, or to "this present age," or to natural objects, does tie us down, enchaining and enslaving the human spirit. Moreover, Jews, Christians, and Muslims view the restless, wandering figure of Abraham as a model of the deeply religious calling to leave the narrowness of "home" in pursuit of deeper fulfillment. In heeding the call to religious life it seems that we are encouraged to pursue a life of detachment. Christianity, following ancient biblical patterns of thought, sees our life here on earth as an exodus journey, a pilgrimage, a desert wandering. In the New Testament, Jesus, the "Son of Man," is portrayed as having "no place to lay his head," and in Luke's Gospel he calls his followers to set their eyes on Jerusalem and not to look back toward what they have left behind. The Kingdom is more important than home and family.

If we turn to the East we notice that the Buddha also has to leave home, to cease clinging to things and even to family, so as to find "enlightenment." And in Hinduism the *sannyasin* finally forsakes home and family also, wandering to the edge of a forest or some other remote spot, so as to get closer to God. A great deal of the world's religious instruction, especially since the Axial Age, persuades us to accept the fundamentally homeless character of our existence as a condition of redemptive liberation. Accepting this homelessness is apparently essential to the religious adventure. But how do we reconcile religious pilgrimage with the ecological imperative to implant ourselves more deeply than ever in the earth? Can we practice "religious homelessness," in other words, without turning it into an ecologically ominous "cosmic homelessness"?

After some reflection on this question, I have come to the tentative conclusion that it is not the ideal of religious homelessness per se that is problematic. Rather it is our careless and unnecessary translation of religious into *cosmic* homelessness. The former, I propose, does not inevitably entail the latter. The endorsement of cosmic homelessness twists the ideal of religious homelessness into an escapism that makes nature a victim of our religious restlessness. Earth, for example, comes to be seen as a place to get *away from* in order to find salvation. The natural world becomes little more than a "vale of soul-making" in which to prove ourselves worthy of eternal life in some extracosmic domain. But if we love nature how can we keep this affection from slipping toward a pure naturalism that binds our spirits and frustrates our search for the ultimate liberation that faith promises? Can we ever truly learn to love God without turning our backs on earth? Can we come to cherish the natural world without surrendering our longing for the beyond? These are questions, perhaps the main questions, to which a Christian theology of nature must now attend.

I believe that we must admit in all candor that the religious formation that many if not most Christians have received has led them to harbor a deep suspicion that the human species does not essentially belong to nature or to the earth; and so in the name of religious aspiration they sometimes still hold themselves at a distance from nature. Many fear that it would be a capitulation to paganism, pantheism, or romantic naturalism if they allowed the roots of their being to penetrate very far into the terrestrial soil. Unhappily, modern theology has done little to prevent the divorce from nature. Especially in the modern period it has handed over the natural world to science and left to itself the task of interpreting classic religious texts, personal life, and human history. It has left questions about nature and its future out of the field of theological interest. The majority of theologians still have little formal interest in the welfare of the nonhuman natural world.

However, I should hasten to add that it is not only religion and theology that have made us feel that we do not really belong to the cosmos. The so-called modern "scientific worldview" has also left us with the strong impression that we humans are essentially exiles from nature. In recent centuries much scientific thought has come to see nature as lifeless and mindless "stuff." As a result, modern intellectual life has often assumed a materialist and pessimistic philosophy that gives the status of reality primarily to dead matter and views life and human consciousness as ephemeral accidents. Thus, in an essentially lifeless and spiritless world it is not surprising that the human spirit can hardly feel at home.

Together, scientific materialism and religious dualism have perpetuated the ancient Gnostic idea that we are "lost in the cosmos." Can we find a way to reconcile the religious requirement of living homelessly, on the one hand, with the ecological imperative to make nature our home on the other? We are torn—or so it would seem—between two appealing but apparently conflicting persuasions. We are drawn spiritually to the religious ideal of living without clinging to things that will diminish us and ultimately disappoint us. A spiritual homelessness is essential to the religious adventure even if physically we are tied to nature; and spiritual detachment can make us reluctant to see nature itself as an ethical concern. But, at the same time, many of us are now attracted to the ecological sentiment that the natural world has values worth preserving, that it is indeed our home.

How do we hold these two propensities together? Fortunately, and perhaps ironically, recent developments in natural science can come to our aid here. Careful reflection on the implications of contemporary scientific cosmology may allow us to belong to nature while at the same time letting us also pursue the life of religious detachment. Only a little knowledge of what science now teaches us about the universe can help us spiritually and intellectually to link our religious journey of homelessness to the ecological requirement of remaining friendly with and even firmly fixed to nature. We can now reasonably claim, in other words, that religious homelessness may exist harmoniously with a sense of our being quite at home in the cosmos. The following is an attempt to say why this solution is plausible.

Over the last century and a half science has demonstrated that the natural world itself is a restless adventure. No previous age had ever known—at least with the assuredness that we now possess—that the natural world is on a pilgrimage of its own. Our religions, including Christianity, emerged long before science had discovered that nature is itself a historical process and not something fixed or static. Today scientists realize that the physical universe is not changeless, eternal, or necessary, as they formerly may have thought it to be. Although many people still do not believe it, the cosmos is most certainly a process, an evolution, an ongoing story. Humans live, in other words, in a universe that is still being created. The cosmos is not a stationary set of things frozen in essentially the same plodding status from all eternity, but an unfinished adventure open to what is perpetually new.

The famous Jesuit geologist and paleontologist Teilhard de Chardin (1881–1955) has probably done more than any other Christian thinker to demonstrate how we can remain fully a part of the earth and the cosmos while also embarking on a momentous religious journey—along with the universe, not apart from it. Although, like others in his day, Teilhard was not fully aware of the scale of ecological degradation that modernity had unleashed, he developed a deeply incarnational and hopeful spirituality that can now frame our own efforts to construct an ecological theology. He did this by reinterpreting Christian faith in the context of cosmic and biological evolution (Teilhard de Chardin 1969).

What evolution implies first and foremost is that creation is not yet finished. It is *in via,* on the way. The cosmos itself is essentially a pilgrimage. Hence, for us to embrace *this* universe we must align our own human existence with its inherent restlessness. Biology, geology, and astrophysics now converge in challenging the ancient assumption that the universe is eternal and essentially unchanging. Taking seriously the new scientific picture of the world allows—even requires—that we embed our own unsettled lives within the much larger context of a *cosmic* restlessness. Only by accepting the universe's own homelessness, in other words, can we be at home in nature. Billions of years before we humans came along in evolution the universe had already been on the move. During the past century and a half science has filled out in remarkable detail the various episodes of this immense journey. I believe that there are implications for an ecological theology in these new accounts of the cosmic adventure.

At first glance, of course, one may wonder just what ecological-theological significance could possibly be squeezed out of the initially disturbing news that the cosmos itself is not at rest. According to the Big Bang theory, which almost all scientists accept today, the universe has a finite evolutionary past and an irreversible temporal trajectory. For all we know, therefore, our Big Bang cosmos may presently be only in the early stages of a creative process that will last for many more billions of years. The point is, it is now clear that the universe is a still unfolding story. But what does this mean for our own question about the relationship of ecology to theology? It means, most fundamentally, that it is not only the human spirit that has undertaken an immense journey (especially through

its religious wanderings) but that the entire cosmos is partner and prologue to our own homeless religious passage. Therefore, we do not need
to abandon the natural world in order to follow the spiritual counsel to
live homelessly. Indeed, we may even be permitted to say that our religious restlessness is a blossoming forth of the universe's own ageless ad-
venturing. Our human hunger for transcendence is a conscious development of a general leaning toward the open future that has always been a
hidden feature of the physical universe. Our religious striving toward the
infinite is to be satisfied only by our attuning ourselves to the larger and
longer cosmic odyssey into the future, not by extricating ourselves from
it. The new scientific cosmology allows us to belong to the universe without our having to sacrifice the ideal of religious sojourning. Eschatology
can embrace cosmology—"Your promise O Lord is as wide as the heavens" (Psalm 138:2).

So our religious homelessness does not have to be turned into cosmic
homelessness after all. Theologically viewed, we may now say that the
universe—at its very core—is inseparable from promise. And so we may
learn to revere the natural world not simply because faith sees it as sacramentally transparent to God, but even more because it carries in its present perishable nature the seeds of a final, glorious future flowering. This
means, in turn, that our current abuse of nature is not only a violation of
nature's sacramentality; it is also a turning away from the promise that
lies embedded in God's creation. In a properly biblical framework, then,
our ecological recklessness is not just disobedience to our mission of
stewardship, nor simply a sacrilege in violation of nature's sacramentality. It is fundamentally an expression of despair, of the distrust that the
Bible considers to lie at the base of human sinfulness.

This promissory way of looking at nature requires that we give a fresh
understanding to the notion of stewardship. Stewardship, in the framework of a cosmology framed by the theme of promise, must amount to
much more than conservation. Conservation is essential of course. We
need to appreciate the many millions of years of evolutionary striving
and achievement that produced the ecological richness that preceded
human emergence. It goes without saying that there is an intrinsic worth
in earth's biosphere that deserves our best efforts at preservation. But
perhaps the most fundamentally Christian reason to participate in the
saving of living diversity is that nature is always pregnant with the promise of humanly incalculable future outcomes. A Christian vision will lead

us to strive not to get out of the world but to do what we can to shepherd this still unfinished universe toward the fulfillment of the promise that underlies and impels it toward the future.

I do not have space here to consider the anticipated questions that arise from recent astrophysical scenarios of a universe that in the distant future will no longer be able to sustain life. The eventual demise of the cosmos, however, does not vitiate the theme of nature's promise that I have been highlighting. To the Christian there should in principle be no more difficulty trusting that the whole universe-story will be taken redemptively into God's life than there is in trusting that we ourselves will be saved by God's compassionate care. For now I must be content to affirm that it is no longer theologically or cosmologically conceivable that human destiny could ever be separated from cosmic destiny and vice-versa. If we dwell within the compass of God's promise, so also does the entire universe.

NOTE

1. Pope John Paul II, "Peace with God the Creator, Peace with All of Creation" (World Day of Peace message, Jan. 1, 1990), and *The Ecological Crisis: A Common Responsibility*, nos. 1, 15 (Dec. 8, 1989); The United States Conference of Catholic Bishops, (1991); Christiansen and Grazer (1996); Bishops' pastoral letter, "The Columbia River Watershed: Caring for Creation and the Common Good" (February, 2001). Documents and discussion of some of the earliest work on ecological issues by the World Council of Churches may be found in Birch, Eakin, and McDaniel (1990).

WORKS CITED

Augustine of Hippo. 1960. *The Confessions of St. Augustine*. Garden City, NY: Image Books.

Berry, Thomas. 1988. *The dream of the earth*. San Francisco: Sierra Club Books.

Birch, Charles, William Eakin, and Jay B. McDaniel, eds. 1990. *Liberating life: Contemporary approaches to ecological theology.* Maryknoll, NY: Orbis Books.

Christiansen, Drew, S. J. and Walter Grazer, eds. 1996. *And God saw that it was good.* Washington DC: United States Catholic Conference.

Commoner, Barry. 1971. In defense of biology. In *Man and nature: Philosophical Issues in Biology,* ed. Ronald Munson, 33-54. New York: Dell Publishing Co.

Daly, Herman E., and John B. Cobb, Jr. 1989. *For the common good.* Boston: Beacon Press.

Fox, Matthew. 1983. *Original blessing.* Santa Fe, NM: Bear.

Haught, John. 1993. *The promise of nature: Ecology and cosmic purpose.* Mahwah, NJ: Paulist Press.

———. 2000. *God after Darwin: A theology of evolution.* Boulder, CO: Westview Press.

Himes, Michael J. and Kenneth R. Himes. 1990. The sacrament of creation: Toward environment theology. *Commonweal* 117 (2): 42–49.

Moltmann, Jürgen. 1967. *Theology of hope.* Trans. by James Leitch. New York: Harper & Row.

———. 1975. *The experiment hope,* Ed. and trans. by M. Douglas Meeks. Philadelphia: Fortress Press.

Passmore, John. 1974. *Man's responsibility for nature.* New York: Scribner.

Rolston, Holmes, III. 1996. Science, religion, and the future. In *Religion and science: History, method, dialogue,* ed. Mark Richardson and Wesley Wildman, 61-82. New York: Routledge.

Sheldrake, Rupert. 1991. *The rebirth of nature: The greening of science and God.* New York: Bantam Books.

Teilhard de Chardin, Pierre. 1969. *Christianity and evolution.* Trans. René Hague. New York: Harcourt Brace & Co.

United States Conference of Catholic Bishops. 1991. Renewing the earth: An invitation to reflection and action on environment in light of Catholic social teaching. Available at http://www.nccbuscc.org/sdwp/ejp/bishopsstatement.htm (last accessed Sept. 2005).

CHAPTER 9

Ecology and Morality: The Challenge to and from Christian Ethics

Larry Rasmussen

The flux of nature on a humanly dominated planet entails an extended range of ethical choices. This is discussed in what follows as "the ascendancy of ethics" in and for our time. Does the flux of nature also mean the ascendancy of religion? If so, might there be impulses for a religiously contoured ecological vision? Whatever the answers to these questions, the flux and unpredictability of nature mean new challenges to Christian ethics, and from Christian ethics to ecology, morality, and society.

This opening paragraph guides this chapter. So does an argument and conclusion, namely, that well-rooted religious and moral ecologies can help counter the downside of "ecomodernity" as well as accommodate flux. Both the questions of the first paragraph and the conclusion require some distinctions best drawn at the outset. We begin with these.

KEY NOTIONS

The subject of all ethical analysis is the same: ways of life and their logic, practices, problems, and achievements. Not that ethics, as a discipline, is alone. Anthropology and sociology make ways of life their subject, as do history, philosophy, and a sizable chunk of ordinary, everyday conversation. So what distinguishes ethics?

We are, by nature, moral animals. We can imagine different worlds—and better ones. This means we live our lives across a certain gap, a gap few other species experience and none in so defining a manner. From childhood to somewhere near dying day we live in the tension between "what is" and "what ought to be," a tension that gives rise to deliberate choice, act, and responsibility. Ethics spans this chasm and brings to life riveted attention to the kinds of questions moral animals and their ways of living ask: What makes human lives go well? What is the good life? How ought we to live? In short, ethics is the normative investigation of the moral ecologies embedded in human ways of life. Ethics interrogates, ethics recommends, and ethics passes along the record of past human efforts to bridge "is" and "ought."

An essential part of any way of life, and a critical element of its moral ecology, is its "cosmology." Cosmologies differ by kind, function and substance, however. In a book like this, distinctions of "religious cosmologies" from "scientific cosmologies" take on special importance, as does the difference of "scientific ecology" from "religious and moral ecology."

Scientific ecology is "the empirical and experimental study of the relations between living and nonliving organisms within their ecosystems" (Tucker and Grim 2001, 15). Scientific cosmology and evolutionary sciences place these relations within the processes of ongoing life and the evolution of the universe itself—the "cosmos." Religious cosmology also orients life to the cosmos and locates our place in it, but not in the same way. It uses little scientific narrative and rarely subjects its claims to the rigors of scientific method. Rather, religion utilizes "cosmological stories, symbol systems, ritual practices, ethical norms, historical processes, and institutional structures" to situate humans inside a cosmic matrix of meaning and mystery about life as it "emerges, unfolds, and dies" (Tucker and Grim 2001, 14). This elaborate matrix of meaning and mystery constitutes a kind of communal harbor for the numinous and holy, and within it religion forms human character and conscience in keeping with a way of life tethered to its understanding of the cosmos. It instructs people about their moral responsibilities as these are framed by religious cosmology and lived day-by-day. Religious ecologies thus carry inherent moral content. The interdependent elements of any given religion—the stories, systems, instruction, ritual practices, and so on—impact upon the character, outlook, and conscience of serious participants. "Religious ecology" is thus a proper term for the internal logic of religious practice as it belongs to a way of life and its morality.

Religious ecology can also mean something quite different. It can specify "a cultural awareness of kinship with and dependence on nature for the continuity of all life" (Tucker and Grim 2001, 15). In that capacity religious ecology not only offers a basis for studying how religions view nature; it also shows how particular natural environments influence particular religions and cultures and their ways of life. (Desert spirituality mirrors desert life, mountain spirituality reflects mountain vistas and ways.)

Both meanings of religious ecology—how religious systems work and how religions view nature and are influenced by it—hold for the discussion that follows. Both also underscore what the archeological record turns up time and again: humans turn to nature as both metaphor and context to interpret cosmic purpose and to discern moral order itself.

THE ASCENDANCY OF ETHICS

These distinctions in hand, we return to the opening paragraph and the claim that the flux of nature on a humanly dominated planet means "the ascendancy of ethics." Why the ascendancy of ethics? Because modernity, due in no small part to modern science and technology, has vastly amplified human powers. The consequences of wielding these powers have been extended in time, space, and degree. We *can* do more, more than ever before, and we do, from splitting atoms to splitting genes to splitting timbers, mountains, and rivers.

Whenever the scope and impact of human agency broaden or deepen because of new possibilities, or new consequences follow from the cumulative impact of established ways, moral and ethical issues press to the fore. We *can* do more, we *are* doing more. But *ought* we to do all we can, and ought we to have done what we have? What precisely ought we to do now in facing new, enlarged, or otherwise changed circumstances? And what consequences should we now repair, if we can? These are the perennial ethical questions riding in the wake of heightened human power and its real-world consequences.

Take, for example, the cumulative human impact on the rest of nature over the course of the last century. That impact has been dramatic. Humans moved more rocks and soil in the twentieth century than did volcanoes, glaciers, and tectonic plates! We used ten times more energy in the last one hundred years than our forebears did in the last one thousand, and we used it to alter both natural and artificial landscapes in ways and degrees our ancestors would have found stunning and disorienting. The raw numbers for other increases—urban population and industrial output—are thirteen times and forty times, respectively, for the twentieth century, with the bulk of that coming after 1950 and with no signs of abatement in the new millennium (McNeill 2000).

The World According to Pimm: A Scientist Audits the Earth (Pimm 2001) tells the same tale. Pimm's is a present tabulation of forests, croplands, oceans, and species. His conclusion is that "Earth at the turn of this new millennium is suffering from huge and unmistakable human impacts. Some—the loss of species, certainly, and the loss of tropical forests, almost surely—are about to become irreversible" (Pimm 2001, 233). Hamlin and Lodge's own conclusion is similar: "Wherever we look, human impact is overwhelming" (introduction, this volume, 12).

Let me put this differently, albeit in the interest of the same point (the ascendancy of ethics). Life, which has always been a dicey, unplanned experiment, has become an experiment of planetary proportions at the hands of a single remarkable and irrepressible species. This species, "moral" by nature in that its day-to-day choices determine so much of its own and others' lives, presently feels its way on a scale new to the planetary community of life. Expanded efforts to meet the needs and wants of historically unprecedented numbers of people (9.2 billion by 2050 is one estimate) will only ratchet upward the dimensions of this unplanned experiment. The breakthroughs of science and industry—the mapping of genomes and the global investment in biotechnologies, for example—will magnify it as well. So, too, will coming to grips with accelerated climate change. What "humans throw at nature," then, is as vital to nature itself as "what nature threw at humans" (introduction, this volume, 7). The salient point is that "what humans throw at nature" is a matter of moral choices and their life ways above all, in contrast to fate ("what nature threw at humans"). The ascendancy of ethics follows from our greatly enhanced capacities to affect the rest of nature on an increasingly humanly dominated planet.

But a humanly dominated planet is not a humanly controlled one. The flux and unpredictability of nature assures that. It also complicates morality and ethics. Flux and unpredictability do not change the ascendancy of ethics per se. That, as noted, is the outcome of amplified human powers. But when nature, in both religious and scientific cosmologies, was perceived in terms of "balance," "harmony," and "equilibrium," it could be, and was, a source of morality in its own right. Or it was the more-or-less reliable world for moral choices made on other grounds (the "moral law within,"[1] for example, or the dictates of sacred scriptures).

Nature, human nature included, as a source of reliable moral guidance has an impressive record in the moral ecologies of innumerable ways of life. These "natural law" traditions have been at home in numerous human cultures stretching across millennia. They continue in forms as global as the human rights tradition, the substance of international treaties and conventions, and the laws of nations. Yet whether named "natural law" or something else, the gist is the same: the orderliness and intelligibility of nature, together with its resilience, perceived harmony and interdependence, have long been considered trustworthy sources of morally relevant knowledge.

Christian ethics has also long been a welcoming home to natural law traditions. From its onset Christianity has assumed that there is an independent reality to the material world, the ordering and structure of which is intelligible to the human mind. Nature is more than intelligible, however. It is, as intimated above, also reliable; it provides solid ground for human knowledge and choice. Perhaps even more important, from a moral point of view, nature is "good," nothing less than the precious expression of a gracious God who, while shrouded in mystery, is neither arbitrary nor pernicious. Nature carefully observed thus yields knowledge of God and God's ways, and as such is a source of wisdom for God's (human) creatures as they confront their moral responsibilities and fashion their ways of life.[2] Moral wisdom is found in the Book of Nature as well as the Book of Holy Writ.

The Belgic Confession of 1561 nicely illustrates Christian apprehension of nature as a source for morality. It would not be the first source to come to mind for Christian natural law, however. That would be the Aristotelian, Stoic, and Augustinian legacies given classic expression in Roman Catholic moral theology and practice by Thomas Aquinas and his scholastic successors. The Belgic Confession, by contrast, reflects a distinctive mark of the Protestant Reformation, here in Calvinist form, namely, severe doubts about the trustworthiness of unaided human knowing on the part of "fallen" creatures. Given natural law's trust in shared and unaided human knowing, there is all the more reason, then, to listen for the place of nature in this Calvinist confession together with the conclusion it draws for the moral life. We know, the authors write, "[f]irst, by the creation, preservation and government of the universe, which is before our eyes as a most beautiful book, in which all creatures, great and small, are like so many characters leading us to contemplate the invisible things of God. . . . All of these things are sufficient to convince humanity [of its responsibilities], and leave [humanity] without excuse" (McGrath 2001, 23). In other words, even for sinful human beings guidance from creation is clear enough and sound enough that no one is morally off-the-hook.

But what does Christian ethics do when what we know about nature is its propensity to gamble? Where will Christian ethics turn as it discovers the extent to which its own assumptions of reliable nature play out older (Greek) preferences for stability over change and immutability over transience, thereby according greater value to the changeless than the changeable? And what does this investment in stasis mean for moral guidance, if stasis runs counter to present knowledge of nature and counter to guidance from the specific science most directly engaged with interdependent life systems, namely, ecology? If Christian ethics, both as a discipline and as practice, is wittingly and unwittingly deeply rooted in assumptions of the nature of nature as harmony, balance, and constancy, how will an inherently uncertain nature—the current paradigm in ecology—guide us morally? Are nature's days as a source for moral wisdom over? If so, what else is there? Imagination? Random tastes and preferences? Predominating power? Custom and habit? Do we have any idea what it means to lose Mother Nature as a teacher for morality?

In sum, nature's flux and surprise would seem to challenge to the core natural law traditions that have given humans guidance for as long as we have looked to the heavens or contemplated the ground under our feet. Nature's inclination to do the unexpected certainly challenges longstanding notions in Christian ethics. And all this is compounded by the fact that nature's ways are, more than in the past, affected by yet another volatile factor, namely, human choices and actions, both singly and cumulatively.

ECOMODERNITY

The challenge of flux and unpredictability to Christian ethics is min-
iscule, however, compared with its challenge to a present way of life that
prevails for millions, perhaps billions. It is a way of life that assumes engineering precision and managerial control of reasonably reliable nature.
Following Aiden Davison, I will label this way of life "ecomodernity"
(Davison 2001). The gist of ecomodernity, argues Davison, is the transformation and management of nature for human benefit, in a humanly
dominated biosphere, on the terms of commerce and a technocratic
agenda. Biological life systems themselves are among the objects of direct
management and change, as part of our own life system and its drives.
Ecomodernity, then, is an engineering and management ethic that uses
nature as the dynamic material of a humanly constructed and humanly
ordered world.

The challenge of flux and unpredictability to Christian ethics is min-
Yet this assertion, standing alone, is little more than a raw claim. An
extended analysis of ecomodernity itself is required to appreciate the
challenge of flux to a prominent way of life. And while a gloss on Christianity's role will be included, the real agenda here is to carry on the work
of any ethic, namely, to interrogate the moral dimensions of this way of
life and then offer a recommendation of what we ought to do in light of
our findings. What, then, *is* ecomodernity and how ought we to respond,
from a moral point of view?

Davison contends that modernity's project has been the same since its
inception: to organize nature itself as raw material for the technological
production of human well-being. "Eco"-modernity extends this by appropriating recent sciences in dramatic ways—ecology, genetics, and com-
puting sciences, to name prominent ones. At first glance, these sciences
would seem to transform modernity. Modernity's assumption of a mechanistic universe, for example, would seem significantly altered when the
language of organism and organic process is joined to information and
machine metaphors in descriptions of nature. To cite a second case, ecology's holistic thought would seem to displace the logic of tight, linear
cause-and-effect so common to modernity's world. In yet a third example, living interdependence in a deeply relational world—hardly the
theme of modernity's metaphysics—is now offered by ecology and genetics as the nature of nature itself. All three of these major shifts belong
to the "eco" of ecomodernity.

So is it still modernity? Davison says, emphatically, "Yes!" To make his case, he discusses four elements: dualism, subjectivism, anthropocentrism, and productivism.

Dualism

Dualism, though a strong mark of modernity, harkens back to Plato's formative impact on occidental thought. For Plato the search of pure mind for truth and certainty turns away from apparently indifferent materiality. Indeed, the quest of Plato's rational soul carries a certain disdain for materiality (despite all those gorgeous Greek torsos and the ideal of a sound mind in a healthy body)!

Western Christianity and ethics imbibed Greek dualism early and often, with millennial staying power. Particularly influential was the Neoplatonism of Plotinus (205–270 CE). Through his influence, not least upon St. Augustine (354–430 CE), much of Western Christianity's spiritual quest became the Neoplatonic pilgrim journey of the rational soul scaling the cosmic ladder in a life of ascetic ascent. The farther Christians journeyed upward toward union with God as Pure Mind and Spirit, the more Earth, corrupting nature, and the bonds of materiality were left behind.[3] Here a religious cosmology that thought itself accurate as a scientific cosmology also articulated a "Great Chain of Being"[4] that molded ways of both devotion and morality. The Great Chain of Being yielded an ethic and way of life both dualistic and hierarchical, as we shall see in the discussion of anthropocentrism below.

Subjectivism

The point for both modernity's and ecomodernity's ways, however, rests with the most powerful dualism of all, namely, Cartesian. (The heart of Davison's meaning of modernity cum ecomodernity is the persistence of Cartesian dualism.) This dualist "perfection" was reached in the seventeenth century when Rene Descartes neatly cleft the world "out there" from the mind "within." With that cleavage modernity's subjectivism was born. The gist is this: human self-consciousness alone discloses the only "undoubtable" ground of real and reliable knowledge. This is the Enlightenment's fabled turn to the human subject as the center of both knowing and knowledge, a move never made in the same way or degree by Plato or Christian theologians.

Yet this turn was not only about knowing, but valuing as well. Thus was Descartes' thought experiment crucial for both science and ethics—to doubt all things possible except the self-conscious, thinking "I." From the seventeenth century onward, a Western culture that had once considered meaning and purpose to be written into the order of nature and the cosmos by an awesome and incarnate God now assumed that the meaning and end of all nature has its effective value in the rational will and active agency of autonomous and sovereign humanity. Here is modernity in the raw. Here, in scantest form, is the severe subjectivism embedded in the working assumptions of so much of modern culture, ethics, even religion. Namely, the essence of humanity is consciousness and mind; this essence radically distinguishes us from (the rest of) nature. The rest of nature is now "object" to us, rather than "subject," and our relationship to this nature is in the manner of subject-over-object and mind-over-matter. When armed with modern science, technology, and other powers, such subjectivism assures the triumph of humans as effectively a segregated and dominating species. That Cartesian cosmology further pictured nature as mechanism only reinforced this separatist, subject-over-object stance. It is no exaggeration to say that Cartesian (and Baconian, Lockean, and Kantian) humans act upon nature in accord with a morality most reminiscent of master/slave, with nature the slave and humanity the master. This is stark distance and alienation, almost a separate order of being itself.

Anthropocentrism

The anthropocentrism of ecomodernity is as complex as ecomodernity itself, not least because of a subtle and complex relationship to Western Christian ethics. Here we go beyond Davison's discussion to sort three streams: patterns of superiority and inferiority, *contemptus mundi* teaching, and the challenge of modern science. Together they nuance the ethic and cosmology already set in motion by Cartesian dualism and modern subjectivism.

Superiority and inferiority.   Modernity's mind-over-matter, subject-over-object relationship, with humans seemingly a species apart, drew from deep-running currents in Christian cosmology and ethics. Christian sources themselves fostered the anthropocentrism of species pride. They did so with a millennial emphasis on human uniqueness and favor. Never mind that after an initial account in Genesis, the Hebrew Bible offers scant evidence that *imago dei* ("the image of God") plays any major role at all in subsequent biblical articulations of human being and human ways. In the New Testament writings the only reference is Paul's, and it is to Jesus Christ as the image of God, not to *Homo sapiens sapiens* as an elect species. Nonetheless, divinely created uniqueness and high human standing came to have extraordinary influence in Christian ethics. Granted, much of it meant to undergird sober moral responsibility on the part of stewards trying faithfully to live out their place of honor in the cosmic chain. But whether in sober stewardly fashion or not, *imago dei* status merged with the subject-object split-off of "us" vis à vis "them." And it did so in such a way that nonhuman creation is always lodged "below," not only as the created hierarchy of nature but as value or worth. God alone is "above," *and thus* commands respect and allegiance. What is "below" does not. To label someone or something a "low life" is the ultimate put down.

What modernity did was solder species uniqueness to perceived patterns of superiority and inferiority. Yet that, too, was easy for Christians, since Great Chain of Being cosmology had already set superiority in place on both androcentric and species terms. As already noted, this most popular and enduring of Christian cosmologies, current by the fourth century and lasting into the eighteenth century, placed all things on a cosmic ladder of lesser and more. Inorganic matter was at the bottom and valued least, while God as Pure Mind and Spirit rested at the apex as the subject of pure adoration and the only object truly worthy of worship. Humankind rested "just a little lower than the angels," with "lower" life forms— "all sheep and oxen, and also the beasts of the field, the birds of the air, and the fish of the sea, whatever passes along the paths of the seas"— "under [humankind's] feet" (Psalm 8:5–8). Distinctions reigned within species as well—males were "superior" to females, and "civilized" peoples ranked above "uncivilized." Value and place, or status, were thus clarified together on no less than "cosmic" terms, with perfection as the least earthly or soiled. Morality, science, and religious mission all belonged together in the same coherent picture of the Western world.

To round out the power of these patterns of superiority and inferiority for the making of modernity, this Christian cosmology and morality needed only to sanction social orders in keeping with this hierarchy. That it did, literally on a global scale, in the Age of Discovery when, from the fifteenth century onward, European sailors learned to master the wind and water currents of the great oceans, the Atlantic and the Pacific. This meant European contact with peoples, religions, cultures, flora, and fauna across the planet. Sometimes that fateful contact was on beneficent terms. More often it was the cruel side of conquest, colonization, commerce, Christianity, and "civilization" as a package. For Christian participation, important baselines had been laid down as early as Constantine and Theodosius in the fourth century. When Theodosius made Christianity the official and mandatory religion, Christianity became what it was not in its origins, and had never been in any of the centuries before Constantine—namely, a budding imperial religion. All it then needed, in order to "go global" as a domination system, was that initial wave of "globalization" in the fifteenth century. Yet the point here is that this was also the onset of modernity itself and its migration to every continent except Antarctica. Add to the Age of Discovery the European Enlightenment and the Industrial Revolution, and the outcome is that neo-European settlements and systems would reign more than any other and would transform lands and peoples together, nature and culture alike and both at once. Neo-European ways answered in great detail and with great confidence the irrepressible question of how humans ought to live.

In passing, we should note that this global neo-Europeanizing of culture and nature together was served by the most learned European and expatriate minds of the day. Even amidst dissent and the rise of democratic forces, nature and the world itself were understood in both scientific and religious cosmologies as infinite links hierarchically ordered. The transformation of the planet in neo-European ways was thus accomplished with a confidence—and naiveté—that can only be explained by the grip of these imperial Chain of Being cosmologies on the minds of scientists, philosophers, sailors, theologians, preachers, teachers, and merchants alike. Men of science and religion (and they were men) might war with one another at home, but in matters of empire, they made common cause.

Contemptus mundi. Modernity's domination practices (subject-over-object and mind-over-matter, with a global reach) were well-served by a certain twist on another element, the teaching of *contemptus mundi* (contempt for the world). Initially, *contemptus mundi* was the classic protest of early Christianity against the wiles of evil as corrupted and un-just society. The "way of the world"—meaning Greco-Roman culture and imperial rule, in this case—was "the way of death." It contrasted with "the way of life" as the way of devout faith and disciplined living in communities of zealous faith. But *contemptus mundi* in some cases ab-sorbed Earth-denigrating dualism to become subtle disdain for nature as well as culture, including the human body itself. When reinforced with a religious cosmology of cosmic ladders, a paradoxical picture emerged. On the one hand, God is praised "for the beauty of the earth" and "the beauty of the skies" (to remember a popular hymn), and nature as cre-ation is seen as a reliable source for moral instruction. On the other hand, and in the very same moment, we are alienated from the rest of nature, and from our bodies, as the solitary Earthling who is not truly at home here! *Contemptus mundi,* in the subtle but major shift from attention to "this present world" as moral evil to "this present world" as nature and society together, made it "cosmically clear" that humans are not fully at home in this world. Spiritually, and even categorically as a species, we belong elsewhere. To this day, Christians are not of a mind about their relationship to (the rest) of creation.

Perhaps oddly, *contemptus mundi* teaching curiously reinforced the anthropocentrism that in due course would characterize modernity. As creatures of aspiring mind and spirit we are, as moderns, the keepers of a restless transcendence. Ours is a roaming, free agency that constantly breaks the mold of physical and social existence. Breaking the molds that nature and society supply in turn distances us from the rest of nature and sanctions our separation from it in the manner of subject to object and superior to inferior. A subtle, secular *contemptus mundi* thus pervades modernity and ecomodernity. Biophilia, to cite the constrasting orienta-tion, doesn't surface here, except as a stream running against the tide of a humanly centered world.

The challenge of modern science. By now it will have occurred to most readers that ecology, genetics, astronomy, and evolutionary sciences challenge the anthropocentrism and human exceptionalism that typify modernity and that retain a steady beat in much Christian piety and ethics. They likewise challenge religiously sanctioned human alienation from the only home we have ever known and the only place we are fine-tuned to live. These sciences are utterly clear in ways Christianity has not always been; we are, they aver without qualification, creatures of evolution and of Earth. "Humanity is part of a vast evolving universe," to cite the Earth Charter, which then goes on to speak of uniqueness. It is not, however, the sort of uniqueness to which we grown accustomed; namely, our own as a species. Rather, "Earth, our home, is alive with a unique community of life" (Earth Charter, Preamble).

These sciences challenge most Christian natural law traditions as well. The reason is not the one cited earlier, however—nature's flux. The challenge instead is to the nature of "nature" in most natural law traditions, at least most Christian natural law traditions. The full breadth of human relationships as *internally* related members across the whole community of life—Earth's distinguishing mark—has not been typical of most Christian natural law. Christian natural law has instead drawn the circle around human nature and the distinctive rational character of *Homo sapiens sapiens* in a moral universe consisting of intra-human relationships. We are biological creatures, to be sure, and social animals. That is clear in these traditions. But we are not genuinely ecological/evolutionary ones. We have not emerged from the same evolutionary life processes as the rest of life, according to these traditions, nor do we move with all else into the future as sharers in a common destiny. Thus the interests of (segregated) humanity have garnered all the attention in natural law traditions, and the life-claims of the other life-forms with and upon whom we exist in utter interdependence have gone wanting, if not missing altogether. Nature as a moral guide in Christian natural law was never, then, about the conditions for the fullest possible flourishing of Earth's unique community of life and the moral claims such conditions impose upon us. Nature as a moral guide was, at least for the modern era, about human flourishing in an anthropocentric, dualist, and subjectivist moral universe. It was also notably male and European or neo-European, that is, notably "white" in race consciousness and privilege (which means "white" as a determinant of cultural and moral norms).

These sciences, then, challenge much of inherited Christianity. But do they challenge modernity and its ways, including its anthropocentrism? Answering that entails a return to Davison.

Productivism

Cartesian/Enlightenment mind-over-matter, subject-over-object relationships with the rest of nature took on a strongly Promethean character Davison labels "productivism." Prometheus's gift of fire, now in the hands of post-Enlightenment sovereign humanity (the hands of European and neo-European men, in real terms), symbolized the energy and drive of a new political economy and a new social class—Europe's rising bourgeoisie. This was the force that, with help from the zeal and ethic of newborn Protestantism, on the one hand, and the devastation of the Plague, on the other, sent feudalism to the grave. The new political economy would eventually acquire a name of its own—"capitalism." The point here, however, is that "productivism" meant, and still means, the domination of political economic life over the rest of life, whether as the mercantilism and trade of conquest and colonization, the later industrialism of neo-European societies newly in place around the globe, or, presently, political economic globalization that is no longer simply the dominance of "the West over the rest" but a force affecting all countries internally and externally, west, east, north, south. Modernity's master image may always have been mastery itself, as the organization of nature (and subjugated cultures) for human well-being (some humans far more than others). But nothing so served the creation of a world in our human design as this Promethean economic spirit and the ways in which it effectively channeled other forces—science, technology, religion, and culture. And yes, morality and ethics, too, since for modernity the good life is, for millions if not billions, the life of goods created and used as we desire in a world of our own making.

A look at reigning ethical theory adds detail. In practical terms, the social contract traditions associated with John Locke and Anglo-Saxon social and political philosophy have inordinately influenced modernity's treatment of the Earth, its peoples and cultures included. This is due chiefly to the merger of social contract philosophy with the institutional needs and developments of modernity, above all the economic and political practices that have dominated since the initial wave of neo-European globalization. Modern ways of spelling out obligation—duties, rights, justice, law, morality—are considered the product of free contract between rational individuals acting as centers of autonomous agency in a world of subject-over-object, mind-over-matter. Here again biophysical nature is cordoned off and parked at the edge of the moral universe, except as raw material awaiting human transformation into objects of "real value" ("real value" means commodities commanding market exchange).

Mary Midgley has listed those missing in action from this moral world. It turns out that social contract morality—the morality of "economic man" globally, it bears repeating—leaves out our ancestors, posterity, children, the senile, the temporarily insane, the permanently insane, "defectives" ranging down to human "vegetables," embryos, sentient animals, nonsentient animals, plants of all kinds, artifacts (including works of arts), inanimate but structured objects (rivers, rocks), unchosen groups of all kinds (including families and species, ecosystems, landscapes, villages, cities), countries, the biosphere, and God! In short, the most commonly utilized moral universe of our daily lives excludes the greater part of our actual communities and obligations. Why? Because these are noncontractors, and as such they are not moral agents, they are not individual, rational, human bearers of responsibility. They are not, in different words, the only population that truly counts in the practical moral universe of society as social contract.

Midgley, by contrast, urges a morality that would of necessity "arise out of our membership in complex biological and ecological communities that are to a great extent invisible to us" (Midgley 1995, 101). These are communities upon which our lives and other lives depend utterly (ecosystems, for example, or the gases of the atmosphere), and upon which, in a humanly dominated biosphere, our actions impact fatefully. Yet these relevant wholes—what "humans throw at nature"—are rendered little or no moral due and have little or no independent moral standing. Working moral theory thereby systematically overlooks many, maybe most, of the consequences of our actual, wielded power.

Modernity/ecomodernity's moral universe, as embodied in daily habits and the law itself, is thus far smaller than the actual reach of human agency. In Thomas Berry's terms, ours is "microphase" ethics but "macrophase" power (Berry 2000, 101). We don't have a picture of the moral universe in our heads and hearts that is commensurate with our real-life impact. We "do" spiritual-moral formation on a microphase scale attuned to our immediate worlds and in accord with our anthropocentrism and subjectivism. Our sense of obligation and responsibility are thus microphase while the consequences of our actions are macrophase. The upshot is that we make all manner of choices without truly accounting for them morally, religiously, and in terms of relevant time and space. (No one has gone to trial or even suffered serious moral approbation for an act of "uncreation" such as species extinction, to give an example. Nor has accelerated climate change been ably discussed to date as a matter of morality.)

But we must ask again: How does this tale of modernity's making—its dualism, anthropocentrism, subjectivism, and narrow-gauge utilitarian productivism—become ecomodernity's?

RECENT SCIENCE + MODERN PRACTICE = ECOMODERNITY

As noted, evolution as taught by the heirs of Darwin, Mendel, and a gaggle of ecologists embed humans firmly in nature as an extraordinary expression of it. Moral and spiritual qualities such as humility, awe, mystery, reverence, and gratitude could be nurtured in the process of cultivating just such consciousness. Empathy might also be a mark, as well as shared responsibility. Scientists themselves sometimes talk this way, effectively promoting a set of virtues. Stephen Jay Gould brings the thirteen-hundred-plus pages of *The Structure of Evolutionary Theory* to a close with a glance back at "this grandest earthly enterprise, the tree of life." He then asks a question, "Why fret and care [about life as it has evolved]?" to which he replies, "We care because the broad events that had to happen, happened to happen *in a certain particular way.* And something almost unspeakably holy—I don't know how else to say this—underlies our discovery and confirmation of the actual details that made our world and also, in realms of contingency, assured the minutiae of its construction in the manner we know, and not in any one of a trillion other ways, nearly all of which would not have included the evolution of a scribe to record the beauty, the cruelty, the fascination, and the mystery" (Gould 2002, 1342).

Yet this fit of the unlikely (human) "scribe" into "the beauty, . . . cruelty, . . . fascination, and . . . mystery" of "something almost unspeakably holy" is frustrated because ecology and evolution, as practiced science, are embedded in institutional arrangements that fail to dislodge the practical morality of technological ontology and nature's place in it. So argues Davison (and I agree). Here, where entrepreneurs, engineers, bankers, and patent lawyers hold as much sway as sages and scientists and work together with them as players in a larger system, value resides in human ascription, labor, and investment. Plants are just weeds until they serve human purposes, minerals are just rocks, water is just H_2O. Biodiversity may have esthetic and even religious appeal, but its "real" usefulness and value belong to agriculture, pharmaceuticals, and the exploding frontiers of biotechnology. Techno-science is thus merged with market capitalism as a way of life in which commerce essentially co-opts nature to do the bidding of particular interests. Thus does Darwinian naturalism end up serving present-minded utility rather than embedding us more profoundly in nature and the grand scheme of things ("a vast evolving universe" and Earth's "unique community of life," to recall the Earth Charter).

Differently said, while the language of ecology is taken up everywhere, and the metaphors for viewing self, society, and (the rest of) nature are increasingly "ecological" and "holistic," nature outside us is nonetheless absorbed, for all practical purposes, into modern subjectivism. We incorporate (the rest of) nature into human culture on terms we decide and in accord with our own well-being. In this way of life and in this moral universe, nature will not and, it is assumed, *ought* not exist independently of us, with value of its own. Life systems, as we said earlier, become critical and valuable as part of *our* life system. "Natural capital" joins other capital in the stream of human investments and benefits. As such, nature belongs to humanly designed and steered processes of technological evolution. This is the slave status of nature we noted earlier. Only now it belongs to ecomodernity. It thus means, as a matter of morality, what it has always meant for master/slave, or domination, ethics: when and where conflicts of interest arise, the master's interests trump the slave's. Slaves are indispensable, to be certain. We cannot live without them. But they can be replaced by other slaves.

This entire analysis of modernity become ecomodernity is nicely captured in one now forgotten advertisement. On June 2, 1998, New York's American Museum of Natural History opened its new Hall of Biodiversity. A full-page ad appeared that day in the *New York Times*. It displays an eye-catching selection of flora and fauna from around the world. Running across the top in large letters is the sentence: "We believe in equal opportunity regardless of race, creed, gender, kingdom, phylum, class, order, family, genus, or species." The creatures then tumble down the page, followed by somewhat smaller-lettered text:

> All life is interconnected. So without a supporting cast of millions of species, human survival is far from guaranteed. This variety and interdependence of species is what's called biodiversity. And it matters to Monsanto in particular. Our business depends on making discoveries in the world of genetic information. Information that is lost forever when a species becomes extinct. Information that offers solutions in agriculture, nutrition, and medicine never before thought possible. For a population that's growing. On a planet that's not.

The logo—a growing plant—then appears next to the name and trademark: Monsanto: Food Health Hope. The last line is: "Monsanto is honored to be a sponsor of the Hall of Biodiversity at the American Museum of Natural History. www.monsanto.com."

This ad is unthinkable apart from ecology and its impact. Its thought-world appears to be holistic thinking, succinctly put and based in good science. The awareness of complex, living interdependence seems central, though it is not quite so. At the outset the ad even strikes a notion of egalitarian bio-democracy worthy of St. Francis. But by the bottom of the page we are keeping company with the soft utopianism and secular promise-and-fulfillment theology of so much biotechnology: "Monsanto: Food Health Hope" and "solutions in agriculture, nutrition, and medicine never before thought possible." We are also keeping company with human subjectivism in ethics, even if it has been eco-sensitized. That is, this moral universe not only assumes that human beings are the moral agents, it assumes that in the end the only actions that matter are the ones affecting human beings. Humans will, in turn, be the sole judges of those actions, without reference to any court of appeal beyond the human subject. And by the very bottom, right-hand corner of the page, we have placed good science and a viable way of life firmly in the hands of global ecomodern business. Long-standing boundaries of mind and matter, human culture and resistant nature, and sharp distinctions of humans from other creatures have been erased, it would seem, in favor of "equal opportunity regardless of race. . .phylum, class . . . genus, or species" in a world where "[a]ll life is interconnected." Yet their erasure is only apparent. Practice itself features human mind and culture as the creators, controllers, and high-tech bio-cowboys who work ecosystems as they would their ranchlands. These creatures are generic, not particular. They are not even truly creatures, as biological individuals; they are, categorically and simply, "information" and "resources." Humans are thereby re-centered as masters without qualification. The disconnect of humans from the rest of their co-siblings in creation thus remains unmended, as do other elements of modernity's morality of domination. Ecology, molecular biology, genetics, and evolution itself thus find themselves, again as practiced science, in the employ of a morality that views "all things bright and beautiful," "all creatures great and small," even "all things wise and wonderful," as information and resources. This is not Earth Community, this is Genetic Mine, commercial modernity in ecological mode. So in only one striking page, what begins as a confession of bio-democracy ends as (indispensable) user-friendly exploitation that promises, yet one more time, to do good by doing well, for profit and without (human) sacrifice, on the interlocking terms of dualism, subjectivism, anthropocentrism, and productivism.

To say it differently: genetics as a science may render us kin to roundworms, to say nothing of giraffes and bonobos; ecology may map in gratifying detail the awesome webbing of life; and Evolution with a capital *E* may present a dynamic universe still on its way, with us a stupendous expression of it, even if only a wink in its sense of time. Yet these sciences are captured for ecomodernity and an ethic that retains modernity's hubris as that is married to engineering courage and confidence. Life is still chiefly a production, management, and security problem, subject to technological remedies based in rigorous science and the wizardry of the market. Life is not a species problem, or a problem of the human soul or spirit, or a matter of evil and injustice and things going wildly awry on a regular basis. And for all of it, nature is there for us—from kingdom to kingdom, phylum to phylum, species to species, gene to gene, atom to atom, and sea to shining sea.

Ecomodernity's is thus, in the end, a technical upgrade of modernity's ethic of domination of nature-culture as a complex but single reality driven largely by market forces. Does it come as a surprise, then, that Food-Health-Hope Monsanto finds itself entangled in a nasty case of environmental racism in the poor and heavily African-American community of Anniston, Alabama, where it flushed tens of thousands of pounds of PCBs into Snow Creek each year over nearly four decades and millions of pounds more into a nearby landfill (*New York Times* 2002a)? Or does Donna Haraway's list of moral troublepoints surprise? While her discussion is aimed specifically at biotechnology linked to economic globalization, it easily adapts to ecomodernism more broadly. The troublepoints are these:

> increasing capital concentration and the monopolization of the means of life, reproduction, and labor; appropriation of the commons of biological inheritance as the private preserve of corporations; the global deepening of inequality by region, nation, race, gender, and class; erosion of indigenous peoples' self-determination and sovereignty in regions designated as biodiverse while indigenous lands and bodies become the object of intense gene prospecting and proprietary development; inadequately assessed and potentially dire environmental and health consequences; misplaced priorities for technoscientific investment funds; propagation of distorted and simplistic scientific explana-

tions, such as genetic determinism; intensified cruelty to and clear domination over animals; depletion of biodiversity; and the undermining of established practices of human and nonhuman life, culture, and production without engaging those most affected in democratic decision-making. (Haraway 1997, 60–61)

This Monsanto gloss brings the ethical analysis of modernity cum ecomodernity to a close. Dualism, subjectivism, anthropocentrism, and productivism interlock for the transformation and management of nature-culture on the terms of commerce and a technocratic agenda. Biological life systems are subservient to human systems. More precisely, they are subservient to the way(s) of life of the human "haves" who most shape these arrangements and most benefit from them.

FLUX AND ECOMODERNITY

This analysis isn't complete, however, until we broach the thorny question of what nature's flux and unpredictability mean vis à vis ecomodernity. The normal, rather than aberrational, case for most decisions we make is incomplete knowledge and the presence of complexities we do not initially comprehend. We constantly work from inferences and only rarely, if ever, from a complete picture. Risks are inevitable. So is error. Wisdom never wholly aligns with knowledge and knowledge is never comprehensive.

Flux exacerbates this uncertainty. It exacerbates it for modernity in special ways. Modernity built itself on a mechanistic notion of predictable nature. Its master image was mastery itself. Consider but one case in which nature's flux and complexity subverted human expectations, the Glen Canyon Dam. Forty years after damming the Colorado River in northern Arizona at Glen Canyon, scientists and engineers struggle with "colossal loss of sand, shrinking beaches, an invasion of outside fish and plants, the extinction of native species, erosion of archaeological sites and the sudden appearance of an Asian tapeworm," to name only some of the unexpected consequences. The whole experience, resident scientists and engineers now say, underscores factors that in retrospect must be taken into account for future policy: "complex systems are inherently unpredictable," "it is impossible to know the consequences of various

human actions," "a collaborative process" is required "in which everyone with a stake" is involved and is ready "to try something else" "when
experiments fail" (*New York Times* 2002a). The upshot is "adaptive
management" as a new tack. Adaptive management backs away from
modernity's efforts to conquer nature. It does not back away from human
interventions, however. Instead, it tries more carefully to mimic shifting
patterns in nature. It also allows wider margins of error and more lati-
tude for recovery than earlier confidence (and naiveté) thought necessary.
Put differently, adaptive management moves between two extremes and
assumes there are both policy regimes and moral systems other than a
tight and essentially mechanistic management ethic, on the one hand,
and simply "letting nature be," on the other, with humans encamped as
far out on the margins as possible.

How Might Adaptive Management Appear as an Ethic?

What follows is one possibility and it brings us to the final, and constructive, section of this essay. It shares several elements with other conceivable versions of adaptive management (or, as I prefer, "sustainable
adaptability"). In this ethic, questions of prudent use are not the only serious questions asked. Questions about respect across the community of
life, value beyond utility, and justice to the environment for its own independent well-being are accorded a place that is not granted by either modernity or ecomodernity. The gradual formation of a different "moral
habitat" altogether (Erhard 2002) is also a conscious goal, a moral habitat that counters the exploitative hubris of the plastic view of nature that
marked modernity's ethic, and one that combats modernity's consumerism, imperialism, and alienation as well. Not least, this sustainable adaptability ethic assumes, even centers, what many others do not, namely,
religious impulses as a substantive contribution.

At the same time, nature's flux is considered a given for this ethic. This
ethic also recognizes that significant cases of flux may be the consequence
of human agency as increasingly the wild card in the fate of Earth's
unique community of life. Whether or not this is so, however, nature is
assumed to include changing habitats that can give rise to surprisingly altered, and even novel, circumstances. Accelerated climate change may be
the most dramatic instance at our doorstep. The woes of Glen Canyon

pale by comparison. Accelerated climate change will not likely be the only one, however (the death of coral reefs—those key ocean nurseries—and unsustainable rates of fresh water use also come to mind). With this as introduction, we turn to the specific ways in which this ethic centers contributions of religious traditions.

A RELIGIOUS ECOLOGY AND ETHIC

Comparative studies underscore more convergence of "eco"-value among world religions than one might expect. The editors' summary in *Daedalus* lists these: "reverence for the earth and its profound cosmological processes, respect for the earth's myriad species, an extension of ethics to include all life forms, restraint in the use of natural resources combined with support for effective alternative technologies, equitable distribution of wealth, and the acknowledgement of human responsibility in regard to the continuity of life and the ecosystems that support life" (Tucker and Grim 2001, 19). The editors go on to note that each of these shared dispositions might *also* be affirmed by sciences that consistently embed us in the larger drama of life.

Kusumita Pedersen's study (1998) of religious ecologies across world religions offers another tally of shared substance. There is greater or lesser agreement on the following:

- The natural world has value in itself and does not exist solely to serve human ends.
- There is significant continuity of being between human and nonhuman life, even though humans have a distinctive role.
- Nonhuman beings are morally significant, in the eyes of God or the cosmic order. They have their own unique relations to God and their own places in the cosmic order.
- The dependence of human life on the rest of nature can and should be acknowledged in ritual and other expressions of appreciation and gratitude.
- Moral norms such as justice, compassion and reciprocity apply in appropriate ways to both human and nonhuman beings. The well-being of humans and that of nonhuman beings is inseparably connected.

- There are legitimate and illegitimate uses of nature.
- Greed and destructiveness are condemned. Restraint and protection are commended.
- Human beings are obliged to be aware and responsible in living in harmony with the natural world, and should follow the specific practices for this prescribed in their traditions.

This tally, too, could be fertile meeting ground for alliances of science and religion in an ethic of sustainable adaptability (or adaptive management).

There is more. Religious ecologies offer deep traditions of faith and practice that can be tapped for a moral alternative to ecomodernity. We shall do so, with this caveat: these traditions must now account for ecology's challenge to embed human being so profoundly in the story of earth and evolution that Christianity shows itself to be a genuine "earth faith," inclusive of the community of life and at home in the cosmos. Christianity's time for extricating human beings from the drag of matter and excluding nature from the history of salvation is long past, just as is its time for "rescuing" *Homo sapiens sapiens* from humiliating oneness with the rest of nature. We don't live *on* earth, but *in* earth *as* earth. It's ecomodernity that lives *on* Earth, as a stage, and there is no compelling reason to remain its ally.

In any event, religious cosmologies and ecologies, and the moral ethos and practice they carry, are remarkable for their capacity to generate ways of life that find cross-cultural expression over centuries. We will take up four such recurring deep traditions: asceticism, sacramentalism, mysticism, and prophetic-liberative practices. All are living traditions, which means their narratives are not yet complete nor their creativity spent. Challenges to the moral ethos of ecomodernity issue from each of them. So does a relationship to uncertain nature. That these millennial Christian traditions are shared with other faiths and can serve as a basis for interfaith alliance is another point worth noting in passing.

Asceticism

Asceticism is about saying "Yes!" and saying "No!" in a simple, disciplined way of life. Religions have always generated communities of such renunciation and annunciation: "No" is said to one way of life on the basis of "Yes" to another. In their practices of spiritual and moral formation, the varied strains of asceticism seek always to discipline the ego and the will and to nurture a life of virtue that counters a life of distracting attachments: ostentation, conspicuous consumption, and loose sex usually have pride of place on the list. Differently said, asceticism seeks, in the face of a dominant culture it judges as morally corrupt and corrupting, to forge a counterworld nurtured by an alternative ethos. Monasticism is one obvious strand in Orthodox, Roman Catholic, and Anglican communions, but ascetic Protestant communities show similar traits, especially communities of radical Reformation traditions. A close look uncovers both the life of renunciation—those distracting and corrupting attachments—and a simultaneous effort to embody harmony with nature and in society. Such harmony is manifest in the details of life—in clothing, diet, agricultural and healing practices, governance, art, architecture, and liturgy. The kind of asceticism most needed now—in light of a planet in plain jeopardy at human hands—is one that loves the earth fiercely in a simple way of life, with disciplined and heightened senses for the profound and numinous in all of life.

A necessary gloss on ascetic community goes like this. Christian asceticism's own conversion to earth requires that it abandon the metaphysic noted earlier, namely, the Christian life lived as ascetic ascent, life lived as the hard scramble upward on the cosmic ladder of the Great Chain of Being, a life in which the more our passion for God, the less our passion for earthly existence. The concrete practices and underlying theory of an asceticism that loves the earth fiercely in a simple way of life, as the way of loving God fiercely, remain to be worked out.

Asceticism's challenge to ecomodernism is clear. It challenges directly an arrogant consumerism and materialism presented as the good life itself. One illustration suffices. The December 2001 cover of *Woman's Day* magazine proclaims in large, bright, and beautifully crafted letters the hope so many carried into the holidays after the events of September 11: "Peace on Earth!" The white script is superimposed upon a room piled with gifts everywhere, leaving only space for a tree burdened in comparable fashion with gold and silver ornaments. Below "Peace on Earth!" and also superimposed on this excess was: "605 Ideas for Christmas." Yet *Woman's Day* probably received no letters to the editor about the "innocent" juxtaposition of deep wishes for peace on earth in a world of mass poverty with "605 Ideas" as the way to celebrate the birth of a poor Jew who is worshipped by millions, even billions, as the compelling incarnation of a kenotic God.

It only need be added that asceticism's simple, disciplined, conserving life of more with less grants a far greater margin of error when the conditions are those of nature's inherent uncertainties. The drain on resources is markedly less, and recovery from the capricious and unpredictable whims of nature markedly easier, when systems are simpler rather than complex and minimal goods are maximally reused. Not least, the whole posture of this manner of living finds freedom and deep satisfaction in being one (limited) creature among other (limited) creatures, all of whom have need of one another in a shared creation.

Sacramentalism

Another ancient and living tradition that challenges ecomodernism is sacramental communion. In the sacramentalist tradition, life as an unmerited and awesome gift of God and the medium of grace is the great theme. Life in its totality is brought into the worshipful presence of God. There it is renewed in contemplative and sacramental practices. In many traditions, sacramental communion is far more than the gathering of God and humankind it became in some. It is ritually enacted community as the hymn of the universe itself. Its great acts are acts of the cosmic drama of creation and its story proclaims that a God beyond dimensions we can know is nonetheless as near as the grain and the grape, the water and the oil. Creation and its transfiguration, together with human salvation, is the arching theme here, whether in Orthodox communions, Celtic Christianity, Roman Catholicism, or Anglican bodies (to mention only some of its Christian variants).

While a deep and broad tradition, sacramental community is almost the antithesis of the working cosmology and "theology" of modernity's/ecomodernity's institutions and practices. Modern institutions and practices have assumed an utterly plastic view that characterizes nature collectively as simply "natural resources." "Natural resources" and "capital," like "human resources" and "human capital," betray a mindset that is utilitarian with a vengeance and devoid of any sacramental sense. They belong to a disenchanted world where the numinous is beaten from the common and the sacred is leached from the ordinary.[5]

A necessary gloss on sacramental communion as Earth-honoring and Earth-enhancing would include several matters, at least for much of Christianity. One is the continuing legacy of medieval and Reformation preoccupation with human salvation as the primary focus. By contrast, the proper circumference of sacramentalism is the redemption of all creation as the abode of God. Orthodox and Anglican communions have sometimes been better in their reach here. All nature is transfigured in the Orthodox eucharist, for example. But the Orthodox continue, like Rome, Canterbury, and many Protestants, to invest the celebration of the sacraments themselves with a church order governed by that other deep and enduring tradition, patriarchy. So all nature is transfigured, with the notable exception of male-dominated church order and androcentric views! Nor can the metaphysics of sacramentalism continue "Greek" substance metaphysics and Neoplatonism's desire to leave Earth's materiality behind as unessential, even alien, to our true nature and destiny. The theological work now is to offer an evolutionary sacramentalist ontology that resonates with the story of the cosmos itself on its own stunning pilgrimage.

This is far from simply a recommendation. The recasting of the Catholic sacramentalist tradition in the work of such as Thomas Berry has already had great influence in the lives of many communities. The Maryknoll Ecological Sanctuary in Baguio, the Philippines, is but one example. Among many features in which "the new creation story" of science informs religious cosmology and practices is the sanctuary's "Cosmic Journey." The journey is presented as thirteen stations on the mountainside of the sanctuary. In Catholic piety, thirteen stations are associated with the thirteen stations of the cross. But here, beginning with the Big Bang, they are thirteen stations of the epic of evolution told as the flaming forth of the universe from the heart of God. Thus is the Catholic sacramentalist vision recast as Earth-honoring, with humankind truly at home in and as Earth. The way of life in the sanctuary is also wholly nonutilitarian. More precisely said, it is not utilitarian or instrumentalist in the small-world way of anthropocentric modernity. So when three very large pines were removed to make space for the home of the Sisters a ritual of thanksgiving for these trees of life was created. The trees themselves became virtually all the wood used in the house, from floors to cabinets, to stairways, banisters, art and altars. And ten pine seedlings were planted to take their place. Like the other trees' removal and reincarnation, the planting was also enacted as a community ritual.

It does not require much imagination to see that a sacramentalist evolutionary cosmology and moral universe accommodates nature in flux. In this religious cosmology we are truly at home in a universe that was our community long before us and will be creation's community long after we, our planet, and our star are gone. This cosmos will kill us, just as it also birthed us. It is not thereby our enemy. Or if and when it is, it will be an enemy we somehow learn to respect, even love, with ourselves integrally part of it (an earthquake destroyed the Maryknoll Convent in 1991, after which it was rebuilt as the Bio-Shelter).

Mysticism

Mysticism and the contemplative life are yet another long-standing set of practices that reaches across diverse Christianities and most all other faiths to effect a moral habitat different from ecomodernity's. This cosmological orientation and these practices all rest in the conviction that "we can touch with our living hearts the Heart of the World and listen to the secret revelations of its unending beat" (Gottlieb 1999, 149). In ways that parallel asceticism, we can do so in ways transcending the hold that forces around us have upon us. Here is the attempt, made innumerable times by millions over thousands of years, to "move beyond the confines of society and history, to break the bounds of normal human interaction, normal consciousness, and normal physical reality" (Gottlieb 1999, 150) in order to draw from a wisdom hidden within this world or resident beyond it. The struggle is always between such transcending wisdom and the powers around us. Again like asceticism, here is momentary release from the grip of the social ego and the socially constructed sense of the body itself. Here is direct, if transient, experience of the divine beyond the definitions of dogma, institution, even moral stipulation. Here is truth apprehended apart from the authority of society's keepers of the truth. And here is revelation itself as shorn from our attachments and mistaken yearnings. Self falls away, the heresy of "mine" and "thine" falls away as well, and the vision quest of the mystic ends in the cool cosmic fire some name "God" and others refuse to name at all. When the return to routine experience is made, as it must be, and intransigent worldly reality insinuates itself all over again, the mystical community finds itself so identified with a cosmic beauty and harmony that it is permanently dissatisfied with the common ugliness of the world around. It may "accept" that world in an important sense—namely, embrace it with compassion—but that world will not be right until Eden is reborn and its energies sing with the stars. So the mystical community backs into strong moral agency with no sense of heteronomous obligation at all, only the overflow of hearts that cannot deny their moment with God and the burden of their experience of beauty and truth.

Mysticism can, of course, be escapist and thus fail to be Earth-honoring. The people on the block can be forgotten and the mundane tasks of field and factory devalued. These are escapes spiritual mentors commonly warn against.

What is rarely left behind in mysticism is—strikingly—nature. Nature abounds in the mystic's experience and holds unchallenged rank in most mystical visions. God in, as, and through the physical world is often the touchstone of mystical experience. Take for example Hildegaard of Bingen's encounter. She has a vision, and hears God. The God she hears, speaks: "I, the fiery life of divine essence, am aflame beyond the beauty of the meadows, I gleam in the waters, and I burn in the sun, moon, and stars. . . . I awaken everything to life" (Hildegard of Bingen 1990, 91). Mystical experience in fact often happens in the direct encounter with a simple detail of nature, whether the holy that is harbored there is named as God or not.

The mystical tradition, then, may or may not mediate Christian faith as earth faith. It may or may not be life-charged mysticism that stays with earth. But it certainly can be and is for some, with great power. For others, however, nature and earth serve as means on a journey that leaves them behind as useful but discarded cumber. As an earth faith, this tradition and set of practices is inherently no more pristine than asceticism or sacramentalism.

Like sacramentalism, mysticism stands in awe before nature and even enters its own habitat. For much of its history, that meant awe of nature's verdant beauty, its cycles and harmonies. For conditions of flux, no retreat from this beauty or awe is required. They are only recast as untamed and beguiling nature, which we can neither wholly know nor control. But mystics have always known that. Celtic Christian mysticism in fact celebrated both the wildness and fecundity of God as manifest in the tempestuous but fertile nature of the British Isles. The adjustments to uncertain nature are few, then, at least in a broad conceptual sense.

Prophetic-liberative practice.

Prophetic-liberative practice is the last of our efforts to articulate fidelity to God as fidelity to Earth in the face of natural flux and inordinate human power. For the Hebrew prophets, redemption is the redemption of all creation, human and nonhuman, history and nature together. When "the vines languish, the merry-hearted sigh." When "the city . . . is broken down . . . the gladness of earth is banished" (Isaiah 24). This is liberation of all life, from the cell to the community, a struggle inclusive of the poor, the weak, the marginalized, the diseased, disfigured, and exploited, and exhausted nature. The God of mercy and compassion, who is also Judge, "knows" their suffering and goes before in the journey to a teeming land and fertile Sabbath. This prophetic tradition took on a certain decisive shape in the modern period itself, in the face of the social conditions that arose with the spread of industrialism and the unprecedented new wealth and poverty it generated. Aided by social theory and social scientific analysis of society—themselves gifts of the nineteenth and twentieth centuries—it adopted direct efforts to refashion institutions, systems, structures, and policies in the direction of shared and saving power. Rendering society and psyche the subject of rigorous science in this way nudged Christian ethics from an overwhelmingly virtue-oriented ethic (as it remains in much asceticism, sacramentalism, and mysticism) to a value-oriented ethic that seeks to realize social goods directly by attending to how human behavior is patterned through institutions, policies and practices. In different words, through systemic channeling of human action, value-centered ethics tries to fashion a social order that makes it easier for people to do and to be good, and harder for them to be and do evil. The social gospel, Christian realism, liberation, and socio-ecological theologies all belong to recent versions of this ancient moral tradition, as does progressive evangelicalism.

The gloss here need not deter us long. What is needed is chiefly to overcome the remaining anthropocentrism in Christianity's justice-focused traditions, which prophetic-liberative Christianity represents in special measure. What is needed is an account of responsibility that encompasses the biophysical and geoplanetary as well as the socio-communal in an era when the cumulative reach of human power affects all of these. Yet the moral universe of much Christian ethics still draws the line around human populations alone and thinks of power issues as intra-human only. The issue for religious cosmology and flux ecology is how to reorder the moral world so that all creation is considered community and justice is socio-ecological in its reach.

At the same time, prophetic-liberative practice is a challenge from Christian ethics to ecomodernity. Ecomodernity is little better than modernity in rendering Earth a just and comprehensive community, perhaps because its moral universe hardly focuses on justice at all, but rather utility. As we noted earlier from Haraway, ecomodernity pays little note to underrepresented peoples and cultures, together with underrepresented flora, fauna, and land. In other words, ecomodernity pays little note to those who suffer the advantages of the peoples who built their worlds on the first wave of globalization. Ecomodernity is thus very far from ecojustice, and will remain so as long as its practiced science remains largely "innocent" of serious race, gender, and culture analysis.

The focus of prophetic-liberative practice, as specifically justice-centered Christianity, is preoccupied with institutional arrangements and sound day-to-day habits. Prophetic-liberative practice may appreciate the way asceticism, sacramentalism, and mysticism apprehend life and lean into the world, but its own concerns will attend to the details of governing structures, systems, and policies. Giving high attention to how nature concretely functions in a humanly-dominated biosphere and learning the complicated arts of earth-honoring living become critical, since justice, like God and the devil, is in the details. For this tradition, the flux and wildness of nature can never be far away, as reality, as constraint, and as another moment of creativity.

All four of these religious ecologies can come together around creation as community. It might go like this. As co-members of a creation and community of life that is home to us and upon which we are wholly dependent, earth's economy is primary. Ours is derivative. This is a view of nature that is eco- and geocentric rather than homocentric. It means ways of life that adapt "to the limiting conditions of life" set by "the carrying, regenerative, and absorptive capacities of the biophysical world" of which we are part (Nash 2000, 244). Under conditions of flux and unpredictability it also means considerable room for shifts in ecosystem dynamics, whether due to fluctuations in species populations, natural calamities, or the unforeseen and escalating consequences of human ways. Revisions along these eco-/geocentric lines also mean revised moral status for "otherkind" in the community of life, just as it means honoring nature's creativity, itself the result of flux in the drama of evolution and biodiversity.

The essence of a Christian moral and religious perspective is a vision of life in which the material universe is apprehended as sacred and a precious, one-time gift. This means that there are some things, or some dimensions of all things, where value cannot be determined by the market or even by scientific knowledge as such. It also means profound conflict with aggressive market secularism as a dominating way of life, whether in crass forms—"605 Ideas for Christmas"—or eco-sensitive, ecomodern ones—Monsanto as Food Health Hope. Asceticism, sacramentalism, mysticism, and prophetic-liberative practices represent challenges *from* Christian ethics *for* moral possibilities other than consumerism, instrumentalism, and continued oppression as the outcome of entrenched privilege. These religious ecologies can be sources in a science-and-religion alliance for a moral habitat and moral universe far different from the one that prevails. It is also far less dangerous, given nature's tendency to throw curves we don't expect, even though we help create them.

Notes

1. The reference is to one of the most influential traditions in modern philosophy and ethics, the Kantian. See Kant (1898).

2. A classic in this tradition was William Paley's *Natural Theology: or, Evidences of the Existence and Attributes of the Deity, Collected from the Appearances of Nature* (1802). It exercised wide influence for a century and more after its publication.

3. Augustine's mark on Western spirituality and morality is perhaps singular in its influence here, but he was hardly either first or final cause. The cosmic ladder was the frame not only for Christian theology but popular piety, liturgical practices, and church architecture.

4. The phrase itself is taken from Alexander Pope's *The Essay on Man* and used to title an influential work in the history of ideas, Arthur O. Lovejoy's *The Great Chain of Being* (1936). Writing in the eighteenth century, Pope stressed the utter connectedness of all things in this hierarchy of being itself (p. 60):

Vast chain of being! which from God began,
Natures aethereal, human, angel, man,
Beast, bird, fish, insect, what no eye can see,
No glass can reach; from Infinite to thee,
From thee to nothing.—On superior pow'rs

Were we to press, inferior might on ours;
Or in the full creation leave a void,
Where, one step broken, the great scale's destroy'd;
From Nature's chain whatever link you strike,
Tenth, or ten thousandth, breaks the chain alike.
Cited from Lovejoy, p. 60.

5. It need not be so, of course. Science isn't inherently profane in this way. As we noted above, it can do much to cultivate the sacramental virtues of awe, humility, reverence and respect.

Works Cited

Berry, Thomas. 2000. *The great work: Our way into the future.* New York: Bell Tower Books.

Davison, Aidan. 2001. *Technology and the contested meanings of sustainability.* Albany: State University of New York Press.

Earth Charter. Available on-line at www.earthcharter.org or from Earth Charter Secretariat, Earth Council, P. O. Box 319–6100, San Jose, Costa Rica.

Erhard, Nancie. 2002. Moral habitat: Ethos and agency for the sake of earth. Ph.D. diss. Union Theological Seminary.

Gottlieb, Roger. 1999. The transcendence of justice and the justice of transcendence: Mysticism, deep ecology, and political life. *Journal of the American Academy of Religion* 67(1): 149–66.

Gould, Stephen Jay. 2002. *The structure of evolutionary theory.* Cambridge, MA: The Belknap Press of Harvard University Press.

Haraway, Donna J. 1997. *Modest_Witness@Second_Millennium.FemaleMan ©_Meets_OncoMouse: Feminism and technoscience.* New York: Routledge.

Hildegard of Bingen. 1990. The book of divine works. In *Hildegard of Bingen: Mystical writings,* ed. Fiona Bowie and Oliver Davies, 90–107. New York: Crossroad.

Kant, Immanuel. 1898. *Critique of practical reason and other works of the theory of ethics.* Trans. Thomas Kingsmill Abbott. London: Longmans, Green, and Co.

Lovejoy, Arthur O. 1936. *The great chain of being.* Cambridge, MA: Harvard University Press.

McGrath, Alister E. 2001. *A scientific theology.* Vol. 1, *Nature.* Grand Rapids, MI: Eerdmans.

McNeill, J. R. 2000. *Something new under the sun: An environmental history of the twentieth-century world.* New York: W. W. Norton.

Midgley, Mary. 1995. Duties concerning islands. In *Environmental philosophy: A collection of readings,* ed. Robert Eliot, 89–103. New York: Oxford University Press.

Nash, James. 2000. Seeking moral norms in nature: natural law and ecological responsibility. In *Christianity and Ecology,* ed. Dieter T. Hessel and Rosemary Radford Ruether, 227–50. Cambridge: Harvard University Press.

New York Times. 2002a. PCB pollution suits have day in court in Alabama. January 27, 20.

———. 2002b. Restoring an ecosystem torn asunder by a dam. June 11, F1.

Paley, William. 1802. *Natural Theology: or, Evidences of the Existence and Attributes of the Deity, Collected from the Appearances of Nature.* London: R. Faulder.

Pedersen, Kusumita. 1998. Environmental ethics in interreligious perspective. In *Explorations in global ethics: Comparative religious ethics and interreligious dialogue,* ed. Sumner B. Twiss and Bruce Grelle 253–90. Boulder, CO: Westview Press.

Pimm, Stuart L. 2001. *The world according to Pimm: A scientist audits the earth.* New York: McGraw Hill.

Tucker, Mary Evelyn, and John Grim, eds. 2001. The emerging alliance of world religions and ecology. *Daedalus* 130(4).

Ecology and Religion for a Post Natural World

Christopher Hamlin and David M. Lodge

At issue in this book is the integration of religious faith with scientific knowledge as a foundation for action. The issue is not new, but responses must adapt to new modes of analysis and bodies of thought as well as to the changing state of the natural world. We did not ask our authors to integrate disciplines, but rather to present their disciplines as unflinchingly as possible. To do otherwise would have been to run the risk of building a house without a foundation. There is reason for caution. "Ecology" is a widely and variously used term; many versions of "religious ecology" (defined, for example, by Tucker and Grim [2001, 15] as a "cultural awareness of kinship with and dependence on nature for the continuity of all life") are either too general for application or fail to command respect from ecological scientists, committed believers, or both. The challenge is to integrate seemingly disparate endeavors, substantively, without violating their integrity.

In this final chapter, we first return to the theme of this book—the need to incorporate into a religious worldview the paradigm shift in ecology from the balance of nature to the flux of nature. Given that humans are massively reshaping nature, and that nature in flux (even apart from humans) undermines earlier notions of nature as a stable source of wisdom, we are in a post natural world that requires new normative approaches. We reiterate that this shift is not after all so singular, and proceed to draw on aspects of religion that have not been prominent in ecotheology, but which seem pertinent to a "flux of nature" view. Finally, using the case of invasive species, an exemplar of flux ecology, we show how those aspects of religion might apply in practical issues of environmental management.

We begin with some premises and caveats. First, we do not anticipate that concern for other organisms will (or should) trump other goods, including appropriate self-interest, the welfare of other humans, and equity among humans. At the same time, with Rasmussen (chapter 9, this volume), we regard the present as a period of grotesque imbalance. Religious culture is partly to blame. It has been co-opted by extreme self-interest, hedonism, consumerism, and utilitarianism to the extent that nonhuman creation appears to have *no* standing apart from its ability to satisfy immediate needs of existing humans. We are convinced also that reducing human population growth rates, especially in the developing world, is urgent, as is reducing per capita environmental impact, especially in the developed world. And in the face of potentially irreversible ecological change, our perspective is consistent with the precautionary principle now enshrined in some national and international environmental agreements.

Second, we believe that Americans will not choose to significantly reduce their environmental impact unless it becomes a priority of the mainstream religions, Christianity and Judaism, which three-fourths of Americans identify as their faiths. Moreover, those changes will have to come, to a large degree, from resources within those traditions. A designer ecotheology that does not draw from core religious beliefs and practices will not work, nor will an approach that treats religion merely as instrumental to environmental change.

Last, what we offer here does not displace ethical analysis, theological reflection, or quantitative modeling. It is, at best, a foundation for a conversation that is both religious and scientific.

ECOLOGY IN THE FOOTSTEPS OF EVOLUTION AND COSMOLOGY

In flux ecology we encounter a science that in doing what sciences are supposed to do—study nature ever more closely—presents a view that undermines much of what is hoped for from science: a cognitive basis for being comfortable in our world. Knowledge, it is often said, will set us free. Even when knowledge does not bring control, it at least locates the boundaries of our control, making clear human limits, identity, and prospects.

Yet modern ecology seems to be making us less comfortable and confident. As Van Houtan and Pimm (chapter 4, this volume) point out with some despair, the apparent stability of that outer world and the very subject of their science is vanishing. Like light being swallowed by a black hole, species and habitats are ceasing to exist as we watch. It seems absurd to look to ecology for a science to guide stewardship, if what is to be stewarded will not be there. But even in those places that humans are not directly disturbing, change is at least as prominent a feature as stasis, and unpredictability often prevails. As White (chapter 6, this volume) points out, nature changes in ways that are not in accord with anybody's teleology. Large changes may have tiny and transitory causes. Ecosystems may well transform dramatically at the proverbial drop of a hat (or flap of a butterfly wing). Even when environmental phenomena, like those Belovsky (chapter 5, this volume) has outlined, reflect the concordance of a number of cyclical causes whose periods, magnitudes, and dynamics are known, the complexity of the interactions and the randomness that remains may leave us no more reassured than were the ancient Israelites.

This is a different world than many of us have felt we lived in. For much of the history of ecological science there has been a general feeling that the existence of our own and other species could be satisfactorily secured by ensuring the health of something called "Nature." This Nature would guide, provide, and repair itself. If humans knew enough about its workings and applied their knowledge, it would take care of its own, including us. That outlook long predated the term "ecology." In the west, as Stoll (chapter 2, this volume) makes clear, it was well represented in Stoicism, Neoplatonism, and in natural theology, traditions important to those Protestant communities that were central in forging the Anglo-American outlook. This view of nature stressed integration and providence. It promised, if we were but wise and prudent, a stable and sustainable existence.

For like the environmental movements founded on the authority of its twentieth century successor, this older pre-ecology also provided a model for human institutions. Its relations to sociology, to social planning and, indeed, to beliefs about human destiny, were essential, not incidental or accidental. A great deal of utopian thinking, from the mid-nineteenth century onward, has been conspicuously ecological. Often these ecologists and social thinkers sought authority in secular, naturalistic, and positivistic frameworks, and yet, as both Stoll (chapter 2, this volume) and Cittadino (chapter 3, this volume) show, the unarticulated religious heritage and framework is rarely very far below the surface.

Natural theology, which looks to nature for knowledge of God, is not a good ground for an environmental ethic, if only because the nature we confront is one that we, a fallen creature, are significantly responsible for producing. What species exist is a function of what species we have thus far allowed to live. Where they live is often where we have limited them or put them, and even the physical and chemical substrate on which they depend—air, water, soil, exposure to sunlight, and temperature—has been significantly affected by us. One might say that in this regard, humans are no different than any other species, only more powerful. But if, increasingly, that collective entity, nature, is our own co-creation, how can it be used for traditional metaphysical purposes as something exterior to us? And if it can no longer serve as the model for assessing the wisdom and rightness of our various world-changing actions, how then are we to assess those actions? Such is the central problem of a post natural world.

One might argue that the changes occurring in ecology are hardly singular. Ecology had simply been a refuge for natural theology, long after it had been excised from other areas of science. And even the natural theologian Dr. John MacCulloch, a source used by Darwin, had acknowledged that nature was "perpetual flux," with a continual rebalancing among species (MacCulloch 1837). One might say that the metaphor of flux is simply ecology catching up to geology and evolutionary biology or to the quantum revolution or to modern cosmology. It is simply ecology widening its gaze and realizing that nature is not as simple as we hoped.

Second, one might argue that the shock of lost certainty and stability is one that people will get over without losing an ethical fulcrum. The loss of the Aristotelian cosmos, Ptolemaic astronomy, the Newtonian physical universe with its familiar space and time, the stolid dependability of matter itself, and even ordinary notions of causality led, each in turn, to expressions of despair, but society chugged on in orderly fashion. One might ask, "How can we not survive the loss of something that never really existed?"

Indeed, perhaps one should be grateful that this new perspective in ecology promises to extinguish a bad form of reasoning, the naturalistic fallacy—that illogical move from "is" to "ought." All along, it should have been clear that this "Nature" was itself but a noun of convenience. As John Stuart Mill announced in 1867, it was a name we used for matter and force, particularly in nonhuman realms. It was not a thing, or even a set of things, but changing states. To make nature, as did Wordsworth "The anchor of my purest thoughts, the nurse, / The guide, the guardian of my heart, and soul / Of all my moral being" (from "Tintern Abbey") was not only overblown, it was plain misguided. "However offensive the proposition may appear to many religious persons," wrote Mill (1867, 327–28), "they should be willing to look in the face the undeniable fact, that the order of nature, in so far as unmodified by man, is such as no being, whose attributes are justice and benevolence, would have made, with the intention that his rational creatures should follow it as an example." Nature's main characteristics were "perfect and absolute recklessness" and even cruelty: "In sober truth, nearly all the things which men are hanged or imprisoned for doing to one another, are nature's every day performances. Killing, the most criminal act recognized by human laws, Nature does once to every being that lives; . . . All this, Nature does with the most supercilious disregard both of mercy and of justice, emptying her shafts upon the best and noblest indifferently with the meanest and worst upon all those who are engaged in the highest and worthiest enterprises." Civilization, argued Mill, was antinatural.

Yet these reassurances will not quite do. The case is different from that of geology, evolutionary biology, quantum physics, and cosmology. For, in ecology, humans are implicated as victims and as agents of change. The heliocentric arrangement of the universe couldn't be fixed and did no damage. In contrast, humans do not have to resign ourselves to being agents of massive losses of biodiversity, but instead can and should alter these environmental impacts by their choices. And Mill, in inviting us to work to overcome nature, was focusing only on some aspects of what are now recognized as environmental problems. As the most important successor of T. R. Malthus, Mill was well aware that the human enterprise could not flourish if it destroyed, simply by its numbers, the natural systems on which it depended. He treated the wholesale neglect of this truth by many of his contemporaries as the height of human stupidity.

So what happens then when that transcendent, organismic Nature, guide and mother, is replaced with the flux of nature, wherein humans are the dominant mechanism of change? When ecologists and other scholars have addressed these issues, they have often insisted that humans act so that our impact remains within the range of variability that occurs in our absence (see Holling and Meffe 1995; White, chapter 6, this volume). Even those like John Passmore, who, like Mill, reject "naturalness" as grounds for giving moral standing to any particular state of nature, do not abrogate the need to assess ethically states of human-nature relations (Passmore 1974).

Simply to make change the norm would be to circumvent ethical analysis altogether, and, oddly, at the same time to justify an ecology of fatalism, which then becomes an ecology of convenience, an ecology of apology, an ecology of exploitation and of easy expiation, and, possibly, an ecology of widespread human misery and disaster. That is not an answer to which our authors or we are driven or drawn, yet it seems likely that the seeming inescapability of that alternative has prevented many ecologists from directly addressing the shortcomings of the "balance" metaphor. White (chapter 6, this volume) makes clear that flux is not automatically justified, but whence comes the alternative?

To swear off the naturalistic fallacy and pretend ethics has nothing to do with nature is equally absurd if only because so many of the goods and bads that confront any ethicist are states of nature. Talk of health, for example, makes a natural condition a norm. This recognition is what underwrites the view of some ecologists that we can, in fact, define particular states of nature that constitute "ecosystem health" or "ecological integrity," and that these states should therefore be normative.

"Nature," at least in its usual senses, may well be a metaphor that has outlived its usefulness. It is the case that any ethics that touches on the real problems of human living at all must commit the naturalistic fallacy to some degree: the ethicist may perhaps decide *how* to go from "is" to "ought," but the option of not going—of giving "is" no standing—is not really possible. To make the flux, not balance, the default is not necessarily to give up the basis for assessing change or to assert that all change is equally desirable. It is simply to recognize that no good reason for doing anything gets really stronger by having "natural" put in front of it.

RELIGION IN THE FOOTSTEPS OF ECOLOGY

If Nature Cannot Supply an Ethic, What about Religion?

From Lynn White onwards, the focus of much writing on ecotheology and environmental ethics has been on nature as divine creation, even if unfolding or evolving creation. Often that approach isolates environment and seeks to deduce or discover from scripture (chiefly the book of Genesis) or tradition a basis for stewardship of that creation (or some other appropriate stance toward it). As we have seen, an ecology of flux has made this approach harder to defend: the very components of nature it will privilege may seem arbitrary, ambiguous, and transitory. Nor has it been conspicuously successful. For nearly a half century, a call to stewardship has been widely sounded, and yet, as Van Houtan and Pimm (chapter 4, this volume) point out, the extinction rate of the species we are called to steward has not slowed (although progress has been made with respect to air and water pollution, for example).

Why might this be? Perhaps because adding "duty to nature" as an axiom at this late date in the history of Christianity and Judaism so easily looks like making up religion as we go. It can seem as objectionable as making religion merely an instrument to achieve an end external to it. This hazard is evident in a set of questions asked to experts on different faiths by the editors of a recent issue of *Daedalus*. (These editors were also the organizers of ten conferences and books that have emerged since 1996 from the Harvard Divinity School's Religions of the World and Ecology project.) Prominent among their questions was: "What are the core values from this tradition that can lead to the creation of an effective environmental ethics?" (Tucker and Grim 2001; see also http://environment.harvard.edu/religion). Yet in most faiths, the state of the creation has been less central than one's relation to God. Scriptures that may seem full of environmental import may be construed quite differently. Cohen (1989) notes, for example, that medieval Jews did not find Genesis 1:28 and similar passages to have anything to do with environmental issues, much less provide the stewardship mandate apologists have wanted to find there. In short, such an approach can seem to be more concerned with what people ought to believe rather than what they do believe.

The approach seems also to draw on academic theology at the expense of other elements of religious life: charismatic preaching, witness, prayer, prophetic teaching, and committed living. When one thinks of the great social achievements for which religion has been (and continues to be) responsible, such as the missions against slavery and poverty, or the activism to create community and justice, the practices of religious life are at least as important as the theological discourse.

Lynn White bears much of the blame for elevating the faith that should be over the faith that was and is. In casually suggesting that Christians highlight a single and marginal tradition—the complicated and ambiguous heritage of St. Francis—White seems to suggest that Christians become environmentally responsible by ceasing to be Christians (Cunningham 2000, 2001). Likewise, calls to learn from more earth-centered faiths may be helpful, but to the degree that they are perceived to foster a facile eclecticism, attempting to remake a religion into something it has not been, they are unlikely to have much purchase. One might agree that it would be better if more people saw their relation to the creation as Francis did, and yet resent the representation of faith as subject to any expediency that comes along. One might add that the strategy is more likely to have the opposite result if the audience grants any validity to the following syllogism that seemed implicit in White's argument:

> One cannot be a traditional Christian (or Jew or Muslim) and an environmentalist.
> I am a traditional Christian (or Jew or Muslim).
> Therefore I cannot be an environmentalist.

To approach primarily through theological revision—without recognizing the richness of religious teaching and practice in any tradition—risks depriving faith of its very vitality and power to effect change. If we let matters of the moment make up the faith, how then is faith to change or challenge matters of the moment? Such representations of faith risk becoming unrecognizable or even repugnant to the faithful (Tirosh-Samuelson 2001), who will continue to sit on the sidelines of environmental politics, the situation deplored by Van Houtan and Pimm (chapter 4, this volume).

A Look Inward

Fleming (chapter 7, this volume) invites us to ground ethics in metaphors. What can no longer be satisfactorily supplied by the metaphor of a stable nature, whether drawn from superseded maxims of ecology or from Biblical texts, can perhaps be supplied by metaphors of humanness. Such metaphors would highlight the importance of humans as determining a direction: they would enforce a new level of honesty and rigor in justifying that direction and focus responsibility more narrowly on individuals, as well as on institutions. The metaphors of humanness highlighted here are aspects of religious belief and practice. They draw largely on the historical record of humans grappling with uncontrollable, unpredictable nature, expressed not only in the genres of theology and philosophy, but in sermons, poetry, and devotional works. They are metaphorical in that they supply an identity to the human enterprise and to individual human lives, just as balance once supplied an identity to "Nature."

How then can we uncover a religious environmentalism that comes from the ground up, and in a society that is both pluralistic and highly religious, as America is? Perhaps by exploring common elements of religious practice. For most of us, our self-identification as religious persons comes neither from theological analysis nor great familiarity with doctrine, but from inspiration and the cultivation of conscience within communities (Bellah 1986). The fact that, in cases ranging from environmental responsibility to civil liberties to humanitarian issues, people often come to similar conceptions of duty, regardless of religious heritage, suggests its independence from doctrine, however important doctrine may be in the commitments any individual forms. For many, such religious commitments will be the bedrock of their lives—their ultimate concern, as Paul Tillich defined religion—around which life's everyday decisions and behaviors are organized.

The elements considered below—anthropocentrism, reason, sin and repentance, prayer, sacrifice, sacraments, and prophecy and justice—are not uniquely, or even particularly, associated with matters environmental. These elements supply a powerful, and perhaps even an adequate, basis for a moral response to the new ecology of flux. We present them in Christian terms, but one might argue that each is present in some form in every religious tradition, though other elements may be more prominent. In Judaism and Islam, for example, the interpretation of divine law holds pride of place, as Lawrence Slobodkin suggests.[1]

Anthropocentrism　Much of the scholarship on ecotheology and environmental ethics critiques the privileging of the values and viewpoint of the human species (or, more accurately, of some who claim to speak on its behalf). Rightly so: to privilege, uncritically, our own species' welfare over all other things is not only likely to backfire, it is also impious in the extreme, as God makes clear at the end of the book of Job (McKibben 1994). Anthropocentric perspectives are subject to much the same critiques as egocentric or ethnocentric perspectives. And yet it is of course impossible to discard fully the particular embodiment of our species (or equally of self or culture). To the two authors of this essay, a non-anthropocentric perspective seems unavailable—not only conceptually, but also practically, because humans have disturbed the environment so pervasively that even those parts of it which we allow to be "natural" bear the human stamp and continually require managerial decisions. To many Christians and Jews it will also be theologically unavailable: whether or not we would prefer it, we confront the world within a set of religious heritages that distinguish us from other beings and emphasize our history and our condition. A doctrinaire biocentrism is likely to bewilder, perhaps alienate, Christians and Jews, and be hard to apply. But if our religious tradition does not readily give us the means to escape our humanness, it does, we think, give us a framework to confront, accept, and integrate that biological nature.

Letting go of the wise, fair, balanced "Nature" that many biocentrists implicitly invoke as a normative bottom line may well mean for some losing an ideal that inspires and humbles and puts us in our proper places, but it can also be thought of as getting rid of a crutch, which we have expected to guide our behavior and resolve our disagreements. In losing this "Nature," we lose no ability to constrain human action. On the contrary, we are accepting the responsibility that properly accrues to so disruptive a creature as we are. Nor will the character of our actions necessarily differ: we will do what we have been doing all along, trying to manage nature and ourselves, more or less (sadly, often less) prudently, justly, and humanely. Such a situation does not lock us into a narrow utilitarianism—we may still recognize the worth of species and wildernesses, yet we are admitting that we, unavoidably, are the creatures who must recognize that worth. The problem is not anthropocentrism per se, but a particular image of humanness. We have simply recognized that no argument really becomes stronger by appealing to "Nature" or "natural."

Reason   In the Christian heritage in particular, reason has a checkered history—one captured in the notion of an eternal tension between Athens (philosophy) and Jerusalem (holiness). From time to time there have been those, like Blaise Pascal, who have disparaged reason as untrustworthy. And yet theology no less than science (including Pascal's own science) is the product of reason, and the strongest forms of fideism have been regarded within Christianity as heretical. The issue is important because it is sometimes suggested that a spiritual response to environmental matters is distinct from and antithetical to a scientific response. Science closes the door to value, some will say. Readers of John Muir, Rachel Carson, or Henry David Thoreau will quickly recognize the absurdity of that view and the implicit dichotomy on which it rests. Recognition of value often rises with greater understanding. The very science that disabused us of the notion that nature is transcendent and balanced is the same science that gives us what hope we have of translating our values into truly prudential action. Reason can accommodate multiple sources of insight. It gives us the tools with which to move among them. It does not require us to privilege science or any other sort of knowledge (cf. Callicott 2001). What is most important is to jettison the view that separates the life of faith from that of reason and suggests that we are being properly religious when we are most neglecting reason.

Sin, Finitude, and Repentance   A concept of sin exists in many faiths. For much of the history of Christianity, it was central. It has been less so in recent decades, and the term is never uttered in many churches because of the unpleasant feelings that it produces in listeners. Sin has also played a relatively small role in ecotheological discussion. A survey in the University of Notre Dame library of 40 volumes classified under one of the main headings of ecotheology (BT 695.5), shows entries for "sin" in the indices of slightly more than half; frequently, however, the discussions to which these entries refer treat the concept incidentally. More recently, sin has begun to gain traction in Christian discussions of environmental issues: the 2002 *Common Declaration by Pope John Paul II and the Ecumenical Patriarch Bartholomew I* (see www.rsesymposia.org) recognizes sin explicitly as the root cause of environmental degradation and repentance as the beginning of solutions.

Too often "sin" has been seen as an arbitrary accusation in conflicts, something you are committing and I am not. In the public arena such accusations have often sounded inappropriate if only because they seem to circumvent discussion. Thus while ethicists may make reasoned analyses of options, those who shout "sin" are seen as ideologues who declaim because they cannot muster more broadly acceptable arguments. And yet, one might argue that a concept of sin, in all but name, underlies almost all environmentalist critique: the uses we have made of nature reflect our vanity, greed, gluttony, sloth, and, as the mid-nineteenth century Anglican clergyman Charles Kingsley put it, our sheer stupidity (C. Kingsley 1899, 8–9; F. Kingsley 1894, 2:96–98).

Thus the concept of sin is far too important to be excluded from inward examinations. Its value is in tying together three elements: a moral failing, a practical error, and the presumption of a conscience that can recognize the error and feel guilt for the failing. Of these, the conscience seems particularly important to nurture. We are thinking of conscience in a broad sense, including the recognition of particular sins; active engagement in repentance, that is, changing one's behavior; and the ability to see ourselves from an external perspective, as God might.

Closely associated with the recognition of sin is the acceptance of human finitude, important both to theology and to modern existential philosophy (Heidegger 1962; Sheehan 1998). Historically for Christians and Jews, a central source of this finitude—the acknowledgment of our own inadequacy, partiality, and earthly impermanence, understood as the correct appraisal of the human condition—has been the concept of original sin. As an antidote to pride, a sense of finitude can remind us that the world does not revolve around us, that we are not better than others, that we do not know or control as much as we think we do, that we do not always act as we should, that what we often desire is not good for us or for others, and that righteousness is a hard rather than an easy road. In other words, sin reminds us both that we are not God and that we have responsibilities to other humans and other creatures (McKibben 1994). Much of what is called for by those who urge a biocentric perspective has been historically supplied through reflection on the fallen state. A sense of sin reminds us of the physical elements of our inadequacy, of what we share with other forms of life, including our mortality. In some earlier eras of Christianity, that sense went far toward a biocentric vision that severely reined in human ambition: we were vile, dirt, clay, worms (Hamlin 2005).

Finally, the heritage of the concept of sin, even including repentance, reminds us not to expect an earthly state of perfection when the problems will all have been solved and the ecosystems will be wholly sustainable. Instead, it reminds each of us that we are a member of a species, and ingrains in us the expectation that it will always be necessary to struggle with problems of how to live successfully and appropriately with respect to the needs of other creatures.

Prayer   Prayer too, defined broadly as conversation with the divine, is a widely shared religious practice. In Christianity, it is part of the repentant response to sin and occupies a number of roles in private spirituality:

reflection, praise, commitment, supplication, and acceptance. Like sin, it is oddly absent from most environmental discourse. Its absence leaves us without a public language in which to be joyous and thankful, but also critical and questioning, and without a way of underwriting a commitment that is more than good intention. Without it, we are also left impoverished in ways to reflect, in a cosmic context, on what we should be supplicating for.

It is true that prayer may be looked upon as, and surely sometimes is, incompatible with the recognition that human beings exist within rather than outside a natural order. People often pray for transgressions of nature: let the cancer, plague, or storm stay away—at least from those one loves especially. Some pray for personal prosperity or security that effectively translates to gluttony, arrogance, or contempt for other humans or other creatures. At issue here is the acute problem of appropriate desire. Some ethicists, ecotheologians, and church groups (including some of those surveyed by Van Houtan and Pimm [chapter 4, this volume]) have criticized environmentalists for disparaging compassion to humans in favor of biocentrism. As is so often the case, the great problem is where to draw the line, where to find the balance.

In 1866 Charles Kingsley delivered a sermon at Trinity House, headquarters of the British Admiralty, on storms at sea (C. Kingsley 1868, 23–39). He was trying to solve a longstanding theological problem: on the one hand was the Newtonian Christian conception that God works by "fixed and regular laws"; on the other hand was the longstanding faith in the providence of a personal God who "watches over all our actions, . . . that . . . not a sparrow falls . . . without some special reason why that particular sparrow should fall at that particular moment and in that particular place." Kingsley's theological reconciliation—that natural law is the integral of particular providence—was not original, but his thoughts on what to pray for are helpful. His audience of sailors knew it was their duty to learn all they could of natural laws, to try to understand storms, to avoid as far as possible the places they hit, and to take precautions against them. It was perfectly appropriate, Kingsley held, to pray that one would survive the storm, but one should also pray that God's will be done. It was inappropriate to pray that storms not exist; one was to remember that they were, "on the whole, useful" in what we now call the global hydrological cycle. In the framework of Kingsley's natural theology, it was sometimes necessary that the well-being of individuals be sacrificed for the operation of the systems which sustain life generally.

While the case with which Kingsley deals may seem remote, hard issues remain of how to reconcile the legitimate desires for self, family, community, humanity, and other creatures. These issues will be all the harder for Americans and others of the affluent world, precisely because that affluence gives rise to so great a range of seemingly legitimate expectations. For most of us, the greatest problem where acceptance and supplication will arise is in regard to the deaths of ourselves and others. It seems plain that the workings of the world require these deaths, but that realization offers little solace to any sufferer's grief. "Thy will be done" may not be a terribly specific prescriptive, and yet it may still serve as an integrating attitude that reminds us that it is our job to accommodate our own wills with God's and not the other way around.

Sacrifice   We may be encouraged in our supplications on behalf of other creatures by the exemplary place of sacrifice in Christianity. The problem we confront of what to pray for is experienced by a Christ who is both incarnate as a human and divine, and who may be understood to feel fully both the anguish of that sacrifice and to recognize its importance, even necessity. That sacrifice, of course, is not simply one of accepting human limitation; it is a giving up for a much greater good. In Christ's case it is a redemption for sin; in our own cases it might be something simpler: "living simply that others may simply live."

Here too, Kingsley has something to say. Rejecting the commonplace Victorian vision that the laws of political economy should be borrowed from a state of nature in which each being pursued only its self-interest, he argued that it was sacrifice that distinguished humans: "not self-interest, but self-sacrifice, is the only law upon which human society can be grounded with any hope of prosperity and permanence" (F. Kingsley 1894, 2:65–66). Kingsley was not thinking of a kind of universal charity that rejected market forces or capitalism. He accepted the market as a means that rationalized and encouraged production. His point, rather, was that our participation in the market ought to be based on the mandate of working hard to benefit others rather than making a fortune at others' expense to support one's subsequent gluttony and sloth. In Kingsley's view, what united all we did as parents, as citizens, as scientists, as workers, as capitalists, was not really self-interest, since as individuals we must die anyway, but sacrifice for others, for the future. This is a perspective that runs headlong into our current western culture of unbridled self-interest, consumerism, and the celebration of wealth as an end unto itself. Kingsley's perspective, which is consistent with longstanding Christian tradition, must prevail if other creatures are to be protected to any degree.

Sacramentalism   Both of the theologian-authors in this book, Haught (chapter 8) and Rasmussen (chapter 9), highlight sacramentality. They recognize that the nonhuman elements of nature are often the means by which humans apprehend God. While many faiths regard nature or elements of it as sacred, Christians and Jews commonly make a sharp distinction between Creator and creation. But that clear doctrinal distinction does not stop holders of those faiths from sensing and celebrating the divine in nature, the immanence of God. At the key points of passage in our lives—at sexual maturity and in mating, in the generation and birth of children, at death, and in burial—we are recognizing ourselves as natural beings dependent on and participating in systems that are beyond and outside ourselves. Sacraments, then, can be as much ecological as theological celebrations. Often the means of our sacramental celebrations highlight those dependencies and connections: the living water, the bread and wine, the oil, the flowers, the dirt and dust. In all these cases, the connection to God is mediated by the connection to the nature of which we are a part. Indeed, it is not clear that environmental concerns warrant any great expansion or transformation of the concept of sacrament. What is needed is to take sacramentality more seriously.

Prophecy and Justice   All these approaches suggest that in giving up a concept of a balanced nature that guides our conduct and even fixes our errors, one loses nothing but a weak way of arguing. A turn inward, a more serious cultivation of traditional religious practices, can do better what we thought could only be done by a concept of a stable, benevolent, and transcendent "Nature." But spiritual renewal does not substitute for interpreting the signs of the times, determining obligations to them, and acting. For, as Haught (chapter 8, this volume) and Rasmussen (chapter 9, this volume) also point out, a central part of the Christian and Jewish heritage has been a providential understanding of the unfolding of history, an understanding guided by biblical prophecy, both in the sense of foretelling the future and entreating changes in human behavior to create a future. Prophecy, in the Jewish and Christian traditions, provides a direction and framework for human action. But like sin, prophecy has not figured explicitly in most of the ecotheological literature. Indeed, in some quarters a focus on prophecy suggests an uncritical biblical literalism that is the antithesis of a science-based appraisal. And yet much environmental writing is equally concerned with interpreting signs of the "last days."

These are "special times," writes Bill McKibben, in regard to the increasingly rapid doubling of the human population, and they require special response: we must recognize that the command to humans to multiply and fill the earth has been met, and move on to a new stage of human history (McKibben 1999). As Stoll (chapter 2, this volume) and others (Dunlap 2004) have shown, it is no coincidence that environmental literature seems prophetic. Millenarian concerns—concerns with the end times—have profoundly shaped American environmentalism. As Whitney (chapter 1, this volume) points out, they are also implicated in the creation of a "second nature" by the Christian West beginning in the middle ages. The perception of a cultural gulf between the Christian prophetic vision and the environmentalist vision is, therefore, mistaken and unfortunate. What split exists is not between sacred and secular, but rather between different responses to the "cosmic homelessness" that Haught (chapter 8, this volume) finds characteristic of Judeo-Christian tradition. Despite this apparent split, there is a good deal of common ground between the religious and environmentalist prophetic traditions: a call to action, felt, perhaps, by the few who apprehend the seriousness of the age. Both traditions have usually existed on the social margins: they are concerned not with the status quo but with the revolutions that must come. Most troublesome is an arbitrary invocation of providence by those in both camps, in a tendency to read as providential plan those changes that can be fit into prophetic narratives, while ignoring those that cannot as transitory, accidental or incidental, and unimportant.

The prophetic tradition is extremely important now for two reasons. First, it highlights change—including chaotic and seemingly purposeless change—over stability or cyclicity. Providence is recognized as a peculiar and unique history, not a general and rational one. Thus the recognition of apparent randomness in natural systems need not disturb anyone's faith. The enormous contingency of human history suggests this as the norm. Second, it invites people to think about their own actions in terms both of history and of destiny—the issue Rasmussen raises in this volume (chapter 9). For providence does not unfold automatically. Rather it requires the actions of individuals who see clearly and act boldly. The prophetic tradition is full of ordinary people—people who did not seek the opportunity to participate in, much less lead, major changes—who come to lead religious, cultural, or political change. In suggesting that anyone may be called, it can suggest equally that all are, and thus puts an immense responsibility on each to be aware of what the times demand. What the late pope wrote about the environment in 1988 remains true now, and perhaps always: at the "present time . . . *it is not permissible for anyone to remain idle*" (John Paul II 1988, 15; emphasis original). The tradition also suggests that the results of actions may not be immediate or straightforward, but they are no less essential. The environmental mantra, "think globally, act locally," is a prophetic teaching.

Finally, the prophetic tradition highlights justice. We have in mind here an environmental justice broader than concern with inequitable exposure to air or water pollutants or toxic wastes. Rather, breaking the positive feedbacks that often exist between poverty and environmental degradation requires a conception of justice that explicitly incorporates the fluxes of human and natural conditions. It requires not only a concern with human rights, but recognition of the changing relations among the human and nonhuman members of ecosystems. What constitutes justice shifts with changing conditions: a distribution of wealth seen as just prior to a drought may not be just during and after a drought. And justice demands that the needs of future humans and other organisms be considered along with those of today's humans.

These aspects of environmental justice were central in the "green revolution" campaign of the National Catholic Rural Life Conference that began in the 1930s, probably the most concerted and longlasting campaign for environmental change by a quasi-official organ of a mainline American church (and not to be confused with the global agricultural revolution of the 1950s and 1960s). The earlier green revolution was a response to the ecological and economic disasters of the dustbowl and depression, the most striking episode in American history of the transformative power of nature's variability. Its goal was to secure an agricultural sector of sustainable family farms and to oppose short-term, speculative exploitation of natural resources (Hamlin and McGreevy, forthcoming; Liguitti and Rawe 1940; Worster 1979).

The campaign was concerned with justice among humans, underlain by a particular notion of what human flourishing entailed, rather than with protection of nature per se. Some of the policies and values it endorsed (particularly TVA-type projects for the Columbia River basin) are now widely criticized on environmental grounds. Yet the focus on justice brought with it a sense of the value of nature, economically and estheti-cally, though not ethically. Emphasis on sustainability and subsistence put a premium on careful management of soil, water, and woodland. The campaign also recognized the dangers of permanent, fat-soluble, toxic DDT over a decade before Rachel Carson's book and fought a "gam-bling" mentality in agriculture. The approach was defended as a response to the flux of nature as experiencd by American farmers. In the face of environmental and social instability, the campaign recognized that the survival of farmers depended on long-term protection and enrichment of natural systems.

Overall, the goals of the campaign recall the pastoral and agrarian set-ting of the Old Testament. Good times are times of peace when flocks and orchards prosper. Notably, this prophetic perspective presents envi-ronmental responsibility prescriptively as a good that humans will enjoy rather than proscriptively as a desire we must not follow.

A RELIGIOUS RESPONSE TO INVASIVE SPECIES

How might these elements of religiosity arise in the work of scientists addressing environmental problems? Loss of biodiversity and changes in the level of goods and services that ecosystems provide to humans are major environmental changes underway. Here we will briefly consider the leading causes before focusing on one of them. We first describe the situation in the usual scientific terms, implicitly emphasizing the role of reason embedded in scientific research, before turning to how the other religious elements discussed above should assist us in reflecting and act-ing on environmental issues.

On a global basis, five major forces cause large shifts in species abun-dance, including extinctions: (1) destruction of natural habitats and over-harvesting; (2) climate change; (3) deposition of excess nitrogen; (4) in-troduction of nonnative species; and (5) increasing carbon dioxide in the earth's atmosphere (Sala et al. 2000). Human activity—even to some de-gree human existence—is a cause of all of them. Destruction of habitats for other species is a cost of providing housing, roads, lumber, and food for an ever increasing number of humans, many of whom—including most readers of this book—cause far more destruction of habitat per capita than is essential for basic or even luxuriant human needs. Climate change and increasing carbon dioxide in the earth's atmosphere are caused by fossil fuel combustion, predominantly in vehicles occupied by single individuals. Nitrogen is derived not only from fossil fuel combustion, but also from fertilizer applications, which increase the productivity of agriculture per unit of land (and thereby decrease the amount of land needed in agriculture). In the developed world, lawn care is also a major source of nitrogen runoff. Excessive nitrogen causes the eutrophication of rivers and lakes, and the "dead zones" of coastal oceans; these in turn accelerate losses of water quality and fisheries. Excessive nitrogen and sulfur (also derived from fossil fuel combustion) cause the acidification of lakes and rivers worldwide, resulting in the loss of fishes and other organisms. Finally, nonindigenous species—species introduced into an area they had not previously occupied—sometimes become invasive, spread widely, cause economic damage, cause changes in ecosystem goods and services, and drive native species to extinction.

The order of relative importance of these five causes differs among ecosystems. Invasive species, for example, are the leading cause of loss of native biodiversity in freshwater ecosystems across the globe. In general all these environmental problems result from activities that bring substantial benefits to existing humans (if not to subsequent generations), but also bring financial losses, changes in ecosystems, and losses of biodiversity. As with most environmental problems, those who derive the benefits are often not those who suffer the losses, raising the importance of integrating issues of equity and justice among humans into environmental discussions.

As an example, we focus on nonindigenous species, especially those that are invasive. Nonindigenous species that cause net environmental or economic harm are referred to as invasive (National Invasive Species Council 2001). This designation involves value judgments and is not therefore solely a conclusion of science (Rosenzweig 2001; Slobodkin 2001). Because reducing the occurrence of invasive species has become a major focus of scholarly research and environmental management, and because it involves explicit value judgements, it has led to controversies within and beyond the scientific community. The unavoidability of such value judgments in most environmental management, even if the judgments are often more implicit, requires the involvement of more than scientific expertise in policy development. The arrival of a new species, whether from human action or not, often significantly transforms the relations of native species, some of which may be extinguished. Thus it raises fundamental questions about what our obligations to nature are (Lodge and Shrader-Frechette 2003).

Flannery (2001, 345–47) suggests that lions and elephants be reintroduced into North America to replace those that disappeared 13,000 years ago, probably from overhunting by North America's first human colonists. Depending on the temporal frame of reference, these *are* native species. The lions were apparently the same species that exist on the plains of Africa today. The elephants would replace the ecologically similar mammoths and mastodons that once were part of the continent's herbivorous megafauna. Without these large herbivores, with which North American plants co-evolved, some native plants can barely reproduce and cannot thrive (Barlow 2001). By contrast, Flannery notes that other species, like Creosote bush, which is more recently arrived from South America, have been accepted as native, even though they continue to do great damage to some human purposes (Flannery 2001, 141).

Such considerations remind us that extinctions and invasions are part of the flux of nature. Even if humans were responsible for the extinction of the North American megafauna in the last few thousands of years, similar changes have characterized earth for long before humans existed (Flannery 2001). Even on shorter time scales of years and decades, species ranges change. Invasions of new habitats allow the persistence of species, as populations in old habitats are extirpated in the face of environmental change. Such invasions are "natural and, more important, necessary for the persistence of life" (Botkin 2001, 261). The very designation of "nonindigenous" thus often hinges on what time frame and spatial scale is being considered. Thus setting targets for environmental management or ecological restoration—as is often done in the frameworks of ecological health or integrity—is not straightforward. Decisions about such benchmarks require much more discussion—both scientific and otherwise—than has typically been the case.

While humans are as natural as any other species, in recent centuries human influence has increased far more dramatically than that of any other species. Human-induced species invasions have increased dramatically, in concert with the growth and spread of the human population over the last few hundred years (Levine and D'Antonio 2003). More recently, travel and commerce have increased even more rapidly than the human population itself. The result has been burgeoning rates of discovery of nonindigenous species in every ecosystem that has been monitored (e.g., Cohen and Carlton 1998). Both the rate of invasions and the distances traversed by species now exceed by orders of magnitude the rates and distances of only a few hundred years ago. Thus, a robust scientific description establishes that humans have made a large quantitative, if not qualitative, change in the movement of species around the planet. And many of those species have, in the end, contributed to extinctions of other species and changed ecosystems in ways that are harmful to humans.

Demarcating where nature leaves off and the human domain begins is thus difficult, if not impossible. Ethical decisions are often a matter of degree, not category. Environmental management is thus unavoidable. We cannot, in other words, abandon the anthropocentric perspective—the first of the common religious elements outlined above—even if it were deemed desirable to do so. Being left with the problem of management, we must then ask how to manage—toward what ends and with what tools? How are we to reconcile human desires (including the opposing desires of different humans) with responsibilities toward the rest of creation?

The "what" and "how" of management relies heavily on reason, employed not only in the descriptions of the consequences of human activity, but also in the more normative process of identifying questions and goals of management. In the case of invasive species, for example, unless society is prepared to halt global transport of humans and commercial goods, science must be put to good use to quantify the risk of invasion from given levels of introductions. Science and engineering must also be used to provide the techniques to reduce introductions to acceptable levels (while acknowledging that nature's changeability and nonlinearities render any such analyses highly probabilistic), and, to enhance justice, internalize what have previously been economic externalities.

Ecologists study these issues by focusing both on the "pathways" by which species are transported and on the species themselves. Despite the continued existence of substantial uncertainty in making predictions about what species a given pathway is likely to transport, and which nonindigenous species are likely to be invasive, ecologists are making rapid strides in addressing these issues (Groves, Pancetta, and Virtue 2001). Both qualitative (e.g., Ricciardi and Rasmussen 1998) and quantitative assessments (e.g., Reichard and Hamilton 1997; Kolar and Lodge 2001) on a variety of aquatic and terrestrial taxa are paving the way for screening mechanisms to distinguish species that are more likely than others to be harmful. Such information is necessary to better target prevention and control efforts, and avoid unnecessarily reducing the benefits people derive from benign species in trade. Much scientific work remains, though, on an enormous diversity of taxa, and on improving the metrics for making different sorts of benefit and harm (environmental and financial) commensurable so that competing claims can be adjudicated fairly.

Clearly, this is a tricky business. Because the ecosystems under study are themselves partly products of human action, even the empirical modeling of those systems raises questions that encroach on elements of religion, particularly questions about what is the scope for change in human behavior and what are the possible human responses to management initiatives. Sometimes invasive species are clearly the consequence of purposeful human action. Pet-keeping and horticulture, which often involve nonindigenous animals and plants, are often driven by affection for creation and pleasure in "tending the garden." In turn, they provide people with substantial psychological and spiritual benefits. Yet some of the tended species escape or are released and cause a great deal of ecological and economic harm. Here, we can see that the very scientific problem involves an estimation of the determinants of human behavior, which affects the likelihood of such releases of organisms. These parameters are a topic of study for the social as well as the natural sciences, but also for management through education, including religious reflection (Toulmin 1982).

Beyond those species we willfully introduce (or invite to invade), however, are the thousands of species that move into new environments wholly unintentionally. For example, millions of individual organisms hitchhike in the ballast tanks of every ship and in containers of goods transported around the world in ships and planes. Pathway management is the most appropriate response to these threats, and effective techniques exist or are currently under development. For example, research is underway on improved ballast water exchange (currently practiced); treatment with heat, ultraviolet light, ozone, chlorine or other toxins; and filtration. Such pathways pose particular ethical and policy problems, though, because the benefits of the commercial activity accrue to a few producers and transporters, while the costs are difficult to trace to any particular ship or container, given the probabilistic nature of invasions. There is thus a benefit that is easy to quantify, which satisfies consumer demand, and that has an organized constituency (the industries involved); the costs, on the other hand, are much more difficult to quantify and are borne by millions of disparate individuals in society. This is typical of the social injustice that accompanies many environmental problems, and illustrates the difficulty of quantifying and internalizing existing externalities.

Therefore, the very scientific problem of determining the risks and consequences of such events is only in part a matter of estimating probabilities of physical and biological events. Solving the scientific question in a satisfactory manner must involve not only making decisions about how to quantify and respond to the uncertainty in nature, for instance about the particular organisms that may be contained in any ship's ballast tanks or the behavior in new environments of species we had not considered. It must also involve the consideration of why and how human beings make decisions that drive the movements of other species—how in essence one lives with the power of being human.

The questions of whether a situation should be categorized as problematic, how serious a problem it is, and what things it is acceptable to change to fix it are normative questions, not usually recognized as problems of science per se. Of course, scientists do influence such determinations simply because the frameworks within which such matters are discussed incorporate current understanding of the natural world; the "is" is at least a partial determinant of the "ought." Such determinations are typically made through institutions that seek the policy with the greatest advantage and the least disadvantage; such institutions range widely in terms of access to knowledge and degrees of fairness (Shogren 2000).

Some environmentalists have decried cost-benefit analyses on the grounds that they can never accommodate intrinsic or other forms of environmental value because such values cannot adequately be converted into economic values (Brown 2001). Existing institutions and cost-benefit analyses as often practiced are indeed grossly inadequate, and it is difficult to identify common currencies. Nevertheless, we do not see any alternative that is practical or even desirable. Always there will be trade-offs to be made, goods to be balanced (Leung et al. 2002).

The image of nature as a flux co-produced by human action highlights the choices we constantly make and correspondingly undercuts our ability to appeal to any value inherent in "natural" patterns or processes per se. Even if appealing to "Nature" were consistent with widely held religious values, to eliminate the human effect on nature in the name of some value entirely independent of humans will rarely be a practical option. Usually, when we say something has a value other than what a financial market may have assigned to it, we mean that the market has *undervalued* it. We do not usually mean that its value is such as to transcend *any* comparison with competing goods. In practice, to argue that some state or thing has such value, which should trump the need to choose between options on the basis of costs and benefits, may often be to doom that entity to extinction. A mandate to protect something of value can hardly be ethical if it cannot be operationalized or enforced. Instead, other questions arise: Are the ends for which we cause those impacts sufficiently important? Are there other, and ultimately less costly, ways of meeting those ends? At issue then, is not whether one applies cost-benefit analysis, but how one defines costs and benefits, and what values one assigns to particular things or states. Here, economics, the science of responding to scarcity, is equally the template through which each person confronts the broader existential dilemmas of choosing how he or she shall live.

Our focus here then must be on the *valuer* as much as on the *value*. The effectiveness of any ethical mandate will ultimately depend on the choices of humans in acting on it. Flux ecology, by depicting a nature that is the changing vector sum of actions, many of them made by the creature who claims to value, highlights actions and makes each of us responsible. It is here that most of the other religious elements come into play, particularly the concepts and practices of sin and repentence, prayer, sacrifice, and sacramentality.

Economists often describe market behavior in terms of utility. Without denying the importance of utility—and it is clear that in many cases the problem with nonindigenous species is that they will do significant damage of the most clearly utilitarian kind—it is worth recognizing the term's limitations. As environmental economists have sometimes complained, the use of "utility" can be tautological; it is simply a collective label to describe the choices we've made, which smuggles in a notion that there is something truly useful in utility, perhaps something like a vague proxy of thermodynamic efficiency. But for much of our economic behavior, other terms could serve at least as well or better—propriety, for example. In cemeteries, we devote productive agricultural or residential or wild land to the memory of dead ancestors (or increasingly to nonhuman species) from a sense of propriety. Similarly, a sense of propriety has led most of us in recent years to demand that the skins of rare big cats not be available to us in the marketplace, regardless of how warm they might keep us, how well they might serve as rugs, or even the sexual advantage one might gain by representing oneself as a great hunter. These cases alert us to the fact that the values we express in the market do change.

They are products of our culture, our time, our personal values, and our moral choices. In western culture these values have changed relatively recently, and other cultures will have different senses of propriety.

What is going on in making these choices is an inner dialogue, often informed by changes in the outer world. "What should I value? What is it good to want?" Changes in the value that humans attach to environmental goods entail changes in concepts of legitimate desire, which are in turn dependent on changing concepts of human identity and the identities of other natural things. In short, changing values reflect changes in what we think life is about. The importance of the religious elements of sin, prayer, sacrifice, and sacramentality is that they are the framework for this dialogue. The concepts of sin and finitude ask us to see ourselves from outside of ourselves. While the concept of sin differs to some extent among faiths and denominations, it often includes recognition of an inherent tendency toward sinfulness as well as concepts of particular sins that human moral agents commit. It is through a concept of sin, or something like it, that we come to a recognition that what we desire is not necessarily what is good—for us or for anything else—and that the long term is more important than the short term. We also make tradeoffs: to live I must kill and destroy, but I should not to do it cruelly or wantonly. I am sinful if I act carelessly when I might have acted cautiously and prudently, for example, when I have not considered the harmful effects my actions may have on other humans and other creatures.

If sin takes place as a dialogue with conscience, prayer is a dialogue with the divine. Prayer also recognizes our own finiteness and God's infiniteness. We put ourselves in a framework in which we can both express our desires as to how the universe should work, but also reflect on how it does, and even acknowledge "Thy will be done." Sacrifice, so central to Christianity but hardly unique to it, calls upon us to recognize that we live for other entities and for those who will follow us, and suggests that we may as well do that enthusiastically and joyfully. Finally, sacramentality, the seeking of a direct connection with the divine, will often be, as it was so powerfully for John Muir, the basis for a high valuation of nonhuman things and for the systems on which life depends.

All these inner reflections are invitations to regard ourselves with a seriousness commensurate with our potential and actual impact on the outer world. One might argue that when we have taken actions to secure the survival of things that we might otherwise have destroyed, or to avoid undesirable consequences—such as the introduction of invasive species—

that we might otherwise have allowed, it is through some combination of public and private reflection involving these elements. They are the manifestations of taking our power seriously and thereby acquiring a humility that comes through awareness of the actions we might take, their implications, and the legitimate perspectives and needs that other persons, creatures, and God might have. One might go so far as to assert that the more we value ourselves, looking into the mirror at a moral agent possessed of great dignity and great power, the more we value the things over which we have power. As Martin Luther said, "I have so much to do (today) that I should spend the first three hours in prayer." Such reflection is a foundation and complement to scientific assessment, careful ethical analysis, theological guidance, and action. We must use all these tools if we are to manage nature prudentially.

Why then do fewer people engage in such reflection than might do so? By focusing on the dignity of the "human person" as a criterion of justice that societies are obliged to meet, Catholic social teaching makes it possible to identify some of the impediments. One of these is the absence of economic justice. Human beings, it is maintained, cannot acquire the dignity appropriate to the human person as a moral agent when living in economic desperation (John Paul II 1988). While it would probably be wrong to say that most irreversible environmental change is the product of the dire necessity of persons who must survive by destroying the usufruct, some certainly is. It is both futile and unfair to expect it to cease so long as people remain desperate.

Another impediment is the absence of political power. What point can there be for reflection if the institutions of power have disenfranchised and disempowered many people who cannot therefore act as responsible citizens, or if the society is one that recognizes no common good, but only an endless zero sum game?

Finally, and probably most relevant to the developed world, the absence of such reflection might be ascribed to a culture that is thoroughly materialistic, consumerist, and selfish, with many individuals alienated from God, nature, and other human beings alike. With an overweening emphasis on freedom and rights in our culture, the essential connection between responsibilities and rights has been lost. This is the world that Rasmussen (chapter 9, this volume) describes as ecomodernity.

These considerations suggest, then, that desired responses on environmental matters will come about not solely by addressing those matters directly, but by engaging broader social, political, and cultural needs that may have no direct relation to these matters. For environmentalists, this is good news. The efforts to alleviate human misery and desperation, ensure human rights, and reduce materialism and selfishness are more central concerns in most religions than is protection of nature per se. It is on those fronts that environmentalists must engage the connection between human well-being and the well-being of other creatures.

It is here that the final religious element, prophecy, arises. The religions of the book see the human endeavor as a project, something that we must continually work at. The precise end toward which we are to work is sometimes a matter of disagreement, but the general features of it are not: it will be a state of peace, of beauty, of justice, of good. If most ecologists probably find Isaiah's coexistence of lion and lamb problematic, the very recognition of invasive species as a problem requiring a solution demonstrates that ecologists share a broad vision of the world as it rightly should be.

The current association of ecological issues with utopianism, and accordingly with millennialism, is hardly new. What distinguishes an ecology that depicts a world of continual flux from one predicated on balance is not the abandonment of normativity. Rather what most distinguishes the two worldviews is the abandonment of the expectation of an early end to history and the arrival at the problem-free regime of world management. But the realization that we can't get there doesn't mean that we don't get closer, that there are not better and worse options, or that we stop striving. It suggests simply that however long humanity occupies the planet, there will be problems to solve, nature to manage.

Inhabiting a Post Natural World

As bodies of knowledge, bases for the recognition of problems, and frameworks for guiding moral choice, ecology and religion have coexisted—indeed have been integrated—since long before the establishment (and naming) of the scientific discipline of ecology and, probably, also long before organized religion and any particular religious vocabulary existed. To think either that they can usefully be severed or that one can and should be subordinated to the other is both dangerous and futile. But to maintain and nurture their essential integration is equally difficult.

To represent these matters as we have done is simultaneously to make them easier and harder to address. We have shifted attention from profound exegesis to the challenges of moral life (though only in part, for the two must enrich one another). Simple ethical rules or scripture-based dictums are unlikely to provide specific directions on how to solve environmental problems. Rather, we must draw on religious traditions, cultivated in the recognitions that we are not autonomous (that is, we must recognize prayerfully that we are dependent creatures); that we tend to value our desires exclusively, often ignoring the value of other species and their habitats (i.e., we sinfully ignore our responsibilities to other humans and to other creatures); that we resist limiting our insatiable appetites (rather than sacrificing our desires for other humans or other species); that we tend to view the rest of nature solely in instrumental terms (rather than sacramentally acknowledging the sacred presence in and mandate for creation); and that in our pride we tend to ignore the true prophetic calls—from Job to John Muir to Larry Rasmussen—to be better stewards. Finally, though, these habits of heart and mind—these spiritual disciplines—must be implemented through the rigorous exercise of reason. If ultimately most environmental problems are problems of good vs. good, then we must negotiate them by employing our reason—reason that is tempered with the humility embodied in the recognitions listed above.

We arrive at this conclusion by way of first realizing that nature itself can provide only the most indirect guidance about how we should treat it. The reasons for this are worth reiterating. First, the balance of nature to which many generations have previously appealed does not exist. Although "a desire to protect the balance of nature" is one of the primary reasons that Americans support environmental protection (Biodiversity Project 2002) and the theme of many nature books, videos, and news stories, nature is characterized as much by change as balance. These days, most ecologists feel that the "flux of nature" better describes the nature they apprehend. Second, whether nature is characterized more by change than constancy, descriptions of nature cannot by themselves provide prescriptions for the place of humans in nature. Any move from "is" to "ought" is not straightforward. Finally, we are a part of that nature and one of the agents of flux, for better or worse: we can accept neither the view that humans are above nature and can therefore use it in whatever way is useful nor the view that nature is above humans and all human uses of nature are vile. Rather, humans are a special member of nature, and must subject to careful scrutiny their desired uses of other organisms. Thus, our standing with respect to nature *has* changed: nature is not what we thought it was, what is natural is not necessarily what is good, and nature is not "other." In these three senses, we inhabit a post natural world.

Given that we inhabit a post natural world, we must cultivate our inward compass to guide our individual and societal behavior toward the world around us. It is ultimately in our spiritual self-interest, as well as in our aesthetic and economic self-interest, that we approach other species and their habitats with humility. The traditional disciplines of Christians and Jews are entirely consistent with nurturing this inward compass toward greater sensitivity to the environment. Unfortunately, in the ages before the dramatic magnitude of the human impact on other organisms was realized, these disciplines were not usually directed toward the treatment of the rest of nature by humans. We hope that this book encourages the broadening of the traditional scope of these disciplines to include the environment.

NOTE

1. Slobodkin made these remarks in his commentary on the conference out of which this book came. His remarks are unpublished.

WORKS CITED

Barlow, C. 2001. Ghost stories from the ice age. *Natural History* 110 (Sept.): 62–68.

Bellah, R. 1986. *Habits of the heart: Individualism and commitment in American life.* New York: Harper and Row.

Biodiversity Project. 2002. *Ethics for a small planet: A communications handbook on the ethical and theological reasons for protecting biodiversity.* Madison, WI: Biodiversity Project.

Botkin, D. B. 2001. The naturalness of biological invasions. *Western North American Naturalist* 61:261–66.

Brown, D.A. 2001. The ethical dimensions of global environmental issues. *Daedalus* 130:59–76.

Callicott, J. B. 2001. Multicultural environmental ethics. *Daedalus* 130:77–98.

Cohen, A. N., and J. T. Carlton. 1998. Accelerating invasion rate in a highly invaded estuary. *Science* 279:555–58.

Cohen, J. 1989. *Be fertile and increase, fill the earth and master it: The ancient and medieval career of a Biblical Text.* Ithaca, NY: Cornell University Press

Cunningham, A. 2000. Science and religion in the thirteenth century revisited: The making of St. Francis the protoecologist, part 1; Creature not nature. *Studies in the History and Philosophy of Science* 31(4): 613–43.

———. 2001. Science and religion in the thirteenth century revisited: The making of St. Francis the protoecologist, part 2; Nature not creature. *Studies in the History and Philosophy of Science* 32(1): 69–98.

Dunlap, T. 2004. *Faith in nature: Environmentalism as religious quest.* Seattle: University of Washington Press.

Flannery, T. 2001. *The eternal frontier.* Melbourne: Text Publishing.

Groves, R. H., F. D. Panetta, and J. G. Virtue, eds. 2001. *Weed risk assessment.* Collingwood, Australia: CSIRO Publishing.

Hamlin, C., and J. McGreevy. Forthcoming. The greening of America, Catholic style, 1930–1950. *Environmental History.*

———. 2005. Good and intimate filth. In *Dirt, Disgust and Modern Life,* ed. Ryan Johnson and William Cohen, 3–29. Minneapolis: University of Minnesota Press.

Heidegger, Martin. 1962. *Being and time.* Trans. John Macquarrie and Edward Robinson. Oxford: Blackwell.

Holling, C. S., and G. K. Meffe. 1995. Command and control and the pathology of natural resource management. *Conservation Biology* 10:328–37.

John Paul II. 1988. *Christifideles laici: On the vocation and the mission of the lay faithful in the world.* Boston: Pauline Books and Media.

Kingsley, Charles. 1868. Prayer and science. In *Discipline and other sermons.* Philadelphia: Lippincott.

———. 1899. Town geology. In *Scientific lectures and essays.* London: Macmillan.

Kingsley, Frances. 1894. *Charles Kingsley: His letter and memories of his life, edited by his wife.* 2 vols. London: Macmillan.

Kolar, C. S., and D. M. Lodge. 2001. Progress in invasion biology: Predicting invaders. *Trends in Ecology and Evolution* 16:199–204.

Ligutti, Luigi, and John C. Rawe. 1940. *Rural roads to security: America's third struggle for freedom.* Milwaukee: Bruce.

Leung, B., D. M. Lodge, D. Finnoff, J. F. Shogren, M. Lewis, and G. Lamberti. 2002. An ounce of prevention or a pound of cure: Bioeconomic risk analysis of invasive species. *Proceedings of the Royal Society of London B* 269: 2407–13.

Levine, J. M., and C. M. D'Antonio. 2003. Forecasting biological invasions with increasing international trade. *Conservation Biology* 17:322–26.

Lodge, D. M., and K. Shrader-Frechette. 2003. Nonindigenous species: Ecological explanation, environmental ethics, and public policy. *Conservation Biology* 17:31–37.

MacCulloch, John. 1837. *Proofs and illustrations of the attributes of God, from the facts and laws of the physical universe: Being the foundation of natural and revealed religion.* 3 vols. London: James Duncan.

McKibben, B. 1994. *The comforting whirlwind: God, Job, and the scale of creation.* Grand Rapids, MI: Eerdmans.

———. *Maybe one: A case for smaller families.* New York: Plume.

Mill, John Stuart. 1969. *Nature.* In his *Autobiography and Other Writings,* ed. J. Stillinger. New York: Houghton Mifflin, 1969.

National Invasive Species Council. 2001. Meeting the invasive species challenge: national invasive species management plan. Available at http://www.invasivespeciesinfo.gov/council/mpfinal.pdf (last accessed Sept. 2005).

Passmore, J. 1974. *Man's responsibility for nature: Ecological problems and Western traditions.* New York: Scribners.

Reichard, S. H. and C. W. Hamilton. 1997. Predicting invasions of woody plants introduced into North America. *Conservation Biology* 11:193–203.

Ricciardi, A., and J. B. Rasmussen. 1998. Predicting the identity and impact of future biological invaders: A priority for aquatic resource management. *Canadian Journal of Fisheries and Aquatic Sciences* 55:1759–65.

Rosenzweig, M. L. 2001. The four questions: What does the introduction of exotic species do to diversity? *Evolutionary Ecology Research* 3:361–67.

Sala, O. E., F. S. Chapin III, J. J. Armesto, E. Berlow, J. Bloomfield, R. Dirzo, E. Huber-Sannwald, et al. 2000. Global biodiversity scenarios for the year 2100. *Science* 287:1770–74.

Sheehan, T. 1998. Heidegger, Martin. In *Routledge Encyclopedia of Philosophy.* London: Routledge. Available at http://www.rep.routledge.com (last accessed Sept. 2005).

Shogren, J. 2000. Risk reduction strategies against the "explosive invader." In *The Economics of Biological Invasions,* ed. C. Perrings, M. Williamson, and S. Dalmazzone, 56–69. Glasgow: Edward Elgar Publishing.

Slobodkin, L. B. 2001. The good, the bad and the reified. *Evolutionary Ecology Research* 3:1–13.

Tirosh-Samuelson, H. 2001. Nature in the sources of Judaism. *Daedalus* 130:99–124.

Toulmin, Stephen. 1982. *The return to cosmology: Postmodern science and the theology of nature.* Berkeley: University of California Press.

Tucker, M. E., and J. A. Grim. 2001. Introduction: The emerging alliance of world religions and ecology. *Daedalus* 130:1–22.

Worster, D. 1979. *The dust bowl: The southern plains in the 1930s.* Oxford: Oxford University Press.

CONTRIBUTORS

Dr. Gary E. Belovsky
Department of Biological Sciences
University of Notre Dame

Dr. Eugene Cittadino
Gallatin School of Individualized Study
New York University

Dr. Patricia Ann Fleming
Department of Philosophy
Creighton University

Dr. Christopher Hamlin
Department of History
University of Notre Dame

Dr. John F. Haught
Theology Department
Georgetown University

Dr. David M. Lodge
Department of Biological Sciences
University of Notre Dame

Dr. Stuart L. Pimm
Nicholas School of the Environment and Earth Sciences
Duke University

Dr. Larry Rasmussen
Union Theological Seminary

Dr. Peter H. Raven
Missouri Botanical Garden

Dr. Mark Stoll
History Department
Texas Tech University

Kyle S. Van Houtan
University Program in Ecology
Duke University

Dr. Peter S. White
Department of Biology and North Carolina Botanical Garden
The University of North Carolina at Chapel Hill

Dr. Elspeth Whitney
Department of History
University of Nevada